THE PHILOSOPHICAL THEOLOGY OF

John Duns Scotus

THE PHILOSOPHICAL THEOLOGY OF

John Duns Scotus

ALLAN B. WOLTER, O.F.M.

Marilyn McCord Adams, *editor*

CORNELL UNIVERSITY PRESS

Ithaca and London

First published 1990 by Cornell University Press.

International Standard Book Number 0-8014-2385-6
Library of Congress Catalog Card Number 89-46162

Printed in the United States of America

*Librarians: Library of Congress cataloging information
appears on the last page of the book.*

♾The paper used in the text of this publication meets the minimum requirements of American National Standard for Information Sciences—Permanence of Paper for Printed Library Materials, ANSI Z39.48-1984.

Contents

PHILOSOPHICAL THEOLOGY

Foreword

Medieval philosophy is at last assuming its rightful place in the philosophy curricula of American colleges and universities. One outward and visible sign of this change was the formation of the Society for Medieval and Renaissance Philosophy in 1977. Forty years ago, things were different. Most non-Catholic universities adhered to the traditional two-part history of philosophy sequence (Greek and Modern Classical Philosophy), complacent in their omission of a thousand formative years. Catholic schools, on the other hand, tended to focus on Aquinas. Research tools were not yet available and preparation of modern critical editions of Anselm, Scotus, and Ockham was only in beginning stages. English translations of their important works were spotty, making it impossible to teach medieval surveys with a focus on primary sources.

John Duns Scotus (c. 1266–1308) was one of the neglected giants. His interests focused by philosophical theology, Scotus' voluminous works are topically wide-ranging (from metaphysics, epistemology, and natural philosophy, through action-theory to ethics and soteriology), distinctive, and innovative. Like contemporary analytic philosophy (of the seventies and eighties as opposed to the forties, fifties, and sixties), his writings are highly theoretical and systematic, developed with sophisticated technical machinery and explicated with subtle distinctions (hence Scotus' nickname, "Subtle Doctor"). So great were his intellectual power and penetration that, despite his early death and the intellectual independence of the Franciscan tradition, Scotists vied with Thomists and Ockhamists in Scholastic debates down through the seventeenth century, when Luke Wadding published a purported Opera Omnia of Scotus. More recently, Charles Sanders Peirce celebrated Scotus as the greatest of medieval philosophers and one of the most profound metaphysicians of all times.

Over the last four decades, Allan B. Wolter, O.F.M., has done more than anyone else to make the philosophical theology of John Duns Scotus accessible to the English-speaking world, by preparing English translations of primary sources as well as interpretative essays introducing readers to Scotus' central ideas.

These tasks have been both hindered and made more urgent by the painfully slow progress of the new Vatican edition of Scotus' writings (volume 1 containing the Prologue of Scotus' Oxford commentary on the *Sentences* appeared in 1950; as of 1988, only nine volumes have been published, and the critical edition of the Oxford commentary is not yet complete). Although useful, the seventeenth-century Wadding edition is unreliable both in its attributions and readings. Difficult issues of authenticity, dating, and the interrelation of Scotus' works remain. Thus, beginning with his dissertation, Wolter formed the habit of reverting to the manuscripts to produce his own provisional editions, consulting with Vatican editors on the Scotus Commission where possible.

Wolter's career as a Scotus translator began in 1947, when Paul Weiss requested some material for the first volume of his new journal *Review of Metaphysics*. Remarking on Scotus' notoriously tangled Latin, Wolter described the work of translating it as "a special vocation" and vowed never to do it again. Necessity is a sign of calling, however, and Wolter began translating topical selections for summer-school students at the Franciscan Institute in the early fifties. Many of these were published, with Wolter's Latin editions on the facing pages, in *Duns Scotus: Philosophical Writings: A Selection* (first published by Thomas Nelson, 1962, and English only in Bobbs-Merrill's Library of Liberal Arts series, 1962; reprinted by Hackett, 1987). Over the years, Wolter has made many more of Scotus' works available, always preferring the format of publishing the English and Latin together: principally, *John Duns Scotus: God and Creatures, the Quodlibetal Questions* (with Felix Alluntis); *John Duns Scotus. A Treatise on God as First Principle. A Latin Text with English Translation of the De Primo Principio*; and *Duns Scotus on the Will and Morality*. By now, Wolter has given us enough for a reasonably comprehensive and balanced course on Scotus.

Duns Scotus is not called "the Subtle Doctor" for nothing, however. Diving into his highly technical philosophical corpus without benefit of an interpretive guide is heroic at best. Yet, when Wolter began, reliable guides were unavailable. While not without value, the secondary literature was on the whole confused and confusing, and/or marred by polemical distortion. Together with Wolter's pioneering first book on Scotus, his published dissertation *The Transcendentals and Their Function in the Metaphysics of Duns Scotus* (finished in one semester of intensive interaction with Philotheus Boehner), Wolter's interpretive essays over the last forty years supply us with our needed map. Collected here from many (often inaccessible) journals and books, they are a paradigm of method and a treasure of illuminating insights. Wolter's consistent response to interpretive puzzlement has been to return to the primary sources and to offer readings as detailed and philosophically subtle as the texts themselves. Thus, in the early days, when Scotus' ideas were "known" and criticized mostly from hearsay, Wolter refuted misguided attacks with careful analyses of the texts (see chapters 10 and 11 below). Throughout, Wolter's own philosophical penetration of the material has enabled him to make clear what seems in Scotus complex and confusing (e.g., regarding the formal distinction, chapter 1, and Scotus' theory of universals, chapter 2). Again, Wolter's identification of Scotus' doctrine of the will as the key to his ethics resolves old and false puzzles (see chapters 7–9). At the same time, Wolter's sensitivity to philological issues and to the historical development of Scotus' thought has enabled him to illuminate Scotus' notion of intuitive cognition (see chapter 5) as well as his account of Divine foreknowledge (see chapter 13). All of the essays reflect Wolter's philosophical and historical curiosity and a reasoned and reasonable open-mindedness. Paying Scotus the respect due a great philosopher, Wolter was glad to return to old topics because he always learned something new (e.g., his treatment of formal distinction in chapter 1 makes new points not found in his dissertation). Wolter's interests in analytic philosophy surface as he relates Scotus' semantics and metaphysics to twentieth-century analytic thought (see chapters 3 and 12).

I owe most of what I know about Duns Scotus to arguments with Wolter and his essays. I therefore take great pleasure in commending them to you.

MARILYN McCORD ADAMS

University of California, Los Angeles

THE PHILOSOPHICAL THEOLOGY OF

John Duns Scotus

Introduction

As with many of the medieval Schoolmen, little is known of the early life of John Duns, the Scot (or Scotus). From the record of his ordination to the priesthood by Bishop Oliver Sutton at Northampton on March 17, 1291, it is inferred he was born early in 1266 . . . Popular tradition . . . states that his father was the younger son of the Duns of Grueldykes, whose estate was near the present village of Duns in Berwickshire. As a bachelor of theology, Scotus lectured on the *Sentences* of Peter Lombard at Cambridge (date unknown), at Oxford about 1300, and at Paris from 1302 to 1303, when he and others were banished for not taking the side of King Philip the Fair against Pope Boniface VIII in a quarrel over the taxation of church property for the wars with England. The exile was short, however, for Scotus was back in Paris by 1304 and became regent master of theology in 1305. In 1307 he was transferred to the Franciscan study house at Cologne, where he died the following year.

Works Scotus' early death interrupted the final editing of his most important work, the monumental commentary on the *Sentences* known as the *Ordinatio* (or in earlier editions as the *Commentaria Oxoniensia* or simply the *Opus Oxoniense*). An outgrowth of earlier lectures begun at Oxford and continued on the Continent, this final

I

version was dictated to scribes, with instruction to implement it with materials from his Paris and Cambridge lectures. A modern critical edition of the *Ordinatio*, begun by the Typis Polyglottis Vaticanis (Vatican Press) in 1950, is still in progress. Though less extensive in scope, Scotus' *Quaestiones Quodlibetales* are almost as important; they express his most mature thinking as regent master at Paris. Also authentic are the *Quaestiones Subtilissimae in Metaphysicam* on Aristotle's *Metaphyscis*; the *Quaestiones super libros Aristotelis de Anima*; some forty-six shorter disputations held in Oxford and Paris and known as *Collationes*; and a series of logical writings in the form of questions on Porphyry's *Isagoge* and on Aristotle's *Categories, De Interpretione*, and *De Sophisticis Elenchis*. The *Tractatus de Primo Principio* is a short but important compendium of natural theology; drawing heavily upon the *Ordinatio*, it seems to be one of Scotus' latest works. Like the *Theoremata*, a work whose authenticity has been seriously questioned, the *Tractatus* was apparently dictated only in an incomplete form and left to some amanuensis to finish.

Theology and philosophy Like the majority of the great thinkers of the late thirteenth and early fourteenth centuries, Scotus was a professional theologian rather than a philosopher. One of the privileges accorded mendicant friars such as the Franciscans and Dominicans was that of beginning their studies for a mastership in theology without having first become a Master of Arts. The philosophical courses they took in preparation were pursued in study houses of their own order and were, as a rule, less extensive than those required of the candidate for an M.A. As a consequence of this educational program their commentaries on the philosophical works of Aristotle were usually written later than those on biblical works or on the *Sentences* of Peter Lombard; also, the most important features of their philosophy are frequently found in the context of a theological question. This does not mean that they confused theology with philosophy in principle, but only that in practice they used philosophy almost exclusively for systematic defense or explication of the data of revelation. But in so doing these theologians assumed that philosophy as a work of reason unaided by faith played an autonomous role and had a competence of its own, limited though it might be where questions of man's nature and destiny were at issue.

This critical attitude concerning the respective spheres of philosophy and theology became more pronounced around the turn of the fourteenth century. Thus, we often find Scotus not only distinguishing in reply to a particular question the answers given by the theologians from those of the "philosophers" (Aristotle and his Arabic commentators) but also pointing out what the philosophers could have proved had they been better at their profession. On the other hand, the genuine interest in the logical structure of "science" (*episteme*), as Aristotle understood the term, led to an inevitable comparison of systematic theology with the requirements of a science such as Euclid's geometry.

Paradoxically, it is in the attempt of the Scholastics to show to what extent theology is or is not a science that we find the most important expressions of their ideas of a deductive system. This is particularly true of the lengthy discussions on the nature of theology in the Prologue of Scotus' *Ordinatio*. Similarly, if we look for the origin of some important and influential philosophical concepts that lie at the heart of Galileo's mechanics, we find them in the medieval discussions of "the intension and remission of forms" (that is, how qualities like hot and white increase in intensity). It was in his analysis of how a man might grow in supernatural charity, for instance, that Scotus introduced his theory of how variations in the intensity of a quality might be treated quantitatively. This key notion, developed by Merton Schoolmen and extended to the problem of motion, made possible Galileo's description of the free-fall of bodies.

Scotus was most concerned with what philosophy has to say about God and the human spirit. Though his ethical views and philosophy of nature are not without interest, Scotus was primarily a metaphysician.

METAPHYSICS

Scotus was thoroughly familiar with the writings of Avicenna, whose concept of metaphysics Scotus brought to the service of theology. Avicenna agreed with Averroës that Aristotle's metaphysics was meant to be more than a collection of opinions (*doxa*) and had the character of a science (*episteme*) or body of demonstrated truths, where "demonstration" is understood in the sense of the *Posterior Analytics*. They also agreed that this science was in great part concerned with God and the Intelligences responsible for the movement of the planetary spheres. But Averroës believed that the existence of God is proved by physics or natural science (by Aristotle's argument for a prime mover), whereas Avicenna developed a causal proof within the framework of metaphysics itself. Scotus argued that the Averroistic view subordinates Aristotle's "first philosophy" to physics when it should be autonomous. Moreover—and more important—one needs a metaphysician to prove that the "prime mover" is the First Being, and that metaphysics provides more and better arguments for God's existence than this particular physical proof. Part of the difficulty with the physical proof stems from Aristotle's axiom that "whatever is moved is moved by another." Scotus did not regard this as intuitively evident or deducible from any other such principles. Furthermore, he saw numerous counterinstances in experience, such as man's free will or a body's continued motion after external force is removed.

The transcendentals   Scotus saw metaphysics as an autonomous science concerned with the transcendentals, those realities or aspects of reality that transcend the physical. Its subject matter, as Avicenna rightly maintained, is being as being and its transcendental attributes. In contrast with Saint Thomas, who restricted transcendental to such notions as have the same extension as "being," Scotus treated any notion applicable to reality but not included in one of Aristotle's ten categories as transcendental. At least four classes of such can be enumerated. Being (*ens*) is the first of the transcendental notions. It is an irreducibly simple notion of widest extension that is used to designate any subject whose existence implies no contradiction. "Existence" refers to the real or extramental world. Next come the three attributes coextensive with being—"one," "true," and "good"—for to be capable of existing in the extramental world, the subject must have a certain unity and be capable of being known and being desired or willed. Third, there are an unlimited number of attributes such as "infinite-or-finite," "necessary-or-contingent," "cause-or-caused," and so on, that are coextensive with being only in disjunction. Finally, there are many other predicates whose formal notion or definition contains no hint of imperfection or limitation. These are known as pure or unqualified perfections. In addition to being (*ens*), its coextensive attributes, and the more perfect member of each disjunction, this class of transcendentals includes any attribute that can be ascribed to God, whether it pertains to him alone (such as omnipotence or omniscience) or whether it also is characteristic of certain creatures (such as wisdom, knowledge, free will).

DISJUNCTIVE ATTRIBUTES   Like Avicenna, Scotus regarded the disjunctive transcendentals as the most important for metaphysics, but being Christian, he conceived these supercategories of being somewhat differently. Avicenna held that creation proceeded from God by a necessary and inevitable process of emanation, whereas for Scotus creation was contingent and dependent on God's free election. Therefore, for Scotus the less perfect member of each disjunction represents only a possible type of real being, whereas for Avicenna these possible types must all eventually be actualized, and therefore the complete disjunction is a necessary consequence of "being." Scotus expressed this difference in what might be called his "law of disjunction":

> In the disjunctive attributes, while the entire disjunction cannot be demonstrated from "being," nevertheless as a universal rule by positing the less perfect extreme of some being, we can conclude that the more perfect extreme is realized in some other being. Thus it follows that if some being is finite, then some being is infinite, and if some being is contingent, then some being is necessary. For in such cases it is not possible for the more imperfect extreme of the disjunction to be existentially predicated of "being" particularly taken, unless the more perfect extreme be existentially verified of some other being upon which it depends. (*Ordinatio* I, 39)

The task of the metaphysician, then, is to work out the ways in which the various transcendental concepts entail one another. One of the more important conclusions that will emerge from such an analysis is that there is one, and only one, being in which all pure perfection coexists. Such an infinite being we call God.

Proof for God's existence Scotus suggested that the metaphysican might use any pair of disjunctives to prove God exists (and here he seems to be in the tradition of William of Auvergne and the "second way" of Saint Bonaventure). However, the one metaphysical proof he chose to work on in any detail seems to be a synthesis of what he considered the best elements of all the proofs of his predecessors. Henry of Ghent, whose writings so often served as the springboard for Scotus' own discussion of any problem, had tried to bring some order into the many proofs advanced during the Middle Ages by grouping them under two general headings, the way of causality and the way of eminence. The first drew its inspiration from Aristotelian principles, whereas the second was Augustinian in tone and stemmed from the School of Saint Victor and the *Monologion* of Saint Anselm. The way of causality was further divided by Henry accordingly as God is treated as the efficient, the final, or the exemplar cause of creatures.

Scotus simplified the causal approach by eliminating the exemplar cause as a distinct category. He treated it merely as a subdivision of efficiency and implied that the cause in question is intelligent and does not act by blind impulse of nature. As for the way of eminence, it was treated not simply in terms of its Platonic or Augustinian origins, but as having a foundation in Aristotelian principles as well. The proof was developed in two principal parts, one dealing with the relative attributes of the infinite being—efficiency, finality, and eminent perfection—and the second with the absolute property of his infinity.

Given the infinity of God, Scotus essayed to show there can be but one such being. Each section is a concatenation of closely reasoned conclusions, some thirty-odd in all.

The argument was perhaps one of the most elaborate and detailed proofs for God's existence constructed during the Middle Ages, and apart from any intrinsic merit as a whole it is of considerable historical interest (see chapters 10, 11, and 12 below). From the time Scotus first formulated it, he subjected the proof to several revisions, mainly in the direction of greater conceptual economy and logical rigor. In what seems to be the final version (in the *Tractatus de Primo Principio*), the proof is prefaced by two chapters that represent an attempt to formalize what a Schoolman at the turn of the fourteenth century must have regarded as the basic axioms and theses of the science of metaphysics. Other interesting aspects of the argument appear in answer to possible objections to the proof. One anticipates Kant's causal antinomy. Aristotle and his Arabic commentators maintained that the world with its cyclic growth and decay had no beginning. How, then, can one argue to the existence of an uncaused efficient cause? Scotus' solution reveals the influence of Avicenna. On the ground that whatever does not exist of itself has only the possibility of existence as something essential to itself, Avicenna argued that this holds not only of the moment a thing begins to be but of every subsequent moment as well. The true cause of any effect, then, must coexist with and conserve the effect and therefore must be distinguished from the ancillary chain of partial causes that succeed one another in time.

Scotus developed this distinction in terms of what he called an essential versus an accidental concatenation of causes. A series of generative causes such as grandparent, parent, and child, or any sequence of events such as those later analyzed by Hume, would be causes only accidentally ordered to one another in the production of their final effect. Where an essential ordering or concatenation exists, all the causal factors must coexist both to produce and to conserve their effect. This is true whether they be of different types (such as material, formal, efficient, and final) or whether they be a chain of efficient or final causes, such as Avicenna postulated for the hierarchy of Intelligences between God and the material world. While infinite regress in accidentally ordered causes may be possible, Scotus said, the chain as a whole must be essentially ordered to some coexisting cause that guarantees the perpetuity of what is constant or cyclic about such repetitive productivity. But no philosopher postulates an infinite regress where the concatenation of causes is essential and all must coexist. One does not explain how any possible effect is actually conserved, for instance, by assuming an infinity of links upon which it depends.

TECHNICAL DEMONSTRATION   How is any proof that begins with factual propositions demonstrative or scientific in Aristotle's sense of demonstrative? Are not all such premises contingent? With Avicenna obviously in mind, Scotus explained that pagan philosophers could admit that every factual proposition is necessarily true because of the deterministic chain of causes that links it to the first creative cause, God. According to pagan philosophers, this is true not only of eternal entities like primary matter or the inferior or secondary Intelligences but also of all temporal events brought about by the clockwork motions of the heavenly bodies that these Intelligences cause. Empirical explanations of temporal events are required only because the human mind is unable to trace all the intricate links of causal efficacy that make any given event a necessary and inevitable consequence of God's essential nature.

If such a theory were true, Scotus argued, it would eliminate all genuine contingency from the world and thus conflict with one of the most manifest truths of human experience, namely, that we are free to act otherwise than we do. Should one deny such an obvious fact, it is not argument he needs but punishment or perception. "If, as Avicenna says, those who deny a first principle should be beaten or exposed to fire until they concede that to burn and not to burn are not identical, so too ought those who deny that some being is contingent be exposed to torments until they concede that it is possible for them not to be tormented" (Ordinatio I, 39). If true contingency exists, however, it can only be because the first cause does not create the world by any necessity of nature. But if the whole of creation depends upon God's free will, then every factual or existential statement about it will be radically contingent. How, then, can any proof from effect to cause satisfy Aristotle's demand that demonstration begin with necessary premises? One could argue legitimately, but not demonstratively, from such an obvious fact as contingency. Yet, Scotus maintained, it is possible to convert the argument into a technical demonstration by shifting to what is necessary and essential about any contingent fact, namely, its possibility. For while one cannot always infer actuality from possibility, the converse inference is universally valid. What is more, Scotus added, statements about such possibilities are necessary; hence, he preferred to construct the proof from efficiency in the mode of possibility thus: something can be produced, therefore something can be productive; since an infinite regress or circularity in essentially concatenated causes is impossible, some uncaused agent must be possible and hence actual, since it cannot be both possible and incapable of being caused if it is not actually existing.

One can argue similarly of the possibility of a final cause or of a most perfect nature. (Scotus' argument in this connection bears a curious parallel to Wittgenstein's about simple objects in the *Tractatus Logico-Philosophicus*.) Scotus saw God as the necessary or a priori condition required to make any contingent truth about the world possible; these possibilities must be a part of God's nature, "written into him from the beginning"; as source of all possibility, he himself cannot be "merely possible." It is in God's knowledge of, and power over, these limitless possibilities that we discover what is fixed, essential, and noncontingent about not only the actual world but about all possible worlds as well. Since God is the fixed locus in which all possibilities coexist, he must be infinite in knowledge, in power, and therefore in his essence or nature. Since contradictions arise if one assumes that more than one such infinite mind, power, or being exists, there can be but one God.

THEORY OF KNOWLEDGE

After establishing the existence of an infinite being to his own satisfaction, Scotus undertook an analysis of the concepts that enter into statements about God, and in so doing he threw considerable light upon his own theory of knowledge, particularly upon how he considered notions that transcend the level of sensible phenomena to be possible.

Univocity and the transcendentals Some of the earlier Schoolmen like Alexander of Hales, Saint Bonaventure, and Henry of Ghent fell back upon various theories of innatism or illuminationism (in which elements from Saint Augustine and Avicenna were grafted upon the Aristotelian theory of knowledge) to account for such knowledge as seems to have no foundation in the data of the senses. These hybrid interpretations of Aristotle had this in common: this theory was used to explain only how general or universal concepts applicable to the visible world are abstracted from sense images. But where any notion applicable to God was involved, some illumination from a transcendent mind was thought to be required. Not only did this hold for notions obviously proper to God—such as "necessary being" and "omnipotence"—but also for such seemingly common transcendentals as "being," "true," and "good." Although the latter terms were predicated of creatures as well as of God, their meaning was not univocal. Associated with each term were two similar, and hence often indistinguishable meanings, both simple and irreducible to any common denominator. One was believed to be proper to creatures and to be abstracted from sensible things by the aid of an agent intellect; the other was proper to God, and since it transcended in perfection anything to be found in creatures, it must be given from above. It was maintained that these innate ideas, impressed on the soul at birth, lie dormant in the storehouse of the mind, to be recalled like forgotten memories when man encounters something analogous in sensible experience. The discovery of God in created things, then, was explained much like Plato's account of how man recalls the transcendent world of ideas.

As Aristotle's own writings became better known, however, the popularity of such theories diminished. More and more Scholastics followed Aquinas in rejecting any special illumination theory to explain man's knowledge of God, but like Aquinas they failed to see that this required any modification of the traditional doctrine of analogy of being and other transcendental terms. Scotus seems to have been the first to see the discrepancy between the two positions. He pointed out that if all of our general notions (including those of being and its transcendental attributes) are formed by reflecting upon sensible things, as Aristotle explained, then some notions, such as being, must be univocally predicable of God and creatures, or all knowledge of God becomes impossible. Arguing specifically against Henry of Ghent, who claimed we have either a concept of being proper to God or one common to finite creatures, Scotus insisted on the need of a third or neutral notion of being as a common element in both the other concepts. This is evident, he said, because we can be certain that God is a being, while remaining in doubt as to whether he is an infinite or a finite being. When we prove him to be infinite, this does not destroy but adds to our previous incomplete and imperfect notion of him. The same could be said of other transcendental notions, such as wisdom or goodness. Indeed, every irreducibly simple notion predicable of God must be univocally predicable of the finite and created thing from which it is abstracted. Any perfection of God is analogous to its created similitude, but we conceive such a perfection as something exclusive or proper to God through composite concepts constructed by affirming, denying, and interrelating conceptual elements that are simple and univocally predicable of creatures. For even though every element is itself general, certain combinations thereof may serve to characterize one, and only one, thing. Although such concepts are proper to God, they retain their general character and do not express positively the unique individuality of the divine nature. Hence the need for proving that only one God exists.

Scotus also held that the transcendental notion of being (ens) is univocal to substance and accidents as well as to God and creatures.

We have no more sensible experience of substance than we do of God; its very notion is a conceptual construct, and we would be unable to infer its existence if substance did not have something positive in common with our experiential data.

The formal distinction (See chapter 1 below.) The concept of the formal distinction, like univocity of being, is another characteristic metaphysical thesis connected with Scotus' theory of knowledge. Though usually associated with his name, the distinction did not originate with him. It represents a development of what is sometimes called the "virtual distinction" or "conceptual distinction with a foundation in the thing." The latter is an intermediate between the real distinction and that which is merely conceptual. The difference between the morning star and evening star, for example, is purely conceptual. Here one and the same thing, the planet Venus, is conceived and named in two different ways because of different ways or contexts in which it appears to us. The real distinction, on the contrary, concerns two or more individual items, such as Plato and Socrates, body and soul, or substance and its accidents. Though two such things may coexist or even form a substantial unity or accidental aggregate, it is logically possible that one be separated from the other or even exist apart from the other. The Scholastics generally recognized the need of some intermediary distinction if the objectivity of our knowledge of things is to be safeguarded. How is it possible, they asked, to speak of a plurality of attributes or perfections in God when the divine nature is devoid of any real distinction? How is it possible for a creature to resemble God according to one such attribute and not another? Similarly, if the human soul is really simple, as many of the later scholastics taught, how can it lack all objective distinction and still be like an angel by virtue of its rational powers and unlike the angel by reason of its sentient nature? All agree that it is possible for the human mind to conceive one of these intelligible aspects of a thing apart from another and that both concepts give a partial insight into what is objectively present to the thing known.

To put it another way, there is a certain isomorphism between concept and reality, in virtue of which concept may be said to be a likeness (*species*) or picture of reality. This "likeness" should not be construed in terms of the relatively simple way a snapshot depicts a scene, but perhaps something more akin to Wittgenstein's "logical picture," being based upon what shows itself in both the world of facts and our thoughts about the world. In virtue of this intelligibility of form, we can speak of *ratio* (the Latin equivalent of the Greek *logos* or the Avicennist *intentio*) either as in things or as in the mind. To the extent that this *ratio* or intelligible feature is a property or characteristic of a thing, we are justified in saying that the individual possessing it is a so-and-so. Though such *rationes* can be conceived one without the other because their definitions differ and what is implied by one is not necessarily implied by the other, nevertheless, as characteristic of a specific individual, they constitute one thing. They are not separable from that individual in the way the soul can be separated from the body, or a husband from his family. Not even the divine power can separate a soul from its powers or the common features of the individual from what is unique (his *haecceity*).

Aquinas spoke of this nonidentity as conceptual, with the qualification that it does not arise merely in virtue of a thinking mind but "by reason of a property of the thing itself." Henry of Ghent called it an intentional distinction, but he added that the distinction is only potential prior to our thinking about it. Scotus, however, argued that if something has the native ability to produce different concepts of itself in the mind, each concept reflecting a partial but incomplete insight into the thing's nature, then the distinction must be in some sense actual. Put in another way, there must be several "formalities" in the thing (where "form" is understood as the objective basis for a concept and "little form" or formality as an intelligible aspect or feature of a thing that is less than the total intelligible content of a thing). Here again Scotus argued (on a line later followed by Wittgenstein) that a thing's possibilities, unlike their actualization, are not accidental but are essential to it and must have some actual basis. If a thing is virtually two things inasmuch as it is able to be grasped in two mutually exclusive ways, this nonidentity of intelligible content must be prior to our actually thinking about the thing, and to that extent it exists as a reality (*realitas*) or in other words, objectively. This nonidentity of realities, or formalities, is greatest in the case of the Trinity, where the peculiar properties of the three divine persons must be really identical with, but formally distinct from, the divine nature they have in common. This formal nonidentity holds also for the divine attributes, such as wisdom, knowledge, and love, which although really one are virtually many.

The formal distinction was also used by Scotus to explain the validity of our universal conceptions of individuals, a Scotistic thesis that influenced C. S. Peirce. Unlike the "nominalists," Scotus did not believe that the common features of things can be accounted for fully in terms of their being represented by a common term or class concept (see chapter 2 below). Some objective basis for this inclusion is required, and this similarity or aspect in which one individual resembles another he called its common nature (*natura communis*). This common nature is indifferent to being either individualized (as it invariably is in the extramental world) or being recognized as a universal feature of several individuals (as it is when we relate the concept of this "nature," such as "man," to Peter or Paul). The common nature is individualized concretely by what Scotus called its thisness (haecceity), which is a formality other than the nature, a unique property that can characterize one, and only one, subject (see chapter 4 below). Scotus consequently rejected the Aristotelian-Thomistic thesis that the principle of individuation is identified somehow with matter by reason of matter's quantitative aspect. This thesis would seem to make individuality something extrinsic to the thing itself, or at least the effect of something really other than the thing itself, since matter or matter signed with quantity is really distinct from form. The requirement of haecceity is a logical one, according to Scotus, for in practice we do not differentiate individual persons or objects because we know their respective haecceity (that is, their Petrinity, Paulinity, their "thisness," or "thatness"), but because of such accidental differences as being in different places at the same time, or having different colored hair or eyes. However, this individuating difference, he insisted, is known to God and can be known by man in a future life, where his intellect is not so dependent upon sense perception.

Knowing as an activity Though Scotus rejected illumination in favor of what is basically an Aristotelian theory of knowledge, his teaching on the subject shows the influence of some other of Augustine's ideas, notably the active role of the intellect in cognition. Scotus' position is midway between the Aristotelian passivism (the "possible intellect" as a purely "passive potency" receives impressions from without) and Augustine's activism (the intellect as spiritual can act on matter, but matter cannot act upon the spirit or mind). Scotus believed that the so-called possible intellect actively cooperates in concept formation and other intellectual operations. This activity is something over and above that which is usually ascribed to the "agent intellect." Intellect and object (or something that is proxy for the object, such as the intelligible *species* where abstract knowledge is involved) interact as two mutually complementary principles (like man and woman in generation) to produce concepts. Since these concepts reflect only common or universal characteristics of individuals rather than what is uniquely singular about them, it cannot be the singular object itself that directly interacts with the mind, but an intelligible likeness (species) that carries information only about the "common nature" of the object and not its haecceity. The formation of such a likeness or species is the joint effect of the agent intellect and sense image working together as essentially ordered efficient causes. It is in this way that Scotus interpreted the Aristotelian distinction of agent and possible intellect.

Intuitive versus abstractive cognition (See chapter five below.) Although the above description accounts for man's abstract intellectual knowledge, Scotus believed that man's mind is capable of intuitive knowledge as well. By this he understood a simple (nonjudgmental) awareness of an object as existing. Where abstract cognition leaves us unable to assert whether a thing exists or not, one can assert that it exists from intuitive cognition of anything. In such a case no intelligible species of the object need intervene, for the mind is in direct contact with the thing known. While most Scholastics limited intuitive knowledge to the sense level, Scotus argued that if man's intellect is capable only of abstract cognition—what can be abstracted from sense encounters in the way described by Aristotle—then the face-to-face vision of God promised to us in the afterlife becomes impossible. Consequently, our ideas of the proper object of the human intellect must be expanded to account for this.

Scotus thought that rational considerations also require us to admit some degree of intuitive power in man even if the full ambit of this power cannot be established by a philosopher. There are many primary contingent propositions of which we are absolutely certain (such as "I doubt such and such" or "I am thinking of such and such"). Since this certitude cannot be accounted for by any amount of conceptual analysis of the propositional terms, we must admit some prior simple awareness of the existential situation that verifies the proposition. This cannot be mere sensory knowledge, since the existential judgment often involves conceptual or nonsensory meanings, as in the examples given above. It is not clear that Scotus wished to assert that in this life we have intuitive knowledge of anything more than our interior acts of mind, will, and so on. This would seem to limit intellectual intuition to reflective awareness and would be consistent with his statements that we have no direct and immediate knowledge of the haecceity of any extramental object. However, he believed that in the afterlife man by his native powers will be able to intuit any created thing, be it material or spiritual, and to that extent man's mind is not essentially inferior to that of the angel. On the other hand, it is not merely because of man's lapsed state that his mind is at present limited to knowing the intelligible features of sense data but also because of the natural harmony of body and mind that would obtain even in a purely natural state.

Certitude Man's capacity for certitude was also discussed, with Henry of Ghent as the chief opponent. Henry, Scotus explained, appealed to illumination, not for the acquisition of our everyday concepts about the world, since these are obtained by abstraction, but for certitude of judgment. Although the "mechanics" of the process are not fully clear, two "mental images" or species are involved, one derived from creatures, the other imparted by divine illumination from above. Since both the human mind and the sensible object are subject to change, no species or likeness taken from the sensible object and impressed upon the mind will yield invariant truth. Something must be added from above. Scotus made short shrift of this theory. If the conclusion of a syllogism is no stronger than its weakest premises, neither does a blending of an immutable and a mutable species make for immutability. Furthermore, if the object is so radically mutable that nothing is invariant under change, then to know it as immutable is itself an error. By way of contrast, Scotus set out to show that certitude is possible without any special illumination. This is certainly the case with first principles and the conclusions necessarily entailed by them. Such necessary truths assert a connection or disconnection between concepts that is independent of the source of the concepts. It is not, for example, because we are actually in sense contact with a finite composite that we can assert that a "whole" of this kind is greater than a part thereof. Even if we erroneously perceive white as black and vice versa, a judgment like "white is not black" precludes any possible error because it depends only on a knowledge of the terms and not on how we arrived at that knowledge.

A second type of certitude concerns internal states of mind or actions. That we are feeling, willing, doubting are experiential facts that can be known with a degree of certitude equal to that of first principles or the conclusions they entail.

A third category concerns many propositions of natural science where a combination of experience and conceptual analysis gives us certitude. Reposing in our soul is the self-evident proposition: "Whatever occurs in a great many instances by a cause that is not free is the natural effect of that cause." Even if the terms are derived from erring senses, we know this to be true, for the very meaning of nature or natural cause is one that is neither free nor acts haphazardly. If experience reveals recurrent behavior patterns where no free intelligent agent is involved, then we are evidently dealing with a natural cause. If the same situation occurs, we can be certain at least of what *should* result therefrom. That the effect expected actually does occur depends on two further conditions: that the natural course of events is not interrupted by some unforeseen causal factor and that God does not miraculously intervene. Even sensory perception can be analyzed critically to exclude any reasonable doubt. Conflicting sense reports produce such illusions as the stick immersed in water that feels straight yet appears to be bent. Yet there is always some self-evident principle possessed by our mind that enables us to decide which sense perceptual information is correct. Here it is the proposition "Any harder object is not broken by something soft that gives way before it." There are many areas of knowledge, then, where man is perfectly well equipped to arrive at certitude without any special divine enlightenment.

THE DOMAIN OF CREATURES

Exemplar ideas Scholastics generally accepted Augustine's theory that before creatures are produced, they preexist in God's mind as archetypal ideas. Scotus differed from Bonaventure and Aquinas, however, by denying that God knows creatures through such ideas. Every creature is limited and finite as to intelligible content. To make God's knowledge of a creature dependent on this limited intelligibility of any given idea denigrates the perfection of his intellect; if there is any dependence of idea and intellect, it must be the other way around. Only the infinitely perfect essence can be regarded as logically, though not temporally, antecedent to God's knowledge of both himself and possible creatures. Since possible creatures are written into the divine nature itself, in knowing his nature God knows each possible creature, and in knowing the creature he gives it intelligibility and existence as an object of thought. Like the creative painter or sculptor who produces an idea of his masterpiece in his mind before embodying it in canvas or stone, God, if he is not to act blindly but intelligently, must have a guiding idea or "divine blueprint" of the creature that is logically prior to his decision to create it. Creatures, then are dually dependent on God; they depend on his infinitely fertile knowledge for their conception as examplar ideas, and they depend on the divine election of his omnipotent will for their actual existence. This tendency to distinguish various "logical moments" in God, and in terms of their nonmutual entailment to set up some kind of order or "priority of nature" among them, is characteristic of much of Scotus' theological speculation and became a prime target for Ockham's subsequent criticism.

Theory of matter and form The hylomorphic interpretation formerly attributed to Scotus was based on the *De Rerum Principio*, now ascribed to Cardinal Vital du Four. Scotus, unlike most of his Franciscan predecessors, did not accept the view of Ibn-Gabirol (Avicebrón) that all creatures are composed of matter and form. He considered both angels and human souls as simple substances, devoid of any real parts, though they differ in formal perfections they possess.

Since Scotus did not equate matter with potency (as did Saint Bonaventure), nor did he consider it in any way a principle of individuation (as did Saint Thomas), there was no reason to postulate it in spiritual creatures either to explain why they are not pure act like God or to account for the possibility of a plurality of individuals in the same species. Hence, against Aquinas, Scotus argued that even though angels lack matter, more than one individual of the same species may exist. More important, Scotus, like John Peckham and Richard of Middleton before him, insisted that matter must be a positive entity. Peckham's view grew out of his Augustinian theory of matter as the seat of the "seminal reasons," but Scotus rejected this germinal interpretation of inchoate forms and argued that if matter is what Aristotle thought it to be, it must have some minimal entity or actuality apart from form. It is true that primary matter is said to be pure potency, but there are two types of such passive potency: one is called objective and refers to some thing that is simply nonexistent but that can be the object of some productive creation. Matter as the correlative of form, however, is a "subjective" potency or capacity; it is a neutral subject able to exist under different forms and hence is not really identical with any one of them. Absolutely speaking, God could give matter existence apart from form, either accidental or substantial. In such a case, matter would exist much like a pure spirit or the human soul.

Ockham followed Scotus on this point, as well as in his view that the primary matter of the sun and planetary spheres is not any different from that found in terrestrial bodies, though the substantial form in question may be superior to that of terrestrial elements and compounds.

The human soul as form   From man's ability to think or reason, Scotus argued that the intellective soul is the substantial form that makes man precisely human. But to the extent that reason can prove the soul to be the form of the body, it becomes correspondingly more difficult to demonstrate that the soul will survive the death of the body. While the traditional arguments for immortality have probabilistic value, only faith can make one certain of this truth. On the other hand, if the soul must be a spiritual substance to account for the higher life of reason, at least one other perishable "form of corporeity" must be postulated to give primary matter the form of a human body. Though to this extent Scotus agreed with the pluriformists against Saint Thomas, it is not so clear that he would postulate additional subsidiary forms. A virtual presence of the lower forms (elements and chemical compounds) in the form of corporeity would seem to suffice. The form of corporeity has dimensive quantity, that is, it is not the same in each and every part of the body, as is the human soul. The same may be said of the "souls" of plants and animals. Though the human soul has the formal perfections of both the vegetative and animal souls, these components are not really distinct parts. A formal distinction between the soul's faculties or powers suffices to account for this.

Free will Particularly in his conception of free will, Scotus departed in many respects from contemporary positions (see chapter 8 below). The will is not simply an intellective appetite, a motor power or drive guided by intelligence rather than mere sense perception. Freedom of will, in other words, is not a simple logical consequence of intelligence but is unique among the agencies found in nature. All other active powers or potentialities (*potentiae activae*) are determined by their nature not only to act but to act in a specific way unless impeded by internal or external causes. But even when all the intrinsic or extrinsic conditions necessary for its operation are present, the free will need not act. Not only may it refrain from acting at all but it may act now one way, now another. The will has a two-fold positive response toward a concrete thing or situation. It can love or seek what is good, or it can hate or shun what is evil. Moreover, it has an inborn inclination to do so. But unlike the sense appetites, the will need not follow its inclination. Scotus rejected Aquinas' theory that man is free only if he sees some measure of imperfection or evil in a good object and that the will is necessitated by its end (the good as such), though it is free to choose between several means of attaining it.

But Scotus saw a still more basic freedom in the will, one that Aristotle and Plato failed to recognize. Their theory of man's appetites and loves can be called physical in the original sense of that term. All striving, all activity stems from an imperfection in the agent, whose actions all tend to perfect or complete its nature. *Physis* or "nature" means literally what a thing is "born to be" or become. Since what perfects a thing is its good, and since striving for what is good is a form of love, we could say that all activity is sparked by love. The peculiarity of such "love," however, is that it can never be truly altruistic or even objective. It is radically self-centered in the sense that nature seeks primarily and above all else its own welfare. If at times we find what appears to be altruistic behavior, it is always a case where the "nature" or "species" is favored at the cost of the individual. But nature, either in its individual concretization or as a self-perpetuating species, must of necessity and in all that it does seek its own perfection. This is its supreme value, and the ultimate goal of its loves. Such a theory presents a dual difficulty for a Christian. How can one maintain that "God is love" (1 John 4.16) and how can man love God above all things if self-perfection is his supreme value? Aquinas tried to solve the problem within the general framework of the Aristotelian system by making God the perfection of man. In loving God as his supreme value, man is really loving himself. Love of friendship becomes possible to the extent that he loves another as an "other self." This solution had its drawbacks, for certain aspects of Christian mysticism must then be dealt with in a Procrustean way. It leaves unexplained certain facets of man's complex love life. Finally, the theory commits Saint Thomas, as it did Aristotle, to maintain that the intellect, rather than free will, is the highest and most divine of man's powers—a view at odds with the whole Christian tradition and particularly with Augustine.

Scotus tried another tack, developing an idea suggested by Saint Anselm of Canterbury (see chapters 6, 7, and 9 below). The will has a twofold inclination or attraction toward the good. One inclination is the affection for what is to our advantage (*affectio commodi*), which corresponds to the drive for the welfare of the self described above. It inclines man to seek his perfection and happiness in all that he does. If this tendency alone were operative, we would love God only because he is our greatest good, and man's perfected self (albeit perfected by union with God in knowledge and love) would be the supreme object of man's affection; it would be that which is loved for its own sake and for the sake of which all else is loved. But there is a second and more noble tendency in the will, an inclination or affection for justice (*affectio justitiae*), so called because it inclines one to do justice to the objective goodness, the intrinsic value of a thing regardless of whether it happens to be a good for oneself or not. There are several distinguishing features of this "affection for justice." It inclines one to love a thing primarily for its own sake (its absolute worth) rather than for what it does or can do for one (its relative value). Hence it leads one to love God in himself as the most perfect and adorable of objects, irrespective of the fact that he happens to love us in return or that such a love for God produces supreme delight or happiness in man as its concomitant effect. Third, it enables one to love his neighbor literally as himself (where each individual is of equal objective value). Finally, this love is not jealous of the beloved but seeks to make the beloved loved and appreciated by others. "Whoever loves perfectly, desires co-lovers for the beloved" (*Opus Oxoniense* III, 37). Recall the tendency to make others admire the beautiful or the sorrow felt when something perfectly lovely is unloved, desecrated, or destroyed. If the *affectio commodi* tends to utter selfishness as a limiting case, the first checkrein on its headlong self-seeking is the *affectio justitiae*. Scotus wrote:

> This affection for what is just is the first tempering influence on the affection for what is to our advantage. And inasmuch as our will need not actually seek that towards which the later affection inclines us, nor need we seek it above all else, this affection for what is just, I say, is that liberty which is native or innate in the will, since it provides the first tempering influence on our affection for what is to our own advantage. (*Ibid.*, II, 6, 2)

The will's basic liberty, in short, is that which frees it from the necessity of nature described by Aristotle, the need to seek its own perfection and fulfillment above all else. Here is the factor needed to account for the generous and genuinely altruistic features of human love inexplicable in terms of physicalist theory.

Scotus therefore distinguished between the will with respect to its natural inclinations and the will as free. The former is the will considered as the seat of affection for the advantageous. It views everything as something delightful, useful, or a good for oneself and leads to the love of desire (*velle concupiscentiae*). As free or rational (in accord with right reason), the will is the seat of the affection for justice that inclines us to love each thing "honestly" or as a *bonum honestum*, that is, for what it is in itself and hence for its own sake. Since only such love recognizes the supreme value and dignity of a person and finds its highest and most characteristic expression when directed toward another, it is usually called the love of friendship (*velle amicicitae*) or of wishing one well (*amor benevolentiae*).

ETHICAL AND POLITICAL PHILOSOPHY

Although not primarily an ethicist, Scotus did solve enough specific moral problems from the standpoint of his general system of ethics to make it clear that his ethical system falls well within the accepted code of Christian morality of the day. Yet it does have some distinctive features, most of them growing out of the theory of the will's native liberty (see chapter 9 below). Without some such theory, Scotus did not believe a genuine ethics is possible. If man had only a "natural will" (a rational or intellectual appetite dominated by the inclination for self-fulfillment), he would be incapable of sin but subject to errors of judgment. On the other hand, if the will's freedom is taken to mean nothing more than simple liberation from this inclination of nature, its actions would become irrational and governed by chance or caprice. What is needed is some counterinclination that frees man from this need to follow his natural inclination yet is in accord with right reason. This is precisely the function of man's native freedom. Man's reason, when unimpeded by emotional considerations, is capable of arriving at a fairly objective estimate of the most important human actions in terms of the intrinsic worth of the goal attained, the effort expended, the consequences, and so on. By reason of its "affection for justice" the will is inclined to accept and to seek such intrinsic values, even when this runs counter to other natural inclinations of self-indulgence. But being free to disregard the inclination for self-indulgence and to follow the higher dictates of justice, man becomes responsible for the good or evil he forsees will result from either course of action. It is the exercise of this freedom that is a necessary, though not a sufficient, condition for any action to have a moral value.

The other requisite conditions become apparent if we consider the nature of moral goodness. An action may be called good on several counts. There is that transcendental goodness coextensive with being which means simply that, having some positive entity, a thing can be wanted or desired. But over and above this is that natural goodness which may or may not be present. Like bodily beauty, this accidental quality is a harmonious blend of all that becomes the thing in question. Actions also can have such a natural goodness. Walking, running, and the like may be done awkwardly or with a certain grace or beauty. More generally, an activity or operation of mind or will can be "in harmony with its efficient cause, its object, its purpose and its form and is naturally good when it has all that becomes it in this way" (*Opus Oxoniense* II, 40). But moral goodness goes beyond this natural goodness. "Even as beauty of body is an harmonious blend of all that becomes a body so far as size, color, figure and so on are concerned," Scotus wrote, "so the goodness of a moral act is a combination of all that is becoming to it according to right reason" (*ibid.*). One must consider not only the nature of the action itself but also all the circumstances, including the purpose of its performance. An otherwise naturally good action may be vitiated if circumstances forbid it or if it is done for an evil end.

Right reason tells us there is one action that can never be inordinate or unbecoming under any set of circumstances: the love of God for his own sake. "God is to be loved" is the first moral principle or ethical norm. This and its converse, "God must never be hated or dishonored," are two obligations from which God himself can never grant dispensation. He is the one absolute intrinsic value, which cannot be loved to excess; but "anything other than God is good because God wills it and not vice versa" (*ibid.* III, 19).

Scotus argued here as in the case of the divine intellect that the intelligibility of a creature depends upon God's knowing it, and not the other way around. So too its actual value or goodness depends upon God's loving it with a creative love and not vice versa. This obviously applies to transcendental goodness, which is coextensive with a thing's being, but it also holds for natural and moral goodness as well. If the infinite perfection of God's will prevents it from being dependent or necessitated by any finite good, it also ensures that creation as a whole will be good. God is like a master craftsman. For all his artistic liberty, he cannot turn out a product that is badly done. Yet no particular creation is so perfect, beautiful, or good that God might not have produced another that is also good; neither must all evil or ugliness be absent, particularly where this stems from a creature's misuse of his freedom. Nevertheless, there are limits to which God's providence can allow evil to enter the world picture. He may permit suffering and injustice so that mankind may learn the consequences of its misbehavior and through a collective sense of responsibility may right its social wrongs.

While certain actions may be naturally good or bad, they are not by that very fact invested with moral value; they may still be morally indifferent even when all circumstances are taken into consideration. Only hatred and the "friendship-love" of God are invested with moral value of themselves, and as the motivation for otherwise naturally good or indifferent actions they may make the actions morally wrong or good. Otherwise, the action must be forbidden by God to be morally wrong or commanded by him to be morally good. To that extent, moral goodness too depends on the will of God. However, it is important to know that some actions are good or bad only because God commands or forbids them, whereas he enjoins or prohibits other actions because they are naturally good or bad, that is, they are consonant or in conflict with man's nature in the sense that they tend to perfect it or do violence to it. Such are the precepts of the natural law embodied in the Decalogue and "written into man's heart." But note that what makes obedience to this instinctual law of moral value is that it be recognized and intended as something willed by God; otherwise, good as it may be naturally, the action is morally indifferent. This too is a consequence of man's native liberty, which can be bound only by an absolute value or the will of its author. To the extent that the first two commandments are expressions of the first moral principle and its converse, God can never make their violation morally right or a matter of indifference;

the same does not hold of the last seven, which regulate man's behavior to his fellow man. God granted genuine dispensations from natural law, permitting polygamy to the patriarchs so that the children of God might be multiplied when believers were few. This might be permitted again if plague or war so decimated the male population that race survival was threatened. In such a case, God would reveal this dispensation to man, probably through his church.

Human society Although Scotus wrote little on the origin of civil power, his ideas of its origin resemble Locke's. Society is naturally organized into families; but when they band into communities they find some higher authority necessary and agree to vest it in an individual or a group, and decide how it is to be perpetuated—for example, by election or hereditary succession. All political authority is derived from the consent of the governed, and no legislator may pass laws for private advantage or ones that conflict with the natural or divine positive law. Private property is a product of positive rather than natural law and may not be administered to the detriment of the common good. More striking, perhaps, than Scotus' social philosophy was his theological theory (which influenced Suárez and, more recently, Teilhard de Chardin) that the second person of the Trinity would have become incarnate even if man had not sinned. Intended as God's "firstborn of creatures," Christ represents the alpha and omega not only of human society but of all creation.

CONCLUSION

Known to posterity as the "Subtle Doctor," Scotus is admittedly a difficult thinker. Almost invariably his thought develops through an involved dialogue with unnamed contemporaries. Although this undoubtedly delighted his students and still interests the historian, it tries the patience of most readers. His style has neither the simplicity of Thomas' nor the beauty of Bonaventure's, yet as late as the seventeenth century he attracted more followers than they. Like students who unconsciously mimic the worst mannerisms of their mentor, many of Scotus' disciples seemed bent more on outdoing him in subtlety than in clarifying and developing his insights, so that for both the humanist and reformer "dunce" (a Dunsman) became a word of obloquy. Yet there have always been a hardy few who find the effort of exploring his mind rewarding. Even a poet like Gerard Manley Hopkins regarded his insights as unrivaled "be rival Italy or Greece," and the philosopher C. S. Peirce considered Scotus the greatest speculative mind of the Middle Ages as well as one of the "profoundest metaphysicians that ever lived." Even existentialists, who deplore the efforts to cast his philosophy in Aristotle's mold of science, find his views on intuition, contingency, and freedom refreshing. Scotus' doctrine of haecceity, applied to the human person, invests each individual with a unique value as one wanted and loved by God, quite apart from any trait he shares with others or any contribution he might make to society.

Despite his genius for speculation, Scotus considered speculation merely a means to an end: "Thinking of God matters little, if he be not loved in contemplation." Against Aristotle, he appealed to "our philosopher, Paul," who recognized the supreme value of friendship and love, which, directed to God, make men truly wise.

METAPHYSICS AND EPISTEMOLOGY

1 / The Formal Distinction

Ockham once remarked that the formal distinction was as much a mystery as the Trinity itself.[1] Though he required it to explain why the expository syllogism

> This divine essence is the Father.
> This divine essence is the Son.
> Therefore, the Father is the Son.

is invalid without having recourse to the "supernatural logic" used by some of his contemporaries, he was loath to admit it elsewhere. Much of the mystery disappears, I think, if we view the distinction in the comparatively simple context in which Scotus introduced it rather than against the more sophisticated set of distinction employed by some of the later scholastics.

Medieval philosophers generally admitted a threefold distinction: (1) the real distinction that exists between individuals in the extramental world, (2) the purely mental distinction created by the mind, and (3) an intermediate distinction which, though defined with reference to a mind, has some kind of basis in the thing. Historically the formal

Originally appeared in *John Duns Scotus, 1265–1965*, ed. John K. Ryan and Bernardine M. Bonansea (Washington, D.C.: Catholic University of America Press, 1965).

[1] *Guillelmus de Occam O.F.M.: Opera plurima*, Vol. III, *In Sententiarum 1* (Lugduni, 1495), d. 2, q. 1, F [no pagination].

distinction had its origin in the attempt to clarify the precise nature of that foundation in reality.[2]

Since the real distinction also was not always understood in the same way, we must keep in mind what it meant to Scotus. In the works of Aquinas, for example, the term seems to have two basically different meanings, only one of which corresponds to the usage of Scotus, Ockham or Suárez.[3] For the latter, the real distinction is that which exists between individuals, be they substances or some individual accident or property. It invariably implies the possibility of separating one really distinct thing from another to the extent that one of the two at least may exist apart from the other. The mental distinction on the other hand involves separability only in a thinking mind. The things to be distinguished are, so to speak, created in the very act of thinking about them. They are *entia rationis*. The need for some intermediary distinction, so the scholastics argued, stems from the fact that individuals are characterized by certain objective properties which, though inseparable in reality, are separable in concept, since neither notion includes the other. The inseparability of these properties from the individual, however, should be understood as follows. As an individual characteristic, this property cannot be separated from that individual in the way a loose stone may be removed from a particular wall, or an organ transplanted from one body to another. In this sense, there is no real distinction between the property in question and other features which inseparably accompany it in a particular individual. Nevertheless, it may be possible to discover other individuals which possess this property yet lack some of the associated features found in the first individual. A favorite example of the scholastics was the case of the human soul. As the seat not only of the higher life of reason, but also of that which man has in common with the brute animal or insensate vegetable, the soul was said to possess intellective and vegetative properties. Yet not all the scholastics regarded these as so many really distinct parts since the soul, as immortal, should be substantially simple.[4] God

[2] For a history of the formal distinction see B. Jansen, S.J., "Beiträge zur geschichtlichen Entwicklung der Distinctio formalis," *Zeitschrift für katholische Theologie*, LIII (1929), 317–344; 517–544; M. Grajewski, O.F.M., *The Formal Distinction of Duns Scotus* (Washington: The Catholic University of America Press, 1944), pp. 102–123.

[3] Thomists speak of a real distinction even where the *distinguenda* are separable only in thought (e.g. the soul and its faculties, essence and existence). Contrast this with the distinction between body and soul, mind and its thoughts, matter and any given form. At the time of Scotus and Ockham, it had become customary to restrict the name real distinction to the latter type.

[4] A common view among the scholastics during the mid-thirteenth century, especially at Oxford, seems to have been that the human soul was a composite substance consisting of really distinct parts. One of the theses condemned by the Dominican

might create it or destroy it as a unit, but even he could not alter its properties in such a way that it would become a purely animal or vegetable form such as the brute or plant possessed. Neither could he transform it into a pure intelligence such as the angel was said to be. Still the angel, so they argued, has the property of intellectivity without either sensitivity or the ability to vegetate, whereas the brute beast has a capacity for sense knowledge while lacking what is essential to the higher life of reason.

There are two ways of describing this intermediary distinction. Viewed from the vantage point of the mind which separates these properties in concept, the distinction is mental (*distinctio rationis*). Considered in terms of the intelligible features to which these concepts refer, however, the distinction is in some sense real. Thus St. Thomas insists that the distinction arises "not merely by reason of the one conceiving it but in virtue of a property of the thing itself,"[5] whereas Scotus speaks of it in the terminology of Peter Olivi as a distinction between *rationes reales*.[6]

This distinction was adopted primarily for the epistemological purpose of saving the objectivity of concepts that express a partial insight but not the whole truth about a reality which lacks really distinct parts in the sense explained above. It should not surprise us then that there is a certain unanimity among the scholastics about its objective nature. On the other hand, they differ considerably as to whether what such distinct concepts denote can be said to be nonidentical even before we begin to think about them. On this point there seems to be a marked development of thought from the time Aquinas composed his commentary on the second distinction of Book I of the *Sentences* to the day Scotus lectured on that work of Peter Lombard.

Kilwardby in 1277 was *quod vegetativa, sensitiva et intellectiva sint una forma simplex*. Though this idea of the soul as a composite unity was frequently associated with the thesis of the plurality of forms (e.g. Roger Bacon, Philip the Chancellor, John Peckham), this was not always the case. In a letter written to his confrere, Peter of Conflans, Archbishop of Corinth, Kilwardby makes the interesting statement: "Positio de unitate formarum nisi plus dicatur non satis est mihi. Scio tamen, quod unus homo habet unam formam, quae non est una simplex, sed ex multis composita, ordinem ad invicem habentibus naturalem et sine quarum nulla perfectus homo esse potest, quarum ultima completiva et perfectiva totius aggregati est intellectiva." Confer A. Birkenmajer, "Der Brief Robert Kilwardby's an Peter von Conflans und die Streitschrift des Aegidius von Lessines" in *Vermischte Untersuchungen zur Geschichte der mittelalterlichen Philosophie* (Beiträge zur Geschichte der Philosophie des Mittelalters, Bd. XX, Heft 5, Münster, 1922), p. 63.

[5] St. Thomas Aquinas, *Commentum in Librum I Sententiarum*, d. 2, q. 1, a. 2, *Opera omnia* (Vivès edition), VII, p. 36.

[6] Duns Scotus, *Quaestiones subtilissimae in Metaphysicam Aristotelis*, lib. VII, q. 19, n. 10, *Opera omnia* (Vivès edition), VII, p. 470.

The area of general agreement, I believe, includes the following points: (1) Some kind of isomorphism exists between thought and reality in virtue of which the former may be said to be a likeness or picture of the latter. This "likeness" should not be construed in terms of the relatively simple way a snapshot depicts a scene; it is something more sophisticated—not unlike Wittgenstein's "logical picture," perhaps—and is based upon what "shows itself" in both the world of facts and our thoughts about that world. (2) In virtue of this community of intelligible form, we can speak of *ratio* (the same would be true of the Greek *logos* or the Avicennian *intentio*) either as in things or in the mind. (3) To the extent that this ratio is a property or characteristic of the thing, we are justified in asserting that the individual in question is a "so and so." (4) Though such *rationes* can be conceived one without the other, since their definitions differ and what is implied by one is not implied by the other, nevertheless as characteristic of extramental reality they constitute one thing. In a word they are not individuals or really distinct parts in the way the real distinction was explained above.

The main area of difference concerns the meaningfulness of saying that one *ratio* is actually not identical with the other prior to our actually thinking of one apart from its mate. Though Aquinas does not raise this question in so many words, what he writes in his commentary on the *Sentences* about the attributes of God (which are so many *rationes*) might well be interpreted as favoring such an actual nonidentity, despite Cajetan's denial that such is the mind of the saint. Thus, for example, St. Thomas tells us that when we speak of a *ratio* as a property of a thing what we mean is

> ... that in the thing outside the mind, there is something which corresponds to the conception of the mind as the significatum corresponds to the sign ... and this occurs in a proper sense when the conception of the intellect is a likeness of the thing.[7]

To speak of different *rationes* in God in this sense, however, does not introduce a real distinction or plurality into the divine essence. And while

> ... we must say that wisdom, goodness and such like are in God, each of these is the divine essence itself and thus all are one thing. But because each of them in its truest sense is in God and what wisdom means is not what is meant by goodness as such, it follows that they are concep-

[7] Op. cit., a. 3, p. 37.

tually different not just in virtue of the one conceiving them but by reason of a property of the thing itself.[8]

And he insists further that

> ... from all eternity when creatures were non-existent, and even if they never were going to exist, it was still true to say that he [God] is wise, good and the like. Neither does one notion signify what the other does in the way that the same thing is signified by synonyms.[9]

Henry of Ghent, writing several decades later, however, takes some pains to point out that the intentional distinction, as he calls it (*intentio* being a term he uses as a synonym for Aquinas' *ratio*), is merely potential prior to the act of thought, whereas it becomes actual only in the mind when the latter conceives one intention apart from the other.[10]

Perhaps one of Scotus' more illuminating remarks is that the formal distinction does not deny the intentional distinction of Henry but merely postulates what is needed in things to account for it.[11] With reference to Henry's version he writes:

> In such notions as these, does the intellect, I ask, have as object something in the thing? If not, we have a mere fiction of the mind. If it is the same thing, then the object of both concepts should be identical unless you grant that one and the same extramental thing formally generates two objects in the intellect. But in this case, it does not seem that the thing or anything of the thing is the object of my knowledge, but that the latter is something produced by the thing. But if the intellect knows something different in each concept, then our thesis is granted, since a difference is there prior to the concept.[12]

Unless I am mistaken, the precise difference between Scotus and Henry is this. If you grant their common scholastic assumption that our concepts and reality are somehow isomorphic, then the mere possibility of conceiving one property without the other requires some actual nonidentity or distinction of properties a *parte rei* which is logically prior to, and a condition for, our thinking of one apart from the other.

Scotus' point here, I believe, is well taken. As every great philosopher

---

[8] Ibid., a. 2, p. 35.

[9] Ibid., a. 3, p. 39.

[10] Henry of Ghent, *Summa quaestionum ordinarum*, art. 27, q. 1 (Parisiis, 1520), Tom. I, fol. 162r O; *Quodlibet* V, q. 6 in *Disputationes quodlibeticae* (Parisiis, 1518), Tom. I, fol. 161rv. See also Duns Scotus, *op. cit.*, n. 4, p. 465.

[11] Duns Scotus, *op. cit.*, n. 10, p. 470.

[12] *Ibid.*, n. 5, p. 466.

from Aristotle to our own day has noted, what a thing *can be* (or in this case, *can do*) is part and parcel of *what it is*. As Ludwig Wittgenstein pointed out, a thing's "possibilities," unlike their actualization, are not something accidental to the thing. They "must be written into the thing itself," so to speak, "from the beginning."[13]

That is why the acute Aquinas insisted that this distinction cannot be reduced purely and simply to a distinction of reason; it arises in part at least *ex proprietate ipsius rei*. Scotus, with his usual subtlety, is simply spelling out what such a statement implies, viz. that such "property-differences" are based upon what a thing is or is not in actuality. Two objects are not formally identical *a parte rei*, if one can be imitated without the other or if one can be distinctly known for what it is apart from the other. Some way of expressing this nonidentity or distinction of intelligible content, or imitable perfection, is needed. To say it is purely potential does not do justice to the actual basis that makes such a conceptual distinction possible. All concede that the positive basis for the distinct concept is not created by the mind in the very act of knowing it. Neither then, Scotus argued, is the nonidentity of what is known by each of two isomorphic concepts. To argue that the precise objective correlate of each of the two is in all respects actually identical seems to commit one to the dilemma pointed out by Scotus. Either but one true concept of the thing is possible or else, if we do have two concepts, they cannot be concepts of what is actually present, but are concepts of objects produced by the thing.

Scotus ascribes various names to the objective correlate of such concepts. His usual designation for it is *realitas* or *formalitas*, though he occasionally refers to it as an *intentio* or a *ratio realis*.[14]

---

[13] L. Wittgenstein, *Tractatus Logico-Philosophicus*, 2.012–2.0121, trans. D. F. Pears and B. F. McGuinness (London: Routledge and Kegan Paul, 1961), pp. 7–9.

[14] See especially the *Ordinatio* I, d. 2, nn. 399–407, *Opera omnia* (Vatican edition) II, pp. 355–358; also Scotus' remark in *Reportata Parisiensia* II, d. 1, q. 6, n. 20, *Opera* (Vivès ed.), XXII, p. 556: "Intelligit idem ipse Avicenna per aliam intentionem quod ego dico per aliam formalitatem." The neologism "formalitas" or "little form" invites comparison between the properties of a formality and those traditionally ascribed to the Aristotelian "form" (such as its being the principle of intelligibility and actuality, or its being equated with essence). One thing is certain, by means of the formal distinction Scotus was able to simplify a doctrine that seems almost traditional among Franciscan thinkers, that of a plurality of forms in man. On the one hand, Scotus recognizes the need of a *forma corporeitatis* that is really distinct from and other than the rational soul as the highest form in man. But differing from some of the earlier thinkers of this century like Roger Bacon, Kilwardby and others (confer T. Crowley, *Roger Bacon, The Problem of the Soul in His Philosophical Commentaries*, Louvain: Editions de l'Institut Supérieur de Philosophie—Dublin: James Duffy and Co., 1950, especially pp. 136–152 for an account of the divergent views at this time), Scotus saw no need to postulate any real composition or distinction of forms in the human soul. For him the sensitive and vegetative "parts" are only formally distinct from the rational. While the same solution

The distinction or nonidentity that obtains between such correlates he prefers to call "formal" but adds that you may also speak of it as a "virtual distinction"[15] since what you find in the thing is not really two things but "one thing which is virtually or preeminently, as it were, two realities."[16] You may even call it *distinctio rationis*, he says, apparently referring to St. Bonaventure's terminology,[17] where *ratio* means not something created by the mind, but rather expresses something of what the thing is insofar as the "whatness is an object of the intellect."[18]

This raises the interesting question as to how far Scotus himself may be responsible for the usage of latter day Thomists who commonly label this intermediate distinction as "virtual"? For while we find this term in Boethius, neither he nor Aquinas apply it in this connection. Suarez, on the other hand, seems to prefer this designation and Cajetan in trying to delineate more precisely how Scotus differs from Thomas declares that where Scotus postulates in the object an "actual formal distinction," Aquinas admits only a "virtual formal distinction."[19]

More important perhaps is the fact that Scotus calls the distinction one of reason (*distinctio rationis*). This fact alone should make it clear that he did not claim the nonidentity in question could be defined or described apart from some reference to an intellect. If no intellect could exist, there would be no formal distinction. While Scotus insists the distinction is prior to the *act* of thinking (and hence is not created by the mind), he never says it is prior to the possibility of thought. Indeed, the possibility of knowing (which is one way of describing the intellect)

---

might conceivably be adopted to eliminate a plurality or hierarchy of further forms within the *forma corporeitatis*, not all interpreters of Scotus hold that he postulates only one organic form for the entire organism and its various parts. Some believe that he used "form of corporeity" as a collective term for a hierarchy of subordinate forms corresponding to the different organs of the body. In this connection see B. J. Campbell, *The Problem of One or Plural Substantial Forms in Man as Found in the Works of St. Thomas Aquinas and John Duns Scotus* (Philadelphia: University of Pennsylvania, 1940); B. Baudoux, "De forma corporeitatis scotistica," *Antonianum*, XIII (1938), 429–474; B. Vogt, "The *Forma corporeitatis* of Duns Scotus and Modern Science," *Franciscan Studies*, III (1943), 47–62.

[15] *Ordinatio, loc. cit.,* p. 355.

[16] *Ibid.,* p. 356.

[17] St. Bonaventure, *Commentaria in quatuor libros Sententiarum,* lib. I, d. 5, art. 1, q. 1, ad 1, *Opera omnia,* Tom. I (Ad Claras Aquas: Ex typographia Collegii S. Bonaventurae, 1882), p. 113; *ibid.,* d. 26, q. 1, ad 2, p. 453; *ibid.,* d. 45, art. 2, q. 1, p. 804.

[18] *Ordinatio, loc. cit.,* p. 355.

[19] *Commentum in Summam theologicam* I, q. 39, art. 1 in *Sti. Thomae Aquinatis Summa theologica cum Commentariis Thomae de Vio Card. Cajetani,* Tom. I (Patavii: Ex typographia Seminarii, 1698), p. 261. See also F. Suarez, *De SS. Trinitatis mysterio,* IV, c. 4, n. 15 (Borgnet edition), Vol. I, 627; *idem, Disputationes metaphysicae,* disp. 7, sec. 1, Vol. 25, pp. 250ff.

and the possibility of being known (which is another way of saying "formality") are correlative terms. Each entails the other. Neither is logically nor ontologically prior, but they are technically *simul natura*.

It is a historical fact that Scotus did not invent this distinction but took it over from his contemporaries. On the other hand, those who adopted it after him were not loathe to cite him as a fore-runner of their own views on the subject. As Ockham himself warned, we must not attribute to the Subtle Scot all the exaggerated claims made by others for this distinction. For one thing, I think it would be a mistake to believe that he, like some of the later formalists, regarded realities or formalities as some kind of "ontological bricks" characterized by fixed dimensions. A careful reading of what he says on the subject lends no support to such an interpretation. His account of the distinction is perfectly consistent with the admission that there is something fluid about the way we think of things, and hence about the way we draw the lines that separate one intelligible aspect from another. The one essential point seems to be that however we may choose to divide the perfections of a thing, if our concepts reflect something about the latter, there must be something positive in that thing which corresponds to these concepts. This positive entity or reality is not something the thing has only because we happen to be thinking about it at the moment. Perhaps a better analogy than "ontological bricks" would be that of a stage upon which different spotlights are playing, where each illuminated area represents what we grasp in one of our concepts. It is not necessary that the spotlights remained fixed; they may move about, and the areas illumined may even intersect in part. Scotus' point, I believe, would be this. Even before you switch the spotlights on, or, what is more, if you never turned them on or even had any lights, it would still be meaningful not only to speak of what they would reveal if you had them to turn on, but there would also be grounds for denying that one part of the stage is simply identical with the other as regards what a light will reveal. For each possibly separate area of illumination would still be just what it is and would contain what is proper to itself. And it is what each has, and not just what we reveal or think it has, that makes the one area not simply identical with the other. For some nonidentity of what exists on the part of a thing, Scotus argues, must be logically prior to and a necessary condition for our being able to think of one without the other. Though Scotus repeatedly stresses that the formal distinction is logically prior to actual thought, I can find no passage where he suggests the distinction can be defined without reference to the possibility of separating the formalities in thought. In fact the whole historical context in which the distinction was born argues to the contrary.

Though no individual thing is so simple that is does not contain more than one formality, nor are formalities so distinct that they do not form one real thing, there are different ways in which formalities may be said to be one.

Consider, for the moment, the attributes of God. Though each is infinitely perfect, one attribute is not formally the other, since their definitions differ and one asserts what the other does not. Even the mode of infinity does not fuse the formal concepts. For to say that God's knowledge, for instance, is infinite, is to say that it comprehends all that can be known. Yet this is something quite different from saying that knowledge is formally love or that the sense of their several definitions are identical. But because each of God's attributes is infinitely perfect, we have no grounds for claiming that one formality perfects another in the way that parts are mutually perfected by their forming one whole.

But, says Scotus, the same need not hold for creatures. Here we can speak of a quasi-composition, not of course in any real or proper sense as would be the case were the parts really distinct. But if, in a thing characterized by two or more formalities, their combination, as it were, turns out to be something more than we might expect of the simple sum of the two, we may say that their togetherness constitutes a *per se*, rather than a *per accidens*, unity. In man or in the human soul, where both sensitivity and intelligence are present, each adds something as it were to the perfection of the other. The creative imagination of the artist, for example, which is born of their union, is something neither the brute beast with its sensitivity nor the angel with its intellectual life as such possess. Because of this we may say that in man, or in human nature, the abstract formalities of animality and rationality, though formally distinct, are so related that together they form not a mere aggregate of intelligible items which the mind lists in catalogue fashion, but they are so ordered to one another that they constitute a single intelligible whole.[20]

Not only must the attributes of God be formally distinct, says Scotus,[21] but some formal nonidentity must be postulated between the divine essence and what is proper or peculiar to each Person, if fallacies like the one mentioned at the beginning of this essay are to be avoided. If the Father communicates his nature to the Son, and together with the latter to the Holy Spirit, his paternity is something he shares with neither. Far from depending upon the divine intellect's actual knowl-

---

[20] *Ordinatio* I, d. 8, nn. 103–107, *Opera* (Vatican ed.) IV, pp. 200–202; *ibid.* nn. 218–221, pp. 274–276.
[21] *Ibid.*, nn. 186–217, pp. 254–274.

edge, this nonidentity is a logically prior condition for God's awareness of the same.[22] Ockham will admit the existence of a formal distinction only in this case, but not in creatures or even between the attributes of God. Scotus, on the contrary, speaks of various degrees of the distinction and admits some form of it not only in the latter case, but also between the generic perfection and that expressed by the specific difference,[23] or between the unique haecceity or individuating difference of a thing and those features it has in common with other individuals.[24] He adds that the transcendental attributes of being are formally distinct from each other as well as from being. The same holds for the soul and its powers such as intellect and will.[25]

Since Scotus denies the real distinction between essence and existence some Scotists thought he might wish to substitute a formal distinction for the same, or at least a formal modal distinction.[26] The latter is the type of distinction found between a formality and its intrinsic mode such as "wisdom" and "infinite" in God, or "being" and "finite" in a creature.[27] Whereas the proper concepts of two formalities may be mutually exclusive, the concept of an intrinsic mode includes somehow the notion of the formality of which it is the mode. Yet the formality, let us say, of "being" or "wisdom," is not so identical with the mode or manner in which it exists in a concrete instance that it is impossible for the mind to prescind from the mode and still say something true and objective. Thus, for instance, one could say in all truth that God possesses the formal perfection of being or wisdom and still leave open whether the perfection in question is present in a finite or infinite degree.

It does not seem sufficient, however, to characterize the formal modal distinction as nothing more than a non-mutual formal distinction such as would hold, for example, between the perfection of animality and corporeity. For animality not only includes corporeity, but adds something to the formal character of the latter, viz., what is required for sense and vegetative life. Such is not the case

[22] Ibid., d. 2, nn. 388–410, II, pp. 349–361.

[23] Ibid., d. 8, n. 219, IV, p. 275; Quaest. in Metaphys., loc. cit., n. 8, p. 468.

[24] Opus oxoniense II, d. 3, q. 6, n. 15, Opera (Vivès ed.) XII, p. 144.

[25] Ibid., d. 16, q. unica, n. 17, XIII, pp. 43–44.

[26] For a survey of the problem see A. J. O'Brien's unusually perceptive study "Scotus on Essence and Existence," The New Scholasticism, XXXVIII (1964), 61–77. In addition to those interpreters he mentions who ascribe to Scotus a formal distinction between essence and existence are S. Day, Intuitive Cognition: A Key to the Later Scholastics (St. Bonaventure, N.Y.: Franciscan Institute, 1947), p. 63; J. Weinburg, A Short History of Medieval Philosophy (Princeton, N.J.: Princeton University Press, 1964), p. 218.

[27] Ordinatio I, d. 8, nn. 136–150, IV, pp. 221–227.

with an intrinsic mode. One is tempted to say that what is added to our knowledge in the latter case pertains to the order of quantity rather than quality. This is true if we do not take quality and quantity as Aristotelian categories, but in an extended or transcendental sense, viz., that one represents a reply to a question of the form: "What kind of perfection does this have?" or "What type of thing is it?" whereas the other answers a query of the form: "How great is the perfection in question?" or "To what degree is such and such a characteristic present?" (Scotus, we know, was one of the first scholastics to show how variations in quality intensity might be treated quantitatively—an insight applied by the Merton schoolmen to the problem of motion, which made Galileo's description of the free-fall of bodies possible).[28]

But in differentiating the modal from the strict formal distinction, Scotus seems to have had more in mind than this. In speaking of the comparative simplicity of various concepts used to describe God, Scotus makes the somewhat puzzling statement that "infinite being" is a simpler concept than "good being" or "true being" since "infinite" is not a quasi-attribute of being like "good" or "true," but expresses an intrinsic mode even as a certain intensity of whiteness expresses not some formal composition but an intrinsic mode of the quality.[29] What Scotus seems to be struggling to express, if somewhat obscurely because of a lack of analytical tools, is a problem not unfamiliar to the contemporary philosopher. The ontological structure of reality is not always faithfully reflected in language or thought. Though an expression like "infinite being" bears a superficial resemblance to "true being," it has a different logical form. The reality referred to by composite terms like "infinite being" or "infinite whiteness" is so simple, says Scotus, that if it were known intuitively rather than in an abstract way, the distinction between a formality and its mode would be erased. Where two formalities are known intuitively, however, they still appear as two distinct formal objects.[30] Yet infinity is not so much a part of God's goodness, wisdom, or other formal perfection that if we teach a child, for instance, that God is good, wise, loving and so on without conveying in any way the information that he is such in an infinite

[28] M. Clagett, *The Science of Mechanics in the Middle Ages* (Madison: University of Wisconsin Press—London: Oxford University Press, 1959), p. 206. For a concise historical account of the development of the problem of intension and remission of forms see A. Maier, *Zwei Grundprobleme der scholastischen Naturphilosophie*, 2 ed. (Roma: Edizioni di Storia e Letteratura, 1951).

[29] *Ordinatio* I, d. 3, n. 58, III, p. 40.

[30] *Ibid.*, d. 8, n. 142, IV, p. 224.

degree, we have deceived the child and have not told the truth. Granted the information is not complete or perfect, what we know by means of such imperfect concepts is still true.[31]

Even though Scotus' remarks on the formal modal distinction leave much to be desired as to how far he would be willing to apply it, what he does say makes it clear enough that he considered even the formal distinction inadequate to express all the intelligible differences characteristic of reality. If we pursue this point farther, I think we could say that Scotus would not reject every distinction *a parte rei* between essence and existence, even if he would not necessarily consider it to be a strictly formal, or even perhaps a formal modal, distinction.[32]

The proper way to distinguish essence from existence, however, would seem to be in terms of what is required *a parte rei* for intuitive versus abstractive cognition and not, primarily at least, in terms of the objective basis for different types of concepts.

Unlike some current interpretations of the Thomistic position, Scotus does not hold that existence is first grasped in and through an existential judgment, but rather by a simple act of intellectual awareness called intuition. For like the generality of the scholastics, he considers every judgment—as "an act of composition and division"—to presuppose logically, if not psychologically or temporally, some prior act of simple apprehension. There are many primary contingent propositions of which we are absolutely certain (e.g., "I doubt such and such" or "I am thinking of such and such," etc.). Since this certitude cannot be explained by a knowledge of the conceptual terms of the proposition in question, we must admit some prior simple awareness of the existential situation that verifies the proposition. This cannot be mere sensory knowledge, since the existential judgment often involves conceptual or non-sensory meanings as in the examples cited above.

Some form of intellectual intuition precedes not only every existential judgment, but probably every abstract concept which the mind forms. This is certainly the case according of Ockham, who develops

[31] *Ibid.*, nn. 143–145, pp. 225–226.

[32] In the *Quaestiones quodlibetales*, q. 13, n. 10 (Vivès ed.), XXV, p. 522, Scotus speaks of "aliqua distinctio objecti" between what is grasped by abstractive and intuitive knowledge respectively, but goes on to add that this distinction becomes apparent only when existence is grasped abstractly. This means that a formal difference between what is known through abstract knowledge (viz., what the object is) and what is known by intuitive knowledge (viz., the object as existing and present here and now) concerns not so much the content of what is known as the way in which the object known moves the intellect, viz., in itself and by reason of existing and interacting with the mind, or (in the case of abstract knowledge) in and through a species.

the Scotist doctrine of intuition, but it seems to be implicit, at least, in what Scotus says on the subject.[33]

Simple apprehension, then, can be either an intuitive or an abstractive cognition. The latter is concerned with "essences" or essential features in the sense that the concepts which are the end product of such simple awareness represent answers to questions of the form *Quid est?*, that is to say, they are questions that are answerable in terms of the categories to which the features in question belong. We might note that an intrinsic mode such as infinity or finitude, or the degree of intensity of a quality like whiteness, would seem to be an essential feature in this broad sense of the term. Intuitive cognition, on the other hand, while it may include all the data or information found in a corresponding abstractive cognition, invariably includes something more, viz., that additional knowledge or information of the fact that it exists.

The proper way of distinguishing essence from existence for Scotus then would seem to be in terms of that objective feature of any object, situation or thing that makes it possible not merely to identify what it is, but to assert that it is. At the primary level at which this datum is presented, existence is not strictly speaking "conceivable"; neither is intuitive awareness properly speaking a concept. For as we ordinarily understand this term, a concept is always the result of abstractive cognition. By reflection upon what is common to all instances of intellectual intuition, the mind can form an abstract concept of existence. And it is this concept that seems to be related to the concept of what a thing is as something formally other, or as an additional modality. But it would be a mistake, Scotus recognizes, to argue from the superficial likeness of concepts like "rational animal," "intense whiteness," and "an existing person" to the same ontological structure or distinction *a parte rei*.[34]

If our analysis of the reasoning that led Scotus to postulate the formal distinction is substantially correct, then it would seem that the strict formal distinction, the formal modal distinction and that between essence and existence have something in common and yet, for all that, differ by reason of the objective basis for the distinction.

---

[33] For a collection of texts of Scotus and Ockham on this subject see S. Day, *Intuitive Cognition: A Key to the Significance of the Later Scholastics* (St. Bonaventure, N.Y.: The Franciscan Institute, 1947); P. Boehner, *Ockham, Philosophical Writings* (Edinburgh: Thomas Nelson and Sons, 1957), pp. 18–27; *idem*, "The Notitia Intuitiva of Non-Existents According to William Ockham," *Traditio*, I (1943), pp. 223–275.

[34] See the discussion in *Ordinatio* I, d. 3, n. 58, III, p. 40 and d. 8, n. 138ss, IV, p. 222ff; also Scotus' remarks in *Collationes seu Disputationes subtilissimae*, collatio 13, n. 5 (Vivès ed.), V, p. 202.

All three arise from the desire to distinguish those characteristics of reality that make it possible to have different types of knowledge about it. The features known, however, are separable only in concept, though at the point where this becomes possible, the concepts may not represent the same level of abstraction or perhaps refer to reality in the same manner. To put the matter briefly in modern terminology, they have not the same "logical form." On the other hand, to speak of the distinction as one that is simply created by the mind does not do full justice to the fact that more is required of reality to justify one type of knowledge or concept than is needed to justify another. The meaning of "more" can be explicated as follows. If the information conveyed or expressed by *A* includes the information conveyed or expressed by *B*, but not vice versa, where *A* and *B* stand for two types of knowledge (e.g., intuitive versus abstractive knowledge of the same object), or for two concepts (e.g., infinite wisdom versus wisdom) or sets of concepts (e.g., rational animal versus animal), then what is denoted by *A* is not simply identical *a parte rei* with what *B* denotes, and the distinction or nonidentity in question is one of a greater or lesser degree of intelligibility.

But this way of describing the three distinctions obscures the fact that it was made possible only by conceiving the *distinguenda* abstractly, for only at the level of abstractive cognition do they appear as formally different objects of intelligibility. Two of the distinctions (the formal modal and the essence-existence distinction) evaporate as it were if the reality in question is known intuitively. Scotus made an initial attempt to indicate how the first of these differs from the formal distinction proper in terms of what he calls the relative "simplicity" of the concepts in which these objective differences are mirrored. Admittedly this mode of description may not have proved particularly enlightening to Scotus' contemporaries or immediate followers. It does seem to make a bit more sense, perhaps, in view of Russell's and Wittgenstein's early attempts to determine to what extent it is possible to express the metaphysical structure, or what they called the "logical form," of the world in thought or language.

Had Scotus been cognizant of their speculations on the subject, I think he might have pointed out that if the essence-existence distinction resembles in some respects a formal distinction, or still more the distinction between a formality and its mode, the ontological "structure" is quite different in the three cases. And, though it is far from adequate and deserves to be pursued further, it might do for a beginning at least to say that one way in which the existence of a real object differs from both a formality or an intrinsic mode like the finitude of a creature or the intensity of a color is that it is possible to grasp it primarily and perfectly only in an intuition. What a formality is, or what intrinsic mode characterizes a given object, however, is something that can be known through an abstract form of cognition with an immediacy and perfection that is not the case with the modality called existence (e.g. by infused, yet abstract, knowledge such as Scotus suggests was granted to St. Paul or the prophets).[35] In its "here and now-ness" the existence of an existing essence, quality or situation is something unique and non-universal. Only when it is grasped in some secondary and abstract form of knowledge does it appear to have a commonness or universal features, and as having such, to be related to "whatness" or quiddity as a mode to its subject.

[35] This seems to be the whole point of Scotus' remark: "De quocumque objecto scientiae potest haberi cognitio simpliciter distinctissma abstractiva objecti citra intuitivam... Omnis scientia est re non praecise, ut existens est, quod intelligo sic, quod ipsa existentia, etsi sit ratio intellecta in objecto, vel citra objectum, tamen non necessario requiritur, ut actualiter conveniens objecto, inquantum objectum est scibile" *Quaest. quodlibetales*, q. 7, n. 8; XXV, 290. An intrinsic mode like finitude in creatures or infinity in God, however, pertains to what is necessarily connected with the essence and hence what is *scibile* in the technical sense of *sciri* according to the requirements set down by Aristotle at the beginning of the *Posterior Analytics*.

2 / The Realism of Scotus

The realist-nominalist controversy in the fourteenth century owes its origin to Duns Scotus and William Ockham, the two men whom C. S. Peirce in his Harvard lectures on British logicians praised as "decidedly the greatest speculative minds of the middle ages, as well as two of the profoundest metaphysicians that ever lived."[1] Scotus' reputation as a realist, even if his realism be what neo-scholastics call "moderate" and Peirce "halting," rests on his conception of how the specific nature of anything exists in individuals of any given kind.

Like Aquinas, Scotus was impressed by Avicenna's statement that "equinity is just equinity"[2]; that is to say, of itself, it is neither one nor several, neither universal nor particular.[3] And since "one," as contrasted with "several," refers to individual or numerical unity, rather than to specific or generic unity, Scotus went a step further, insisting that even in the existing individual one could speak of its specific nature as possessing a "unity that is real, yet less than numerical unity" (*Opus oxon.*, N 2; p. 7).

This assertion, however, is based upon another of Scotus' pet theories: that between the individual's nature and that positive and unique

Reprinted with permission from *The Journal of Philosophy* 59 (1962), 725–36.

[1] C. Hartshorne and P. Weiss, eds., *Collected Papers of Charles Sanders Peirce*, vol. I (Cambridge, Mass.: Harvard University Press, 1931), p. 10, §29.

[2] Avicenna, *Metaphysica*, tract. 5, cap. 1 (Venice, 1508, fol. 86va).

[3] Cf. Scotus, *Opus oxoniense* II, D 3, Q 1, N 7 (Vivès ed., vol. 12, p. 48); also *Quaestiones in Metaphysicam* VII, Q 18, N 8 (Vivès ed., vol. 7, p. 458).

feature which differentiates it from all other individuals there is a formal distinction.

The difference between the realism of Scotus and Ockham's nominalism (some would prefer to call it a "realistic conceptualism") lies, so far as I can see, in the denial by Ockham of this formal nonidentity on the part of the object known.[4]

Each of these statements merits a word of explanation. Let me begin with the formal distinction, since this seems to be the key to understanding the rest.

THE FORMAL DISTINCTION

Scholastics generally admit a threefold distinction: (1) the real distinction that exists between individuals in the extramental world, (2) the purely mental distinction created by the mind, and (3) an intermediate distinction which, though defined with reference to a mind, has some kind of basis in the thing. Historically the formal distinction developed as an attempt to clarify the precise nature of that foundation in reality.

The real distinction proper that exists between individuals (be they substances or some individual property or accident) implies, for Scotus, Ockham, and Suarez, the possibility of separating one really distinct thing from another to the extent that one of the two at least may exist without the other. The mental distinction on the other hand involves separability only in a thinking mind, because the things to be distinguished are, so to speak, created in the very act of thinking about them (entia rationis). The need for some intermediary distinction, so the scholastics argued, stems from the fact that individuals are characterized by certain objective properties, which, though inseparable in reality, are separable in concept, since neither notion includes the other. The inseparability of these properties from the individual, however, should be understood as follows. As an individual characteristic, this property cannot be separated from that individual in the way a brick can be removed from a particular wall, or an organ transplanted from one living body to another. In this sense, there is no real distinction between the property in question and other associated features that inseparably accompany it in a particular individual. Nevertheless, it may be possible to discover other individuals that possess this property but lack one or more of the associated attributes that characterize the first individual. A favorite example of the scholastics was the human

[4] Ockham, Ordinatio (Sent. I), D 2, Q 1 F (Lyons, 1495; no pagination).

soul as they conceived it to be. As the seat not only of the higher life of reason, but also of that which man has in common with the brute animal or insensate vegetable, the soul was said to possess intellective, sensitive, and vegetative properties, but not as so many really distinct parts, since the soul, as immortal, was regarded as substantially simple. God might create it or destroy it as a unit, but even he could not alter its properties in such a way that it would become a purely animal or vegetable form such as the brute or plant were assumed to possess, nor could he transform it into a pure intelligence such as the angel was said to be. And yet the angel, so they argued, possesses the property of intellectivity without either sensitivity or the ability to vegetate, whereas the brute beast has a capacity for sense knowledge while lacking what is essential for the higher life of reason.

There are two ways of describing this intermediary distinction. If we consider it from the vantage point of the mind that separates these properties in concept, it is a mental distinction (*distinctio rationis*). Viewed in terms of the intelligible features to which these concepts refer, however, it can be said to be in some sense real. Thus Aquinas insists the distinction arises "not merely by reason of the one conceiving it but in virtue of a property of the thing itself,"[5] whereas Scotus refers to it in the language of Peter Olivi as a distinction between *rationes reales*.

Since this distinction was adopted primarily for the epistemological purpose of saving the objectivity of concepts that express a partial insight but not the whole truth about a reality which lacks really distinct parts in the sense explained above, it should not surprise us that there is a certain unanimity among the scholastics about the objective nature of this distinction. On the other hand, they differ considerably as to whether what such distinct concepts connote can be said to be nonidentical even before we begin to think about them.

The area of general agreement, I believe, includes the following points:(1) Some kind of isomorphism exists between thought and reality in virtue of which the former may be said to be a likeness or picture of the latter. This "likeness" should not be construed in terms of the relatively simple way a snapshot depicts a scene; it is something more sophisticated—along the lines, perhaps, of Wittgenstein's "logical picture"—and is based upon what "shows itself" in both the world of facts and our thoughts about that world. (2) In virtue of this community of intelligible form we can speak of *ratio* (the same would be true of the Greek *logos* or the Avicennian *intentio*) either as in things or in the mind. (3) To the extent that this *ratio* is a property or characteristic

---

[5] *Commentum in lib. I Sent.*, D 2, Q 1, A 3 (*Opera Omnia*, Vivès ed., vol. 7, p. 36).

of a thing, we are justified in asserting that the individual in question is a "so and so." (4) Though such *rationes* can be conceived one without the other, since their definitions differ and what is implied by one is not what is implied by the other, nevertheless as characteristic of extramental reality they constitute one thing; i.e., they are not really distinct parts in the way the real distinction was explained above.

The main area of difference concerns the meaningfulness of saying that one *ratio* is actually not identical with the other prior to our actually thinking of one apart from its mate. Though Aquinas does not raise this question in so many words, what he says in his commentary on the *Sentences* about the attributes of God (which are so many *rationes*) might be interpreted as favoring such an actual nonidentity. Thus, for example, Thomas tells us that when we speak of a *ratio* as a property of a thing what we mean is

> ...that in the thing outside the mind, there is something which corresponds to the conception of the mind as the significatum corresponds to the sign and this occurs in a proper sense when the conception of the intellect is a likeness of the thing (*Sent.* I, D 2, Q 1, A 3; p. 37).

To speak of different *rationes* in God in this sense, however, does not introduce a real distinction or plurality into the divine essence. And while

> ...we must say that wisdom, goodness and such like are in God, each of these is the divine essence itself and thus all are one thing. But because each of them in its truest sense is in God and what wisdom means is not what is meant by goodness as such, it follows that they are conceptually different not just in virtue of the one conceiving them but by reason of a property of the thing itself (A 2; p. 35).

And he insists further that

> ...from all eternity when creatures were non-existent, and even if they never were going to exist, it was still true to say that he [God] is wise, good and the like. Neither does one notion signify what the other does in the way that the same thing is signified by synonyms (A 3; p. 39).

Henry of Ghent, however, writing several decades later, takes some pains to explain that the intentional distinction, as he calls it (*intentio* being a term he uses as a synonym for Aquinas's *ratio*), is merely potential prior to the act of thought, whereas it becomes actual only in the mind when the latter conceives one intention apart from the other.[6]

Perhaps one of Scotus' most illuminating remarks is that the formal distinction does not deny the intentional distinction of Henry but merely postulates what is needed in things to account for it (*Quaest.*, p. 470). With reference to Henry's version he writes:

> In such notions as these, does the intellect, I ask, have as the object something in the thing? If not, we have a mere fiction of the mind. If it is the same thing, the object of both concepts is identical unless you admit that one and the same extramental thing formally generates two objects in the intellect. And in this case, it does not seem that the thing or anything of the thing is the object of my knowledge, but rather something produced by the thing. But if the intellect knows something different in each concept, then our thesis is granted, since a difference is there prior to the concept (N 5; p. 466).

If I am not mistaken, the precise difference between Scotus and Henry boils down to this. If you grant their common scholastic assumption that our concepts and reality are somehow isomorphic, then the mere possibility of conceiving one property without the other requires some actual nonidentity or distinction of properties *a parte rei* logically prior to and as a condition for our thinking of one apart from the other. (Recall in this connection what Wittgenstein says in *Tractatus Logico-Philosophicus* 2.012–2.0121). One can of course deny the isomorphism as Ockham does, but if you concede it as Aquinas and Henry do, it seems difficult to escape Scotus' conclusion.

Scotus ascribes various names to the objective correlate of such concepts. His usual designation for it is *realitas or formalitas*, though he occasionally refers to it as an *intentio* or a *ratio realis*.[7] The distinction or nonidentity that obtains between such correlates he prefers to call "formal" though, he adds, you may also speak of it as a "virtual distinction" since what you find in the thing is not really two things but "one thing which is virtually or pre-eminently as it were two realities" (N. 402; pp. 355–356). You may even call it a *distinctio rationis*, so long as by *ratio* you do not mean "something formed by the mind" but something of "what the thing is insofar as the 'whatness' is an object of the intellect" (N 401; p. 355).

Since Scotus did not invent this distinction, but took it over from

---

[6] Cf. Henry of Ghent, *Summa quaestionum ordinarum*, A 27, Q 1 (Paris: 1520, tom. I, fol. 162r O); and *Quodlibet* V, Q 6 (*Disputationes quodlibeticae*, Paris: 1518, tom. I, fol. 161rv). See also Scotus, *Quaest.* VII, Q 19, N 4; vol. 7, p. 465.

[7] Compare especially the *Ordinatio* I, D 2, pars. 2, QQ 1–4 (*Opera Omnia*, Vatican edition, vol. II, pp. 355–357).

his contemporaries, as Ockham himself warned, we must not attribute to the Subtle Scot all the exaggerated claims made by others for this distinction. For one thing, I think it would be a mistake to believe that he, like some of the later formalists, regarded realities or formalities as some kind of "ontological bricks" with fixed dimensions. For from the examples he gives there seems to be a certain fluidity about our way of regarding things and, hence, about the way we draw the lines that separate one intelligible aspect of a thing from another. The one essential point he returns to again and again is that howsoever we may choose to conceive the thing, if our concepts reflect something about the latter, there must be something positive in that thing which corresponds thereto, and this positive entity or reality is not something that thing has only because we happen to be thinking about it. Perhaps a better analogy than "ontological bricks," then, would be that of a stage upon which different spotlights are playing, where each illuminated area represents what we grasp in one of our concepts. It is not necessary that the spotlights remain fixed; they may move about, and the areas illumined may even at times interest in part. Scotus' point, I believe, would be this. Even before you switch the spots on, or, what is more, if you never turned them on or even had any lights, not only would it still be meaningful to speak of what they would reveal, if you had them to turn on, but there would also be grounds for not speaking of one part of the stage as simply identical with the other. For each possibly separate area of illumination would still be just what it is and would contain what is proper to itself. And it is what each has, and not just what we reveal or think it has, that makes the one area not simply identical with the other. For some nonidentity of what exists on the part of a thing, Scotus argued, must be logically prior to and a necessary condition for our being able to think of one without the other. Though Scotus repeatedly stresses that the formal distinction is logically prior to actual thought, he nowhere suggests that the distinction can be defined without reference to possibility of separating the formalities in thought. And that is why he agrees that this nonidentity on the part of the thing can be characterized as a *distinctio rationis*.

Though no individual thing is so simple that it does not contain more than one formality, nor are formalities so distinct that they do not form one real thing, there are different ways in which formalities may be said to be one.

Consider, for example, the attributes of God. Though each is infinitely perfect, one attribute is not formally the other. For to say that God's knowledge, for instance, is infinite, is to say that it comprehends all that can be known, but this is something quite different from saying that knowledge is formally love or that the sense of their several definitions are identical. But because each of God's attributes is infinitely perfect, we have no grounds for claiming that one formality perfects another in the way that parts are mutually perfected by their forming one whole. But the same need not hold of creatures. Here we can speak of a quasi-composition, not of course in any real or proper sense as would be the case were the parts really distinct. But if, in a thing characterized by two or more formalities, their combination, as it were, turns out to be something more than we might expect of the simple sum of the two, we may say that their togetherness constitutes a *per se*, rather than a *per accidens*, unity. In man or in the human spirit, where both sensitivity and intelligence are present, each adds something as it were to the perfection of the other. The creative imagination of the artist, for example, which is born of their union, is something neither the brute beast with its sensitivity nor the angel with its intellectual life as such possess. Because of this we may say that in man, or in human nature, the abstract formalities of animality and rationality, though formally distinct, are so related that together they form not a mere aggregate of intelligible items which the mind lists in catalogue fashion, but they are so ordered to one another that they constitute a single intelligible whole.

THE FORMAL CONSTITUTION OF THE INDIVIDUAL

With this in mind, consider what Scotus says of the formal constitution of singulars.[8] Each individual, he declares, differs from every other individual of its kind by some positive entity or reality, which, though really one with, is formally distinct from, that reality or specific complex of formalities which makes it the kind of thing it is. This latter, Scotus calls the nature of the thing (or less frequently, the *natura communis*), whereas the former is referred to as the thing's *haecceity* or individuating difference. The *haecceity* (literally the "thisness") of this individual and that of another individual are so radically and absolutely diverse that neither the one nor the other can be grasped in itself or as such by a concept that is universal. Like Russell's individuals or Wittgenstein's simple objects, Scotus' individuating differences are realities one can know or identify only by acquaintance; and, like these other philosophers, he concludes that there are such entities by way of a reasoning process, for, because of the complex mechanism by which we come to know, he does not claim that we intuit the *haecccity*

[8] Cf. *Opus oxon.* II, D 3, Q 1–6; also *Quaest.* VII, Q 18.

of any of the ordinary things that go to make up our everyday world. In practice we differentiate things in terms of their accidental differences, not by anything that might be called an intrinsic constituent or property thereof. He does believe, however, that if our mind could know things as he believed it will know them in the life to come, we could know these unique differences by acquaintance and not merely by descriptions. As it is, however, we infer that such differences exist because individuals exist; yet nothing we can say or know about them as such turns out to be unique or would explain why another might not duplicate their every known trait. Such differences must then be described in terms of what is extrinsic to their uniqueness, such as what they are not or their relations to such other realities as the nature of the thing. In this way, for instance, Scotus describes the "haecceity" as being related to the individual's nature in a fashion similar to the way the specifying difference is related to its generic nature. But where the latter produces a difference in kind, the former results in the numerical distinction that sets one individual apart from every other of its kind. Furthermore, just as the formalities corresponding to the generic and specifying notions can be considered as *per se* constituents of the individual's specific nature, so also can the particular *haecceity* be called a *per se* part of the individual possessing it.

But Scotus, we recall, insisted that, even as found in the individual, the nature has a real unity less than numerical unity. What he means is this. Numerical unity is really the name of a disjunctive concept, an umbrella term if you will—to cover the many diverse combinations where we find a kind of thing (a nature) with just this *haecceity* or just that *haecceity* or "thet" or "thot" *haecceity*—to use Wisdom's expanded vocabulary for individuals. Each such combination represents, for Scotus, a real and *per se* togetherness which is something over and above that togetherness characteristic of the nature of the thing. To the extent that it is over and above, numerical unity is a greater unity, and, conversely, the unity of the formalities that constitute the nature of the individual must be a lesser *per se* unity.

Where we are speaking of those formalities which constitute the specific nature of the individual we can call this *per se* unity specific, provided we keep in mind that we are referring not to a unity between two individuals but between two formalities of the same individual. That is why Scotus insists that "this real unity is not that of some entity which exists in two individuals but in one" (*Opus oxon* II, D 3, Q 6, N 10; p. 133). In similar fashion he speaks of a real unity in the individual that is less than the unity of the specific nature, that characteristic of its generic nature.

But if these minor unities are characteristic of the nature (generic, specific, transcendental, etc.) as it is found in the individual, is there not some sense in which we can speak of this nature as numerically one also?

Of course, replies Scotus, for the nature and the thing's *haecceity* are only formally distinct, but are really one and therefore inseparable so far as the existing individual is concerned. But keep in mind that by 'numerically one' Scotus does not mean primarily simply "having some or other haecceity," for in this sense it is necessary for a nature qua existing that it be individual and hence have some individuating difference. When Scotus says the nature as characteristic of the individual is not as such numerically one, the oneness he has in mind is the unique oneness that "this" does not have in common with "that" or "thet" or any other individual. And what is primarily numerically one about the individual is its "thisness" or "thatness" or "thotness." What is *per se* "this," "thet," or "thot" is the individual that has the "thisness," or "thotness" as a *per se* constitutive part. And by association or *denominative*, the nature is also numerically one in the same way that the animal nature in man can be called "rational" denominatively. And in this sense, it is true to say that the nature in a thing is individual or is just this (i.e., not that or thet or thot). "I grant you," says Scotus, "that whatever is in this stone is numerically one, either primarily or *per se* or denominatively" (*ibid.*, N 10; p. 134).

In justification of this theory Scotus appeals to the basic fact both that we seem to know something about concrete or individual objects and that there is nothing we know about them that seems to be primarily numerically one. And if we don't know that, then neither do we know their numerical unity as such, since we are ignorant of the most important item it involves, viz., the unique *haecceity* that this and only this individual possesses. Our notions of individuality and of what and why an individual is an individual, in other words, are really universals. 'Numerically one' itself is a universal predicate, since it can be asserted of "this" and "that" and so on.

What we are continually faced with and what is being presented to us as a "given" is not an individualized nature, but a nature formally indifferent to being just "this" and not "that" or "thot." And what is true of the nature is true of its properties and relations.

It seemed obvious to Scotus, then, that what we know or can know directly must be something less than the numerical or individual unity of a thing. What we use to differentiate individuals (at least the ordinary individuals that form the people and furniture of our every day world) is what is extrinsic or accidental to them. And while, if an infinite regress is to be avoided, there would seem to be some accidents (though certainly not all) whose individuality we are acquainted with, even in such cases, there must be something other than their bare individuality that we know—if nothing else, the generality that they are all individuals. Otherwise there seems to be no way even of inferring that what they are other things may also be, viz., individuals.

Furthermore, Scotus argues, since the numerical unity must be something which is irreducibly unique, if things differed from each other only by reason of their individuality, everything would be equally different from everything else and there would be no gradations of differences. Neither would it be possible to classify things in any ordered fashion. There would be no grounds, in other words, for saying that Socrates resembles Plato more than he does a chalk line.

It is clear from all this why Scotus insisted that what is the *given* in what we understand about things is not the intelligible nature as formally individualized but as formally indifferent to being just this. What we must explain, then, he goes on to say, is how this indifferent nature is individualized in existing things, and how it becomes completely universal. That is to say, how is it that we are able to conceive the nature apart from its *haecceity?* A minimal condition for such separation would seem to be that nature and *haecceity* are not formally identical and that this, though the mind discovers it, is not something the mind creates. And what seems also true, he argues, is that insofar as our knowledge is caused somehow by individual objects, the effective ingredient, so to speak, on the part of the object must be not the individual characteristics as such but precisely such characteristics as are not of themselves such, namely the common nature.

On the other hand, some other agency is obviously required, for the object is individual and the intellect that knows is, according to Aristotle, passive or receptive. It is here that Scotus appeals to the agent intellect. Through a complex process which we will not go into, the agent intellect and the sense images function as a complex but integrated efficient cause to produce a real though accidental modification of the possible intellect, namely the intelligible species.

Turning now to the principal problem of our symposium, we can ask with Scotus: Does the universal then exist in things? (*Quaest.*, p. 466 ff.) The word 'universal', he explains, can be given three meanings.

1. We may wish to refer to that logical relationship the predicate bears toward that of which it is predicated, and we may use either the concrete name 'universal' or the abstract term 'universality' to signify this relationship. Understood in this way, 'universal' is the name of a second intention, i.e., a concept whose referent is some other concept

and whose sense expresses the way in which one concept is related to another. As such it is clear that a universal never exists outside the mind.

But second intentions are applied to first intentions, i.e., to concepts whose referent is always some real or individual thing. And the name 'universal', consequently may signify by association (*denominative*) either the first intention (in the mind) or that intelligible feature (*ratio or realitas*) in its referents which this intention depicts or mirrors. Thus the word 'universal' may have two additional significations.

2. As a name it may signify that reality or formality which we called the thing's nature, when the latter is regarded absolutely (i.e., according to its formal definition of what it is in itself). Since the nature of the thing is not of itself just "this" rather than "that" or "thet" or "thot," there is nothing about, the formal features of such a nature that would prevent it from being linked with the *haecceity* of this rather than of that or thet or thot. And to this extent, it may be regarded, says Scotus, "as a kind of remote subject" of this relationship we called "universal" in the first sense (*ibid.*, p. 456).

3. But the true or proximate subject of this relationship is not the nature as it exists in things, for there it is *de facto* determined by just this *haecceity*, and, as so determined, it is a characteristic of just this, not of that, or of many individuals. It is rather, the first intention itself, i.e., the concept we have in our mind of such a nature. And in this sense, it is only in the intellect that the nature in question is present in its complete universality, that is, as actually undetermined by a particular *haecceity*. In the thing, however, that nature was only formally, not really distinct from, or indifferent to its "thisness"

But while we may say that the complete universal is only in the mind, this is not to say simply that universality (in the sense of being actually undertermined by *haecceity)* is simply created by our act of knowing the thing, for this would seem to imply that when we predicate such a notion of an individual we really don't know the individual but something created by our mind, and our assertions, therefore, would be false. For an Aristotelian like Scotus, the intellect that actually knows would be the possible intellect. Something is required to trigger such actual knowledge, and this for him, as we said, is the intelligible species (a co-product of the agent intellect working with information of the common nature of things outside, which comes through the medium of the senses). The intelligible species, we might say, contains the "logical form" of nature or natures in the external world without their individual content. And to this extent, it goes proxy for that nature as it were, enabling the mind to know not the species but the intelligible nature or formality as such. And to this extent, it is the agent intellect together with sense information about such aspects of the individual as are not of themselves just "this" that is the total or integral cause why the latter are represented abstractly, i.e., as actually undetermined by the "thisness."

When Avicenna says then that a nature like equinity is just equinity, that is, of itself it is neither universal nor particular but just nature, we must understand it in this way. Considered abstractly or in terms of its sense, "the nature is in remote potency to both the determination of singularity and to the indetermination of the [complete] universal." It becomes concretized, as it were, by being produced in the extramental world; it becomes universalized by the agent intellect producing in the possible intellect an intelligible species. Though the latter is an effective cause of the intellect's knowing, it is not the formal object of that knowledge, for this is the nature as such, denuded of "thisness" or "thatness."

Scotus speaks of this intelligible nature in somewhat the same way as Wittgenstein spoke of logical form in the *Tractatus*. It is something which "shows itself" both in the world and in thought; it is something which is simply given and must be accepted as the irreducible and fixed aspect of things, the hardest thing that there is.

But if this is the given, then Scotus' problem is twofold. He must explain why this indifferent nature is individual in reality, and why it is universal in the mind.

Ockham as we know rejected the formal distinction, not because he considered it a contradiction, for he admits at least one case of it in the case of the Trinity to save the universality of logic, but because he regarded it as almost as much of a mystery as the Trinity itself. By denying the distinction in creatures, he simplified matters in one sense by reducing Scotus' twofold problem to one. What is given is not the indifferent or common nature but the individual; what we must explain is how we come to know the individual through universals. On the other hand one might ask whether his use of the razor really simplified things after all or whether it so complicated the remaining problem as to render it insoluble. But the discussion of that question I leave for another occasion.

3 / A "Reportatio" of Duns Scotus' Merton College Dialogue on Language and Metaphysics

In the never-never land of science fiction and fantasy time barriers break down and Merton College, Oxford, witnessed a dialogue between Scotus *redivivus* and an Oxford analyst. Before the meeting Duns Scotus paid a visit to the Bodleian and Blackwell's and, being a speed reader with a computer-like memory, he was able to digest much of Russell, Wittgenstein and other analysts like Ayer and Carnap. When the chairperson came to escort him to the lecture hall, she found him buried deep in the *Collected Works of Charles Sanders Peirce*. The entire dialogue is too long to be given here, but its substance according to a reliable source roughly came down to this.[1]

Scotus began by presenting his semantical theory as to how names signify. Primarily, he said, they signify things, but associated with them are concepts in the mind.[2] The ability to use a name properly (*cognitio*

Reprinted with permission from *Miscellanea Mediaevalia*, Band 31/1; *Sprache und Erkenntnis im Mittelalter*, ed. Albert Zimmermann (Berlin: De Gruyter, 1981), pp. 179–191.

[1] Allan B. Wolter, "An Oxford Dialogue on Language and Metaphysics," *The Review of Metaphysics* 31 (June 1978), 615–648 and 32 (December 1978), 323–348. This "Reportatio" of the original dialogue was first given orally at the Bonn Conference and subsequently expanded somewhat as the result of discussions with Prof. M. M. Adams during my tenure as visiting professor of philosophy at the University of California, Los Angeles, in the Spring of 1978 under the sponsorship of the Center for Medieval and Renaissance Studies.

[2] *Ordinatio* I, dist. 27, n. 83 (VI, 97); *Lectura* I, dist. 27, n. 2 (XVII, 343).—Unless otherwise indicated all references are to the Vatican edition *Ioannis Duns Scoti Opera Omnia* (Civitas Vaticana, 1950–). For an account of the *magna altercatio* Scotus refers

54

quid nominis) is first in the order of time, whereas the ability to define a word precisely or definitional knowledge (*cognitio quid rei*) comes later. Furthermore, though the name zeroes in on the concrete individual, it is not a proper but a common name that is used initially to classify it. Hence the associated concept is universal, but most specific (*cognitio speciei specialissimae*).[3] Scotus seemed to be saying that when a name is used with reference to a particular individual, it may have associated with it a wide spectrum of concepts (more or less distinct) that bear only a "family resemblance" to one another. It is meaningless, then, to ask for *the* meaning of a name, except with respect to an instant of time contemporal with one's mental span of attention. Rather one ought to ask for the *meanings* or set of concepts that may pass through the mind when the name is used referentially or with personal supposition.[4] Contemporary historians of medieval philosophy point out that Ockham's more popularized semantical theory had its roots in this earlier version of Duns Scotus.[5] Some of these seem to assume that when Scotus speaks of the possibility of words being direct signs of things, he understood this to mean that the common names one uses refer directly to the realities or formalities embodied in the individuals, e.g. in the explanatory statement that "Shep

---

to, see his commentary on *Perihermenias* I q. 2 (*Joannis Duns Scoti Opera Omnia* Parisiis: L. Vivès, 1891–1895—hereafter referred to as the Vivès edition) I, 540ff.

[3] *Ordinatio* I, dist. 3, nn. 71–82 (III, 49–56); *Quaestiones subtilissimae super libros Metaphysicorum Aristotelis* VII, q. 15, n. 8 (Vivès ed. VII, 439).

[4] Wolter's interpretation, see *An Oxford Dialogue*, pp. 620 and 624–628. This interpretation is based on Scotus' insistence that the name designates or can designate the individual "ut haec" even though we may have no proper notion of it, and that the "individual" here seems to be in the category of substance, something we know only by way of inference and that, based on previous sense perceptual observations. See *Ordinatio* I, dist. 22, nn. 5–8 (V, 343–346). Even Henry of Ghent, whose views Scotus is opposing here, admitted that "intellectus negotians possit plures conceptus causare et fabricare circa illud obiectum [reale]," and that there is a progressive clarification going on in the adult mind as it moves from a state of ignorance to distinct knowledge. See *ibid.* n. 3, 343 and what I have written elsewhere in *The Transcendentals and Their Function in the Metaphysics of Duns Scotus* (St. Bonaventure, N.Y.: The Franciscan Institute, 1946), pp. 59–65, about confused knowledge of the "species specialissima" preceding temporally even such distinct knowledge as "hoc aliquid" or "haec lapis"— to use the example of distinction 22. When Scotus writes that "confuse intelligitur quando concipitur sicut exprimitur per nomen" (*Ord.* I, d. 3, n. 71; III, 49), I submit he means that we know how to apply a *common* name *properly*, where "properly" means not only correctly, but in the manner of a proper name, namely to point to, indicate, or name an individual subject. This seems to be the whole point of his insistence that we can name something more precisely than we can think of it. See note 9 *infra*.

[5] Stephen F. Brown alluded to this earlier in his plenary session paper at the Bonn Conference, "A Modern Prologue to Ockham's Natural Philosophy." See supra, *Sprache und Erkenntnis im Mittelalter, Miscellanea Mediaevalia*, ed. Albert Zimmermann (Berlin and New York: Walter De Gruyter, 1981), pp. 107–129.

is a dog of mine," "dog" refers to the *natura communis* or dog-ness of the particular dog I call "Shep."[6] One can of course use a name to do that job, as when I point to Shep as a concrete instance of what I mean by *natura communis canis familiaris*.[7] But if you consider what Scotus says in *Ordinatio* I, distinction 22 (and not just distinction 27 of that book) one fact becomes clear. If Scotus correlated *concepts* with objective formalities of things in some isomorphic fashion,[8] this has little or nothing to do with the process of *naming* or how a name (whatsoever be its etymological meaning) zeroes in on the particular or individual subject to which it refers.[9] Put in another way, when one uses a classificatory name or common noun to refer to one or more individuals of that kind, such as "dog," "horse," "cow," "table," "man," and the like, the name refers to (denominates, designates, supposits for) the individual thing in question, and not the individual's "caninity," "equinity," "bovinity," "tabular nature," or "humanity," as the case may be. What the *sense* of the accompanying concept may be in the mind of the one using a name significantly is, of course, another question.[10] But the common opinion that we can refer to things with no

---

[6] See Armand Mauer's sectional paper, "William of Ockham on Language and Reality," *ibid.*, Bd. II, pp. 795–802.

[7] The analyst interlocuter in the dialogue thought a good illustration of this linguistic usage was the enthusiastic exclamation of a fellow student during his college days: "To think is Wittgenstein!"

[8] On the isomorphic structure of thought and reality according to Scotus see chapters 1 and 2 in this volume.

[9] *Ord.* I, dist. 22, n. 4 (V, 343): "Potest dici ad quaestionem [Utrum Deus sit nominabilis a nobis aliquo nomine significante essentiam divinam in se, ut est 'haec'] breviter quod ista propositio communis multis opinionibus scilicet quod 'sicut intelligitur, sic et nominatur'—falsa est si intelligatur praecise, quia distinctius potest aliquid significari quam intelligi." As a persuasive argument for the correctness of this view, he cites the fact that we use classificatory names that refer to specific sorts of substances even though the only simple positive notion we have of substance is *ens* (in the sense of "a being" or "an extramental thing"). *Ibid.* nn. 5–6; 343–344: "Quod videtur persuaderi ex hoc, quod cum substantia non sit intelligibilis a viatore nisi in communi conceptu entis (sicut probatum est distinctione 3), si non possit distinctius significari quam intelligi, nullum nomen impositum a viatore significaret aliquam rem de genere substantiae, sed sicut praecise concipitur ab intellectu viatoris aliqua proprietas a qua imponitur nomen (quae proprietas communiter exprimitur per etymologiam nominis), ita praecise talis proprietas significaretur per nomen: puta, per nomen lapidis non significaretur aliquid de genere substantiae, sed tantum aliquid de genere actionis, puta 'laesio pedis,' quam exprimit etymologia et fuit a qua nomen imponebatur. Et ita potest argui de omnibus aliis nominibus, impositis rebus de genere substantiae, quod nullum illorum significat aliquid nisi proprietatem accidentalem aliquam quae intelligebatur ab imponente,—vel oportet dicere quod nomen distinctius significat quam intellexit imponens."

[10] The *sense* of a word, as distinct from its reference, is usually described as its definitional meaning or what we understand by the word. For Scotus, strictly speaking, "definitional knowledge" is *distinct* and is opposed to knowing something "confusedly"

greater precision than we can think of them in descriptive terms, Scotus believes to be false.[11]

This becomes particularly clear in his criticism of Henry of Ghent and many others as to how God-names, derived from creatures, signify the unique individual deity we call by the proper name of "God." Objectively, there is no formally distinct "haecceity" and "essentia" in God, such as Scotus postulates in the case of individual created things.[12] Furthermore, we have no simple proper notion of "haec essentia" or this essence "ut haec" as we would have, could we intuit God like the blessed in heaven or as some mystics seem to have done.[13] Such knowledge would be what Russell calls "knowledge by acquain-

---

or as expressed by means of a name. *Ord.* I, dist. 3, n. 72; III, 50: "Confuse aliquid dicitur concipi, quando concipitur sicut exprimitur per nomen; distincte vero quando concipitur, sicut exprimitur per definitionem." *Ibid.* n. 80, III, 55: "Cognoscere 'distincte' habetur per definitionem, quae inquiritur per viam divisionis, incipiendo ab ente usque ad conceptum definiti." There is obviously some *sense* associated with the correct use of a common name, something that makes the confused concept a sign of the 'species specialissima' of what is most forcibly impressed upon the senses, but it cannot be clearly defined or analyzed as a definition can. See *Lectura* I, dist. 3, n. 69 (VII, 250): "Tunc dicitur aliquid confuse cognosci quando cognoscitur per nomen tantum et indistincte, non per resolutionem in ea in quae est resolubile." Since being or *ens* can only be known distinctly, it is not included in this initial confused knowledge that precedes distinct knowledge in the temporal process of knowing. *Ibid.*, nn. 78–79 (253–54): "Dico quod cognitio confusa simpliciter prior est cognitione distincta . . . quia cognitio confusa media est inter cognitionem distinctam et potentialem . . . cum intellectus noster procedat de imperfecto ad perfectum." *Ibid.*, n. 69 (250): "Ens non potest indistincte et confuse cognosci."

[11] See note 9 *supra*; also *Lectura* I, dist. 22, nn. 2–3 (XVII, 301): "Ut mihi videtur, haec propositio falsa est quod 'nihil potest nominari a nobis magis proprie quam intelligatur,' sicut quidam dicunt quod sicut intelligimus sic significamus, et quia non intelligimus Deum nisi ex creaturis, ideo non significamus nisi per nomina accepta a creaturis. Hoc enim falsum est. Video enim albedinem in pariete, et video quod manente quantitate parietis—quae est sensibilis per se—variatur albedo; item video quod alias potest paries dealbari et manente albedine quantitas mutari ab una figura in aliam. Ex hoc ego concludo quod est aliquod tertium, substratum utrique, alterum ab eis: illi nomen impono *a*, vocando ipsum corpus in genere substantiae,—quod tamen intelligo tantum sub intentione communi quod sit 'hoc ens' et nullo modo propriam speciem eius habeo (sicut quilibet potest experiri in se ipso), et ideo verius possum illud nominare quam intelligere."

[12] *Ord.* II, dist. 3, nn. 39–40 (VII, 408).

[13] *Ord.* I, dist. 3, n. 56 (III, 38): "Dico quod Deus non cognoscitur naturaliter a viatore in particulari et proprie, hoc est sub ratione huius essentia ut haec est in se." *Lectura* I, dist. 3, n. 35 (XVI, 238): "De facto, nisi fiat per revelationem, non cognoscitur Deus a nobis in particulari, ita quod cognoscatur ut haec essentia et distincta ab omni alia, quia quod concipitur in particulari ut distinguitur ab omni alio, concipitur sub conceptu qui contradicit alteri; sed nihil concipimus in Deo quod repugnat contradictorie alteri, et cui repugnat esse in altero." *Ibid.*, dist. 22, n. 4 (XVII, 301–302): "Intelligo essentiam divinam non secundum quod est 'haec essentia,' sed tantum sub intentione communi quod sit 'hoc ens infinitum a nullo dependens.' "

tance."[14] and scholastics *cognitio propria ex propriis*.[15] By contrast, our "proper" concepts of God, at best, are what Russell would call "knowledge by description" or scholastics *cognitio propria ex communibus*. They are constructed, if you will, from positive, negative and relational elements in much the same way that the theoretical physicist forms notions of microcosmic entities that he assumes refer to the real underpinning structure of the material universe.[16]

Often, however, in ordinary usage of common names we have only a confused, rather than a distinct notion (in the technical sense Scotus defines these terms) associated with the name in question. Even where we have some distinct or clear conception in mind, it is often far removed from the original meaning of the term. Thus, Scotus says, a word like "stone" (*lapis*; genitive case, *lapidis*) which derives etymologically from a purely incidental feature (*laesio pedis* or "foot injury"), is rarely, if ever, used today to denote this accidental characteristic of stones, though a philosophically-minded individual like Samuel Johnson might use it to try to refute radical idealism. In ordinary usage, says Scotus, "stone" refers to a substance.[17] And the only common denominator conceptually that he would admit can be carried over and incorporated *in some fashion*[18] in every first intentional use of a prop-

---

[14] Bertrand Russell, "Knowledge by Acquaintance and Knowledge by Description," *Mysticism and Logic* (London: Allen and Unwin, 1917), pp. 209–232.

[15] Georg Cantor makes use of this well known distinction in explaining that our knowledge of irrational and transfinite numbers represents "proper knowledge" only in this secondary sense. "Nach unserer Organisation sind wir nur selten im Besitz eines Begriffes, von dem wir sagen könnten, daß er ein 'conceptus rei proprius ex propriis' ware, indem wir durch ihn eine Sache adäquat, ohne Hilfe einer Negation, eines Symbols oder Beispiels, so auffassen und erkennen, wie sie an und für sich ist. Vielmehr sind wir beim Erkennen zumeist auf einen 'conceptus proprius ex communibus' angewiesen, welcher uns befähigt, ein Ding aus allgemeinen Pradikaten und mit Hilfe von Vergleichungen, Ausschließungen, Symbolen oder Beispielen derartig zu bestimmen, daß es von jedem andern Ding wohlunter schieden ist. Man vergleiche z. B. die Methode, nach welcher ich in den 'Grundlagen' (1883) und schon fruher in den Math. Ann. 5 (1871), die *irrationalen* Zahlgrößen definiert habe." Georg Cantor, *Gesammelte Abhandlungen*, hrg. v. Ernst Zermelo (Berlin: Verlag von Julius Springer, 1932), pp. 402–403.

[16] *Ord.* I, dist. 3, n. 61 (III, 42); *Lectura* I, dist. 3, n. 56 (XVI, 246): "Sicut imaginativa imaginatur 'montem aureum,' tamen tantum extrema sunt in re et non ipsum coniunctum, sic igitur, abstrahendo a creaturis intentiones communes et coniungendo eas, possumus cognoscere Deum in universali, et etiam illum conceptum dictum de Deo qui maxime sibi convenit prout a nobis cognoscitur ... Potest abstrahere summitatem ab hac summitate et illa, et sic cognoscere quid sit summum, et coniungere intentionem summitatis intentioni entis vel boni et sic cognoscere summum ens vel bonum, et sic de infinito ente." For a parallel use of "constructionism" in mathematics see note 15 *supra*, and in the physical sciences, see Mary Hesse, "Models and Analogies in Science," *Encyclopedia of Philosophy* (New York and London: Macmillan and Free Press, 1967), V, 354–359.

[17] See notes 9 and 11 *supra*.

[18] *Lectura* I, dist. 3, n. 75 (XVI, 252): "Ens non potest cognosci nisi distincte, quia

ositional term seems to be that of "ens" in the sense of an extramental sort of thing or being.

As far as this reporter could make out, Scotus' point here was this. If names can single out things more specifically or distinctly than our associated concepts upon reflective analysis can classify the objects in question, then there is at best a "free-wheeling" association between an identical word used referentially as a sign of an object in the everyday world about us, and the universal concept associated with it. All our simple or unconstructed concepts of the extramental world, according to Scotus, seem to be universal, or common, at least in terms of their "sense"—for though we know singulars, it is not because we conceive their, "haecceities" as such directly, but by reflection upon the sense images.[19] While we can

---

non est resolubile in plures conceptus priores; sed ad hoc quod aliquid distincte cognoscatur cognitione distincta, oportet quod ens praecognoscitur, quia in omni conceptu est ens." Just how this is to be understood is spelled out more clearly in the *Ordinatio* I, dist. 3, nn. 150–151 (III, 92–94) where Scotus explains the "double primacy of being"; see Wolter, *Transcendentals and Their Function*, pp. 77–98. See also the several senses in which "ens" and "res" can be taken, one of which embraces all "intelligibilia per se," according to the multi-level analysis Scotus gives in his *Quodlibet*, q. 3 (confer note 30, *infra*).

[19] It is frequently stated that Scotus holds we can have an intellectual intuition of material singulars, presumably of *this stone* qua 'this' and qua 'stone', for example. This is clearly an unwarranted oversimplification of the processes that go on, according to Scotus, in knowing a singular qua singular. A particular sense, like sight, hearing, etc. can have an intuitive cognition of its proper sensible both as individual and as here and now present, and the phantasy or sense imagination can abstract from existence while retaining the sensible's singularity as an abstract "image" or phantasm. *Ord.* II, dist. 3, n. 323 (VII, 554): "Declaratio huius distinctionis [inter intuitivam et abstractivam cognitionem]—per simile—est in potentiis sensitivis: aliter enim sensus particularis cognoscit obiectorum, aliter phantasia. Sensus enim particularis, est obiecti secundum quod est per se et in se existens,—phantasia cognoscit idem secundum quod est praesens per speciem, quae species posset esse eius licet non esset existens vel praesens, ita quod cognitio phantastica est abstractiva respectu sensus particularis." The intellect understands *what* is being sensed or imagined, first confusedly and later distinctly (to some degree at least). Scotus theorizes that agent intellect and phantasm cooperate as essentially ordered causes to produce an intelligible species reflecting the *common nature* rather than the *haecceity* of what is being sensed or imagined. At the level of confused knowledge (*sicut exprimitur per nomen tantum et indistincte*) this would be the most special species (e.g. the whiteness) rather than a more generic notion (e.g. color in general). *Lectura* I, dist. 3, n. 32 (XVI, 236–237): "Simul intelligitur aliquod universale ab intellectu et phantasiatur singulare eiusdem universalis in virtute phantastica. Unde si intelligo album, etiam imaginor hoc album, et quanto propinquius est illud universale—quod intelligitur—singulari quod phantasiatur, tanto est propinquius intellectui. Unde non ita firmiter stat intellectus in colore sicut in albedine, quia singulare albedinis plus propinquat albedini quam colori"; also *Ordinatio* I, dist. 3, n. 187 (III, 113–114) and *Ord.* II, dist. 3, n. 289f. (VII, 535): "Intellectus noster pro statu isto non est natus movere vel moveri immediate, nisi ab aliquo imaginabili vel 'sensibili extra' prius moveatur." Note, however, that a color, like blue, can be perceived not merely as a background (such as

use any name to supposit for or refer to an individual thing, if we are asked to specify what it is we are talking about, we normally reply with some definite description rather than a proper name, for example, "this stone" or "the table," and so on.

---

the boundless sky or sea) but as concretized in a specific "Gestalt" of definite size and shape. *Ibid.*, n. 295 (VII, 541): "... de colore, cuius receptivum 'secundum esse materiale' est superficies coloris terminati, receptivum autem eiusdem 'sine materia' est corpus perspicuum sive non-terminatum. Et ita oppositae dispositiones requiruntur in organo sensu; quod debet esse receptivum sensibilis sine materia, et in eo quod debet recipere objectum secundum esse materiale." Furthermore, the sense imagination as a 'synthetic sense' can combine a number of accidental features not only from the same sense but from many senses, and if the imagination has this combinatory power, so too, says Scotus, does the intellect. From the "multa accidentia mutuo se contrahentia" in the phantasy, "intellectus intelligendo universale, abstrahit quodcumque illorum; intelligendo tandem ut intelligat singulare secundum naturam, quae est haec, non inquantum haec, sed cum accidentibus propriis, huic componit subjectum cum accidentibus... Unde dicitur, quod non tantum sunt nomina secundae intentionis conditiones singularis exprimentia, ... sed etiam aliqua primae intentionis, ut *individuum, unum numero, incommunicabile*, etc. Natura igitur determinata istis, intelligitur, et est conceptus non simpliciter simplex, ut ens, nec etiam simplex quidditativus ut *homo*, sed tantum quasi per accidens, ut *homo albus* [cf. *Lectura* I, dist. 3, n. 68 (XVI, 250)], licet non ita per accidens; et iste est determinatior conceptus, ad quem venimus in vita ista, nam ad nihil devenimus, cui de ratione sua inquantum a nobis cognoscitur, contradictorie repugnat alteri inesse, et sine tali conceptu nunquam concipitur singulare distincte" *Quaest. in Metaphysicam Aristotelis loc. cit.* Note further that while the mind is studying the nature of something present here and now in sense perception, the idea of what it is before us (for instance, a stone, or a man), etc. that is immediately associated with such a sense perceptual object may be indeed theory-laden (confer *Ord.* I, dist. 22 and the parallel passage in the *Lectura* cited earlier in notes 9 and 11), and in giving it a common name or a definite descriptive denomination we may indeed intend to refer to the concrete individual subject before us, whatever it may be, even if we do not grasp it directly as "this substance" intuitively. *Lect.* I, d. 3, nn. 110 ff. (XVI, 265–66): "substantia non habet propriam speciem in intellectu possibili, sed tantum conceptum entis abstrahendo a speciebus accidentium ... quia si esset propria species substantiae in intellectu possibili a virtute phantastica, igitur quando ibi esset—vel formaliter vel virtualiter—gigneret speciem suam in intellectu possibili, et quando non, non gigneret, nec immutaret intellectum; et sic posset sciri per naturam quando panis esset sub speciebus panis et quando non in sacramento altaris, quod falsum est. Unde ita perfecte repraesentatur species substantiae—si substantia non esset et accidens esset—sicut si substantia esset sub accidentibus, et non magis perfecte; et ideo sicut si subtantia non esset, non faceret propriam speciem in intellectu possibili, ita nec etiam si esset sub speciebus accidentalibus. Unde si per impossibile Deus ostenderet intellectui tuo essentiam hominis—vel per possibile—et non daret tibi aliud lumen, sed tantum eam faceret intellectui tuo esse praesentem, et non ostenderet tibi descriptiones accidentium quae intelligis vel quibus cognoscis substantiam, nescires utrum esset essentia hominis vel non. Unde dico quod intellectus noster primo cognoscit accidentia, a quibus abstrahit intentionem entis, quod praedicat essentiam substantiae sicut accidentis; et tantum intuitive cognoscimus de substantia, et non plus. Hoc, sicut dixi, experitur quilibet in se, quod non cognoscit plus de natura substantiae nisi quod sit ens. Totum autem aliud quod cognoscimus de substantia, sunt proprietates et accidentia propria tali substantiae, per quas proprietates intuemur ea quae sunt essentialia substantiae." But because the intellect has the ability to be reflectively aware, in a single integral intuitive act, (1) of itself as

There is a temptation to think that Ockham had Scotus in mind when he insists (to quote Armand Mauer's abstract) that his position differs from others:

> St. Thomas claims that a general word like "man" directly signifies a concept and not a reality, for it designates human nature in abstraction from individual men. Scotus, on the contrary, argues that general words can directly signify realities, for in his view there are real common natures.
>
> In this dispute Ockham agrees with Scotus, that words like "man" are first of all signs of things and not of concepts; but he insists that the things they signify are only individuals. General words are not signs of general objects, for there are no general objects or universal things.[20]

That Ockham rejected Scotus' conception of the ontological-formality structure of individuals is clear enough[21] but it is also clear that a number of ultra-realistic positions existed, even on the basis of some "formal distinction" (which after all was not Scotus' own invention, and existed in various forms among his contemporaries),

---

knowing here and now, (2) a real object other than itself presented as a whole (the *totum* of "properties and proper accidents" referred to above), (3) plus some notion of the sort of thing this *totum* really is (the latter's presence here and now being explained if you will by what was once reasoned to but now exists as habitual knowledge), Scotus can speak of an "intellectual intuition" while it is here and now present (perfect intuition) and refer to its later recall (as an imperfect intuition). Thus he writes of this "confused" object, in the sense that a *confusum cognitum* is not to be confused with something known *confuse* [confer *Ord.* I, dist. 3, n. 72 (III, 49–50; *Lectura* I, dist. 3, n. 69 (XVI, 250)], "ita terminus *a quo et ad quem* reflexionis, est confusum, et in medio est distinctum" (Q. *in Metaphys. loc. cit.*) and "idem enim intellectus potest esse 'ipsemet' realiter, et in actu per habitum realiter, et tamen receptivus intellectualiter et sui et habitus sui et cuiuscumque informantis eam realiter; et ratio tota est, quia talia sic recepta intellectualiter, non requirunt in recipiente determinatam dispositionem, oppositam enti intelligibili reali" *Ord.* II, dist. 3, n. 296 (VII, 542).

[20] A. Mauer, *art. cit.*, p. 797f. Mauer's carefully worded statement is correct as it stands, for Aquinas's remarks, in *Summa theologiae* 1, q. 13, art. 1 corpus and the second "lectio" on *Perihermenias* 1, seem to exclude the possibility of words signifying directly (i.e. immediately or primarily) the extramental thing. Confer A. B. Wolter, *An Oxford Dialogue on Language and Metaphysics* (First Day), p. 625. It is also true that for Scotus "general words *can* directly signify realities," though our contention is that this is not what they denote, but what they connote, implicitly at best, in ordinary discourse. For Ockham, on the other hand, absolute general terms denote all those individuals that possess a certain sort of objective similarity, rather than sameness. See M. M. Adams, "Ockham's Theory of Natural Signification" in *The Monist* 61, no. 3 (July 1978), 444–459.

[21] M. M. Adams, "Ockham on Identity and Distinction," *Franciscan Studies*, vol. 36, Annual XIV (1976), 5–74.

which realists at Ockham's time associated with Scotus, but which were not—in Ockham's opinion—that of the Subtle Doctor himself.[22]

So much for the way in which names signify. But what of the abstract concepts associated with those names in actual use? Here the *Dialogue* shows Duns Scotus making use of four types of abstraction familiar to the analyst, to clarify his own position. Two of these were borrowed from C. S. Peirce, one from Bertrand Russell, and one from an American called Allan Wolter. These Scotus employed to explain how he thought names applied to transempirical objects, like God or primary matter, can be given some conceptual meaning. And since this dialogue was advertised as a discussion about metaphysical language specifically, Scotus, at the analyst's suggestion, made extensive reference to a number of philosophical confusions associated with the metaphysician's use of the term "being."

The first type of abstraction is what Peirce calls "prescissive"[23] and seems to have been what the scholastics customarily had in mind when picking out one feature of the object under consideration while ignoring the others. The example Scotus used was "The Bodleian Library is *large*"—a statement which concentrates on the size of the library and prescinds from the materials of which it is built, its location, style of architecture, etc. etc. Of abstraction in this sense, one could say that to abstract is not to falsify.

However, there is a second quite different type of "abstraction" which Peirce called "subjectification,"[24] or more usually, "hypostatic abstraction."[25] Here we take the abstract feature of prescissive abstraction, whatever be the Aristotelian category it might fall under, and make it the *subject* of consideration. We put it, speaking grammatically, in the nominative case. Thus we speak of the "largeness" of the Bodleian. Now Scotus thought this led to considerable confusion when one inquired about the concept, or better, concepts, associated with the word or noun "being." For, as speculative grammarians in his day pointed out, *ens* was always used as a noun, never as a participle, and what is more, was said to be contained implicitly in every other noun

[22] Guillelmi de Ockham, *Scriptum in librum primum Sententiarum (Ordinatio)*, dist. 2, qq. 4–7 (*Opera theologica* II, St. Bonaventure, N.Y., 1970, pp. 100–266).

[23] *Collected Papers of Charles Sanders Peirce*, vols. I–VI, ed. C. Hartshorne and P. Weiss (Cambridge, Mass.: Harvard University Press, 1931–1935), 5.449. References to this work are customarily given in this form where the number before the period indicates the volume, here vol. V. and the number after the period, the paragraph, here 449. See also 1.549 note, 2.364, 2.428. For a Scotistic example of different levels of prescissive abstraction see *Ord.* I, dist. 3, n. 61 (III, 42).

[24] *Ibid.*, 2.428, 4.332.

[25] *Ibid.*, 4.235, 4.549.

or name *(nomen)*.[26] Hence, by hypostatic abstraction we can make "things" or "beings" out of the objective correlates of every modification or qualification used to contract either the notion of transcendental being as *ens communissimum predicabile in quid* or any notion falling under it, such as substance, intermediate genera, species or individuals. By this device "ultimate differences" or *qualia*, like "finite," "infinite," "material," "rational," or the formal principle of individuality in "Peter," can be transformed linguistically into "quiddities" in their own right. It is in this way that the linguistic puzzle or paradox arises: Is it the case that "infinity," "finitude," "materiality," "Petrinity," "rationality" and the like, are included extensionally under *ens*, or is *ens* (which upon analysis seems to be what remains after all differences or qualifications are stripped off) predicated *in quid* not only of determinable concepts, but primitive determining ones as well?[27] Scotus suggested a solution to the puzzle in terms of a distinction between different levels of language. He was careful to point out, however, that he did not want to say that all higher level words are of secondary imposition (or involve cognate concepts that are second intentions), but only that one never predicates a modifier or qualification except of some subject. For instance, if one is inquiring whether the "largeness" of the Bodleian is something, namely, in the category of quantity, we do so only if we have some subject (i.e. something Aristotle would call a primary or secondary substance) of which to assert it—in this case, a thing we call properly "the Bodleian" (a proper name) or "the library of Oxford restored by Sir Thomas Bodley and re-opened in 1602" (a definite description). Now the subject term ("Bodleian" or "the library etc.") already includes the note of *ens in quid*. That is to say, it is essentially a thing or being in its own right. And as subject it is prior logically or by nature to whatever further qualifications it may be said to posses, among them being "largeness." But if we persist in treating this "largeness" itself as something falling under the extension of the quidditative concept *ens* (and refer to it as "a thing" or "a being") rather than treating it essentially as an aspect or qualification of a thing, and hence as including "being" or *ens* only *"sicut additum"* or *ek prostheseos*, we become entangled in the con-

---

[26] *Grammatica Speculativa of Thomas of Erfurt*, ed. G. L. Bursil-Hall (London: Longmans, 1972), ch. 8, n. 16, p. 154; see also A. B. Wolter, *An Oxford Dialogue*, pp. 630–31, for an account of "metaphysical muddle" this leads to in determining the meaning of "being."

[27] This sort of confusion is apparent in the reaction of a number of medieval thinkers to Scotus' intepretation of what Avicenna meant by "being qua being." See Stephen F. Brown, "Avicenna and the Unity of the Concept of Being," *Franciscan Studies* 25 (1965), 117–150.

ceptual or linguistic morass Aristotle refers to in *Metaphysics* VII, chapters 4 and 5 and in the *Posterior Analytics* I, chapter 4.[28] Scotus cited, as an example of the sort of analysis needed, his distinction between cases where "being" or *ens*, as an univocal term, could be predicated *in quid* and where it could not.[29] And he cited his *Quodlibet*, question three[30] as an example of a multi-level analysis of "being" or *ens* as an equivocal term. Among other things, he pointed out how at the highest level "being" may be treated as logically equivalent to "intelligible" and in this sense, if we do not press too far the issue of how "something intelligible" is *one* concept—in the broad sense of Wittgenstein[31] or, in his own day, Henry of Ghent[32]—"being" could be said to be the "object of the intellect." On the other hand, he claimed the *Ordinatio* question[33] showed how he understood this "oneness" and how it should be further analyzed into lower level quidditative and qualitative notions.

The third type Scotus referred to was Bertrand Russell's "principle of abstraction" that Sir Bertrand claimed could just as well be called "the principle which dispenses with abstraction," since it "clears away incredible accumulations of metaphysical lumber."[34] It is used by mathematicians like Peano, who spoke of it as "definition by abstraction," and was pointed out to Russell by A. N. Whitehead as a device for avoiding disputes about the metaphysical status of common properties, theoretical entities, etc.

> This principle asserts that, whenever a relation, of which there are instances, has the two properties of being symmetrical and transitive, then the relation in question is not primitive, but is analyzable into sameness of relation to some other term.[35]

Scotus found this interesting because it raises a challenge to anyone claiming objectivity for any so-called "common property" and

[28] See A. B. Wolter, *The Transcendentals and Their Function*, p. 88f.

[29] *Ordinatio* I, dist. 3, nn. 131–151.

[30] *Quodlibet*, q. 3, nn. 2–3 (*Obras del Doctor Sutil Juan Duns Escoto*, ed. bilingue *Cuestiones Cuodlibetales*, de Felix Alluntis, O.F.M. [Biblioteca de autores Cristianos] Madrid, 1968, pp. 92–97). For an English translation by F. Alluntis and A. B. Wolter, see *John Duns Scotus, God and Creatures: The Quodlibetal Questions* (Princeton and London: Princeton University Press, 1975), pp. 61–63.

[31] Ludwig Wittgenstein, *Philosophical Investigations*, Part I, § 71.

[32] Henricus Gandavensis, *Summa quaestionum ordinarium*, art. 21, q. 3 ad 3 (Paris, 1520), I, fol. 125 S.; confer Scotus, *Ordinatio* I, dist. 3, nn. 20, 30 (III, 11–12, 20).

[33] *Ordinatio* I, dist. 3, nn. 129–151 (III, 80–94).

[34] Bertrand Russell, *Our Knowledge of the External World*, Mentor ed. (New York: New American Library, 1960), p. 40.

[35] Bertrand Russell, *The Principle of Mathematics*, 2d ed. (New York: W. W. Norton, 1951), p. 166.

particularly for his own realistic claims for the *natura communis*. For in terms of logical properties alone, it makes little difference whether you treat a common nature or characteristic accident as an absolute entity or *realitas a parte rei* (the moderate realistic position on universals he himself defended) or deal with it relationally as an *ens rationis*, something a set of objectively similar objects have in relation to the common concept or term used to categorize them naturally (Ockham's so-called "nominalism" or realistic conceptualism). After reading Russell, Scotus had to admit that genuine prescissive abstractions with some absolute basis in reality are difficult to distinguish from logical constructs that refer to extramental realities, for both sorts of terms may be regarded as first intentional. Scotus himself conceded he made use of Russell's principle of abstraction in dealing with the problem of individuation, for his "haecceity" is precisely such a construct, which lumps together formalities that have nothing in common absolutely, being *primo diversa in se*. Their communality is *purely relational*, being described in terms of the common way in which each unique haecceity is related to the *natura communis* or essential sortal features shared by each individual of a specific class.

Russell himself admitted that his "principle of abstraction" did not settle the question of the objectivity or non-objectivity of such "abstracted properties" but merely enabled one to by-pass the deeper metaphysical problem, which he personally regarded as insoluble. Scotus, on the contrary, felt, like Peirce, that while the nominalist's claim might seem to be a *prima facie* plausible solution to the problem of universals, for an important class of formalities—those that served as essential or defining characteristics—a moderate realistic position could be effectively argued, but he did not wish to pursue the matter in the present dialogue.

The fourth type of abstraction Scotus used was what Wolter calls "Augustinian abstraction." It is based on the famous text in the *De Trinitate*:

> Bonum hoc et bonum illud. Tolle hoc et illud et vide ipsum bonum, si potes; ita Deum videbis![36]

"This" and "that" obviously refer to differences in kind, and what St. Augustine appears to be doing is starting with everyday things like the earth, mountains, a farm, conversation with a friend, a philosophical discussion, or what have you; then prescinding from all qualitative

---

[36] Augustine, *De Trinitate* VIII, c. 3 (PL 42, 949; CCSL 50, 272).

features, he comes up with a common denominator. Scotus comments that if one substitutes "being" for "good," the point he wishes to make is more striking. The notion one ought to arrive at by such a succession of prescissive abstractions should be what Scotus calls a quidditative notion of being. With each successive abstraction, the resulting conceptual concept diminishes in comprehension or intensional meaning, while the extension or application of the notion increases. But what happens at this point? Something for want of a better term we can call a "Gestalt-shift." Instead of a notion minimal in comprehension and maximal in extension, we have a notion maximal in comprehension and minimal in extension, so minimal that it is applicable to one and only one Being or Good, namely, God.[37] Scotus and the analyst relate this sort of gestalt-shift to the flash of insight (Köhler and Koffka called it "intelligence") involved in learning the "meaning" of a word, or making a revolutionary scientific discovery,[38] or the grasping of a complex of notional elements as a single "concept" and so on.

Specifically as regards metaphysics, Scotus thought there was a great deal of confusion about the meaning of "being," whether we have one concept or many, or—on the assumption that we do have one concept of sorts (à la Avicenna),[39] whether it should be called "univocal" or "analogous," or whether the concept associated with the word "being," when used reduplicatively in the expression "being qua being," extends to all that is not nothing, or includes only the barest of descriptive content. He suggested that much of this confusion results from the fact that sense and referential meanings are not distinguished, and that over the time period in which one reflects upon what the precise meaning of "being" might be, various "gestalt-shifts" occur, so that our concept associated with the term *"ens communissimum"* seems at one moment almost devoid of descriptive content or sense and a moment later as something including the totality of real being, if not actually, at least implicitly.

---

[37] Though Scotus understandably does not refer to any "Gestalt-shift," he is well aware of the two ways in which Augustine's *Ipsum Bonum* can be understood. Thus he writes in *Ordinatio* II, dist. 3, n. 399 (VII, 564): "Et licet Augustinus dicat de hoc bono et illa (forte singularibus bonis quae occurrant animae) 'Tolle hoc et tolle illud, et vide ipsum bonum, si potes' etc., tamen non intelligit hoc nisi quia ista bona particularia includunt limitationem; qua limitatione ablata, statur in illimitatione boni in communi,—et in hoc intelligitur Deus in universali, sicut dictum fuit in I libro distinctione 3; vel ulterius, statur in bono universalissimo secundum perfectionem,—et tunc intelligitur Deus magis in particulari (et illud bonum nec est hoc nec illud), per ablationem gradus boni limitati."

[38] See for instance N. R. Hanson, *Patterns of Discovery* (Cambridge: Cambridge University Press, 1957), pp. 8–15.

[39] Confer S. F. Brown, *Avicenna and the Unity of the Concept of Being, loc. cit.*

Scotus also wished to use these ideas to explain what happens when one forms a concept of infinity, something Hobbes regarded as the paradigm of a nonsense-word, devoid of all conceptual content.[40] Scotus and the analyst discussed how many thought they had proved that an actual infinitude of discrete entities could neither exist nor be conceived. Cantor, on the other hand, refuted their arguments and showed that Augustine, in contrast to Origen, had a true idea of the *transfinite* as something intermediary between a potential and an absolute infinity. Cantor also explicitly referred to some "Scotists" who held similar views.[41] Scotus went on to state that while he was well aware of the difficulty involved with the very concept of an actual infinite multitude, he personally believed that one could form a constructed or higher level concept of it at least, and if one could, by some flash of "insight," conceive this as a whole, it would be a step towards giving some sense to what he regarded as the peak of metaphysical thought, where one reaches the very limits of language and of abstract speculation.[42]

The analyst concluded the discussion with an observation made by one of his mentors during his student days: "If Aquinas begins with his feet on the ground, he soon takes off like the angels." Scotus—he thought—tried at least to file a flight plan.

[40] Hobbes, *Leviathan*, Part I, chap. 3 (Oxford: James Thornton, 1881), pp. 16–17.

[41] Georg Cantor, *Gesammelte Abhandlugen*, p. 405.

[42] One condition for conceiving anything as a whole or *per se* unity in a single act of understanding would be that the parts are related as act and potency. See for example, *Quodl.* q. 1 (*God and Creatures* 1.12, p. 9). See especially *Lectura* I, dist. 3, n. 68 (XVI, 250) where Scotus distinguishes between a "conceptus simplex, qui concipitur una intellectione et uno actu intelligendi" (which may be subdivided into (a) primitive or irreducibly simple notions like *ens*, or the ultimate differences or primitive qualifications, and (b) those capable of definition, and hence resolvably into further, or—as Scotus calls them—"prior concepts," like "man" into "rational" and "animal") and a concept that is "non-simplex qui pluribus actibus concipitur sicut ens per accidens, ut "homo albus," et etiam alia complexa." Even our explicit notions of an individual as "hic homo" or "hoc aliquid," being constructs, are "quasi per accidens" (see *QQ. in Metaphysiciam*, *loc. cit.*). As for the notion of "infinite being," Scotus tries to make a case for a greater unity than can be achieved with either non-simplex or simple concepts that can be defined (*Ordinatio* I, dist. 3, n. 58; III, 40) and that the compatibility of "infinity" and "being" is something we have some intuitive psychological evidence for (*ibid.*, dist. 2, n. 136; II, 208).

4 / Scotus' Individuation Theory

INTRODUCTION

Because of its theological implications, the problem of individuation in the latter portion of the thirteenth century became one of the more controversial and hotly discussed issues in university circles, especially at Paris and Oxford. Not surprisingly, then, do we find Scotus devoting considerable attention to the topic in four of his more important writings,[1] and even participating in a public dispute on the question with

[1] Besides passing references to his theory, Scotus deals with the problem of individuation in detail in the second book of his several commentaries on the *Sentences*. At Oxford he treated the topic in distinction three as a part of his discussion of the angels, whereas in Paris it was in distinction 12 that deals more specifically with matter. For it was especially the Aristotelian claims about matter that provoked the theological controversy about the angels. This is clear from Scotus' fourth treatment of individuation in book 7, q. 13, of his *Quaestiones subtilissimae super libros Metaphysicorum Aristotelis*, which he introduces with the Philosopher's remark about Callias and Socrates being distinct individuals because of having "this flesh and these bones." The subject also surfaces briefly in question 2, art. 1, of Scotus' magisterial quodlibet. Fortunately, the as yet incomplete critical edition begun in 1950 by the Vatican Polyglot Press (*Ioannis Duns Scoti O.F.M. opera omnia*) contains the questions on individuation (d. 3, pars 1, qq. 1–7) in both the early Oxford *Lectura in librum secundum Sententiarum* (vol. XVIII, published in 1982) and its final revision or *Ordinatio* (vol. VII, published in 1973). Since the paragraphs within each distinction are numbered consecutively irrespective of the question we refer to these two works hereafter simply as *Lect* and *Ord* followed by the number and page. For the other works we refer to the Wadding-Vivès edition (*Ioannis Duns Scoti, O.F.M. opera omnia*, 26 vols., Parisiis: Apud Ludivocum Vivès, 1891–95). The report of the Paris lecture (referred to as *Rep*), qq. 3–8 is found in vol. XXI, pp. 20–41; the *Quaestiones subtilissimae super libros Metaphysicorum Aristotelis* (referred to

William Peter Godin, O.P.[2] The origins of the dispute like many of the day stem from the difficulty of reconciling certain remarks of Aristotle (the Philosopher) with the mainstream of systematic theology.

As an Oxford bachelor, Scotus tells us the dispute centered on "the personality of the angels."[3] If this strikes us as strange, remember that Peter Lombard, whose *Sentences* by the mid-century had become the introductory textbook to systematic theology,[4] begins Book II with the creation, nature, and properties of the angels.[5] Each angel, he argued, is a distinct person, for as "an individual substance of a rational nature" it fulfills the Boethian definition of such.[6] But as pure spirits angels, like the "Intelligences" of the Philosopher, have no matter, and yet Aristotle, his admirers insisted, proves that "all individuation stems completely from matter." It is questionable, therefore, whether a plurality of angels of the same species is possible, and hence whether angels are technically "individuals" or "persons."

By 1277 this controversial interpretation had become so widespread

in the text as "Scotus' *Metaphysics* or in the footnotes as *Meta*) in vol. VII; and the *Quaestiones quodlibetales*, q. 2, art. 1 (referred to as *Quod*) in vol. XXV, pp. 61–62, 90–91. For these last three works it is helpful to indicate the question, marginal number, and page.

[2] In Codex Amplonianus Fol. 369 (Stadtbibliothek Erfurt), ff. 71vb–75rb we find an unedited disputation between Scotus and Godin entitled "Utrum materia sit principium individuationis." F. Pelster, S. J., thinks the disputation probably took place in 1305. See his "Handschriftliches zu Skotus mit neuen Angaben über sein Leben," *Franziskanische Studien* 10 (1923), 15–16.

[3] In his earliest lecture he writes: "Concerning the third distinction (which treats of the personality of the angels), the first question is raised about the singularity in material substances. For it is on the basis of the divergent views about the cause of individuation in material substances that their proponents think differently about the personality of the angels, and about their personality or unity in one species" (*Lect* n. 1229.). See also the reference to personality in the parallel passage in *Ord* n. 1, 391: "Circa distinctionem tertiam quaerendum est de distinctione personali in angelis. Ad videndum autem de ista distinctione in eis, primo quaerendum est de distinctione individuali in substantiis materialibus, de qua sicut diversi diversimode dicunt, ita consequenter dicunt de pluralitate individuorum in eadem specie angelica."

[4] Alexander of Hales seems to have been the first regent master of theology to adopt it for his ordinary lectures and in his *Glossa* to divide it into the distinctions subsequently used. See I. Brady, "The Distinctions of Lombard's Book of Sentences and Alexander of Hales," *Franciscan Studies* 25 (1965), 90–116; also his unsigned "Prolegomena" to his critical edition (*infra* note 5) vol. I, pp. 117*–18*; 143*–44*.

[5] *Magistri Petri Lombardi Sententiae in IV libris distinctae*, lib. II, 3, cc. 1–2 (Grottaferrata [Romae]: Editiones Collegii S. Bonabenturae ad Claras Aquas, 1971) vol. I, pp. 341–42. Peter Lombard took his description of the angelic properties from Hugh of St. Victor's *De Sacramentis* I, 5, 7–8 (PL 176, 250). Hugh ascribed four characteristics to the angels at the time of their creation, viz., first, an immaterial simple substance; second, a distinct personality; third, a rational nature, and fourth, the power of free choice.

[6] Scotus discusses the Boethian definition and what Richard of St. Victor's did to correct it. See, e.g., *Ord* I, d. 23, n. 15 (Vatican ed. V, 355–56).

that several relevant propostions were included among the "errors" condemned by Bishop Stephen Tempier, on the advice of the Parisian theologians.[7] Though in his late *Quodlibetal* Scotus seems to think it still worth while to mention these condemnations as relevant to the question of angelic individuation, he qualifies his claim that it is only "prima facie" they seem to be directed against this theory.[8] He may have had in mind the fact that no less an authority than Godfrey of Fontaines had declared these matters still open to theological discussion.[9] At any rate, in all of his *Sentence*-commentaries, Scotus discusses the question of individuation of material substances, and in particular Godfrey's theory, on purely philosophical grounds with but a passing reference to its theological implications for the theory of eucharistic transubstantiation.

If we compare his various treatments of the subject, it seems that Scotus' basic notions on individuation underwent little or no change in the course of his academic career. With the exception of the involved treatment in his *Metaphysics*,[10] part of which Maurice O'Fihely described as "that scotistic metaphysical chaos,"[11] Scotus' account in his three principal commentaries on Book II of the *Sentences* is quite orderly and systematic. In a series of six questions, he explains and criticizes each of the more prominent theories of his day. In his early Oxford lecture as well as its *Ordinatio* revision, these questions are raised in distinction three as a prelude to a seventh question of whether each angelic nature, as an immaterial substance, represents technically an individual, rather than a monoatomic species. In the Paris lectures, however, only this last question is left in that distinction and the remaining six, with a slight change of order, are relegated to distinction

---

[7] H. Denifle and A. Chatelain, *Chartularium Universitatis Parisiensis*, vol. I (Paris, 1891), p. 549, art. 96: "Quod Deus non potest multiplicare individua sub una specie sine materia"; also art. 81: "Quod, quia intelligentiae non habent materiam, Deus non posset facere plures eiusdem speciei" (p. 548); art. 191: "Quod formae non recipiunt divisionem, nisi per materiam.—Error, nisi intelligatur de formis eductis de potentia materiae" (p. 554).

[8] *Quod* q. 2, n. 4, 61.

[9] Godfrey of Fontaines, in question 5 of his twelfth *Quodlibet*, written around 1296 or 1297, asks: "Does the Bishop of Paris sin because he fails to correct certain articles condemned by his predecessor?" and pointing specifically to articles 96 and 81 according to which God cannot multiply individuals within a species without matter, and God cannot produce many intelligences (or angels) in the same species because they lack matter, declares these matters are still open to discussion for they have been defended by many Catholic teachers. See J. F. Wippel, *The Metaphysical Thought of Godfrey of Fontaines*, pp. 382–83.

[10] *Meta* 7, q. 13, 402–26.

[11] Mauritius de Portu (O'Fihely): "Pertransibis lento passu illud chaos metaphysicale Scoticum," "Annotationes" to q. 13, bk. 7, in the Wadding-Vivès ed. of Scotus, *Opera omnia*, vol. VII, p. 429a.

twelve, which treats of the creation of matter, since all six questions refer specifically to the individuation of a *material* substance. In his *Metaphysics* Scotus introduces his own question ("Is the stone nature of itself a 'this' or is it such only by something extrinsic to the form, such as matter?") with a number of quotations from Book VII of Aristotle.[12] One of them reads: "When we have the whole, such and such a form in this flesh and these bones, this is Callias or Socrates; and they are different in virtue of their matter (for that is different), but the same in form (for the form is indivisible or atomic)."[13] This seems to imply that matter is somehow required to individuate a nature, since in virtue of its form, the nature or essence of anything is as such a sortal principle. Only when matter is combined with form do we have individuals of the same specific nature.

Scotus, of course, does not agree that this is what Aristotle meant by "matter" as an individuating principle and, because of his respect and admiration for "the Philosopher," will give his interesting and subtle interpretation of how to gloss such texts.[14] However, the quotations cited are indicative of the Aristotelian source of the problem.

Since in his early *Lectura* Scotus already gives us an extensive presentation of his views, one that he seemed to feel needed only minor alterations to stand in the *Ordinatio* as an expression of his most mature thinking on this topic, I base this chapter mainly on these two works, with an occasional clarification from his Paris lectures or his *Metaphysics*.

SCOTISTIC REALISM

If we read any of these works, however, it soon becomes apparent that Scotus in raising these questions on individuation was far less concerned with the problem of the metaphysical composition of either angels or matter than with a more fundamental epistemological and psychological question, namely, the objective nature of our intellectual knowledge. The problem arose because the human intellect with its gift of generalization invariably grasps some common or potentially universal characteristic of sense perceptual objects, and yet discovers no reason why the nature (i.e., the essential constitution or general

[12] See Wadding-Vivès ed., *Meta*, 402.
[13] Aristotle, *Metaphysics* VII, ch. 8 (1034a5–7).
[14] *Lect* nn. 192–95, 290–92; *Ord* nn. 201–11, 490–94; *ibid.* n. 238, 505; *Rep* qq. 3–4, n. 10, 24; see also F. Alluntis and A. B. Wolter, eds. *John Duns Scotus, God and Creatures: The Quodlibetal Questions*, 2.57–59 (Princeton: Princeton University Press, 1975), pp. 48–49.

defining characteristics) of what it abstracts could not be multiplied indefinitely. In this sense, what is known about a thing is not what is uniquely individual, but some common property or feature it shares with other things. Even if one grants that formal universality arises only when the concept in the intellect is perceived as common and predicable of many individuals, there still seems to be something in the nature of each thing that is isomorphic with the sort of thing we think it to be.

Various attempts have been made by philosophers to deal with this dual aspect of what they regard as real. Charles Sanders Peirce, who admitted he was profoundly influenced by Duns Scotus and even went so far as to call himself a "Scotistic realist,"[15] tried various semantical ways to express the difference between what he regarded as the two basic metaphysical options of nominalism or realism. His distinctions between token and type, or between indexical and sortal names come to mind. Scotus chose the term "common nature" or "natura communis"[16] to express what he believed Avicenna had in mind with his famous statement:

> For the definition of equinity is apart from the definition of universality, neither is universality contained in the definition of equinity; for equinity has a definition that does not need universality, but is that to which universality is added incidentally, hence equinity itself is nothing other than equinity; for of itself it is neither many nor one, existing in sense perceptible things or in the soul; neither is it some one of these as a potency or as an actual effect, so that it was something contained intrinsically in the essence of equinity, but on this score it is only equinity.[17]

---

[15] [Peirce], *Collected Papers of Charles Sanders Peirce*, ed. C. Hartshorne and P. Weiss, 6 vols. (Cambridge, Mass.: The Belknap Press of Harvard University Press, 1931–35). References to this edition are given not to the pages but to the paragraphs preceded by the volume number. For example, 4.51 refers to volume 4, paragraph 51, where Peirce styles himself "a Scotistic realist." In 1.4 he admits: "The works of Duns Scotus have strongly influenced me. If his logic and metaphysics, not slavishly worshipped, but torn away from its medievalism, be adapted to modern culture under continual wholesome reminders of nominalistic criticism, I am convinced it will go far towards supplying the philosophy which is best to harmonize with physical science."

[16] See A. B. Wolter, *The Transcendentals and Their Function in the Metaphysics of Duns Scotus* (St. Bonaventure, N.Y.: Franciscan Institute, 1946), pp. 107–11.

[17] Avicenna, *Metaphysica* V, ch. 1 (*Avicenna... opera*, vol. 2 [Venice, 1508]), f. 86va: "Definitio enim equinitatis est praeter definitionem univeralitatis, nec universalitas continetur in definitione equinitatis; equinitas etenim habet definitionem quae non eget universalitate, sed est cui accidit universalitas; unde ipsa equinitas non est aliquid nisi equinitas tantum: ipsa enim ex se nec est multa nec unum nec est existens in his sensibilibus nec in anima: nec est aliquid horum potentia vel effectu, ita ut hoc contineatur intra essentiam equinitatis, sed ex hoc quod est equinitas tantum." In *Ord* nn. 31–32, 403, Scotus explains precisely how he understands this dictum of Avicenna.

By "nature" therefore Scotus had in mind the quiddity or whatness (i.e., the essence, which Aristotle described as the "to ti ēn einai"[18] [literally the "what the thing was" or "quod quid erat"] and by "common" he meant that this intelligible form or quiddity could exist either mentally or extramentally, either as singular or universal). "Individual" on the other hand means etymologically something that is "undivided." Division in this sense does not refer to a partition or dissection into either integral parts (like the organs in a body) or essential parts (like matter and form), but into what were called technically "subjective parts," that is, into logical subdivisions and instantiations. In this sense generic natures are divided into species and specific natures into subspecies, or, if they are atomic or the most special species, into individuals.

If a "nominalist" protests that this is a purely logical or conceptual division, a realist might counter that a more realistic analogy of what he means by division into subjective parts would be biological cloning, where the cloned cells are identical qualitatively but are quantitatively or numerically distinct. Though each individual clone has the same nature as its parent cell or sibling, Scotus would say, each also has its own individuality, and this is something that cannot be cloned. The basic question for Scotus is why not? In these questions on individuation, then, it is this sense of individuality that Scotus is talking about. And it is helpful to keep in mind that it is always his "Scotistic realism," as Peirce called it, that inspires both his exposition and critique of the theories competing with his own.

Though the sequence in which they are presented differs notably in the Paris lectures, his arrangement even there is presented in such a way as to enable him to introduce his "common nature" conception relatively quickly into the discussion. In the *Lectura* and *Ordinatio* he does this in the body of the opening question, and in all three commentaries he concludes in the sixth question with his own theory of what needs to be added to the individual's nature qua nature to make it unique to that individual and incapable of being imitated.

The five competing theories in contrast to his own are the following: (1) The first argues that real natures are individual as such. The same four Aristotelian causes that account for the reality of a material substance account for both its nature and its individuality. No added principle is needed; hence, it is meaningless to ask what makes an extramental thing individual; the real question is why does it become universal in thought? (2) The second theory admits the question is not meaningless, but the answer to it is expressed in a double negation;

---

[18] Aristotle, *Metaphysics* VII, ch. 3, 1028b34.

the remaining theories counter that mere negations no matter how multiplied will not explain why only the nature of an individual can be cloned but not its own unique individuality; hence, some additional positive factor is required. These theories offer different proposals as to what that positive factor might be: (3) one suggests a general explanation, viz., existence, since real things are composed of essence and existence; the other two apply only to material substances, namely (4) quantity, or (5) matter. Against these Scotus argues that something intrinsic to the individual nature is required, not something logically external or incidental to it as it were. If existence is not precisely an accident, it is neither unique qua existence nor is it predicated *per se* of any nature except the divine. What is more, if quantity and matter are really distinct things, be they accidents or substance, substantive or modal, they too require a principle of individuation. Hence, (6) Scotus concludes with his own speculation as to what this positive individuating difference must be. Because it is unique, and not general, and proper to each individual, it can only be known adequately by direct acquaintence, and only generally and analogically by description, and referred to by proper names or such general indexical terms as "haecceity" or "thisness."

Although Scotus discusses each theory at great length in his Oxford lecture, and his discussion becomes more elaborate and involved in his subsequent works, I shall treat only the initial and final questions of the *Lectura* in any detail and deal only summarily with specific theories that provoked the other four questions.

First Theory: Real Natures Are Individual as Such

Scotus' first question reads: "Is a material substance by its very nature a 'this,' that is, singular and individual?" And he adds immediately that the terms "substance" and "singular" refer to things that make up the world of real existence, not to the fictive being or existence substances and individual things may have in thought or discourse. As he puts it technically:

> Here 'singularity' is not understood as a second intention [i.e. a concept of a concept] corresponding to 'universality' as its opposite, but the question concerns the material substance itself. Is a material substance of its very nature numerically one, incapable of division into several individuals?[19]

[19] *Lect* n. 1, 229; also *Ord* n. 1, 391. In the Paris lecture he goes to even greater lengths to clarify that it is the real world the question is about. See *Rep* qq. 3–4, n. 3, 21.

As noted above, the advocates of this theory claim the question as formulated is meaningless, since it is looking for a reason or cause specifically for individuality, which has no specific cause.[20] "Some say to this question that there is no intervening cause between the nature of a thing and its singularity. One should not look for any further reason . . . for those causes that give a nature its existence also account for its singularity."[21] On the other hand, to ask what form of thing is this? or what is it made of? or what agent produced it? or what is its purpose? are all properly worded questions and one can answer them by giving as a reason one of the four kinds of causes distinguished by Aristotle. But "singularity" and "universality" have no specific causes other than what causes things or natures to exist in reality or in the mind.

Scotus makes this point even clearer in his Paris lectures.

> The same causes that make it substance, make it both *this* and *substance*, for as it is substance effectively and finally from extrinsic causes, and materially and formally from intrinsic causes, by these same causes is it made *this substance*, so that it is not first a nature before it is this nature. Indeed there seems to be no question to raise as to what makes this substance a "this." For just as in its extramental existence it is universal. And the proof for this is that "existence" in the mind or soul is existence only in a qualified sense, whereas existence extramentally is existence pure and simple with no qualification; thus the two divide all being or existence. And hence there is no need to ask further why it [i.e., this nature] has in the soul universal being as such, though one may well ask what gives it such existence effectively, since the intellect does so by considering it and causing it and the "existence" it gives is of a diminutive sort. But there is no more reason either to ask by what is this nature formally "this" as it exists extramentally in simple unqualified existence. One may ask only what produced it, or why was it produced? Intrinsically, however, it is the singular thing that it is by its intrinsic causes.[22]

Scotus presents two arguments against this, both based on his realistic theory of knowledge. His first is brief and stresses the admittedly

---

[20] As the editors of the *Lectura* indicate, Scotus may have had in mind Roger Marston or Peter de Falco, who had proposed such views a decade or so earlier. They cite the view of Roger Marston, who objected to those who speak "as if all individuation stemmed completely from matter, which is false. For individuation is from the efficient cause that generates or gives it being, from the matter as providing the occasion, from the form, however, as formally constituting; for this gives being formally and consequently makes it distinct and one. I concede therefore that God could make several forms of the same species, apart from any matter." (*Quodlibet* I, q. 3, ed. G. F. Etzkorn and I. C. Brady [Quaracchi, Florentina: Ex Typographia Collegi S. Bonaventurae, 1968], p. 13).

[21] *Lect* nn. 5–7, 230–31; see also *Ord* nn. 5–6, 393–94; *Meta* n. 9, 410.

[22] *Rep* q. 5, n. 7, 28.

different way in which the intellect conceives the real object. If the real is by its essence and nature individual, then knowing it only in terms of what is not individual but universal is no knowledge of it at all, for such so-called knowledge is radically opposed to the nature's singularity.[23]

This suggests a second elaborate argument that allows Scotus the opportunity to explain in some detail the way he considers the "natura communis" to exist in a real or extramental thing.[24] If what we conceive of the thing is isomorphic with its quiddity or nature, then this nature qua nature has a peculiar "unity" of its own which is less than the sort of unity characteristic of this nature qua individual. Using our clone model we might say Scotus' claim comes down to this. God, at least, could conceivably clone any individual nature qua nature but even God could not clone its unique individuality. This implies that even in one unique individual, such as Peter the Apostle, what makes him human is less opposed to being multiplied than what makes him Peter and not his identical twin, if this be his brother Andrew, for otherwise he would not be like his twin or resemble Paul, his fellow apostle, without being either his brother or Saint Paul as such. "Petrinity" is not "Paulinity," if we may designate their respective "haecceities" properly rather than in general. Since we never made the direct acquaintance of either, we must fall back on what Bertrand Russell called "knowledge by description,"[25] which is always couched in general or decriptive terms. Here, however, Scotus is not concerned with how "haecceities"[26] might be known by acquaintance, if they are known as such, but solely with proving that lesser unities than that which "haecceity" brings to the individual are real and objective.

[23] *Lect* n. 8, 231; *Ord* n. 7, 394. In his Paris lectures, this first theory appears as the last of the three discussed under question 5, and all essential points made in the two arguments here appear in a somewhat different form; see *Rep* nn. 7–11, 28–30.

[24] *Lect* nn. 9–11, 231–32; see the parallel passage in *Ord* nn. 8–10, 395.

[25] Bertrand Russell, "Knowledge by Acquaintance and Knowledge by Description," in *Mysticism and Logic* (London: Allen and Unwin, 1917), pp. 209–32.

[26] In the *Lect*, *Ord*, and *Quod* Scotus always refers to the individuating principle as "differentia individualis." He seems to have first referred to it as "haecceity" in his Paris lectures and his *Metaphysics*. See *Rep* nn. 25, 29, 31, and 32; *Meta* n. 9, 410 and n. 26, 426. In subsequent decades, however, this designation was widely used, both by those who accepted and those who rejected his theory. See, for example, Antonius Andreus: "Individuum addit super naturam speciei, puta proprietatem sive differentiam individualem, quae est individuationis praecisa causa, et vocatur haecceitas" (*Expositio textuali librorum Metaphysicorum*, lib. 1, summa 2, cap. 4, n. 61, in *Joannis Duns Scoti opera omnia* [Vivès ed., V, 506]); see also pseudo-Scotus, *Super lib. I Posteriorum*, q. 36, n. 4, in the same edition (II, 298–99). By Suarez' time the name seems to have become customary, for he says "solet vocari haecceitas vel differentia individualis" (*Disputationes Metaphysicae*, disp. 5, section 2, n. 5). At one stage of his development Peirce identified it with "secondness." See *Collected Papers of Charles Sanders Peirce, Passim*.

Scotus usually styles his arguments in strict syllogistic form in an attempt to make his often involved and elaborate proofs of the truth of each premise and the logical validity of the inference somewhat easier to follow. Using "stone" as an example of a real nature, Scotus words his *Lectura* version as follows:

> Anything whose proper unity is less than numerical unity, is not numerical unity; but the unity of a stone's nature is less than numerical unity; therefore the unity which a stone's nature has of itself is not numerical unity.
>
> The major is sufficiently evident, for a lesser unity is consistent with the opposite of a greater unity; therefore, since what is the opposite of numerical unity (for instance, a numerical multitude) is logically compatible with a unity less than numerical, whereas the same thing is not logically compatible with the opposite of its very self; therefore, that unity [of a stone's nature] that is less than numerical unity is not numerical unity.
>
> But the minor is also true, namely, that the unity characteristic of the nature in this stone is less than the numerical unity of this stone, for if this unity were not less than numerical unity, there would be no "real unity" less than numerical unity; the consequent is false, therefore the antecedent is likewise.[27]

Note that Scotus is taking "stone" as an example of a sortal nature that is most specific or atomic, something the mind immediately recognizes this real individual stone to have. As he points out elsewhere we first learn to name things correctly before we can define them more exactly or scientifically. As the child learns to recognize common or sortal characteristics it points to individual instances, e.g. this stone (an indexical gesture in lieu of a proper name applicable to it as "this") and gives it the most specialized sortal name it can, a name of what applies to "the most special species" or *species specialissima*. Scotus calls this initial recognition of its "nominal essence" or *quid nominis*, "confused knowledge" because one has not learned how to distinguish those generic or analogical similarities that permit one to define or describe this stone more precisely. Such "distinct knowledge" comes later.[28]

Hence, Scotus asks us as "proof of the validity of his second argument" to consider any unity other than that of the nature (for instance, the generic or analogical features of that nature) that allow us to specify what is really there more precisely. If we are loath to admit the reality

---

[27] *Lect* nn. 9–11, 231–32; see the parallel passage in *Ord* nn. 8–10, 395.

[28] *Lect* n. 12, 232; in *Ord* nn. 8–10, the argument is reworded in such a way as to incorporate this proof as part of the proof for the minor.

of a less than numerical unity in this stone that justifies our calling it "stone," then there is nothing real about this stone that justifies a more precise scientific definition or description of what it is.[29] The realist, in short, sees many sorts of real unities that are less or not as great as numerical unity; while the taxonomic classifications into various genera and species may represent names we give to what the Scholastics called "second intentions" whose referent is some thought object or "fiction of the mind," the real similarities and differences that justifies our calling such classifications objective or scientific has to be something in the individual other than its individuality. Indeed, as Peirce later pointed out, the very reality of the laws of nature are based on these "lesser unities" Scotus refers to here.[30]

Duns Scotus goes on to give seven arguments why he considers the denial of any real unity other than numerical unity to be false.[31] Not all are of equal merit, since they reflect antiquated Aristotelian notions that might well be questioned today, but they give us a good outline of the extent of his realistic epistemology that appealed so much to Peirce.

[Argument 1] The first is an argument for generic unity based on the

[29] See A. B. Wolter, *The Transcendentals and Their Function in the Metaphysics of Duns Scotus*, pp. 59–65, on the technical distinction between confused and distinct knowledge, and the opening pages of chapter 3, "A 'Reportatio' of Duns Scotus' Merton College Dialogue on Language and Metaphysics," for Scotus' semantical theory as to how names signify.

[30] Peirce, *Collected Papers of Charles Sanders Peirce*, passim; see, e.g.: "General principles are operative in nature. That is the doctrine of scholastic realism" (5.101); "Let a law of nature—say a law of gravitation—remain a mere uniformity—a mere formula establishing a relation between terms—and what in the world should induce a stone which is not a term or a concept but just a plain thing, to act in conformity to that uniformity? . . . There is no use talking reason to a stone. It is deaf and it has no reason. I should ask the objector whether he was a nominalist or a scholastic realist. If he is a nominalist, he holds that laws are mere generals, that is, formulae relating to mere terms; and ordinary good sense ought to force him to acknowledge that there are real connections between individual things regardless of mere formulae" (5.48); "Mill . . . speaks of the 'uniformity of nature.' Before asking exactly what this phrase means, it can be noted that, whatever it means, the assertion of it is an assent to scholastic realism, except for a difference of emphasis" (6.100).

[31] *Lect* nn. 13–27, 232–36. The same seven arguments with the last two reversed are found in the *Ord* (nn. 11–28, 396–402) but are scattered in the *Reportatio* where Scotus tries a different classification scheme, based on whether individuation is intrinsic to the substance individuated or whether it is through something only really distinct from the substance and logically connected with it only *per accidens*. Godfrey's view that the individuating principle is somehow intrinsic to the nature of a material substance and the theory of Giles of Rome and others that quantity signs or modifies the very substance of matter are combined with that attributed to Marston and Peter de Falco as three distinct versions of the view that a material substance is by its very nature individual. See *Rep* q. 5, nn. 2–7, 25–28.

implications of Aristotle's statement that "to be 'one' means 'to be indivisible, being essentially a "this" and capable of being isolated either in place or in form or thought'; ... but most of all it means to be the first measure of each genus, and most properly, of quantity, for it is from this that it has been extended to the others."[32] Scotus uses this text in Book X coupled with what Aristotle had said earlier in Book III, chapter 3[33] about the differences between the unity of the generic nature, the unity of the specific nature, and the unity of the individual, to make three points.[34] First, that Aristotle was struggling to defend the idea that the generic oneness is something real and not a mental fiction. This is what he meant by claiming that in every genus there is a first measure that is "one" and "indivisible" and is "capable of being isolated either in place or in form or in thought." This generic nature is in each species, since it is predicable essentially of each as a whole or unit, and as such seems to be a quasi principle though of less degree than a species. Second, it is not separable from the species of which it is predicable as a separate substance or a Platonic idea might be, and hence Aristotle admits the difficulty of determining what sort of "principle" it might be, since principles and causes are separate from what they cause to be the sorts of things they are. Third, the generic oneness is not identical with the numerical unity, for a measure enjoys a logical and essential priority with respect to what it measures, whereas there is no priority or posteriority among the "individuals" or the "indivisibles" of which an atomic species is predicated essentially.

It is questionable just what Aristotle had in mind, and Scotus claims even Averroës, the Commentator, interpreted him badly. But in thinking that generic unity is based upon something real in the nature of every species, even if inseparable from those species, and claiming further that its unity is of a lesser degree than specific unity, Aristotle was admitting the existence of some real unity less than both specific and numerical unity.[35] In fact, says Scotus, "the Philosopher intended to give a reason why Plato had postulated the notion of a separate species but not a separate genus, because among species there is an essential order since the posterior can be reduced to the prior, (and therefore according to Plato it was not necessary to postulate an idea of the genus 'through participation in which the species are what they

---

[32] Aristotle, *Metaphysics* X, ch. 1, 1052b18.
[33] Aristotle, *Metaphysics* III, ch. 3, 999a12–13.
[34] *Lect* nn. 13–16, 232–33; *Ord* nn. 11–15, 396–97.
[35] In this argument Scotus, however, argues only for the reality of the generic unity and leaves the fact that it is less than specific unity for his second argument.

are'; but in individuals, according to both Plato and according to the Philosopher quoting him, there is no such order."[36]

[Argument 2] Scotus' second argument stresses more specifically Aristotle's distinction of specific and generic unities, falling back on what the Philosopher says in his *Physics*[37] about the atomic species containing one nature whereas in the genus there are many hidden equivocations. This distinction cannot be justified simply in terms of how we think of the two, for though our concept of the genus is one just as much as our concept of the species is (otherwise we could not predicate it essentially of each species), nevertheless we cannot predicate it of individuals in the way the species can be predicated. Its reference to real things is ambiguous in a way that the reference of a species-concept is not. A realist, like Scotus, will argue that this difference in reference stems from some sort of real difference in the nature of what we conceive.[38]

[Argument 3] A third argument is based on what Aristotle in his *Metaphysics* says about similarity. Like identity and equality, it is one of the three distinct "relationships" based on unity.[39] Similarity, however, is a real, not just a conceptual, relation and hence it requires some real basis in the object. This cannot be numerical unity or singularity, for it is of a qualitative rather than a quantitative nature. It is not proper to speak of one and the same individual as being either similar or equal to itself.[40]

[Argument 4] Scotus' next argument is in some respects an anticipation of Peirce's observation about the laws of nature requiring a real foundation.[41] He writes "the opposition between two real extremes, is real ... Now heat destroys cold apart from any thinking about it. Each of the opposite extremes, therefore, is something real and their opposition is really one by a real unity." Certain things, like heat and cold, by reason of their physical nature form a functional unit or are dynam-

---

[36] *Ord* nn. 14–15, 396–97.

[37] Aristotle, *Physics* VII, ch. 4, 249a3–8: "Must we then say that, if two things are to be commensurable in respect of any attribute, not only must the attribute be applicable to both without equivocation, but there must also be no specific differences either in the attribute itself or in that which contains the attribute—that these, I mean, must not be divisible in the way colour is divided into kinds? Thus in this respect, one thing will not be commensurable with another, i.e., we cannot say that one is more coloured than the other where only colour in general and not any particular colour is meant; but they are commensurable in respect to whiteness."

[38] *Lect* nn. 18–20, 233–34; *Ord* nn. 16–17, 397–98.

[39] Aristotle, *Metaphysics* V, ch. 15, 1021a9–12: "Those things are called 'the same' whose substance is one, those are called 'like' whose quality is one, those are called 'equal' whose quantity is one."

[40] *Lect* n. 21, 234–35; *Ord* n. 18, 398.

[41] See note 30 *supra*.

ically interrelated. The basis for this is not their numerical unity, for then all physical things would be interrelated in the same way, since they are all individuals.[42]

[Argument 5] Scotus' fifth argument is based on the fact that when we see a white object we actually do not discern it as just *this* white object rather *a* white object. Indeed, if God were, unknown to us, to make two such distinct objects each with its own unique singularity, and present them to our vision sequentially, but uninterruptedly, then apart from any other clues we would be unable to discriminate between this whiteness and any whiteness not this. In his Paris lecture Scotus suggests that if God miraculously presented two distinct white objects of identical shape and form in one and the same place, we would see the twin objects as one.[43] One might add that if God miraculously bilocated one such object, we would see the one individual as twins. To Scotus this thought experiment indicates that we do not perceive the individuating difference of singulars, but only their sortal nature. He sees an actual instance of such a situation in the case of the sun rays. According to the medieval theory current in his day, as the sun moves, its rays are continually changed so that one individual ray replaces the other without interruption, yet we perceive this numerical diversity as a simple continuity.[44]

[Argument 6] In the *Ordinatio* Scotus cites as his sixth an argument based on the degrees of difference among real things.[45] One cannot claim these degrees are objective, if the only real diversity stems from individual differences alone. Socrates differs less from Plato than he differs from something purely quantitative such as a line, yet everything should be equally different from everything else, if the only basis for real difference is the fact that each thing is singular. Some contemporary critics of nominalism have constructed an analogous argument based on degrees of resemblance.[46]

[Argument 7] This final argument in the *Ordinatio* is not numbered explicitly and in the *Lectura* it precedes the previous argument.[47] It is introduced with the observation that fire generates fire and corrupts

---

[42] *Lect* n. 22, 235. In the *Ord* Scotus uses another example that is stranger to us but was popular in his day, namely, that the way blackness and whiteness are transmitted from object to eye is physically different, one contracting the medium, the other dilating it. See *Ord* n. 19, 398–99.

[43] *Rep* 10, 30.

[44] *Lect* nn. 23–24, 235–36; *Ord* nn. 20–22, 399–400; *Meta* n. 24, 425.

[45] *Ord* nn. 23–28, 400–402. The *Lectura* reverses the sequence of the sixth and seventh arguments and fails to number either of them. See *Lect* nn. 25–27, 236.

[46] See D. M. Armstrong, *Universals and Scientific Realism*, vol. 2, *A Theory of Universals* (Cambridge: Cambridge University Press, 1978), pp. 105–8.

[47] *Ord* n. 28, 401–2. In the *Lectura* it precedes the sixth argument.

water apart from the existence of any mind that might know or discover this about the physical world. Here Scotus is not concerned so much with the physical law aspect as he was in the fourth argument, but with the identity of form that exists between what generates and what is generated. Technically, "like generating like" is known as univocal generation, as when fire produces fire or members of a biological species reproduce. Where the agent produces something unlike itself, the generation is called by contrast "equivocal," as in human production of artifacts or divine creation. In the *Lectura* the argument is worded as follows: "Fire generates fire by a univocal generation, even if no intellect existed; but in a univocal generation the generated is similar in form and nature to the generator; therefore, they have a real unity that is not numerical."[48] The conclusion is obvious since they are numerically distinct though alike in nature. In the *Ordinatio* Scotus notes that the intellect, by considering the situation, does not make the generation univocal but perceives it to be such, the point being that reality is prior by nature to the act of knowing it.

Scotus winds up his lengthy proof with this formal answer:[49]

> To the first question, then, I say that a material substance of its nature is not of itself "this" for then as the first argument proves, it could not be thought of under an aspect unsuited to what is proper to such an object. Also, the second argument with all its proofs shows there is a certain real unity in a thing apart from any operation of the intellect. And this unity of a nature in itself is less than numerical unity or the unity proper to a singular. And since a nature is not of itself one with that unity, it is according to its own proper unity indifferent to the unity of singularity.
>
> One can get some idea of how this should be understood from the dictum of Avicenna (*Metaphysics* V) that "equinity is just equinity; of itself it is neither one nor many, universal nor singular." I understand: "it is not of itself one" of numerical unity, and "it is not several" of the plurality opposed to that unity; and that it is not actually "universal" (viz. in the sense that, as an object of the intellect, something is universal), nor is it of itself "singular." For though it is never in reality without some one of these features, of itself it is not any one of them, but it is something naturally prior to all of these—and according to this natural priority the "what it is" is the *per se* object of the intellect, and as such it is considered by the metaphysician and is expressed by an [essential] definition; and propositions in the first mode of *per se* predication are true of it under this aspect, for nothing is asserted *per se* in the first mode of the quiddity as abstracted from everything that is naturally posterior to it unless included in the quiddity essentially.
>
> Not only is the nature of itself indifferent to existence in the intellect

[48] *Lect* n. 25, 236.
[49] *Ord* nn. 31–34, 402–3; see the parallel passage in *Lect* nn. 28–32, 236–37.

and in a particular, and hence to universal and particular (or singular) existence; but also, in having existence in the intellect it does not have universality primarily of itself. For even though it falls under the concept 'universality' so far as the mode of understanding it is concerned, still universality is not a part of its primary concept, since the concept 'universality' does not belong to metaphysics, but rather to logic. For according to Avicenna himself, the logician considers second intentions applied to first intentions. Thus what is known primarily is the nature apart from any accompanying mode whether it be that characteristic of it in the intellect or outside it. And although universality is the mode of conceiving this nature, it is not this mode that is understood!

And just as a nature is not of itself universal as it exists in the intellect, but universality is something that accrues only incidentally to this primary notion of it as an object, so also in external reality, where the nature is invested with singularity, but is not of itself limited to singularity. Rather it is naturally prior to that characteristic contracting it to this unique singularity, and insofar as it is naturally prior to what contracts it, it is not repugnant to that nature to exist without what contracts it. And just as an object in the intellect would have true intelligible being in the intellect according to that primacy and generality it has, so too according to that entity it has a true real being outside the soul, and according to that entity it has a proportional unity appropriate to it that is indifferent to singularity, so that it is not repugnant to that unity as such that it be associated with any uniquely singular unity. It is in this way I understand the expression "the nature has a real unity less than numerical." And even though it does not have this unity of itself so that it would be included in the formula used to define it, for "equinity is just equinity" according to Avicenna (*Metaphysics* V), nevertheless it is a proper attribute of that nature according to its primary entity. Consequently, of itself it is "this" neither internally, nor according to the proper entity included necessarily in that very nature by reason of its primary entity.

In the *Lectura* he explains that this primary entity is what is technically known as "quidditative" or "essential" being, and gets expressed in real definitions, and is the basis in any real thing for predicating propositions that are true in the first mode of *per se* predication (i.e., those that assert one or all of its defining characteristics).[50] By contrast necessary attributes of that essence are predicated only in the second mode of *per se* predication. It was in this sense he admitted in the quotation above that the "unity less than numerical" that is proper to any nature as such "would not be included in the formula used to define it."

With this realistic position in mind, Scotus turns to evaluate other theories. His second question reads: "Is a material substance individual through something positive and intrinsic to itself?"[51]

SECOND THEORY: INDIVIDUATION AS A DOUBLE NEGATION

Henry of Ghent, who so frequently provides Scotus with the spring-board for a discussion, claimed all that is needed is a double negation, for "individual" means first a lack of division internally and second a non-identity with anything else. Any nature can be duplicated, but each individual is unique. The first negation expresses this lack of division in the individual nature itself and its inability to be multiplied. The second negation denies its identity with any other individual nature.[52]

Scotus rejects this as too simplistic a solution. The fact that some-thing is numerically one or individual, does not mean simply that the individual happens to be one of a kind, but that its uniqueness is incapable of being duplicated. Henry's double negation theory might account for factual indivision, but it cannot explain why it is logically repugnant that an individualized nature should be further instantiated. Only some positive feature of a thing can explain such repugnance. This is clear, for individual uniqueness is a perfection and it cannot stem from a mere privation or negation. Furthermore, according to Aristotle, every negation stems from and presupposes something pos-itive that is naturally prior to what is negative. It remains, therefore, to discuss what such a positive feature might be.[53] The subsequent questions give some suggestions.

THIRD THEORY: EXISTENCE INDIVIDUATES

The first of these reads: "Is a material substance individual through actual existence, or is something else the principle of individuation?"[54] Scotus says the main reason cited for this view is that, according to Aristotle, it is the function of act to distinguish, and of the ultimate act to make the final or ultimate distinction, which is that based on individuation.[55] Peter de Falco, a Franciscan master who flourished around 1280, held an opinion of this sort and may be the possible proponent Scotus had in mind.[56]

---

[52] In his Ord Scotus refers explicitly to question 8 of Henry's 5th Quodlibet. The editors cite the relevant text in a footnote.

[53] Ord nn. 48–56, 412–16; Lect nn. 45–51, 241–43.

[54] Ord n. 59, 418. See also Lect n. 54, 244.

[55] Lect n. 55, 244; Ord n. 60, 418. The reference is to Aristotle's Metaphysics VII, ch. 13, 1039a3–7.

[56] The editors of the Lectura suggest this (loc. cit., p. 244) and cite a passage from Peter's Quaestiones ordinariae, q. 8.

Scotus' objection is twofold:[57] First, actual existence is not the primary distinguishing feature about individuals; even as possibles they can be distinguished. Logically speaking, they belong to the same coordination or ordered hierarchy as genera and species. In fact, individuals lie at the basis of the whole order.[58] Just as existence does not distinguish species from genera, neither does it distinguish individuals of the same species from one another. "This man" no more includes the notion of actual existence than does "man."

Second, existence itself is not *per se* distinctive, but common. Hence, the same question arises about existence as about the nature itself. Where the specific nature of individuals is the same, their existence is of the same sort. What makes it just this existence and not that existence?

FOURTH AND FIFTH THEORIES: QUANTITY OR MATTER INDIVIDUATES

In question four Scotus asks: "Is quantity that positive thing whereby a material substance is a 'this' and singular, and indivisible in many subjective parts?" and in question five: "Is a material substance this and individual through matter?"[59] Since the notion of quantity or extension is so intimately intertwined with the notion of matter, however, it is not surprising to find Scotus combining the treatment of the two questions in his Paris lectures.[60] But even in the earlier *Lectura* that provides the ground plan for the *Ordinatio*, Scotus devotes more time and space to the subject of quantitative individuation than to any other theory, so much so that any adequate treatment would require a separate study. Here, I can but skim the surface of his criticism, as it were.

Underlying his critique would be such Aristotelian convictions as these. The first concerns the general nature of a category. Nothing

---

[57] *Ord* nn. 61–64, 418–20; *Lect* nn. 56–58, 245.
[58] *Ord* nn. 62–63, 420: "Sed exsistentia, ut determinata et distincta, praesupponit ordinem et distinctionem essentiarum . . . In coordinatione praedicamentali sunt omnia quae per se pertinent ad illam coordinationem, circumscripto quocumque quod nihil est illius coordinationis, quia secundum Philosophus I *Posteriorum* 'status est in quolibet praedicamento in sursum et in deorsum.' Igitur sicut invenitur supremum in genere praecise considerando illud sub ratione essentiae, ita inveniuntur genera intermedia, et species et differentiae; invenitur etiam ibi infimum, scilicet singulare, omnino circumscripta existentia actuali,—quod patet evidenter, quia 'hic homo' non plus includit formaliter exsistentiam actualem quam 'homo.'"
[59] *Lect* n. 61, 246; n. 125, 268; *Ord* n. 66, 421; n. 129, 458.
[60] *Rep* qq. 3–4, 20.

essential to any of the ten categories stems from another category. The second concerns substance as the first category. In his *Categories* Aristotle states that genera and species are substance only in a secondary sense, the primary substance is the individual.[61] A third point concerns quantity in particular and its connection with matter. In its basic metaphysical sense, quantity is the first of the nine accidental predicaments, distinct from the category of substance. Furthermore, like quality, it is an absolute accident, whereas the remaining seven are relational predicaments. As for matter, some notion of quantity or extension seems so basic to its nature that one can question to what extent it can be considered an accident of a material substance, or really distinct and separable from its substantial nature. Hence, we find Scotus devoting special attention to the suggestion of Giles of Rome that quantity modifies or signs the very substance of matter, and puzzling at considerable length over Godfrey's theory that though material things are individuated formally by their substantial form, quantity as the basis for numerical unity plays at least a dispositional role.[62] From what we said of his realistic Avicennian interpretation of "nature," however, it should be clear Scotus is looking beyond the relatively specific question of how material substances are individuated. His quest is for a more universal and metaphysical principal of individuation that can be applied to any really distinct nature, be it substantial or accidental, material or spiritual.

Hence, his detailed criticism of quantity as a specific principle for an individual material substance takes two forms, one based on the priority of substance over accident and the other on the false analogy that leads one to think that either quantity or matter, even if disposed or modified by quantity, will do the individuating job required.

Consider the first of these. In the preceding question, we recall, Scotus argued against actual existence as an individuating principle, because it was extrinsic and logically accidental, as it were, to the essence or quiddity of a real thing. Furthermore, what is essential or intrinsic to any predicamental or categorical order, requires that what is potential be actualized by some difference pertaining to that order, not by something extrinsic to it. Now individuals as well as species and genera belong logically to a specific category, here the category of substance. On the realistic interpretation of nature, however, it is the very substance of each distinct individual of the genus or species that has been uniquely individuated. If whatever pertains to that individual's generic or specific perfection, however, is formally and *per se*

---

[61] Aristotle, *Categories*, ch. 5, 2a11–18.
[62] See Wippel, *Metaphysical Thought*, pp. 359–69.

"less than numerically one," it will not be made an individual by something that is really distinct and separable from that individual's substance. Accidents, however, are really distinct from substance, and by the power of God at least any real substance can be separated from what is accidental to it. In fact, where the substance is material, the Scholastics agreed no divine intervention is required. Even natural or physical causes can alter a material's quantity through rarefaction or condensation without changing it substantially or numerically. How then, Scotus argues, can something that pertains to one of the accidental categories individualize anything substantial?

Actual existence is not precisely an accident in the sense that it falls under any of the nine categories of Aristotle, nor is it a true predicate in the categorical sense. Nevertheless, it is predicated as "secundum adiacens" in contingent statements of the form "Such and such a nature exists," where "esse exsistentiae" behaves like a quasi accident, inasmuch as it is not intrinsic to any nature other than the divine. There, in a quite different sense than in creatures, "existence" is predicate in the first mode of *per se* predication. Hence, in his *Metaphysics*,[63] where Scotus uses the substance-accident dichotomy as his basis for ordering the various theories, he considers existence as a quasi accident and indicates it falls heir to the same criticism leveled here against quantity; nothing extrinsic or distinct from the substance *per se* will individuate that substance.

As for the second, Scotus objects to the reason given for any quantitative form of individuation. In his exposition of the fourth theory, he indicates it was based on Aristotle's definition of quantity.[64] " 'Quantum' means that which is divisible into the parts that constitute it, each of which is by nature a 'one' and a 'this.' " Proponents of this theory, he says, take this to mean that function of dividing things into parts of the same sort pertains primarily to quantity. Now the division of a species into individuals is just such a division, since this is what distinguishes the division of a species into individuals from the division of a genus into species; therefore, individuals of the same species are distinguished by quantity, and as a consequence, material substance becomes singular through quantity.[65]

The whole argument, however, is based on a faulty analogy, namely, the impression that the division of some quantity into its integral parts

[63] He lists five theories, the fourth of which ascribes individuation to actual existence. "What seems common to all five, or at least to the first three opinions about individuation through something accidental, can be refuted in four ways that are sufficiently based on reason" (*Meta* n. 3, 404).

[64] Aristotle, *Metaphysics* V, ch. 13, 1020a7–8.

[65] *Lect* n. 67, 248; *Ord* n. 71–74, 423–26.

is like the division of a specific nature into its subjective parts. Never is any integral part the whole of quantity, yet a subjective part (e.g., Socrates) is always a complete human being. In a word, when one "divides" any atomic species into individuals, each instance is a complete nature of that sort.[66]

What is more, he argues, proponents of this view misinterpret the Philosopher's text. In explaining how quantity is divided, Aristotle's very way of speaking indicates that its parts are not new, but are already present as real constituents. Though not actually separated each portion of a continuum has its own proper extended entity. All division does is to separate one from the other. Separability, for Scotus, was always a criterion of a real distinction. Furthermore, he insists, division of a quantum does not yield parts of the same sort. Consider a quantum consisting of six units; one can divide it into two triads or three pairs or into one section having four parts and another having two. Here we have a division of quantity into parts that are in it, but they are not of the same sort. Also, to have any quantum whole and entire, all its parts must be integrated. This is not true of the interrelation of individuals, and species. Otherwise a species would be an amalgam of individuals. Hence, to appeal to quantity to explain division into parts of the same sort is wholly irrelevant.[67]

Scotus devotes comparatively little space to the fifth theory, because it is primarily an explanation of how the substantial form is individuated, not the material substance as such. For they claim this is individual, he says, "only because its form is received into this or that matter, as though the whole singularity of a material substance stemmed from the matter."[68]

But this theory will not wash either. What is peculiar about each individuating principle is that it is unique and primarily diverse. In other words, there is nothing in two such individuating differences that is identical and provides an objective basis for abstracting a common feature. That is why Aristotle calls the members of an atomic species "indivisibles." As "indivisible" the individuating factor has no "parts" that might be used to define it; only the nature each individual shares with others of its kind can be defined. If "this matter" truly individualizes this material form and "that matter" individualizes that material form, then one cannot abstract a common nature from the two "matters." "Matter," like Scotus' "individual difference" or "haecceity," would be simply a common name for a general description

---

[66] Lect nn. 103, 261; see also Ord nn. 105-6, 443-44.
[67] Lect nn. 104-5, 262; Ord nn. 107-9, 444-45.
[68] Lect nn. 128-32, 269-71.

given to radically different principles. One might object that even if the difference *per se* is unique, it bears the same relationship to the specific nature as any other such difference. Speaking precisely, Scotus would deny this is true; the relationship may be similar but it is never the same sort. For if each "haecceity" is unique, then one term of the so-called common relationship is different and this suffices to make the two relations similar but not identical.

Scotus seems to have this in mind when he proposes this quandary to the advocates of this theory.[69] "If from this matter and that matter one cannot abstract 'matter,' and from this man and that man one can abstract 'man,' then matter does not pertain to the essence of man; but this is clearly false." If so, one can abstract "matter" from this matter and that matter, and therefore, matter is indifferent to being in this or that. In its indifference, matter cannot be the reason why each material substance is unique or individual, and what is more, we have to seek a reason why matter itself is individual or singular.

Consider also the phenomenon of how one of the four physical elements changes into another.[70] "If matter is the cause of individuation and singularity, since matter remains the same when fire perishes and changes to water, the singularity will remain the same, and therefore the same singular will exist." If you say it is no longer the same singular, since it no longer is the same species, this will not do either. For if fire can perish and become water, so too water can perish and become fire again and then since the original fire and the second fire have both the same matter and species, they are numerically the same—which no one admits.

SIXTH THEORY: SCOTUS' THEORY OF HAECCEITY

Scotus' sixth and final question is one to which he will give a positive answer. "Is a material substance individual through something positive determining the nature to be just this individual substance?"[71] After distinguishing the sense in which Godfrey's theory might be listed as a positive answer to this question—which we omit in the interest of brevity—he presents his own personal view.

"I reply therefore to the question that material substance is determined to this singularity by some positive entity and to other diverse singularities by other diverse positive entities."[72] First, he says, I will

[69] *Lect* n. 133, 271–72.
[70] *Lect* nn. 135–36, 272.
[71] *Lect* n. 139, 273.
[72] *Lect* n. 164, 280.

give arguments for this conclusion and afterward explain the nature of this positive individuating entity and how it functions.

His basic argument is that unity logically is always attributed to some positive entity. If this is true of being in general, then it should also be true of that unity of singularity that is opposed to any further division into subjective parts. This sort of unity is not the precise property of the entity that constitutes the nature or quiddity of the individual, for as he stressed in his initial question, this is less than numerical unity, and is not contradictorily opposed to the possibility of there being more than one individual of that sort; hence, it is not of itself an adequate explanation of why this individual is just this individual and not another. This positive entity to which we attribute singularity, therefore, must be formally other than the entity constitute of the specific nature. Though formally distinct, this individuating difference must form with that nature a *per se* unity; hence, its proper "haecceity" is not accidental to any individual.[73]

His second argument is based on the idea that where two things differ, each difference must in the last analysis be reduced to something primitive or radically diverse. Technically, Aristotle claims, things are said to *differ* only if they have something in common. Now individuals (of the same species) differ in the proper sense of the term, that is, they have something in common (their specific nature) and something that is different. This difference must in the last analysis be reduced to something that is primarily diverse. Obviously, this is not the nature, for though the nature of one is not that of the other, the two natures are identical specifically or formally. Otherwise there would be no real resemblance or agreement between the two individuals of the same species; consequently, there must be something else in each whereby they differ. Now this is not privative, but positive, not something accidental like quantity, or contingent like actual existence, as the answers to the preceding questions showed. Therefore, it must be something intrinsic, pertaining to the category of substance, that, logically speaking, contracts the indifference of the specific nature to just one unique individual.[74]

Having presented his arguments for its existence, Scotus tries to clarify more precisely the nature of this positive entity and how it individuates the specific nature of the individual. His promised explanation is based on the triple analogy he believes exists between specific and individual differences, or more precisely, between the formal perfection or entity in an individual corresponding to such differences.

[73] *Ord* n. 169, 474–75; *Lect* n. 166, 279–80.
[74] *Ord* n. 170, 475; *Lect* n. 162, 279–80.

These objective correlates of our real concepts about the existing world he calls "realities" or "formalities" in contrast to *res*, or real separable "things" that are classified under Aristotle's ten categories.[75] Each difference, he says, bears a triple relationship: (1) to what is below it, (2) to what is above it, and (3) to what is side by side with it.[76]

Consider the first likeness. It is repugnant to the specific difference and the reality corresponding to it to be divided further into essentially different species or natures, and through this difference it is also repugnant to the specific subject of which this is an essential part to be so divided. In an individual subject the individuating reality plays a similar role. Primarily it is this individual entity or "haecceity" that is opposed to any further division into subjective parts, that is, into numerically distinct individuals. And this formal difference, as an intrinsic or *per se* part of the individual substance, makes it logically impossible for that substance itself to be so divided. Nevertheless these two sorts of differences differ inasmuch as the unity of the specific nature is less perfect than this unity of the individual as a whole, for the lesser unity is not repugnant to further numerical division, but only to division into essential parts. The individual's unity by contrast forbids both sorts of division. Scotus sees this as confirming his thesis that the individuating element is a positive entity. If the unity less than numerical is a proper attribute of the individual's nature, a subject with its own proper entity, then "it does not seem probable that one ought to deny that that most perfect of unities [viz., individuality] is also the proper attribute of some positive entity of its own," namely, the specific nature as singularized by its haecceity.[77]

As for the second analogy, if we compare the respective differences to what is above them, the formal perfection on which the specific difference is based is actual with respect to that formal perfection from which the notion of the genus is taken; otherwise, says Scotus, the definition would contain a useless repetition, and the genus alone would suffice to define a nature, for it would indicate the entire entity of the defined. Sometimes, what contracts or distinguishes the generic perfection may be a distinct substantial form.[78] (Scotus has in mind, for instance, a living organism. Here the material substance [the generic perfection] is an organic body with its own corporeal form, but the specific difference, "living," derives primarily from the fact that this material substance is enlivened by a really distinct form or living soul.)

[75] See chapter 1.
[76] *Ord* nn. 176–83, 478–81; *Lect* nn. 170–72, 282–84.
[77] *Ord* nn. 177–78, 478–79.
[78] *Ord* n. 179, 479.

At other times, however, the differential perfection is only a distinct formality, or another formal concept of the same real thing. From this standpoint, he says, some specific differences have a concept that is not irreducibly simple, for they include the notion of "a being." The concept we have of other specific differences, however, can be irreducibly simple, and can not contain, but qualify the notion of "being" as a subject.[79] In such a case, the objective reality corresponding to this specific difference is only formally distinct from the reality of the subject it qualifies. Haecceity resembles this second sort of difference, for though it is a "quasi act" adding some real perfection to the quasi-potential specific nature of the individual, it is never a really distinct thing or form, but rather represents the ultimate reality of that individual's form.[80] In the *Lectura* Scotus illustrates this point as follows:[81]

Not only is the concept of the genus qualified by the concept of the difference, but the reality from which the notion of genus is taken is naturally prior to that reality from which the notion of the difference is taken, and that reality from which the genus is taken is determinable and able to be contracted or qualified by the reality of the difference. Similarly, in the individual, the specific nature is determinable and able to be contracted by the reality from which the individual difference is taken. Hence, just as in the same real thing (such as whiteness) there are diverse formal perfections or formal entities, from one of which the notion of the genus (such as that of color) is taken, and another formal entity from which the notion of the difference (that of whiteness) is taken, ... so there is a positive entity in the same real thing from which the specific nature is taken, and an entity formally other from which the ultimate individual difference is taken, an entity which is totally "this," and is opposed to any division whatsoever. And as the reality of the genus is in potency to the differential reality, so the reality of the nature qua nature is in potency to the reality from which the individual difference is taken. But still there is a dissimilarity, for the difference with the generic nature constitutes what sort of being it is, and is also called its quidditative or formal being, whereas the individual difference together with the nature is not constitutive of what sort of thing the individual is, for this difference lies outside the notion of what it is [i.e., of its quiddity or essence], and therefore does not constitute it in its constitutive or formal being, but rather in its material being, insofar as "material" is opposed to "formal" being, in the sense of "formal being" just

---

[79] See Wolter, *Transcendentals and Their Function*, pp. 84–85.
[80] *Ord* nn. 179–80, 479.
[81] *Lect* n. 171, 282–83.

mentioned and in the sense that the Philosopher calls "form" the "what-the-something-was-to-be."[82]

Third, if we compare the specific difference to what is side by side with it, namely, another specific difference, though not everything we conceive of as a specific difference is primarily diverse from every other such difference, if each of our concepts of two such formal differences is primitive or irreducible, that is if each is technically "simply simple," then the formal entities or formalities from which such real primitive concepts are derived are themselves radically diverse. And in this latter case, such formal or specific differences resemble the individual or individuating differences, for each formality or entity that individuates a singular nature is a primitive difference distinct from the primitive difference of a second individual of that nature.[83]

Scotus concludes his explanation of "haecceity" with this reaffirmation of his realism:[84]

If you ask me: What is this "individuating entity" from which the individual difference is taken? Is it matter or form or the composite? I give you this answer. Every quidditative entity—be it partial or total—of any sort, is of itself indifferent "as a quidditative entity" to this entity and that entity, so that as a quidditative entity it is naturally prior to this entity as just this. Now just as, in this natural priority, it does not pertain to it to be *this*, neither is it repugnant to its essential nature to be other than just *this*. And as the composite does not include qua nature its entity whereby it is formally *this*, so neither does its matter qua nature include its entity whereby it is *this matter*, nor does its form qua nature include its entity whereby it is this form.

This [individuating] entity therefore is not the matter or the form or the composite insofar as each of these is a "nature,"—but it is the ultimate reality of the being [i.e., the *ens*] that is the matter or that is the form or that is the composite; so that whatever is common and nevertheless determinable, no matter how much it is only one real thing [i.e., *una res*], we can still distinguish further several formally distinct realities, of which this formally is not that; and this is formally the entity of singularity and that is formally the entity of a nature. Nor can these two realities ever be two distinct real things, in the way the two realities might be from which the genus is taken and that from which the dif-

---

[82] "Quod-quid-erat-esse" was the literal translation of Aristotle's "to ti en einai"; "forma" here is the Latin translation of Aristotle's "eidos," not "morphe"; cf. *Metaphysica* V, ch. 2, 1013a26–28.

[83] *Ord* n. 183, 481; see also *Lect* n. 172, 283–84.

[84] *Ord* nn. 87–88, 483–84. Though the formal distinction between the haecceity and the nature is never based on two distinct real things that could be separated, the reality from which the genus is taken could at times be really distinct from the reality from which the specific difference is taken. As we noted above this would be the case with a living organism.

ference is taken (from which two realities the specific reality as a whole is taken),—but in the same real thing there are always formally distinct realities (be they in the same real part or the same real whole).

When he first presented this theory of individuation in the *Lectura*, one of his auditors must have charged him with extreme or Platonic realism for believing the nature in its extramental existence still retains its "less than numerical unity." For in revising his presentation for the *Ordinatio* he interjects this interesting objection.[85] If the nature in an individual has any real unity, his protagonist insists,

> it is either in the same numerical subject or in some other subject as well. Now it is not in the same numerical subject, for whatever is in that one subject is numerically one; neither is it in two or more subjects, since in two distinct subjects (or persons) there is nothing that is really one, for this is a property of divine subjects or persons (as Damascene points out).

Earlier in the *Ordinatio* Scotus had admitted that the sense in which the three divine persons share the same nature is quite different from the way individuals of the same species share a common nature. For the divine nature by reason of its infinity is unique or individual, it needs no special principle of individuation.[86]

Scotus' answer is philosophically interesting for it indicates the difference between his moderate realism and that of Plato.[87]

> As was stated in the solution to the first question on this matter [of individuation], nature is prior naturally to "this nature," and the unity proper—that follows nature qua nature—is prior naturally to its unity qua this nature. And it is under this prior aspect that there is a metaphysical consideration of the nature, and its definition is assigned and propositions are true in the first mode of *per se* predication. And therefore in the same thing that is one in number there is some entity to which is attributed a unity that is less than numerical, and that unity is real; and that to which such unity pertains is made formally "one *de se*" by numerical unity. Therefore, I concede that this real unity is not something existing in two individuals but in one.

He goes on to explain, that although everything in a real individual is numerically one, it is not for the same logical reason. Peter, for

[85] *Ibid.*, nn. 171–72, 476.

[86] *Ibid.*, n. 39, 408; see also his proof that there can be only numerically one infinite being in *Ord* I, d. 2, pars. 1, q. 3; II, 222–243, and the parallel passages in the *Lect* (XVI, 146–57) and *Rep* I A (A. B. Wolter and M. M. Adams, "Duns Scotus' Parisian Proof for the Existence of God," *Franciscan Studies* 42 (1982), 307–16.

[87] *Ord* n. 172, 476.

example, possesses the essential nature of man, plus an element unique and proper to himself, let us call it "Petrinity." Petrinity is primarily individual or numerically one; Peter as a "this man" is *per se* numerically one, for his individualized humanity contains the formality or haecceity or Petrinity. His human nature with its own less-than-numerical-unity, however, is only denominatively numerically one, in the same way Peter's generic animality is denominatively rational, or color, the genus, in redness is denominatively red. Since the whole discussion has been about a material substance, he reverts to "this stone" as his concluding example:[88]

> And so I concede that whatever is in this stone is one numerically,—either primarily or *per se* or denominatively. That through which such unity pertains to this composite, perhaps would be such primarily; this stone would be such *"per se"* [for] that which is primarily one by this unity [i.e. the individuating difference] is a *per se* part of this; that potential [i.e., the stone-nature, in itself less than numerically one] which is perfected by this actual [individuating difference] is only "denominatively" numerically one, with respect to its actuality.

Before concluding this chapter let me make one comment about the intelligibility of singulars. Scotus' remarks in question one about our inability to differentiate two white objects or two individual sunrays on the basis of their respective "haecceities," indicates that we do not know the individuating difference "per se." In fact, if we could there would have been no need of this long discussion as to what individuates a material substance. Scotus is perfectly willing to accept this conclusion as a small price to pay for what seemed even more important to him, the fact that our generalizations about the real world and the individuals in it have an objective foundation. He is also willing to accept the idea that what first motivates our intellect, in this life at least, is what can be abstracted from sense images.[89] But it is the

---

[88] *Ibid.*, n. 175, 477–78: "Ita concedo quod quidquid est in hoc lapide, est unum numero,—vel primo, vel per se, vel denominative: 'primo' forte, ut illud per quod unitas talis convenit huic composito; 'per se' hic lapis, cuius illud quod est primo unum hac unitate, est per se pars; 'denominative' tantum, illud potentiale quod perficitur isto actuali, quod quasi denominative respicit actualitatem eius."

[89] He deals with this limitation of our intellect as compared with that of the angels later in part 2, question 1 of this same distinction, both in the *Lect* (cf. n. 254, XIII, 309–10), and in even more detail in the *Ord.* See nn. 289–93; VII, 535–93: "Sed quod est istud impedimentum?—Respondeo: intellectus pro statu isto non est natus movere vel moveri immediate nisi ab aliquod imaginabili vel 'sensibili extra' prius moveatur...Et secundum istum modum expositionis movetur intellectus ab obiectis imaginabilibus,—et eis cognitis, potest ex eis cognoscere rationes communes et immaterialibus et materialibus." See also book I, d. 3 of either the *Lect* (n. 300; Vatican ed. XVI, 345–46) or the *Ord* (n. 187; Vat. ed. III, 113–14), where Scotus points out the difference between

accidental features of objects in the real world that impinge upon our senses, and it is these we must use to identify and differentiate individuals. How we know singulars, however, is irrelevant to the question of angelic individuation, which—as we recall—was the problem that triggered Scotus' lengthy metaphysical discussion of individuation.[90] The intelligibility question, however, surfaces briefly in one of the initial arguments used to introduce question six.[91] If haecceity is a positive entity formally distinct from but really identical with the specific nature of a substance, it should be as intelligible as the specific difference itself, particularly if it forms a *per se* unity with the nature in the same way as the specific difference forms a *per se* unity with the generic nature. Obviously, the objector argues, this is not the case, for if haecceity were intelligible, the singular nature would be known qua singular, not qua nature. Aristotle recognized this difference between intellectual and sense knowledge when he pointed out that the intellect has to do with universals, the sense with singulars.[92] Scotus' answer acknowledges the problem but solves it succinctly with a distinction. Just because our intellect cannot apprehend haecceity intellectually does not mean it is *per se* unintelligible. God and the angel can know it directly and *per se*. The reason we cannot grasp it intellectually is due not to any lack of intelligibility on the part of the individuating entity but to the imperfection of our intellect and the way it functions in our present life.[93] And he appeals to Aristotle's famous distinction: "As the eyes of the owl are to the blazing sun, so

how our intellect operates at present and how its optimum operation will differ in the afterlife; see also chapter 6, "Duns Scotus on the Natural Desire for the Supernatural."

[90] "Seventh and finally in this matter," says Scotus, "I ask whether it is possible for several angels to be in the same species?" (*Ord* n. 212, 495); in the earlier version, he centered his query even more specifically on the question of personality: "Can there be several persons in the same species of angels?" (*Lect* n. 196, 293).

[91] *Lect* n. 142, 274; *Ord* n. 144, 464: "Tunc singulare, compositum ex natura et illo per se determinante, esset per se unum; ergo per se intelligibile,—quod videtur contra Philosophum II *De anima* et VII *Metaphysicae*, ubi videtur aperte velle quod intellectio est 'universalis' et sensus et sensatio est 'ipsius singularis.' "

[92] Aristotle, *De anima* II, ch. 5, 417b22–23; *Metaphysics* VII, ch. 10, 1035b33–1036a8.

[93] *Lect* n. 180, 286: "Ad aliud quando arguitur quod tunc singulare erit per se intelligibile alia specie quam natura speciei, sicut species alia similitudine quam genus, quia sicut tunc species addit super genus, ita singulare super speciem,—dico quod singulare non intelligitur intellecta specie, et quod singulare intelligitur per se ab intellectu qui potest omnia intelligere intelligibilia (sicut Deus et similiter angelus). Unde quod non intelligatur per se ab intellectu nostro, hoc non est ex parte singularis, sed ex imperfectione intellectus nostri,—sicut noctua non videat solem, non est ex parte solis sed ex parte noctuae." In *Ord* n. 191, 486: "Concedo quod 'singulare' est per se intelligibile, quantum est ex parte sui (si autem alicui intellectui non sit per se intelligibile, puta nostra, de hoc alias); saltem non est ex parte eius impossibilitas quin possit intelligi, sicut nec ex parte solis est impossibilitas videndi et visionis in noctua, sed ex parte noctua."

is the reason in our soul to the things which are by nature most evident of all."[94]

It is only in his *Metaphysics* that Scotus deals at length with the question of whether the singular is *per se* intelligible.[95] I have summed up what he says there in chapter 5.

[94] Aristotle, *Metaphysics* II, ch. 1, 993b9–11.

[95] In book VII of his *Metaphysics* he has not only the question on the individuation of a material substance we have referred to but also the important q. 15 (Vivès, vol. VII, 434–40): "Is the singular *per se* intelligible to us?" I have analyzed this latter question in some detail in Chapter 5, "Duns Scotus on Intuition, Memory, and Our Knowledge of Individuals."

5 / Duns Scotus on Intuition, Memory, and Our Knowledge of Individuals

Perhaps Scotus' most important contribution to medieval epistemology was his theory of intellectual intuition. He clearly regarded it as a departure from Aristotle, who "frequently talks about an intellection of the quiddity, but seems to say nothing about intellectual vision."[1] The terms *intuition, intuitive* or *intuere*, of course, are of earlier origin, having been applied both to the introspective insight into the soul or its functions as well as to the 'face-to-face' vision of God in the afterlife.[2] But Scotus gave the term a new existential twist, distinguished

Reprinted with permission from *History of Philosophy in the Making: A Symposium of Essays to Honor Professor James D. Collins on his 65th Birthday by His Colleagues and Friends*, ed. Linus J. Thro. Copyright 1982 by University Press of America, Inc., Lanham, Maryland.

[1] *Quaestiones subtilissimae super libros Metaphysicorum Aristotelis*, VII, q. 15, n. 9 (Vivès ed. VII, 404). Hereafter this work is referred to in the text as *Questions on the Metaphysics* and in the footnotes as *Meta.*

[2] M.-D. Roland-Gosselin, "Peut-on parler d'intuition intellectuelle dans la philosophie thomiste?," *Philosophia perennis*, hrsg. von F. J. von Rintelen (Regensburg: J. Habbel, 1930) Bd. II, p. 711, suggests the term "intuitive knowledge" was introduced by the Franciscan school after the death of St. Thomas and entered through discussions with the Franciscans. He distinguishes four senses in which it was used: first as "vision" in opposition to faith (pp. 712–714); "direct insight" as opposed to discourse (pp. 714–715); "immediate knowledge" as opposed to mediate knowledge (pp. 716–720); and "vision of the individual" as opposed to that of the universal (pp. 721–730). On the history of the last sense, see Camille Bérubé, *La connaissance de l'individuel au moyen âge* (Montréal: Presses de l'Université de Montréal/Paris: Presses Universitaires de France, 1964). Henry of Ghent's distinction between the two ways in which we can know (*scire*) the existence of a thing, one "per seipsam ex evidentia existentiae suae apud scientem: ad modum quo scit ignem esse ille qui videt ignem praesentem oculis"; the other by

it sharply from its sense perceptual counterpart, and combined it with a non-intuitive theory of how substances and singulars are known.[3] The cautious and tentative way in which his conception of intuition matured would suggest he believed himself to be playing a pioneering role—an hypothesis confirmed to some extent by the attitudes of William of Ockham and Peter Aureoli. The first cites Scotus to prove his own theory of an intellectual intuition of both sensible and intelligible objects was not an Ockhamistic innovation.[4] The second questions whether we actually have in this life any truly intellectual intuition such as Scotus or Ockham claim.[5] From the time of Scotus onward, however, the subject is never ignored by the late scholastics and continues to surface in various controversial contexts until given a new twist by John Major, Calvin's teacher, where it becomes a turning point in the history of theology.[6]

I would like to sketch briefly the main steps I see in the evolution of Scotus' thought until it reaches full bloom in the key text quoted at length by Ockham, where the implications of intuition for memory are explored. But first a word as to what he means by intuitive cognition.

THE NATURE AND TYPES OF INTUITIVE COGNITION

From the many places where he describes it, intuitive cognition in general is a form of existential awareness.[7] At the intellectual level, it

---

inference (cf. Henricus Gandavensis, *Summa quaestionum ordinariarum*, art 22, qq. 1 & 5 [Paris, 1520, photoreprint St. Bonaventure, N.Y.: Franciscan Institute, 1953], I, 130L & 134C), and his critique of the "species" theory of the vision of God (Quodl. 3, q. 1 [Paris, 1518, photoreprint Louvain: Bibliothèque S.J., 1961], f. 47–48) undoubtedly influenced Scotus. Cf. *Lectura* I, prol. n. 108 (XVI, 40).

[3] C. Bérubé, *op. cit.*, p. 179ff.

[4] Guillelmi de Ockham, *Scriptum in librum I Sententiarum Ordinatio, prol. Opera theologica* I (St. Bonaventure, N.Y.: Franciscan Institute, 1967), p. 44: "Ne autem ista opinio quantum ad notitiam intuitivam sensibilium et aliquorum mere intelligibilum tamquam nova contemnatur, adduco verba Doctoris Subtilis libro IV, distinctione 45, quaestione 3, duas praedictas conclusiones expresse ponentis, videlicet quod intellectus noster intuitive cognoscit sensibilia et quod intuitive cognoscit aliqua mere intelligibilia."

[5] Philotheus Boehner, "*Notitia Intuitiva* of Non-Existents According to Peter Aureoli, O.F.M. (1332)," *Franciscan Studies* 8 (1948), 399–410. "The importance of Scotus in regard to the theory of intuitive and abstractive cognition is shown by the fact that Aureoli, like Ockham, starts the explanation of his own theory with a critical discussion of that of Duns Scotus" (p. 391).

[6] Thomas F. Torrence, "Intuitive and Abstractive Knowledge from Duns Scotus to John Calvin," *De doctrina Ioannis Duns Scoti* (Romae: Commissio Scotistica, 1968), v. 4, pp. 291–305.

[7] Sebastian J. Day has given a virtually complete listing of the passages in the Wad-

is an act of simple awareness or intelligence in which some object is grasped holistically [*simul totum*] as present and existing here and now. Hence it is not to be confused with the subsequent contingent or existential judgments that explicate its conceptual content. Rather it is contrasted primarily with abstractive cognition, which is simple awareness or understanding of the meaning of a term or proposition, and prescinds from whether the object or situation conceived of either exists in actuality or is here and now present.[8] At the level of sense cognition, Scotus attributes abstraction to the phantasy or sense imagination, and intuition to the external sense of sight. The former can conjure up a sensible *species* or representative likeness of an object no longer present or perceived as existing by some external sense.[9] In

---

ding-Vivès edition where Scotus treats the subject, together with a helpful analysis of the implications of each. See *Intuitive Cognition: A Key to the Significance of the Later Scholastics* (St. Bonaventure, N.Y.: The Franciscan Institute, 1947), pp. 48–139. To these should be added the texts from the *Lectura* and some references in Scotus' notes available in the *Ordinatio* or revised commentary on the *Sentences*, parts of which are available in the critical edition edited by the Scotistic Commission *Ioannis Duns Scoti Opera Omnia* (Civitas Vaticana: Typis Polyglottis Vaticanis, 1950–   ). Unless otherwise noted, quotations from the *Lectura* and *Ordinatio* I & II are from the Vatican edition, whereas those from *Ordinatio* III & IV are from Codex A, described at length in C. Balić's "De Ordinatione I. Duns Scoti disquisitio historico-critica," pp. 12*–28* in the first volume of this edition.

[8] To quote from a translation of his most mature work: "It is helpful to distinguish two acts of the intellect at the level of simple apprehension or intellection of a simple object. One is indifferent as to whether the object is existing or not, and also whether it is present in reality or not. We often experience this act in ourselves, for universals and the essences of things we grasp equally well whether they exist extramentally in some subject or not, or whether we have an instance of them actually present or not. We also have an empirical or *a posteriori* proof of this, for scientific knowledge of a conclusion or understanding of a principle can be equally present to the intellect whether what they are about is existing or not, or is present or absent. In either case, then, one can have an equal understanding of that term on which an understanding of the principle or conclusion depends. This act of understanding, which can be called 'scientific,' because it is a prerequisite condition for knowing the conclusion and understanding the principle, can very appropriately be called 'abstractive' because it 'abstracts' the object from existence or non-existence, from presence or absence. But there is another act of understanding, though we do not experience it in ourselves as certainly, but it is possible. It is knowledge precisely of a present object as present and of an existing object as existing. ... This is so when it is attained in itself and not just in some diminished or derivative likeness of itself [i.e. an intelligible species]," *John Duns Scotus, God and Creatures: The Quodlibetal Questions*, trs. with an introduction, F. Alluntis and A. B. Wolter (Princeton and London: Princeton University Press, 1975; reprinted Washington, D.C.: The Catholic University of America Press, 1981), par. 6.18–6. 19, pp. 135–136; hereafter cited as *God and Creatures*.

[9] *Ibid.* par. 13.27 (p. 290): "There is some knowledge of the existent as such, such as that which grasps the object in its actual existence, e.g., the sight of color and in general of any sense perception involving the external senses. There is also knowledge of the object, but not as existing as such, either because the object does not exist or at least

similar fashion at the intellective level, abstractive cognition depends causally upon some naturally prior intelligible species which goes proxy for the object it represents. By contrast, intuitive intellection has the thing itself, rather than a substitute species, interacting with the mind or soul to cause actual knowledge of itself.[10] Unlike Ockham, who critically developed and extended Scotus' conception to include the supernatural possibility of an intuition of nonexistence, Scotus sees the creature's awareness of existence as essential to any intuition it may have.

But because the memory of an initial intellectual intuition can linger on, Scotus found it necessary to expand his notion to include a distinction between perfect and imperfect intuition.[11] The need for such may have become apparent to him when he considered the implications of his argument for intellective intuition in the present life, based on our assurance of the truth of certain primitive contingent propositions. Perfect intuition is the awareness of a present existential situation; imperfect intuition, an opinion about a past or future existential situation. One might speculate as to how intuition of the future should be understood. It seems to refer to the veridical prophecies theologians attributed to Christ and the prophets, but it could also be an allusion to the reputedly high incidence of 'second sight' among the Scots. Be that as it may, it is only the memory of the past that Scotus explains in any detail, and here an antecedent perfect intellectual intuition is a necessary, but not sufficient, condition for our subsequent imperfect intuition. Though perfect intuition dispenses with a naturally prior intelligible species, the same is not true of imperfect intuition. Some form of intelligible species produced by the original perfect intuition must be impressed upon the memorative faculty.[12] And so imperfect

---

the knowledge is not of the object as actually existing. One can imagine color, for example, both when it exists and when it does not."

[10] Day sees the question of whether or not a species is involved in intuitive cognition "a problem that has exercised the ingenuity of Scotistic commentators for centuries" (*op. cit.* p. 105). In what follows, I hope to make clear to what extent a "species," in any capacity, functions in intuitive cognition.

[11] *Ordinatio* III, d. 14, 9. 3; Codex A, f. 155vb: "Loquendo autem de alia cognitione, scilicet intuitiva, quae est de natura vel singulari, ut concernit actualem exsistentiam, dico quod illa est vel perfecta, qualis est de obiecto ut exsistens praesentialiter, vel imperfecta, qualis est opinio de futuro vel memoria de praeterito." Cf. Vivès ed. XIV, 527.

[12] *Ibid.*, ff. 155vd–156ra: "Obiectum isto modo [scil. intuitive] non est cognoscibile nisi ut actualiter praesens in se vel in aliquo in quo habet esse perfectius quam in se [scil. in essentia divina]....Non esset igitur nata cognosci sessio Petri, nisi praesens esset sessio Petri in se; et ita cum multa obiecta nec fuerint nec esse potuerint praesentia illi intellectui [Christi] secundum exsistentiam actualem illorum, non potuit habere cognitionem intuitivam illorum. Et si dicatur quod [Christus] potuit habere cognitionem

intuition, inasmuch as it functions at a time when the object is not intuited as here and now present, introduces features common either to abstractive knowledge and/or Ockham's famed intuition of nonexistence.

A still further expansion of the notion of intuition seems warranted in view of the role Scotus assigns to intellective memory, in terms of its proximate and remote object of recall, a subject I will discuss later vis-á-vis the final stage of development. Before we can trace any growth in his thought, however, some relative dating of the works we shall be using is needed.

---

omnium exsistentium pro quacumque differentia temporis per species infusas, hoc falsum est; tum quia species infusae repraesentant obiectum ut abstrahit ab exsistentia actuali, quia eodem modo repraesentat sive obiectum exsitat sive non exsistat, et per consequens non sunt ratio cognoscendi exsistens ut exsistens; tum quia veritates quae sunt cognoscibiles cognitione intuitiva de exsistentibus ut sunt exsistentia, videlicet veritates contingentes, non possunt cognosci per species qualescumque innatas, quia ex cognitione terminorm contingentium non potest cognosci veritas complexionis contingentium de illis terminis, quia illarum complexionum veritas non includitur in terminis, sicut in speciebus et terminis eorum includitur veritas necessaria complexionis scientialis. Oportet ergo—etiam propter veritates cognoscibiles cognitione intuitiva, quae sunt veritates contingentes quae sunt de exsistentibus ut exsistentia sunt, et propter exsistentia ipsa in se actualiter cognoscenda—habere ipsa obiecta in se praesentia, ut intuitive possint cognosci et intuitive in se videri. Et hoc non potest fieri in ipsis rebus in genere proprio, nisi ipsis rebus in se secundum suam propriam exsistentiam praesentibus et ita potest ista cognitio in genere proprio intuitiva actualis vel habitualis illi animae dari de omnibus. Et quoad hoc necesse est dicere quod profecit sicut alia anima, et obiecta alia aliquo modo cognoscit. Sed quantum ad intuitivam imperfectam, qualis est opinio de futuro et memoria de praeterito, quae relinquitur ex ista perfecta, quia de talibus pluribus perfecte intuitive cognitis derelicta sunt plura experimenta et plures memoriae in intellectu, quibus cognosci possint illa obiecta quantum ad conditiones exsistentiae, non ut praeterita, sed ut praesentia, adhuc dico quod etiam [non] novit omnia in genere proprio. Et si obiicitur quod ex re praesente non derelinquitur nisi species intelligibilis impressa in intellectu et in parte sensitiva, ut in virtue phantastica, species imaginabiles, hoc falsum est, quia de re praesente non tantum derelinquitur species intelligibilis in intellectu qua cognoscitur sub nulla differentia temporis, sed alia in potentia memorativa. Et istae potentiae cognoscunt obiectum sub alia et alia ratione. Una cognoscit obiectum ut exsistit praesentialiter, alia cognoscit ipsum ut in praeterito apprehensum ita quod apprehensio praeteriti est immediatum obiectum memoriae et immediatum obiectum illius apprehensionis praeteritae est obiectum mediatum recordationis. Ita etiam praesente aliquo sensibili sensui, potest virtute illius causari in intellectu duplex cognitio, una abstractiva, qua intellectus agens abstrahit speciem quidditatis, ut quidditas est, a specie in phantasmate, quae reprasentat obiectum absolute, non ut exsistit nunc et tunc; alia potest esse cognitio in intellectu intuitiva, qua obiectum cooperatur intellectui ut exsistens, et ab hac potest derelinqui habitualis cognitio intuitiva importata in memoria intellectiva, quae non sit quidditatis absolute, sicut fuit alia prima abstractiva, sed cogniti ut existens, scil. quomodo in praeterito apprehendebatur. Hoc modo per experientiam dicitur Christus multa didicisse, i.e. per cognitiones intuitivas, hoc est, illorum cognitorum quantum ad existentiam et per memorias derelictas ab eis." Codex S (f. 191va/b) has virtually the same wording.

CHRONOLOGICAL NOTE ON SCOTUS' WORKS

Any attempt at a definitive chronology of Scotus' major works, perhaps, is at present premature. Yet enough data is available to suggest a working hypothesis for the four we wish to compare. There seems general agreement that the *Lectura* came at the beginning, and the *Quodlibetal Questions* near the end of his academic career. It seems fair then to take these as our boundary conditions. As for the *Ordinatio*, or revised commentary on the *Sentences* of Peter Lombard, work on the Prologue was under way at Oxford in 1300, a date mentioned in the second question,[13] and was still in progress at Paris in 1304, for Scotus refers in Bk. IV, distinction 25, to a papal bull he had seen with his own eyes that was issued by Benedict XI in the early months of that year.[14] A note in Scotus' own hand indicating the number of questions yet to be dictated in the last two distinctions of Book IV, reported by the scribe of the important Codex A,[15] would imply the revision was never completed, like that of the last question of the *Quodilbet*, which exists only in a partially emended form.[16] We seem justified in assuming that while Scotus may have by-passed certain particular questions en route, he had pushed on to drafting all but the final portions of Book IV before leaving Paris his final teaching assignment in Cologne, where he died. Hence the questions in distinction 45 of this book we rank with questions six and thirteen of the *Quodlibet* as the most mature expressions of his thought on intuitive cognition. As for the two questions on intuition in his *Questions on the Metaphysics*, for internal reasons as well as Lottin's observations on the subject,[17] we date them after the *Lectura*, but prior to the question in *Ordinatio*, Book III, on Christ's intuitive knowledge. This would permit us to demark four or five very broad steps in the evolution of his ideas on the intellect's powers of intuition.

---

[13] *Ordinato*, prol., n. 112 (I, 77). See A. G. Little, "Chronological Notes on the Life of Duns Scotus," *English Historical Review* 47 (1932), 573, and C. K. Brampton, "Duns Scotus at Oxford, 1288–1301," *Franciscan Studies* 24 (1964), 9–10, for an interpretation of this passage. If it refers to the short-lived euphoria the news of the defeat of the Egyptians by the Turks in alliance with the Christians in the battle of Medjamâa el-Morûdj on Dec. 23, 1299 brought to Oxford in June of 1300, one would have expected Scotus to qualify, or eliminate the remark, had he lived to complete the final revision of the *Ordinatio*. The internal structure of this question (absent from the earlier *Lectura*) suggests it may have been a university sermon.

[14] Little, *art. cit.*, p. 577; C. K. Brampton, *art. cit.*, pp. 9–10.

[15] See C. Balić, "De ordinatione ... disquisitio historico-critica," p. 28*.

[16] *God and Creatures*, p. xxxiii.

[17] Odon Lottin, "L'Ordinatio de Jean Duns Scot sur le livre III des Sentences," *Recherches de théologie ancienne et médiévale* 20 (1953), 102–119.

Lectura I, the Incipient State of Development

In these lectures given before the turn of the century, the technical distinction between abstractive and intuitive cognition appears only in the second book, when Scotus speaks of angelic knowledge. In the first book, the doctrine of intellective intuition seems only implicit, and even the term "intuitive," as opposed to "vision," seems to have been *obiter dictum*.[18] Whereas Ockham introduced his theory of intellectual intuition already in the Prologue to his *Ordinatio* and made it central to his whole epistemology, Scotus sets forth his ideas as to how our intellect functions only in distinction 3, and with no explicit mention of its capacity for intuition. His main concern was what a theologically tenable account of its adequate object might be. His first ideas on the subject appear in simplified form in the *Lectura* as part of the larger question: Is God the first object of knowledge as Henry of Ghent claimed?[19] And the expanded version of the *Ordinatio* devotes an entire question to the topic.[20]

Like most of his contemporaries, Scotus held a basically Aristotelian theory of knowledge, which he modified only slightly in the interests of an earlier Franciscan-Augustinian tradition.[21] Roughly what is relevant about this common theory is that man's intellect lies midway between the cognitive powers of the brute beast on the one hand and the Judeo-Christian "angel" or the philosophers' "Intelligence" on the other. Where the brute knew only material and sensible things and the angel the spiritual and immaterial, man's proper intellectual object is the essence or quiddity of what is sensible or material. Working with the aid of an agent intellect, man's mind is able to grasp the universal or immaterial aspects, whereas his senses by contrast are concerned with the particular material or accidental features. Hence the cognitive maxim: *Intellectus est universalium, sensus particularium.*

While Scotus as a philosopher was willing to accept this tripartite division of cognitive faculties as a fair description of what normally moved brute, man and angel to know, he could not, as a theologian,

---

[18] Of the six explicit uses in *Lectura* I a cursory reading revealed (viz. prol. n. 108; d. 3, n. 59, n. 112; d. 8, n. 174; d. 10, n. 3; d. 13, n. 17), the first three seem to refer to "intuition" as opposed to "discursus" or reasoning; the last three refer to God's intuitive cognition. Only the first of these seems to contrast intuition with abstractive knowledge, and the second is of interest because it suggests that God, at least, has an intuitive cognition of nonexistence: " . . . in essentia cognoscitur creatura intuitive antequam sit" (d. 10, n. 3; XVII, 115).

[19] *Lectura* I, d. 3, nn. 88–123 (XVI, 258–273).

[20] *Ordinatio* I, d. 3, nn. 108–201 (III, 68–123).

[21] On this tradition and Scotus' reaction to it, see the editorial notes re *Lectura* I, d. 3, n. 313 (XVI, 350–351).

regard it as an adequate account of the nature of the human intellect as such.[22] For if the face-to-face beatific vision of God that Paul spoke of was to be explained in terms of some sort of Aristotelian intellectual habit given in heaven, then by its nature, our intellect must at least be able both to know and be moved by something other than sensible quiddities. Hence Scotus' complex counter proposal as to what constitutes the adequate object of our intellect, based on what we can know under optimum conditions and not just what we know at present through the medium of the senses.

Implicit in this enlarged conception of our intellect's nature as a cognitive potency is its natural capacity to know intuitively as well as abstractly, once the soul is freed from the body. Since we have treated elsewhere of the manifold distinctions Scotus makes in this connection,[23] we only note briefly here that he distinguishes between the intuitive cognition we can receive naturally and what can be obtained through the interaction of natural causes. Since no form of intuitive cognition does violence to the intellect, but perfects it as a receptive potency, we can even be said to be "naturally inclined" to receive knowledge impressed directly by anything as existing and present to it, be it the divine nature or the essence of a creature. Nevertheless, even in its separated state, our intellect—which is but little less than the angel's in this respect—can only be moved naturally to such intuitive knowledge by created beings.[24] And in such a case, the intellect is not purely passive, but it cooperates as a partial, essentially ordered efficient cause, with the created object itself (for natural intuitive cognition), just as it cooperates with an intelligible species that represents the object (for natural abstractive cognition).[25] In the supernatural face-

[22] *Lectura* I, d. 3, n. 92 (XVI, 259): "Opinio, quae ponit quod quiditas rei materialis sit primum obiectum adaequatum ipsius intellectus, non est vera....Nullus catholicus potest hoc dicere, quia tunc esset alia potentia quando videret essentiam divinam in patria et alia immaterialia"; *Ordinatio* I, d. 3, n. 113 (III, 70): "Istud non potest sustineri a theologo, quia intellectus exsistens eadem potentia naturaliter, cognoscet per se quiditatem substantiae immaterialis, sicut patet secundum fidem de anima beata."

[23] A. B. Wolter, "Duns Scotus on the Natural Desire for the Supenatural," *The New Scholasticism* 23 (1949), pp. 281–317; see chapter 6, pp. 124–147, below.

[24] *Ibid.*, pp. 294–300. Especially illuminating are Scotus' remarks on how the blessed in heaven can acquire new knowledge of the creatural world. See *Ordinatio* IV, d. 45, q. 2; Codex A, f. 267vb: "Ad quaestionem ergo dico quod anima separata potest acquirere cognitionem prius ignoti, et hoc tam cognitionem abstractivam quam intuitivam.... Patet secundum, scilicet de cognitione intuitiva, nam causae illius sufficientes sunt obiectum in actuali exsistentia praesens, et intellectus agens et possibilis....Sed nec ista intellectio intuitiva haberi potest per speciem praesentem, quia illa repraesentat rem indifferenter exsistentem et non exsistentem, praesentem et non praesentem."

[25] Scotus' concession to the older Franciscan position (ascribed to Augustine) that the intellect is the sole efficient or active cause in intellection, was to admit that Augustine only attributed a partial activity to the soul or intellect; hence his frequent

to-face vision promised in heaven, however, God's essence is not a naturally moving object, nor does the created intellect act or coact with it, but God moves the passive intellect of the blessed through his will, and thus properly speaking he is a voluntary or supernaturally gratuitous object. But because God's will and essence are really identical, the intuition that results is not primarily a knowledge of God's voluntary action as such but rather a vision of the divine essence itself. Here, at least, Scotus seems to have introduced a distinction between the direct causal action of the object known intuitively and what terminates the intentional act of knowing. We shall have occasion to return to this distinction in discussing the dual object that seems to be involved in imperfect intuition of past experiences.

Second Stage: "Lectura" II on Angelic Intuition

In the first distinction, question six, of Book II Scotus discusses the precise formal reason why the human soul and an angel are specifically different, and why the latter is more perfect in nature than the former. But he makes it quite clear that the reason is not to be found in any intrinsic specific difference in their respective intellectual powers. Once our soul is freed from its embodied state, our mind might even equal an angel's.[26] Consequently, when he raises the question of angelic

citation of that text from the *De Trinitate*, Book 9, ch. 12: "Obviously we must hold fast to the principle that everything which we know begets the knowledge of itself within us. For knowledge is born from both the one who knows and the object known." See e.g., *Lect* I, d. 3, n. 320 (XVI, 352); also n. 365 (p. 367) where he asks: "What then is the sufficient and precise cause of the knowledge produced? I say that the precise cause of intellection and of the knowledge produced is the intellective soul ... and the object in itself, if it is present to the intellect according to itself, or the object in some representation, as in a species representing the object. Neither the object *per se* nor the intellect *per se*, but both together, form one sufficient cause." And he goes on to show how these two essentially ordered efficient causes coact to produce either intuitive or abstractive cognition. To the objection that when an intelligible species goes proxy for the existing object in abstractive cognition, it does so as a form in the possible intellect, he insists: "It is only coincidental so far as the basis for causing [*ratio causandi*] is concerned that one [the species] perfects the other [*qua* form]. ... Indeed, if the object itself were present, or if through some [divine] assistance, the species was present in a way other than as an [accidental] form of the intellect, still the intellect would understand in no less degree" (*ibid.* n. 370, p. 369).

[26] *Lectura* II, d. 1, q. 6, n. 291 (XVIII, 58): "Dico quod [anima et angelus] distinguuntur specie, et tamen non in ratione intellectivi et volitivi, nec ut comparantur ad actus; nec intellectiones eorum et volitiones distinguuntur specie, licet limpidius unus intelligat alio." We are grateful to Father Luke Modrić, O.F.M., Praeses of the Scotistic Commission, for supplying page proofs of this forthcoming volume. See also *Ordinatio* II, d. 1, q. 6, n. 319 (VII, 155).

knowledge later in the second part of distinction three, he can appeal to his theory of what we can know in the afterlife to indicate how his account of angelic cognition differs from that of Henry of Ghent, Aquinas and others. Speaking of the created intellect's power he writes:

> Know that an intellect is capable of two sorts of knowledge and intellection, for it can have one that abstracts from all existence, and another of a thing present in its own existence ... The first sort of knowledge, according to which the intellect abstracts from all existence, is called "abstractive," whereas the other, according to which the intellect sees the thing in its existence, is called "intuitive." It is not called "intuitive" because it is not "discursive," however, but rather because it is distinguished from that abstractive knowledge, which knows a thing in itself through a species.[27]

The *Ordinatio* version is essentially the same except that Scotus suggests this technical usage is peculiarly his own. "I may speak briefly, I call knowledge of the quiddity itself 'abstractive' ... [and] that of a thing according to its actual existence or of a thing present in its existence I call 'intuitive intellection.'"[28] Henry of Ghent had used the term "intuitive" as opposed to "discursive" reasoning, and earlier Scotus himself had employed it in this sense when he wrote of the univocal concept of being or *ens*, predicable of substance but abstracted from accidents: "This is all that we know intuitively of substance, and no more."[29] But here he is using it in the sense of an intellectual vision

[27] *Lectura* II, d. 3, nn. 285, 287–288: "Sciendum est quod in intellectu potest esse duplex cognitio et intellectio, nam una intellectio potest esse in intellectu prout abstrahit ab omni exsistentia,—alia intellectio potest esse rei secundum quod praesens est in exsistentia sua.... Quod sit ponenda secunda cognitio in intellectu, patet: quod est perfectionis in potentia inferiore, est in superiore; sed hoc est perfectionis in potentia inferiore (ut in visu) quod potest cognoscere rem secundum suum verum esse exsistentiae; igitur similiter in intellectu hoc ponendum est, quod ipse potest cognoscere rem in exsistentia sua. Praeterea, prima istarum cognitionum, secundum quam intellectus intelligit rem abstrahentem ab omni exsistentia, dicitur esse cognitio 'abstractiva',—et alia, secundum quam videt rem in exsistentia sua, dicitur esse cognito 'intuitiva' (non autem dicitur esse cognitio 'intuitiva' quia non est 'discursiva,' sed prout distinguitur contra abstractivam qua per speciem cognoscitur res in se)."—Some years ago the Scotistic Commission supplied the author with this text reconstructed for its use from Codices V and F by Father Barnabas Hechich, O.F.M.

[28] *Ordinatio* II, d. 3, n. 321 (VII, 553).

[29] *Lectura* I, d. 3, n. 112 (XVI, 266): "Unde dico quod intellectus noster primo cognoscit accidentia, a quibus abstrahit intentionem entis, quod praedicat essentiam substantiae sicut accidentis; et tantum intuitive cognoscit de substantia, et non plus. Hoc sicut dixi, experitur quilibet in se, quod non cognoscit plus de natura substantiae nisi quod sit ens. Totum autem aliud quod cognoscimus de substantia, sunt proprietates et accidentia propria tali substantiae, per quas proprietates intuemur ea quae sunt essentialia substantiae." The "intuemur," perhaps, refers to the non-inferential way of applying substantive names, indicative of the "species specialissima," to objects in the sense

of existence or the existent. And since many of his colleagues, unlike Henry of Ghent, were asserting that the beatific vision of the divine involved a created species infused by God,[30] Scotus insists that even an infused species yields nothing but abstract knowledge, a point he will bring up again in discussing Christ's knowledge.

Though he illustrates the difference between these two types of knowledge with our intellect in mind, and by analogy with our external and internal sense knowledge,[31] in neither the Lectura nor the Ordinatio versions does he hint that we possess intellective intuition already in this life, but only that we look forward to having it in the next. Once he had introduced the intuitive-abstractive distinction in the second book of the Lectura, he had occasion to refer to it several times in revising the first book as an Ordinatio, for instance, in his famous "coloratio" of Anselm's Proslogion argument for God, absent in the Lectura, where he is referring ahead to distinction three that deals with the object of the intellect and the knowledge it possesses.[32] But even in stressing the certitude we have of our own cognition acts, he apparently failed to recognize that this reflective knowledge is itself a clear-cut case of intellectual intuition, as he later did, for instance, in the Quodlibet.[33] Indeed, the admission that we already may enjoy

perceptual field—a vague form of intellectual knowledge that precedes even the abstraction of the distinct notion of being, and is another form of the verbal skills he calls "habitus vocalis de substantis," Meta. II, q. 3 (VII, 114). Cf. A. B. Wolter, "A 'Reportatio' of Duns Scotus' Merton College Dialogue on Language and Metaphysics," Sprache und Erkenntnis im Mittelalter, Bd. 13.1 Miscellanea Mediaevalia, hrgb. von Albert Zimmermann (Berlin/New York: Walter de Gruyter, 1981), 179–191; cf. chapter 3, pages 54–67, above.

[30] Scotus seems to have studied Henry's Quodl. 3, q. 1, extensively where Henry asks: "Utrum ab intellectu creato in vita beata videbitur deus per aliquam speciem mediam" (op. cit.). What prompted the question is that in color vision light is insufficient to determine the organ but the species of color is needed to inform it. This suggests that the light of glory may be insufficient without some created species in the beatified intellect. Henry rejects the theory, as did Scotus, though not for the same reasons.

[31] Lectura II, d. 3, n. 290 (Hechich text): "Ista autem duplex cognitio potest apparere in cognitione sensitiva, nam aliter cognoscit imaginativa quam visiva; visus enim cognoscit rem in existentia sua dum praesens est, sed imaginativa imaginatur res dum absentes sunt sicut quando sunt praesentes; nunc autem quae sparsa sunt in inferioribus, unita sunt in superioribus; et ideo intellectus quando cognoscit rem in exsistentia, tunc dicitur cognoscere sicut imaginativa."

[32] Ordinatio I, d. 2, n. 139 (II, 211): "De differentia intellectionis intuitivae et abstractivae et quomodo intuitiva est perfectior, tangetur distinctione tertia et alias quando locum habebit." In addition to the references cited by the editors, Scotus could well be referring also to the question on the adequate object of the intellect.

[33] God and Creatures, par. 6.19 (pp. 136–137): "Such knowledge of the existent qua existent and present is something an angel has about himself. For Michael does not know himself in the way he would know Gabriel if Gabriel were annihilated, viz. by abstractive cognition, but he knows himself as existing and as existing in a way identical with himself. He also is aware of his intellection in this way if he reflects upon it,

some measure of intellective intuition at present marks the advent of the next step in his thinking.

THIRD STAGE: SCOTUS' QUESTIONS ON THE METAPHYSICS

The first of the two questions relevant to intuition is question three of Book II.[34] It asks whether the essence of God or any other immaterial substance can be known by us in this life. To solve it Scotus turns once more to the parallel between the sense and intellective functions. There are four degrees of sense knowledge, he informs us. The first is the intuition of a thing as present in its own nature and not known either through a species or a process of reasoning. Seeing color is the sense perceptual example given. The second degree is knowledge through a species or likeness produced by the thing itself, e.g. our phantasy imagines some color we have seen. The third degree is through a species fabricated by the cognitive power itself from several proper species initially impressed upon it, for instance, when we picture a gold mountain to ourselves, or imagine something seen as gray or pale black to be pitch black. Beyond these three forms of *per se* knowledge are *per accidens* "perceptions" which involve opposites or a subject consisting of an aggregate of accidents. Each type of sense knowledge has its analogue at the intellectual counterpart in the essential definitions we form by putting together the differential notions arrived at by the classical "via divisionis" or investigative technique of Plato. Beyond these three degrees of *per se* knowledge is the way in which we construct descriptions of what is transempirical, using negative and accidental features which we add to the core notion of "thing" or "being." In analyzing the nature of our God-notions in question 1, distinction 3, Book I of both the *Ordinatio* and *Lectura*,[35] Scotus had made use of this constructive technique. But what is interesting about the present question, so far as intuition is concerned, is his admission: "As for the first degree, namely intuitive cognition, it is doubtful whether it is in the intellect in our present life. It seems however that

considering it not just as any object in which one has abstracted from existence or nonexistence in the way he would think of another angel's knowledge, if such did not actually exist; rather he knows himself to be knowing, that is to say, he knows his knowledge as something existing in himself. This knowledge possible for an angel, therefore, is also simply possible for our intellective power, because we have the promise that we shall be like the angels. Now this sort of intellection can properly be called 'intuitive,' because it is an intuition of the thing as existing and present."

[34] *Meta.* II, q. 3, nn. 23–25 (VII, 112–114).
[35] *Ordinatio* I, d. 3, nn. 58–61 (III, 42–43); *Lectura* I, d. 3, nn. 50–60 (XVI, 244–246).

it is."[36] Here for the first time, if our dating is correct, Scotus recognizes the fact that we may have intuitive cognition in this life. The argument he gives is the familiar one used to prove we shall have it in the afterlife, namely our intellect is not by its nature an inferior power to that of vision in the eye. This is not an apodictic proof and leaves the question open to doubt, however. The reason for the doubt becomes more apparent when he cites an instance of what he had in mind as a possible candidate. "If one could hold that to know intuitively can pertain to the intellect, then one could say that some act of the intellect accompanies every distinct act of the sense, and this intellection is vision."[37] The reason this is open to doubt, I suspect, is that it seems to belong to the indistinct, or seminconscious peripheral intellections he speaks of in another context,[38] and that we can say of it, as he says of a similar intellection later on in the *Metaphysics*.[39] "Here is another act which is reflex, but is not perceived because it occurs simultaneously" with some act of direct knowledge. Even in as late a work as the *Quodlibet*, he admitted "we do not experience it as certainly" as we do abstractive cognition, "but it is possible" to do so.[40] This I think became apparent

---

[36] *Meta. ibid.*, n. 23 (pp. 112–113). There are indications the edited text includes an earlier version of the parallel between sense and intellectual knowledge in nn. 23–25, namely in n. 119 (p. 110), and there Scotus seems to deny categorically that we have such intuition in this life. "In intellectu notitia visionis vel intuitiva, quae est prima cognitio, non est in via possibilis." Day (*op. cit.* p. 97) has attempted to explain away both this and the later version as not indicative of Scotus' views or as referring only to the intuition of immaterial substances. Admittedly we could do with a critical edition of this question, but the manuscripts I have examined contain both versions. The way Scotus introduces paragraph n. 23 ("Ad pleniorem igitur solutionem...") suggests this revision may have been appended later and reflects his growing awareness of the fact that some intellectual reflection is required for "perceiving darkness" (the example he gives of *per accidens* vision) in n. 19. See for instance the note he added to the *Ordinatio* I, dist. 3, n. 140ff. (III,87ff).

[37] *Meta.* II, q. 3, n. 24 (p. 113): "Si vero teneatur quod intellectus hic posset cognoscere intuitive, potest dici quod omnem actum distinctum sensus concomitatur aliquis actus intellectus circa idem obiectum; et ista intellectio est visio."

[38] In an interesting "reportatio" found in the Wadding-Vivès edition (*Opus oxoniense* II, d. 42, q. 4, n. 10; XIII, 460) Scotus explains that "for every single perfect and distinct intellection existing in the intellect, there can be many indistinct and imperfect intellections existing there. This is evident from the example of vision, the field of which extends as a conical pyramid at the lower base of which one point is seen distinctly, and yet within that same base many things are seen imperfectly and indistinctly; but of these several visions, only one is perfect, that upon which the axis of the pyramid falls. If this is possible in the sense, all the more so is it possible in the intellect." The will can focus on any one of these peripheral intellections and "by taking pleasure in it, firms it up and intends it [directly] whereas one that is nilled or in which the intellect does not take pleasure is weakened and diminished." It is in this way the will controls the intellect.

[39] *Meta.* IV, q. 3, n. 7 (VII, 339).

[40] *God and Creatures*, par. 6.19 (p. 136). See text n. 33 supra.

in the subsequent two stages of development, when he discussed the knowledge of Christ in this life and our own ability to recall past existential situations.

But there is still another interesting point about the present text we are considering. Whatever is to be said about whether or not we have such intuition at present, it is quite clear to him that "here at least, no separate substance is known by us according to this first degree of knowledge, or even in the second way, for the species would have to originate immediately from that object—which never happens. For the only species we receive is through the sense, or is fashioned by the intellect from what it receives."[41] And he goes on to show that this limitation imposed on our intellect through its linkage with the senses, excludes it from knowing intuitively not only separate or purely spiritual substances, but any substance whatsoever. And he explains precisely how we construct descriptions of corporeal substances, or a spiritual but not "separate" substance like our soul, in terms of what is accidental to it (acts of intellection and volition). In short, we have no intuitive intellection of material substances as such, and the same holds good for the *haecceity* or individuating difference, as Book VII of the *Metaphysics* makes clear. In all such cases our intellection of substance and the individual *qua* individual is not knowledge by acquaintance, but by description, to use Russell's distinction.

Though Scotus deals extensively with the metaphysical question of what makes creatures individual in both the *Sentence* commentaries and the *Questions on Metaphysics*,[42] it is only in the latter that he devotes a special question to whether the singular is *per se* knowable by us. And in his reply he distinguishes between two aspects. "The question is metaphysical insofar as it asks about the intelligibility in an unqualified sense; it pertains to a treatise on the soul insofar as one inquires about our intellection of the singular."[43] In reply to the metaphysical question, he shows first of all that the singular is intelligible *per se*, something certain "Aristotelians" had called into question; secondly, how it is a primitive intelligible, because the individuating difference or *haecceity* is something positive in addition to a thing's specific nature; and thirdly, how as a primitive intelligible it relates to the two types of intellection, intuitive and abstractive cognition.

---

[41] *Meta.* II, q. 3, n. 24 (VII, 113): "... sed saltem secundum primum gradum cognitionis, nulla substantia separata hic a nobis cognoscitur. Nec secundo modo, quia oportet quod species illa immediate originaretur ab illo obiecto, quod non fit; nullam enim speciem recipimus nisi vel per sensus vel quam intellectus facit ex receptis."

[42] *Ordinatio* II, d. 3, pars prima, qq. 1–7 (VII, 391–516); *Lectura* II, d. 3, nn. 1–229 (Hechich text); *Meta.* VII, q. 13 (VI, 402–426); cf. chapter 4, pp. 68–97, above.

[43] *Meta.* VII, q. 15, n. 3 (VI, 436).

There are two sorts of intellection, one quidditative, which abstracts from existence; the other, called vision, which is of the existent *qua* existing. Though the first usually concerns the universal, it can also be primarily of the singular. And whenever it is, it has to do primarily with the singular [rather than the specific] nature. For the singular as such is further determined by existence, for *qua* singular it abstracts from existence, just as the universal [nature] does. The second sort of intellection is of the simultaneous whole, that is of the singular *qua* existing. And in this way Aristotle's *simul totum* is glossed. It includes no accident, but only existence which is not of the essence of anything, neither as a *quid* nor as an individual that participates in a *quid*. Now the singular is not primarily an object of this second type of intellection, nor vice versa.[44]

Having shown at the metaphysical level that intellection of singularity and intuitive intellection are essentially independent of one another, Scotus takes up the psychological problem. How is the singular known if our intellect only grasps what is common and is intricately linked with on-going sense functions in its initial intellections? Since Scotus has often been misrepresented as holding we intuit the singular intellectually, it is interesting to find him insisting we have no *per se* knowledge of the singular at all, be it intuitive or abstractive, sense perceptual or intellectual. His task, as he sees it, is twofold. "First we must see just why our intellect in its present state does not grasp the singular *per se*, nor does the sense sense it; secondly, how in some way we do understand and sense the singular, while in another way we do not."[45] If twin objects of the same species were to appear at the same time and place, our intellect would judge them to be one individual, not two; nor would our senses discern them as two. Yet each has its own *haecceity*, he argues, and does not lose it because it happens to be in the same place simultaneously with another. How then do we know the singular? By reflecting upon the phantasm, it is said, for according to Aristotle in *De anima* III,[46] we know it by a process that is not straightforward, but like a line that bends back upon itself. Though Scotus does not seem particularly interested *per se* in exploring the precise feedback mechanism involved, he does express dissatisfaction with Averroes' account and suggests an alternative.

Another explanation is that in the sense imagination there is a confused something either of substance with accidents or an aggregate of many accidents modifying one another. Now the intellect in grasping the universal abstracts each of these until finally it understands the universal,

---

[44] *Ibid.* n. 4 (pp. 436–437).
[45] *Ibid.* n. 5 (p. 437).
[46] *De anima* III, ch. 4, 429b15–17.

namely its nature, which is in fact a 'this,' but is not grasped intellectually as such, but rather with those accidents that are proper to it. And to this the intellect joins the notion of a subject with accidents. . . . The resulting concept is neither irreducibly simple like "being," nor is it a quidditative concept like "man," but is only a quasi-*per accidens* notion, like "a white man,"—although it is not really *per accidens* in that way. But this is the more determinate conception we come to in this life. For we never arrive at anything such that, as we conceive of it, to be in another would be contradictory for it, and without such a concept we shall never conceive the singular distinctly.[47]

The same construction process seems operative here as in the case of forming a concept of substance, be it immaterial or material, described in the earlier text from the *Metaphysics*. We are not only not intuitively in contact with the *haecceity* associated with any singular object but we have no proper abstract knowledge of it *per se*. In the first case, that of the substantive aspects of the object holistically presented in the perceptual field, we eventually come up with a description that zeroes in on one particular species. Here, in the case of the individual our description specifies the accidents peculiar to it. I have suggested that here Scotus is using a technique resembling, if not identical with, that of Russell's "principle of abstraction that dispenses with abstraction," but yields concepts that are not second intentions but first intentions directly predicable of the object described.[48]. There is no reason for thinking Scotus ever abandoned the position that the first indistinct concept we have is of the "species specialissima" of that sense object that most forcibly impresses our senses.[49]. "Only an intellect that could receive the action of the object immediately could be moved by its singularity; not one which is only receptive through some intermediary action. Only the angelic intellect is of the first sort; it sees immediately the singular material object. Our intellect is of the second sort where the nature only acts by means of something produced in the sense."[50] Since we are object oriented in our initial awareness of the world, our first intellectual cognition will not be intuitive, as it is for Ockham, but abstractive. Not until Scotus recognizes that the conscious reflection upon our own cognitive acts is a form of intuition, and that these acts as real accidents in the mind or soul are the "things" that interact directly with the intellect without benefit of species, are there grounds for ascribing to him, at least implicitly, the doctrine that

[47] *Meta.* VII, q. 15, n. 8 (VI, 439).

[48] A. B. Wolter, "An Oxford Dialogue on Language and Metaphysics," *Review of Metaphysics* 31 (June 1978), 639–640; *idem*, "A 'Reportatio' . . . ," p. 189.

[49] *Lectura* I, d. 3, n. 70 (XVI, 251); Ordinatio I, d. 2, n. 73 (III, 50).

[50] Meta. VII, q. 15, n. 6 (VI, 438).

we have an intuitive intellection of singular mental events. But this recognition of reflection as a form of intuition, though hinted at here, is asserted categorically only at the next stage in the evolution of his thought.

FOURTH STAGE: CHRIST'S INTUITIVE COGNITION

As Peirce was quick to perceive, it was their meticulous philosophical analysis of what they believed that made the theological speculations of Scotus and Ockham of more than passing historical interest to a philosopher-scientist like himself. In his Christology, which is the subject of the first half of his commentaries on Book III of the *Sentences,* Scotus is content to explore the possibilities open to a human nature in which the Word, a divine person, became incarnate. For here too he has a methodological principle that allows him to move from possibility to probable actuality. "In extolling Christ, I prefer to praise him too much than fail by defect, if through ignorance I must fall into either excess."[51] In distinction 14 he applies this technique to a discussion of what Christ's soul could have known. The Gospel's description of the Word, "through him all things came into being" (Jn. 1, 3) suggested the Son, as the Wisdom of the Father, was in a special way the locus of the archetypal creatural ideas described by Augustine. Medieval theologians generally agreed Christ's soul must have possessed from the outset the most perfect vision of the Word granted to any creature. But how reconcile this with that other Gospel statement, "Jesus, for his part, progressed in wisdom and age and grace before God and man" (Lk. 2, 52). Many intriguing solutions were suggested by contemporaries and their pros and cons weighed carefully by Scotus. One was that of Aquinas.[52] In addition to its vision of the Word with its creatural archetypes and scenario of creation, Christ's soul, like the angels on the morn they were created, was also impressed with the intelligible species or forms of each creature in its own nature. This infused knowledge in Christ's possible intellect permitted no growth. But he also had an agent intellect, whose function it was to make the intelligible species actual by abstracting them from the sense images or phantasms and impressing them in the possible intellect. It was in this way that Luke's Gospel is to be understood.

Scotus' main difficulty with this theory stemmed from its use of

[51] *Ordinatio* III, d. 13, qq. 1–4: Codex A f. 153va: "In commendando Christum malo excedere laudando quam deficere a laude, si propter ignorantiam oporteat in alterum incidere"; cf. Vivès, n. 9 (XIV, 463).

[52] *Summa theologiae* III, q. 9, art. 3; q. 10, art. 2; q. 11, art. 1; q. 12, art. 1 and 2.

'"intelligible species." Since they abstracted from both singularity and existence, according to Aristotle, it was difficult to see how they would do the job Aquinas assigned to them. It would take us too far afield to detail his counter proposal. What is of interest is the new light it sheds on his notions of intuition and abstraction. We can bypass the first two questions which concern Christ's intuitive human knowledge or vision of the Word, and turn to the third, which treats of what his soul could know of things in themselves.[53]

Cognition of this sort is twofold, abstractive and intuitive, as was pointed out in the case of the angels. Both the nature which precedes singularity and the singular itself can be known in either way. Furthermore, it seems probable to attribute to the soul of Christ the perfection the angels had as regards intelligibles, since according to Augustine cognition of things in the Word (cognitio matutina) is compatible with a cognition of things in themselves (cognitio vespertina). If one looks simply to the different kinds of things, one could say Christ's soul knew all universals or quiddities through infused species, since the kinds of things are not infinite, as opposed to the possible individual instantiations thereof. And this would yield what is technically confused knowledge of singulars. And the knowledge would be abstractive and habitual. But since singulars are knowable in themselves, i.e. any possible haecceity could be known by acquaintance, if it existed, and remembered afterwards as something unique and distinct from any other singular, it would also be possible to infuse a distinct form or species proper to the individual, and then one would have to face the problem: could any finite intellect have an infinity of such individualized forms, even habitually? If one did not wish to make this move, one could admit at least that Christ's soul knew habitually and abstractively some singulars, those of the noble natures, by infused species. And one would not have to assume either that his soul knew all these quiddities and singulars actually at one and the same time, since once habitual knowledge is in the mind, one can recall it in thought by a natural process.

But even proper species will not account for Christ's human existential knowledge. Here we need to turn to intuition. This can be of the nature or of the singular, but qua existing. It can also be perfect or imperfect, according to the time factor. Perfect intuition concerns an object existing here and now. Imperfect intuition is an opinion about the future or a memory about the past. Now it is obvious that Christ's soul did not have intuitively acquired knowledge of everything that existed. For Peter's sitting would not be suited to be known in this

[53] Ordinatio III, d. 14, q. 3, Codex A, f. 155va–156ra; cf. Vivès ed. XIV, 521ff.

fashion unless it were present either in itself or in something in which it has existence in a more perfect way than in itself. But since we are not speaking here of what Christ envisioned in the Word, this second alternative is excluded. And since many things never were present nor will be present to that human intellect in this fashion, Christ's soul could not have known all existents irrespective of the time of their occurrence in this fashion. Hence he concludes:

> If one claims [this soul] could have knowledge of all existents for all the different times when they existed by means of infused species, this is false. First because infused species represent the object as it prescinds from actual existence, since it represents things in the same way whether the object exists or does not exist and hence cannot be the ground for knowing the existent qua existent. Second, because truths knowable by intuitive cognition about existing things qua existing, viz. contingent truths, could not be known through any sort of innate species, since from a knowledge of its terms the truth of a combination of contingents could not be known, for the truth of their combination is not included in the terms as the necessary truth of a scientific combination is included in the species and their terms. Therefore, both because of contingent truths knowable by intuitive cognition (which are contingent truths about existents insofar as they are existing) and in order to know existents actually in themselves, it is necessary to have the objects themselves present that they could be intuitively known and intuitively seen in themselves. This could never happen in regard to things themselves on their own unless these things in themselves according to their own proper existence were present. Only in this way could this intuitive cognition, be it actual or habitual, of everything whatsoever in itself be given to this soul [of Christ]...
>
> But so far as imperfect intuition is concerned, which is an opinion about the future and memory of the past, which remains after perfect intuition—because from many such things known intuitively in a perfect way, many experiences and memories are left behind in the intellect, whereby those objects could be known according to their existential conditions, not as past but as present—I still say that this soul does not know all things in themselves.[54]

Here for the first time we find Scotus introducing a new argument for intuition. We need it to know in a non-inferential manner that anything exists, and we need it to account for the truth of contingent existential statements. And as if realizing this statement is not something applicable to what is special about Christ's intellect but assumes

[54] See note 12 *supra* for the Latin text of Codex A, which differs significantly from that of the Vivès ed.

something about the normal mechanism of how we know, he goes on to explain:

> And if it be objected that all that remains behind from the presence of a thing is an intelligible species impressed upon the intellect and in the sensitive portion [of the soul], such as the imaginative power, an imaginable species, this is false, for what is left behind from a thing's presence is not only an intelligible species in the intellect whereby it is known with no time specification added, but another in the memorative potency. And these several potencies know the object under different aspects. One knows it as it exists presentially, the other knows it as something apprehended in the past, so that the apprehension of the past is the immediate object of the memory, and the immediate object of this past apprehension is the mediate object of recall. Also if some sensible is presented to a sense in this way, a twofold cognition can be caused in the intellect in virtue of this: one abstractive, whereby the agent intellect abstracts from a species in the phantasm a species of the quiddity qua quiddity, which represents the object absolutely and not as existing now or then. The other can be an intuitive cognition in the intellect whereby the object as existing cooperates with the intellect, and this can leave behind in the intellective memory an habitual intuitive cognition, which is not of the quiddity absolutely, as was the other abstractive cognition, but of the known object as existing, namely the way it was apprehended in the past. And by this experience Christ could be said to have learned many things, i.e. by intuitive cognitions, of those things known existentially and through the memories they left behind.

It is arbitrary whether we wish to consider this a separate stage or part of the following or final stage, for Scotus has capsulated the essentials of his mature position in what he says of Christ's experiential knowledge. In distinction 45 of *Ordinatio* IV he spells out in greater detail the intuitive powers he ascribes to a human intellect not united to the Word in speaking of what the departed souls could know.

FIFTH STAGE: INTUITION HERE AND HEREAFTER

The first question is whether the intellect could use the habitual knowledge of quiddities acquired in this life when no longer linked to the phantasy or senses. The second asks: Could the soul acquire new knowledge in this state? Or must it be content to work with species or forms infused by God or the angels, as many of his colleagues maintained? He argues this theory denigrates the intellective nature of the human soul by implying it is functionally less perfect than a stone which seeks the center of the earth and rests there on its own. He argues that the soul could acquire both intuitive and abstractive knowledge, intuitive, because the intellect, working with the object itself rather than a substitute object or the phantasm, should be even more effective " Such cognition, which is called intuitive, can be intellective, otherwise the intellect would not be certain about the existence of any object."[55] Abstractive knowledge would also be possible, since the agent intellect could produce intelligible species working directly on material objects just as it now does working with the sense image. This theory is recapitulated in question four to answer the question: Do the blessed know of the prayers we offer? But it is question three that throws light on what intuitive cognition Scotus thought we had in this life. It reads: "Could the separated soul remember past events that occurred when it was joined to the body?" To answer it, he sets forth his most complete analysis of sense and intellective memory.

Assuming as certain there could be in us an act whereby the past *qua* object is known, I add that this act, which we call "remembering," is not immediately about any past event, but only about some act of the remembering subject, and to exclude vegetative acts, chance actions or imperceptible acts generally, we limit ourselves to human acts. For I only remember that you sat here because I recall I saw or knew you sat here. On the other hand, though I know I was born, or that the world was created, I don't remember either, for I recall no act of mine that had this or that as its object. "Remembering is cognition of some past act of the person remembering where the act is recognized as being past." Given this definition of the term, certain things follow from the fact it is known as past and others from the sort of past object involved. From the fact that this knowledge is of the past four conclusions follow: First, we must understand that the potency or capacity to remember has an act after a lapse of time, otherwise it would not be the past *qua* past that is remembered ... Second, memory perceives the flow of time between that instant or time in which the object remembered existed and the present instant of perception. Third, the remembered object confronting the person remembering is not present in itself, otherwise it would not be remembered as past. Fourth, since the object must in some sense be present to the act and it cannot be present in itself, it must be present in a likeness or species and then the memory will be conserving the species ... Because of the special character of the object remembered, however, namely that it is a past act of the individual who remembers, three more certain conclusions follow: First, remembering will involve a double object: one ultimate or remote (viz. the something about which the person remembering had at one time a conscious or human act); the other, the proximate (viz. the past human act whereby he reached out to that other object). Second, since the potency for remembering requires

[55] *Ordinatio* IV, d. 45, q. 2, Codex A, f. 267vb: "Talis autem cognitio, quae dicitur intuitiva, potest esse intellectiva, alioquin intellectus non esset certus de aliqua existentia alicuius obiecti"; cf. Vivès ed. *ibid.* n. 12, p. 305.

a species, speaking of what is required for remembering *in toto*, this could not be impressed by the object when the latter no longer exists or is actually present. But this proximate object is a human act of the past. Therefore, while it did exist, the necessary species was impressed. And since the species of a past human act could not be impressed in any potency other than that which had this act as object, it follows then that the past act of knowing has to be the object of the potency for remembering. Third, only what concerns one's own act—where this is human—is subject to remembrance, for it is only through knowing one's own act as proximate object that we know its object qua remote object. Hence a person cannot remember the same sort of act in another as he can in himself.[56]

Scotus then goes on to discuss to what extent memory is a sense function and whether animals possess it; and then the question of whether Aristotle admitted intellective memory, and eventually continues with the passage Ockham thought embodied much of what he considered original and important, and quoted at length.

As for this article, then, I say that in the intellective part there is memory and remembering, properly so called. For I presuppose that the intellect not only knows universals (which is true indeed of its abstractive ability that the Philosopher speaks of, for it alone is scientific), but also that it can know intuitively what the sense knows (for the more perfect and higher cognitive power in the same subject knows what the inferior power knows) and that it can also know of sensations. Both assumptions are proved from the fact that the intellect knows contingently true propositions and draws inferences from them. For to form propositions and to syllogize is proper to the intellect. But the truth of these concerns objects known intuitively, that is to say, under their existential aspect, which is something known by sense. Hence, all the aforesaid conditions for remembering can be found in the intellect. For it can perceive time, and has an act after a lapse of time, and so on. To put it briefly, it is possible to remember any object whose sense memory can be recalled. For the act which is the proximate object can be intuitively known when it exists and thus can be remembered later. Also many proximate objects that were never matters for sense remembrance, such as any past intellection or volition, can be recollected. Proof that man can remember such: Otherwise he could not repent of his bad will, make use of intellectual experience in the future, or from the fact that he had thought about such matters, set out to explore other consequences thereof. In short, we could do none of this were we unable to recollect past intellections and volitions. . . . Clearly then some remembrance of both objects of its act, proximate and remote, is proper to the intellect. Some re-

[56] *Ibid.* q. 3; Codex A, f. 268rb; the translation was made from a transcript of this MS. Since the text differs only slightly from the edition (Vivès, nn. 4–6, XX, 326–327), it seems unnecessary to cite it in Latin. Prof. M. M. Adams and I plan to publish the MS text with a translation and commentary.

membrance is so proper by reason of the proximate object, too, that it could not pertain to the sense, whereas some which pertains to the intellect in virtue of its proximate object, could also pertain to the sense, for instance, if the intellect intuitively recognized that I see something white and afterwards retains this knowledge and remembers that I saw something white. And here is a case where both proximate and remote objects are matter of intellective remembrance; it occurs whenever on the basis of such a past remembrance we draw a syllogistic inference to something else. In such a case, the proximate object cannot be the sensation of even the highest sense. . . . It can only be a remembrance of something intellective.[57]

Scotus' sharp distinction between remote and proximate objects of imperfect intuition suggests something similar is required for the original intuition. This was recognized by Ockham, and more recently by Bérubé.[58] The latter argues that Scotus professes an immediate realism in enumerating sensible objects before sensation as instances of intellectual intuition, and that this implies a direct and immediate grasp of the exterior object and of the singular by the intellect. Ockham, it seems, drew much the same conclusion, in appealing to Scotus as a precursor of his own position. All this overlooks, however, (1) the difference between Scotus' and Ockham's theories of cognition,[59] (2) the different mechanism Scotus ascribed to intellectual and sense perceptual intuition,[60] and (3) the difference between the existential status of the proximate and remote objects of memory (and presumably of the initial cognitive experience) that is recalled,[61] as well as (4) the different epistemic values Scotus attached to immediate introspective awareness of internal acts and that of "de cognitis a nobis ut nunc per

[57] Ibid. nn. 17–18 (pp. 348–349); Codex A, fol. 269ra. Cf. Guillelmi de Ockham, op. cit., pp. 44–46.

[58] Bérubé, op. cit. p. 201.

[59] Scotus believed that what was given primitively at the conceptual level was "commonness" or the natura communis, and what needed explanation was how it became singular in the concrete individual and how it became universal in the mind; Ockham believed that what was primitively given was the individual and what needed explanation was only how it became universal. Another difference is that referred to in note 61, infra.

[60] Scotus postulated a different "mechanism" for perfect intellectual intuition and ocular vision; the former requires the direct interaction of a real object with the intellect; the latter is mediated in terms of how the "medium" functions in propagating light and the accidental form. See note 30 supra.

[61] Scotus never abandoned the position that the content of thought had the peculiar existential status of an ens diminutum or what Ockham called a fictum. Only something with real esse could interact causally with the intellect, Ordinatio I, d. 13, n. 4 (V, 81); only in a qualified sense could one speak of intentional object as a passio animae; cf. Ordinatio I, d. 3, nn. 386–388; on Ockham's abandonment of the fictum theory, see op. cit. p. 30, note 3.

sensus,"[62] and perhaps most of all (5) Scotus' recognition, as indicated by his frequent references to the opening chapter of Aristotle's and Avicenna's *Physics*,[63] that perception is a process that moves from the indistinct to the distinct, and involves features that are both—upon later analysis—singular and universal, sensible and intelligible, intuitive and abstractive. "Indistinct" is the Anglo-Latin translation of συγχεχυμενον which suggests the initial, unanalyzed, sense perceptual ὅλον, is not like a piece of granite in which the distinct minerals can be pointed out, but is rather like an amalgam or liquid mixture requiring distinct analytic techniques to isolate the components. To show why the second model fits better Scotus' account of how the intellect extracts the intelligible content, or analyzes the initial sense perceptual whole, would require another paper. Let me close, however, on this note. Earlier I suggested why Scotus was slow to recognize intellectual intuition as a distinct, yet integral, component of the perceptual process.[64] It is because the focal point of our initial interest and attention centers on what stands out most impressively in the perceptual field, whereas the awareness of its existence and presence, like that of being awake, lies in the penumbra of indistinct, peripheral

---

[62] Cf. the note Scotus added as a guideline in revising *Ordinatio* I, d. 3 (Vat. ed. III, p. 137). Scotus put introspective certitude of internal acts *qua* acts on a par with self-evident propositions, "for even though there is no certitude that I see white located outside, either in such a subject or at such a distance (for illusion can be caused in the medium or in the organ or in a number of other ways), still for all that there is certitude that I see"; *ibid.* n. 339 (p. 145); for the English translation, see A. B. Wolter, *Duns Scotus: Philosophical Writings*, p. 112.

[63] Cf. *Lectura* I, d. 3, n. 79 (XIV, 254); *Ord.* I, d. 27, n. 74 (VI, 92), etc. for references to Aristotle's Physics I, ch. 1 (184a16–23); and to Avicenna's *Physics*, *Lectura* I, d. 7, n. 55 (XVI, 493), etc.

[64] Confer note 38, *supra*, and the corresponding text. This "reportatio" is a report of Scotus' Paris lectures; it is missing from his Oxford *Lectura* II (confer the Vienna codex latinus 1449, Osterreiche Nationalbibliothek), but is found in a more polished version in the early fourteenth century Codex V (Vat. lat. 876, f. 308 rb), which Wadding tells us he used in his edition of the *Reportata parisiensia* (see his "Censura" in Vivès ed., XXII, 4–5; and XXIII, 220–221 for the corresponding text). Its absence from *Ordinatio* II (e.g. Codices A, P, and S) can be readily explained, if this revision of the Oxford lectures on Book II was finished before Scotus left for Paris in 1302. By the same token, its inclusion in both the *Opus oxoniense* and *Reportata parisiensia* Codex V would attest to its authenticity in the minds of those charged with editing Scotus' works (after his early death). The *Opus axon.* text may even be closer to the actual lecture than the more polished version of Wadding/ Codex V, since the MS (f. 310va) adds: "Expliciunt Additiones secundi libri magistri Ioannis de Duns, subtilis doctoris, extractae per magistrum Willelmum de Alnewykm de Ordine Fratrum Minorum, de Lectura Parisiensi et Oxoniensi praedicti magistri Ioannis, cui propitietur Deus." If the revision contained in *Ordinatio*, books I and II, was complete before Scotus went to Paris, it would explain why his socius and editor, William of Alnwick, thought it necessary to make major additions to these first two books, which we know as the *Additiones magnae* (Book 1) and *Additiones in II Sententiarum*.

intellections and visions. A special act of the will is required to bring to center stage, as it were, what is lurking in the wings. And this is precisely what happens when after the fact, we deliberately try to recall distinctly the bits of information that entered into our initial on-going experience. It is not surprising then that Scotus' most lucid account of intellectual intuition occurs in his description of intellectual memory, or that he feels the need to prove we had some intellectual awareness of the existential situation that serves as evidence for the two types of primitive contingent statements one needs to explicate its cognitive content. As for Bérubé's contention that Scotus deserves to be called an immediate, rather than a mediate realist, if this means nothing more than that *qua* intentional or tendential the cognitive act terminates directly with what is known, one can admit this. But this does not imply Scotus believed our intellect was ever in direct causal, as opposed to intentional, "contact" with the extramental object in the physical world. And it also leaves us with many of the epistemic problems associated with mediate realism. But then Scotus, unlike Ockham, had no desire to make intuition the keystone of his epistemology. Indeed, if one considers his *Reportatio Parisiensia*, one may question whether Scotus' primary interest in clarifying the nature of intuitive cognition was epistemological at all.[65]

[65] Since the original appearance of this article, Stephen Dumont's further study suggests that in view of the heated controversy between Henry of Ghent and Godfrey of Fontaine when Scotus came to Paris, John as a theologian was more interested in abstractive than intuitive cognition, and its relevance for whether theology as a science is possible or not. Cf. Stephen D. Dumount, "Theology as a Science and Duns Scotus's Distinction between Intuitive and Abstractive Cognition," *Speculum* 64 (1989) 579–99. This would explain John of Reading's comment cited by Gedeon Gál in "Quaestio Ioannis de Reading de necessitate specierum intelligibilium defensio doctrinae Scoti" in *Franciscan Studies* 29 (1969), p. 133, and Ockham's point that he was not concerned with whether Scotus attributed the same importance to intuitive cognition as he himself did.

ACTION THEORY AND ETHICS

6 / Duns Scotus on the Natural Desire for the Supernatural

The relation of the natural and supernatural is a vital question in contemporary theological circles. Not that the problem itself is novel. In a sense, it is as old as the history of revelation itself. Both the philosopher and the theologian have come to grips with it. Yet, after a period of relative dormancy, the problem has been revived by Catholic theologians of the present day. The renewal of interest dates roughly from a group of historical studies begun some three decades ago and has culminated in the controversial work of Père de Lubac, *Surnaturel*, which appeared in 1946.[1]

As a group, these studies reveal the chasm between the modern and medieval conception of man's "natural" and "supernatural" end. Owing to certain dogmatic definitions of the Church regarding the supernatural character of grace and glory which seem to support the position of the modern theologians, various attempts have been made to read the modern conception of the supernatural into the writings of the schoolmen. Yet not every interpretation that may satisfy a contemporary theologian can be expected to content the historian of medieval thought. Much of what has been written seems to be an attempt to save the "orthodoxy" of the medieval theologian rather than an objective study of the thought or the position of the man himself.

The crux of the problem lies in this. The medieval theologians, as

Reprinted with permission, in shortened form, from *The New Scholasticism* [Journal of the ACPA] 23 (1949), pp. 281–317.
[1] Henri de Lubac, *Surnaturel, études historiques* (Paris, 1946).

a group, seem to admit that man has a natural appetite or desire for the beatific vision, yet maintain emphatically that grace and vision are truly supernatural gifts freely bestowed on man by a benevolent God. Thirteenth-century theologians apparently never doubted that the ultimate perfection of human nature could be found only in a supernatural state. Consequently, human nature, like all other natures, "desires" its own ultimate perfection, even though this be beyond its natural powers of attainment. Significantly, the early schoolmen never raise the question which troubles the modern theologian. Can a creature be directed to a supernatural end by an intrinsic finality, rooted in the very nature of the being itself? They are rather concerned with another problem. Is not man less perfect than irrational creatures, since his very nature strives for something beyond his natural powers to satisfy?[2] And their solution is not to deny the premises, but rather the faulty consequence. Man is not less, but more, perfect than the brute or inanimate nature. For the latter never desires anything beyond its natural ability to attain, whereas rational creatures, such as man and the angels, have an *appetitus naturalis* for what can be attained only through supernatural agencies. They are *capaces Dei*.

Much has been written on man's natural desire for God from the Thomistic viewpoint.[3] Scotus' position has been less frequently and less extensively treated. And even those studies which have dealt with the Subtle Doctor, have been confined for the most part to an analysis of the natural appetite in regard to the will and stress Scotus' differentiation of *voluntas ut naturalis* and *voluntas ut libera*, a distinction found already in Odo Rigaux, the Franciscan Master, from whom St. Thomas borrowed so much of his doctrine on the nature of free will.[4]

To avoid the charge of repetitiousness, this present essay emphasizes Scotus' teaching on the human intellect and the beatific vision, indi-

---

[2] Odo Rigaux, for instance, raises and solves this problem in the *Quaestio de Gratia*. See the edition by B. Pergamo, O.F.M. "Il desiderio innato del soprannaturale nelle questioni inedite di Oddone Rigaldo, O.F.M., arcivescovo di Rouen," *Studi Francescani*, VII–VIII (1935–1936), 89. The problem reappears again with Scotus, whose doctrine on the natural desire for beatitude is more in accord with the early Franciscan masters than is that of St. Bonaventure. See for instance *Oxon.* prol. q. 1, 26; Vivès-Wadding ed. VIII, 58.

[3] The recent work of W. O'Connor, *The Eternal Quest* (New York, 1947), contains a list of the more important studies on St. Thomas's position as well as on the problem itself. To these we might add the following: J. de Blic, S. J., "Bulletin de morale," *Mélanges de science réligieuse*, IV (1947), 93–113; C. Boyer, S. J., "Nature pure et surnaturel dans le 'Surnaturel' du Père de Lubac," *Gregorianum*, XXVIII (1947), 379–395; P. J. Donnelly, S. J., "Discussion on the Supernatural Order," *Theological Studies*, IX (1948), 213–249; "The Supernatural," *Review of Politics*, X (1948), 226–232.

[4] Dom Lottin, O.S.B., *Psychologie et morale aux XIIᵉ et XIIIᵉ siècles* (Louvain, 1942–1948), I, 216.

cating at the same time the doctrinal connection with the problem of the natural desire for beatitude. We select this phase not merely because it is usually omitted in discussing the Scotist position on man's natural desire for God but primarily for the following reasons. First of all, Scotus has delineated the distinction between the natural and supernatural more clearly in regard to the intellect than he has in regard to the will. Further, in explaining the nature of the *appetitus naturalis* of the will for beatitude, Scotus explicitly adverts to the parallel that exists between the "desire" in the intellect for the face-to-face vision of God and that of the will for the beatific act of love.[5] And lastly, because the intellect is an integral part of our heavenly beatitude, even according to Scotus. For he did not wholly reject the Bonaventurian thesis that beatitude is a joint function of man's two highest faculties, even though he considered it primarily a function of the will.[6]

THE BEATIFIC VISION AS NATURAL TO MAN

Rationalism in the faculty of Arts at Paris had questioned the very *raison d'être* of theology. To justify the very existence of his science, Scotus, as a theologian, opens the prologue to his greatest theological work with the question: "Is it necessary for man in his present state that he receive supernaturally some special doctrine that his intellect cannot attain by the light of natural reason?"[7] Like a dramatist, he reenacts the scene of a public disputation. The contestants are the "philosophers" on the one hand and the "theologians" on the other.

> A controversy appears in this question between the philosophers and the theologians. The philosophers maintain the perfection of nature and deny supernatural perfection. The theologians, however, are aware of the deficiency of nature, the necessity of grace and of supernatural perfections and therefore hold the supernatural perfection in greater esteem.[8]

Who are the philosophers? Obviously, they are partisans of the Averroistic rationalism that had occasioned the condemnations of 1270

---

[5] *Oxon.* 4, d. 49, q. 9, n. 2; Vivès-Wadding ed., XXI, 318.

[6] *Oxon.* 4, d. 49, q. 3. Scotus attempts to mediate between the position of St. Thomas and that of St. Bonaventure.

[7] *Oxon.* prol. q. 1: Utrum homini pro statu isto sit necessarium aliquam doctrinam specialem supernaturaliter inspirari ad quam videlicet non possit attingere lumine naturali intellectus?

[8] *Ibid.* Assisi ms. 137: In ista quaestione videtur controversia inter philosophos et theologos, et tenent philosophi perfectionem naturae, et negant perfectionem supernaturalem; theologi vero cognoscunt defectum naturae et necessitatem gratiae et perfectionum supernaturalium vel perfectionem supernaturalem, et ideo eam magis honorant. Cf. Vivès, VII, n. 3, p. 11.

and 1277 at Paris and Oxford. Like the "Commentator," they would supplant theology with philosophy, for "there is no more excellent state of life than one devoted to philosophy" (Prop. 40) and "the wise of this world are the philosophers only" (Prop. 154).[9] There is no true supernatural, for human nature is perfect. It needs no additional revelation to supply its weakness.

And who are the theologians? We can hardly doubt that they belong to that group so frequently designated as "Augustinians," for they stress the "deficiency of nature," and at least the last of the five arguments they bring against the philosophers presupposes illuminationism.[10]

This introductory question of Scotus has, at times, been portrayed as an out and out defense of the Augustinians against the so-called "integral Aristotelianism." Perhaps it would be more correct to say that if Scotus ultimately sides with the theologians, it is only after he has played the thesis of the philosophers against the antithesis of the theologians, to rise, Hegelian fashion, to a new synthesis. And in so doing, he reveals clearly his conception of the interrelation of natural and supernatural.

The "philosophers" could find nothing supernatural about the beatific vision. Do not even the theologians, they argue, admit that man is naturally ordained to such an end? How then can they call it supernatural? "Man naturally desires this end which you call supernatural."[11] Furthermore, do they not consider being qua being as the adequate object of the human intellect? How then can they fail to conclude that the divine essence, in which the notion of being is most perfectly realized, is also a natural object of our mind?

The "theologians," on the other hand, counter that the beatific vision is something wholly supernatural.[12] It is an action "which exceeds the very nature of this instrument [namely, the agent intellect]," limited as it is to the senses and sense data.[13] Hence, man must be disposed to attain this end through some supernatural knowledge.

---

[9] Theses condemned in 1277. Denifle, *Chartularium Universitatis Parisiensis*, I, 545, 542. Cf. the errors regarding beatitude in *Giles of Rome Errores Philosophorum* (Milwaukee, 1944).

[10] *Oxon. ib.* n. 19; VII, 46. Scotus seems to be citing the reasoning of William of Ware, *Sent.* I, q. 2. See also Henry of Ghent, *Quodlibet* 3, q. 1.

[11] *Oxon. ib.* n. 9; Quaracchi ed. I, 10: Homo naturaliter appetit finem istum quem dicis supernaturalem; igitur ad istum naturaliter ordinatur; ergo ex tali ordine potest concludi iste finis ex cognitione naturae ordinatae ad ipusm.

[12] *Ibid.* n. 18; ed. I, 18: Homo ordinator ad finen supernaturalem, ad quem ex se est indispositus; ergo indiget paulatim disponi ad habendum illum finem; hoc fit per cognitionem aliquam supernaturalem.

[13] *Ibid.* n. 19.

After hearing both sides of the question, Scotus presents his own solution with a clarity that has seldom been surpassed. Neither side is wholly right. If the philosophers are wrong in considering the beatific vision within the natural competency of the human intellect, the theologians—at least those whose arguments are presented by Scotus—are also in the wrong in stressing the limitations of the intellect as such and regarding the beatific vision as in no sense natural. If what they say were true, even divine illumination, which they postulate, or the addition of a special *habitus* of vision would be of no avail.[14]

The real crux of the problem, says Scotus, is to determine just what is meant by natural and supernatural. Answer that, and the problem of the naturality or supernaturality of the beatific vision solves itself.

> To the question, then, I reply first by distinguishing in what sense something may be called supernatural. For a capacity to receive may be compared to the act which it receives or to the agent from which it receives [this act]. Viewed in the first way, this potentiality is either natural or violent or neither natural nor violent. It is called *natural*, if it is naturally inclined towards the form it receives. It is *violent*, if what it suffers is against its natural inclination. It is neither the one nor the other, if it is inclined neither to the form which it receives nor to its opposite. Now from this viewpoint, there is no supernaturality.
>
> But when the recipient is compared to the agent from which it receives the form, then there is *naturalness* if the recipient is referred to an agent which is naturally ordained to impress such a form in such a recipient. *Supernaturalness* is had, however, when the recipient is referred to an agent which does not impress this form upon this recipient naturally.
>
> Applying this to the question at issue, I say that if the possible intellect be compared to the knowledge that is actualized in it, *no knowledge is supernatural to it*, because the possible intellect is perfected by any knowledge whatsoever and is naturally inclined towards any kind of

---

[14] *Ibid.*: Haec ratio videtur concludere contra eum qui fecit eam; secundum enim deductionem istam lux increata non poterit uti intellectu agente ut instrumento ad cognitionem alicujus sincerae veritatis; quia talis, secundum eum, non potest haberi via sensuum sine speciali illustratione. *Oxon.* 4, d. 49, q. 11, n. 4; XXI, 390: Si hoc est verum, tunc nec cum lumine gloriae vel quocumque habitu esset possibile creaturae videre Deum. *Oxon.* 1, d. 3, q. 3, n. 2; Vivès IX, 88 ff.: Contra istud non potest sustineri a theologo, quia intellectus existens eadem potentia, cognoscet quidditatem substantiae immaterialis, sicut patet secundum fidem de anima beata. Potentia autem manens eadem, non potest habere actum circa aliquid, quod non continetur sub suo primo objecto. Quod si dicas, elevabitur per lumen gloriae ad hoc quod cognoscat illas substantias immateriales. Contra, objectum primum habitus continetur sub primo objecto potentiae, vel saltem non excedit, quia si habitus respicit aliquod objectum quod non continetur sub primo objecto potentiae, sed excedit, tunc ille habitus non esset habitus illius potentiae, sed faceret eam non esse illam potentiam, sed aliam.

knowledge. But according to the second way of speaking, that *knowledge is supernatural* which is generated by some agent which by its very nature is not ordained to move the possible intellect in a natural manner. For our present state, however, the possible intellect according to the Philosopher is ordained to be moved to knowledge by the agent intellect and the phantasm; therefore, that knowledge alone is natural to it which is impressed by these agencies.[15]

The soul or intellect of man is in passive potentiality to receive knowledge. If we look merely to the potency to receive and the form received, we discover but three alternatives, says Scotus. Either the form received perfects the recipient, or it does violence to it, or it neither perfects nor does violence to the recipient. In order to perfect the recipient, as the very term *perficere* implies, there must be some element of incompleteness in that which is perfected. For to perfect is merely to "carry through," as it were, what was begun but left uncompleted. This incompleteness, obviously, is intimately bound up with the very nature of the recipient, and hence, whatever is capable of being perfected is said to have a natural inclination towards that which perfects it. On the contrary, if what is received, far from perfecting, does violence to, or even destroys, the receiver, the latter is said to bear a violent potentiality towards the form in question. Where the receiver is neither perfected nor damaged, it is naturally disposed towards what it receives.

If we look merely to the human intellect and the knowledge it possesses, and abstract completely from the nature in which this knowledge is obtained, we must admit with the philosophers, Scotus argues, that "no knowledge is supernatural to it." For no knowledge, even that

---

[15] *Oxon.* prol. q. 1, Assisi ms 137, f. 2rb: Ad quaestionem igitur respondeo, primo distinguendo quomodo aliquid dicatur supernaturale. Potentia enim receptiva comparatur ad actum quem recipit, vel ad agentem a quo recipit. Primo modo ipsa est potentia naturalis, vel violenta, vel neutra. Naturalis dicitur, si naturaliter inclinetur; violenta, si sit contra naturalem inclinationem passio; neutra, si neque inclinetur naturaliter ad istam formam quam recipit, neque ad oppositam. In hac autem comparatione nulla est supernaturalitas. Sed comparando receptivum ad agens a quo recipit formam, tunc est naturalitas quando receptivum comparatur ad tale agens quod natum est naturaliter imprimere talem formam in tali passo; supernaturalitas autem quando comparatur ad agens quod non est naturaliter impressivum illius formae in illud passum.... Ad propositum applicando dico, quod comparando intellectum possibilem ad notitiam actualem in se, nulla est sibi cognitio supernaturalis; quia intellectus possibilis quacumque cognitione naturaliter perficitur, et ad quamcumque cognitionem naturaliter inclinatur. Sed secundo modo loquendo, sic est supernaturalis, quae generatur ab aliquo agente quod non est natum movere intellectum possibilem ad talem cognitionem naturaliter. Pro statu autem isto, secundum Philosophum, intellectus possibilis natus est moveri ad cognitionem ab intellectu agente et phantasmate; igitur sola illa cognitio est ei naturalis quae ab istis agentibus imprimitur. Cf. Vivès, nn. 20–21; VIII, 48.

of the beatific vision, does violence to the intellect in the sense that poison does violence to the organism that absorbs it, or excessively loud sound damages the ear. Neither is the human intellect neutral to such knowledge in the sense that the eye, from the standpoint of vision, is neutral to the infra-red or ultra-violet radiation falling on the retina. On the contrary, the face-to-face vision of the divine essence continues, as it were, the basic or natural perfection of the intellect; for the latter was made to know and is perfected by all knowledge, whatever be its source or manner of production.

Scotus' concession to the Aristotelian-minded philosophers is a recognition of their clear insight into the implications of a metaphysics of act and potency. A necessary prerequisite for receiving any perfection, be it natural or supernatural, accidental or substantial, is that the recipient have the capacity to receive it. No amount of miracles or supernatural additions can supply this basic want.[16] Though Christ might turn stones into bread, He could not give sight to a stone, unless He first turned it into an eye. And that, incidentally, would be changing its nature and doing violence to it as a stone. As the theologians of Scotus' day readily admitted, God could not give an angel or a human soul the breath-taking vision of Himself unless, in making the angelic nature and fashioning the human soul, He had already put into that nature a capacity to receive that vision. And this is equivalent to saying that from this viewpoint, all knowledge, even that of the beatific vision, is natural in the sense that it is in accord with the nature of man.

THE BEATIFIC VISION AS SUPERNATURAL

If in one sense no knowledge is supernatural, from the standpoint of what natural causes can achieve, a distinction between natural and supernatural is very much in order. And because the "philosophers" failed to make this distinction, they were decidedly in the wrong.

To understand better the meaning of this distinction, a digression on Scotus' conception of the human intellect is not out of place.

For Aristotle the possible intellect was not an active but a passive potency and the process of the soul coming to knowledge was primarily one of receiving an impression from without. Godfrey of Fontaines,

---

[16] To argue that the recipient must be conditioned by a habit for the reception of something supernatural does not obviate the difficulty, since the recipient must be capable of receiving the habit which itself is something supernatural.

the Parisian master under whom Scotus disputed as a bachelor,[17] had perhaps the purest form of this intellectual passivism among Scotus' contemporaries. On the other hand, Henry of Ghent was the chief representative of Augustinian intellectual activism. Scotus' position represented a mean between these two extremes.[18] Neither the object alone (whether in itself or in an intelligible species), nor the soul alone, is the complete cause of actual knowledge. The two are partial, but essentially ordered, efficient causes of the effect we know as intellection.[19] This partial concession to the Aristotelian position is important, as we shall see shortly. It makes it possible for Scotus to distinguish between an object which is by nature ordained to act as a partial cause in producing knowledge and one which is not so ordained but, nevertheless, does move the intellect.

But before taking this up, we might point out an interesting aspect of Scotus' conception of the human intellect. It is reminiscent at least of Christian neo-Platonism. The human intellect, Scotus tells us, is capable of far greater intellectual activity than we would dream of if we merely analyzed its functions in our present state of existence. If man's soul is not a fallen angel, as Plato suggested, at least his intellect is not essentially inferior to that of the angel.[20] As we have indicated elsewhere, this is not a philosophical but a theological conclusion.[21] Scotus believes it can be inferred from the promise of the face-to-face vision of which St. Paul speaks. For the beatific vision is an immediate intuition of the divine essence on the part of a created intellect. Now this implies that the intellect as such is capable of intuitive knowledge.[22] According to Scotus, who retained at least in part the intellectual activism of Augustine, object and intellect are partial co-causes of knowledge. Where this knowledge is intuitive it is the actual pres-

[17] Pelster, S. J. "Hat Duns Skotus in Paris zweimal das dritte Buch der Sentenzen erklärt?" *Gregorianum*, XXVII (1946), 227.

[18] *Oxon.* 1, d. 3, q.7; Vivès ed. (q. 9 in Quaracchi edition), tota quaestio.

[19] *Ibid.* nn. 21–22.

[20] *Oxon.* 2, d. 1, q. 5 (Quaracchi ed. q. 6); XI, 192: Intellectualitas angeli, inquantum intellectualitas non differt specie ab intellectualitate animae, inquantum intellectualitas, hoc est, quod licet iste actus primus et ille differant specie, non tamen secundum illam perfectionem quam virtualiter continent, secundum quam sunt principia actuum secundorum. *Quodlibet*, q. 14, n. 12; XXVI, 46: Objectum adaequatum intellectui nostro ex natura potentiae non est aliquid specialius objecto intellectui angelici.

[21] *Transcendentals and Their Function in the Metaphysics of Duns Scotus* (St. Bonaventure, 1946), pp. 73–75; "Theologism of Duns Scotus," *Franciscan Studies*, VII (1947), 382.

[22] Intuitive knowledge is understood by Scotus in the sense of a simple apprehension of an object as present and existing. See for instance, *Quodl.* q. 6; XXV, 243–244; S. Day, O. F. M., *Intuitive Cognition: A Key to the Significance of the Later Scholastics* (St. Bonaventure, 1947), ch. 2.

ence of the object that exercises this co-causality. Where the knowledge is abstractive, it is the intelligible species which substitutes for the object.[23]

But why is it necessary to assume that the intellect as such must be capable of intuitive knowledge? Could not God infuse some intellectual habit or accidental quality which would transform the intellect, making it capable of intuition? No, Scotus replies. A *habitus* or quality of this kind never actually confers the basic active potentiality to perform a specific kind of action. It merely perfects what is already there.[24] Furthermore, it is not by reason of something accidental to man's soul that man is beatified. It is the human intellect itself and not merely the habit of vision which sees God. It is the human will and not the habit of charity that loves God.[25] Scotus, we must remember, denies any real distinction between soul and its faculties, though even here his position is midway between that of St. Thomas and that of the rigid Augustinian, if we may use such a term.[26] If the soul, then, cannot receive the power of intuition as an accidental addition, be it an active potency or an *habitus*, we are faced with this dilemma. Either admit that the soul is intrinsically changed in the sense that it is given a new nature, or grant that it already possesses the potentiality. The first alternative is inadmissible, for it is tantamount to admitting that the soul is destroyed, since what is substantially simple cannot be intrinsically changed. Hence there is no choice but to admit that the intellectual soul possesses the intrinsic capacity of intuitive knowledge.

But Scotus also finds probable reasons for these hidden potentialities of the soul.[27] The first is the fact that we can form an abstract concept of being qua being. If the natural adequate object of our intellect were material or sensible quiddity, why is it that we can form a more universal concept than that of material quiddity? No faculty, Scotus argues, should be able to have something that does not fall under its

---

[23] *Oxon.* 4, d. 45, q. 2, n. 12; XX, 304–305; *Oxon.* 1, d. 3, q. 7 (Quaracchi ed. q. 9), nn. 20–22; IX, 361ff.; *Quodl.* q. 15, n. 7; XXVI, 437: Certum est quod ad actualem intellectionem causandam concurrent aliquid ipsius animae intellectivae, et objectum aliquo modo praesens, scilicet vel se, vel in aliquo repraesentante.

[24] *Oxon.* 1, d. 3, q. 3, n. 2; IX, 88.

[25] *Rep. Par.* 4, d. 49, q. 10, n. 7; XXIV, 673: Tunc sequitur quod anima humana secundum quid perficitur beatitudine, sed habitus simpliciter, et tunc habitus videret Deum, et charitas diligeret Deum, et anima humana non nisi per accidens et secundum quid.

[26] Scotus postulates a formal distinction *a parte rei* between the faculties. See for instance *Oxon.* 2, d. 16, q. 1, n. 17; XIII, 43ff.

[27] See *Oxon.* 1, d. 3, q. 3, n. 3; IX, 89; *Rep. Par.* 1, d. 3, q. 1; XXII, 93; *ibid.* 4, d. 49, q. 7, nn. 4–6; XXIV, 655ff.

adequate object. A second clue from natural reason is the fact that the soul intuits its own intellectual, volitional, and sense activity. But what is capable of the least degree of intuitive knowledge is capable of intuition in general.

This last point, incidentally, illustrates a principle that seems to dominate Scotus' entire discussion of the nature of the soul and its faculties. An intellectual power rooted in a spiritual nature, be it a pure angelic spirit or the soul-form of a body, is incapable of being limited to a certain sphere of objects by an intrinsic limitation. Hence, his objection to the division of cognitive faculties adopted by St. Thomas (*Summa theol.* I, 85, 1) which is based on the very nature of the faculty in question. Sense faculties on the contrary, by reason of their material or organic component, are like harp strings, tuned to vibrate only at certain frequencies. In the latter case, the very nature of each faculty limits its sphere of objects to a very definite and select portion of the total field of stimuli. But an intellectual faculty, considered simply in itself as an active potency, is not basically different because in one instance it is found in an angel and in another in the soul. Hence any limitation of its activity must come from a positive ordination on the part of the Creator, who restricts the scope of its activity in view of the particular end for which He has destined this intellectual substance.[28]

Such a conception, however, makes it imperative for Scotus to distinguish between (a) what is natural to the intellectual as a *faculty* or *power* and (b) what is natural to it in *some particular state.*

---

[28] Scotus seems to hint that in the state of innocence man's intellect might not have been limited to such knowledge as requires the cooperation of the senses and imagination. But "quidquid sit de notitia naturali ... in statu innocentiae ... nunc omnis nostra cognitio oritur ex sensu" (*Metaphy.* 1, q. 1, n. 41; VII, 32). But if Adam did have greater freedom in the use of his intellect than we do at present, then the intimate dependence of intellect on the imagination in our present state could be considered as a consequence of the fall. Hence Scotus concedes that this limitation could be the result (forte propter peccatum, sicut videtur Augustinus dicere) or again, it might be something purely natural to man as a corporeal being (vel forte ista causa est naturalis, prout natura isto modo instituta est). At any rate, "quidquid dicat Augustinus," this union cannot be regarded as an effect "solum ex peccato," but is something demanded by the very nature of our soul's varied and complex faculties taken as a whole (non solum ex peccato sed natura potentiarum pro statu isto). Cf. *Oxon.* 2, d. 3, q. 8, n. 13; XII, 195. To permit the intellectual soul to function in complete independence of the senses would destroy the harmony and unity of man's psychic life. Consequently "etsi cognitio possit acquiri per usum sensuum et per alium modum ab anima separata, non frustra fit unio ... Unio animae ad corpus non est finaliter propter perfectionem corporis, nec solam perfectionem animae, sed propter perfectionem totius consistentis ex istis partibus; et ideo licet nulla perfectio possit accrescere huic parti vel illi, quae non posset haberi sine tali unione, tamen non fit frustra unio, quia perfectio totius, quae principaliter intenditur a natura, non posset haberi nisi illo modo." *Oxon.* 4, d. 45, q. 2, n. 14; XX, 306.

In the first instance, we abstract from the limitations associated with any particular state and consider the intellect under the best possible conditions. In the second instance, we consider the intellect from the viewpoint of the limitations God has associated with a given state, a state being here understood in Augustinian fashion as a relatively stable or permanent condition established by the laws of divine wisdom.[29]

The fact that man's intellect at present is limited to abstracting its primary data from the phantasm, or that its intuitive powers are restricted to the knowledge of our conscious acts, is the outcome of such a positive ordination on the part of divine wisdom.[30] Consequently, the possibility of other states is not excluded. And some of these possible states we know from revelation to be actually realized. Such for instance is the state of the separated soul. In such a state, the reason for the ligation of the intellectual faculty to the internal senses no longer exists. As a result, man's intellect becomes like unto that of the angelic intellect itself. It is capable of intuiting its own substance. It is able to know immediately other created beings, both spiritual and corporeal, and all this by reason of its own native powers and not by reason of any infused species as St. Thomas suggests.[31]

Keeping this doctrine in mind, we can return to our original problem, the distinction between natural and supernatural knowledge. This distinction, Scotus reminds us, is meaningful only if we compare the knowledge which perfects the human intellect with the causes that produced it. Knowledge is natural if it arises through the agencies of natural causes; otherwise it is supernatural.

> If the possible intellect be compared to the knowledge that is actualized in it, no knowledge is supernatural to it, because the possible intellect is perfected by any knowledge whatsoever and is naturally inclined towards any kind of knowledge. But according to the second way of speaking, that knowledge is supernatural which is generated by some agent which by its very nature is not ordained to move the possible intellect in a natural manner.[32]

A natural cause is one which, by its very nature, given the necessary conditions, produces its effect automatically, as it were. For instance,

---

[29] *Oxon.* 1, d. 3, q. 3, n. 24; IX, 148: Status non videtur esse nisi stabilis permanentia legibus divinae sapientiae firmata.

[30] *Ibid.:* Stabilitum est autem illis legibus sapientiae, quod intellectus noster non intelligat pro statu isto, nisi illa quorum species relucent in phantasmate.

[31] *Oxon.* 4, d. 45, q. 2.

[32] See note 15.

hold a red rose before the open eye of a normal, healthy man under sufficient lighting conditions and vision automatically results. The intellect is a necessarily operating faculty. Given the presence of its object under normal conditions, intellection takes place. In differentiating natural from supernatural knowledge, we must consider primarily the role played by the object in intellection. Normally, intellect and object cooperate as two essentially ordered partial causes of intellection. This is true of both intuitive and abstractive knowledge, the only difference being that in one case the object in its concrete existence directly cooperates, whereas in abstractive cognition the object acts indirectly through the medium of the intelligible species. To ask what objects are naturally capable of causing intellection is to ask for the natural motivating object of the intellect. Now this object, Scotus points out, differs for the different states of existence possible to the intellect.

In this life, for instance, sensible quiddity is the proper and adequate motivating object of our intellect.[33] Hence, any knowledge that can be caused by such objects is natural to man in his present state of existence. This includes not merely the concrete phenomena experienced, but any intelligible note that can be abstracted from the same. For an object, either in itself or through its intelligible species, is able to produce a knowledge of whatever is essentially or virtually contained in it. Hence, for example, all such transcendental notions as being, unity, and the like are natural in this sense.[34]

In its state of separation from the body, the soul or intellect can be motivated naturally by many other objects. Thus, for instance, we find Scotus arguing that if the agent intellect can abstract intelligible species from a mere likeness of the object in the phantasm, a fortiori it can act directly on an object such as a stone and extract from it an intelligible species such as abstractive knowledge requires.[35] Furthermore, it can directly intuit objects, both spiritual and material. Thus it can know its angel guardian, its own soul substance, and the like.[36]

---

[33] Oxon. 1, d. 3, q. 3, n. 24; IX, 148: Pro statu isto ei [sc. intellectui] adaequatur in ratione motivi quidditas rei sensibilis, et ideo pro statu isto non naturaliter intelliget alia, quae non continentur sub illo primo motivo. Quod., q. 14, n. 12; XXVI, 46.

[34] Quodl. q. 14, n. 12; XXVI, 46. This has an important application in regard to our conception of God. Cf. "Duns Scotus on the Nature of Man's Knowledge of God," Review of Metaphysics I (1947), 3ff.

[35] Oxon. 4, d. 45, q. 2, n. 12; XX, 305: Intellectus agens cum objecto est sufficiens causa activa speciei intelligibilis, nec minus cum objecto extra, quam cum phantasmate (de quo isti concedunt, quia, ut dictum est, contra opinionem arguendo, nihil est in phantasmate propter quod sufficiat ad causandum speciem intelligibilem, quin eminentius sit in re cujus est phantasma); intellectus autem possibilis est sufficienter receptivus.

[36] Ibid., 305: Ad quaestionem ergo dico quod anima separata potest acquirere cognitionem objecti prius ignoti, et hoc tam de cognitione abstractiva quam intuitiva.

We may further speculate as to what could naturally motivate the intellect in the state of innocence, or again in what modern theologians call the state of pure nature. But as such is purely theoretical, Scotus does little more than allude to it.[37] What he does do, however, is to discuss thoroughly the natural motivating object of the intellect as a power.[38] What is our intellect capable of under the best possible conditions? He answers that the natural adequate motivating object of our intellect as such is *any limited or finite being*.[39] In other words, our intellect, if confronted by any created being, whether substance or accident, material or spiritual, could know immediately and intuitively the being in question, provided only that God cooperate with the causal action of both our intellect and the object in question. Such a cooperation of God as first cause, though voluntary and contingent absolutely speaking, pertains nevertheless to the natural order, in the sense that it is required by the state in which He has placed the intellectual being.

But Scotus insists that in no state whatsoever is the divine essence of God a natural or adequate motivating object for any intellect other than His own. For any created intellect, be it that of the highest angel or the lowliest human, God's essence is a purely voluntary object.[40] His divine essence, simply in virtue of its being the divine essence, has no natural ordination to act as partial cause with the agent intellect of any creature, man or angel. If God is to play the role of the motivating object, such as is necessary in the case of the immediate and intuitive knowledge we call the beatific vision, it is through a free act of His will.

From this it is easy to see why the beatific vision for Scotus is truly supernatural. It transcends the natural causality of all agencies, including that of the divine essence itself. For where a truly natural causality obtains, the operation (in this case, intellection) follows necessarily, given the required conditions. It proceeds *per modum naturae*, to use Scotus' terminology, and not freely or voluntarily.[41]

In the case of all other knowledge that men or angels possess, it is the being or nature of the object that motivates the intellect. In the case of the beatific vision, it is not the divine nature or essence that formally motivates or moves the intellect but the divine will. And

---

[37] See for instance, *Metaphy.* 1, q. 1, n. 41; VII, 32; *Oxon.* 2, d. 29, q. un., *passim*; XIII, 267ff.; *ibid.* 4, d. 45, q. 2, n. 14; XX, 305ff., etc.

[38] *Oxon.* 1, d. 3, q. 3; *ibid.* 4, d. 45, q. 2; *Quodl.* q. 14, etc.

[39] *Quodl.* q. 14, n. 11; XXVI, 40: Pro quocumque statu, cujuscumque intellectus creati praecise, ens limitatum est objectum adaequatum, quia praecise illud potest attingi virtute causae naturaliter motivae intellectus.

[40] What follows is a summary of Scotus' doctrine as elaborated in *Quodlibet*, q. 14.

[41] Regarding this distinction, see also the following q. 15 of the *Quodlibet*.

since this type of motivation is proper to God alone, we can readily understand why Scotus equates voluntary object with supernatural object.

In this connection, the question naturally arises. Could not all knowledge that depends on the free will of a creature, as for instance, the awareness of our own decisions, the will of one angel to communicate its thought to another, and the like, fall under the heading of voluntary objects? And if so, is it legitimate to equate voluntary with supernatural?

Scotus would reply that God's causality in this connection is vastly different from that of any free creature. The peculiarity of the beatific vision lies in this, that the divine will motivates but does not *terminate* the act of the vision. That is to say, God moves us not merely to see His decrees, but moves us to see His essence. No created will, Scotus points out, is capable of producing in an intellect anything more than a knowledge of its own decrees. It is not capable of causing a perfect, immediate, and intuitive vision of any nature. With God's will it is different for His will is not only perfect, but is really identical with His essence. Hence it contains that essence, so to speak, virtually and unitively. In consequence, not only is it able to produce a knowledge of itself and of its decrees, but it is capable of causing a knowledge of the divine essence itself. And in so far as it is intuitive, and not abstractive, knowledge, it is an awareness of the essence of God as existing.[42]

In fact, Scotus goes on to say, so perfect is the causality of the divine will that the human intellect does not need any special disposing habits, such as the *habitus visionis*, to render it capable of receiving this immediate and intuitive knowledge of God. God's will itself is the *lux* illuminating the mind to see.[43] And this is simply another way of declaring that the intellect of a creature is immediately and by its very nature capable of receiving the vision from God. And therefore, under this aspect, the knowledge of the vision is natural, that is, it perfects the intellect, directly and is that towards which the intellect is inclined. For the intellect, Scotus insists, is in obediential potency to receive vision from God immediately and without any intervening disposing habits. On the other hand, however, this capacity to receive the vision of God can only be achieved by a cause which does not act *per modum naturae*, but with perfect liberty and freedom. And for that reason, the beatific vision exceeds both the powers and the exigencies of any created nature.

Using the distinction between an *objectum inclinationis* and *objec-*

---

[42] *Quodl.*, q. 14, nn. 18–19; XXVI, 63ff.
[43] *Oxon.* 4, d. 49, q. 11, n. 10; XXI, 418. See also *Oxon.* 1, d. 3, q. 8 (Quaracchi ed. q. 10), n. 2; IX, 399.

tum attingentiae which Scotus apparently borrowed from William of Ware,[44] we sum up schematically Scotus' position on the object of the intellect in chart 1.

THE WILL AND BEATITUDE

What has been said of the intellect as to the naturalness or supernaturalness of its knowledge can be applied to the will, *mutatis mutandis*. For the will is as much perfected by the beatific love which follows vision as the intellect is by the vision itself. For the sake of brevity, we refrain from discussing the manner in which man is united to God through the act of love, and content ourselves with the observation that the soul or will is perfected through this love. To put it negatively, the beatific love neither does violence to the will nor leaves it unperfected. Consequently, the will must be naturally inclined towards such a love in the same sense that the intellect is naturally inclined to the beatific vision.

Without going into what we might call the "mechanics" of the beatific act, we note that man, or for that matter, any rational creature, does not elicit this act of love, through which beatitude is primarily achieved, without the vision of the divine essence, the habit of sanctifying grace or charity (the two are really identical for Scotus), and the cooperation of God. None of the three, however, is in any sense demanded by the natural order. Hence, this beatific act of love, from the viewpoint of the agencies required to bring it about, is supernatural. In no sense can it be called the result of purely natural causes.

Once more, then, we have the situation that characterizes the relation of the human intellect to the vision of God. Beatitude is both natural and supernatural; natural in the sense that it perfects the will or soul or man; supernatural in the sense that its attainment transcends the natural ability of all created active power combined.

THE NATURAL APPETITE FOR BEATITUDE

With this in mind, we can better understands what Scotus means by the natural "desire" for supernatural happiness. This desire, or better,

---

[44] *Quodl.*, q. 14, n. 11; XXVI, 40: Diceretur quod objectum primum naturale potest dupliciter intelligi: Uno modo ad quod potentia inclinatur. Alio modo ad quod potentia potest naturaliter attingere, scilicet ex concursu causarum naturalium. Wadding refers this distinction to William of Ware, *Com. in Sent.* 1, q. 2.

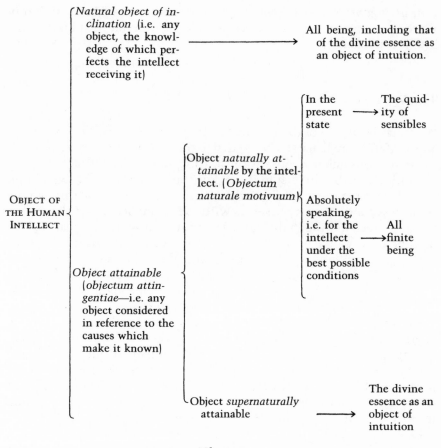

Chart 1

appetitus, is not an act or operation at all.[45] Nor is it something peculiar to the will, or for that matter to an appetitive faculty. For an *appetitus naturalis* is simply an ontological relationship between any faculty (or the soul) and that which perfects it. Thus the intellect has a natural

---

[45] *Oxon.* 4, d. 49, q. 10, n. 2; XXI, 318: Dico, quod duplex est appetitus in voluntate, scilicet naturalis et liber. Naturalem solum dico potentiam voluntatis absolute, sed non aliquid superadditum voluntati. . . . Non est actus aliquis elicitus a voluntate. *Ibid.* 3, d. 17, q. un., n. 3; XIV, 654: Dico quod appetitus naturalis in qualibet re, generali nomine accipitur pro inclinatione naturali rei ad propriam perfectionem, sicut lapis naturaliter inclinatur ad centrum; et si in lapide talis inclinatio sit aliquid absolutum aliud a gravitate, tunc consequenter credo, quod naturalis inclinatio hominis, secundum quod homo, ad propriam perfectionem, est aliud a voluntate libera. Sed primum credo falsum

appetite for truth; the faculty of sight has a natural appetite for seeing; the ear for hearing, and so on. For that reason, to speak of the natural appetite for beatitude as a "desire" or a "longing," and the like, is to use purely metaphorical language.[46] This is brought out in an oft-quoted passage from the *Reportata Parisiensia*.

The appetite or will is twofold; namely, natural and free. For the will can be considered insofar as it is a certain nature and has, like any other nature, an inclination and natural appetite for its own proper perfection. First of all, then, the will should be considered in reference to its natural "willing" as a determinate nature; secondly, in reference to its willing freely. As to the first, we must see just what this natural appetite is.

I say that it is not an elicited act, because the natural appetite of the will is to the will as the natural appetite of the intellect is to the intellect. In the intellect, however, the natural appetite is not elicited; neither then is it in the will. Likewise, the natural appetite is ever present in the will. If then it were an elicited act of the will, the will would be perpetually eliciting some act. But the will does not always have an elicited act, for if it did, we should experience it in ourselves, since it could hardly be admitted that we have some operation ever present in us and that, nevertheless, it still remains hidden from us.... Likewise, if it were an act elicited by the will, two opposite acts would be simultaneously present in the will, for the will can freely will the opposite of that which it seeks by its natural appetite. Thus St. Paul, who in accord with the natural appetite declared: "we do not wish to be unclothed, but rather clothed over" (2 Cor. 5, 4), by his free appetite willed "to depart and to be with Christ" (Phil. 1, 23). Therefore the natural appetite is no more an elicited act in the will than is the natural appetite in a stone.

What is it then? I declare that it is an inclination [of the will] to its perfection, just as in other things which have no free appetite. And of this appetite Aristotle says (in the first book of the *Physics*) that matter seeks the form as the imperfect seeks its perfection.

Concerning this appetite which is not free but natural, it is clear that the

---

scilicet quod inclinatio lapidis ad centrum sit aliquid absolutum aliud a gravitate et aliqua potentia, qua lapis habeat aliquam operationem in centrum, sicut aliqui imaginantur; mirabilis enim esset illa operatio, cum non esset dare terminum illius, et esset actio transiens; et cum centrum sit sibi conveniens, non agit actionem corruptivam ejus, nec etiam salvativam, quia non posset poni qualis esset illa operatio, vel quis terminus illius; ideo naturalis inclinatio lapidis nihil dicit ultra gravitatem lapidis, nisi relationem.... Tunc dico quod sic est de voluntate, quia voluntas naturalis non est voluntas, nec velle naturale est velle; sed naturale distrahit ab utroque, et nihil est nisi relatio consequens potentiam respectu propriae perfectionis. Unde eadem potentia dicitur voluntas naturalis, cum tali respectu necessario consequente ipsam respectu propriae perfectionis, et dicitur libera secundum rationem propriam et intrinsecam, quae est voluntas specifice.

[46] *Ibid.* Cf. O'Connor, *The Eternal Quest, op. cit.* Chapter three contains a very fine summary of Scotus' conception of the *appetitus naturalis* as applied to the will, with the exception of one dubious point which we shall take up later.

will necessarily and perpetually and in the highest degree seeks beatitude, and this means beatitude in particular. That it does so *necessarily* is evident, since a nature cannot remain a nature without being inclined towards its perfection. Remove this inclination, then, and you take away the nature. The natural appetite, however, is nothing more than such an inclination [of the will] to its own perfection. Similarly, the will as nature seeks necessarily its perfection, which above all is beatitude, and this by a natural appetite. That it seeks this *above all* is proved, because a nature is most inclined towards that which perfects it most. If then a nature seeks its perfection, it seeks above all its highest perfection.... But because the highest perfection of the will is beatitude, it follows that the will as nature seeks it above all.... That it thus naturally seeks beatitude *in particular* is evident, because this appetite is towards a perfection in which the will is really perfected. A real perfection, however, is not something universal, but singular. Therefore, it seeks beatitude in particular. Likewise, this "seeking" is not an act consequent upon knowledge, for then it would be free. A universal, however, is an object only of an intellect or is something that depends upon the operation of the intellect. Hence, this appetite in the will is in regard to beatitude in particular.[47]

---

[47] *Rep. Par.* 4, d. 49, q. 9, nn. 3–5; XXIV, 659s: Respondeo ad primam quaestionem, quod duplex est appetitus sive voluntas, scilicet naturalis et libera. Potest enim voluntas considerari, ut est quaedam natura, et inquantum habet inclinationem, et appetitum naturalem ad suam propriam perfectionem, sicut quaecumque alia natura. Primo igitur videndum est de voluntate quantum ad ejus velle naturale, inquantum natura quaedam; secundo quantum ad ejus velle liberum, inquantum appetit libere. Quantum ad primum videndum est, quid sit appetitus naturalis? Dico quod non est actus elicitus, quia appetitus naturalis voluntatis se habt ad voluntatem, sicut appetitus naturalis intellectus se habet ad intellectum; sed in intellectu appetitus naturalis non est elicitus; igitur nec in voluntate. Item, appetitus naturalis perpetuo inest voluntati; si igitur esset actus voluntatis elicitus, aliquis actus elicitus perpetuo inesset voluntati; sed nullum actum elicitium perpetuo habet voluntas, quia illum tunc potuissemus experiri in nobis; inconveniens enim est operationem perpetuo inesse nobis, et illam nos latere; sed hoc est inconveniens, secundum Philosophum, de habitibus. Item si esset actus elicitus in voluntate, essent duo actus oppositi in voluntate simul, quia voluntas potest velle libere oppositum illius, quod appetit appetitu naturali, sicut Paulus, qui dixit secundum appetitum naturalem 'Nolumus expoliari, sed supervestiri,' 2 Cor. 5, voluit appetitu libero ad Philip. 1. 'Dissolvi, et esse cum Christo.' Non ergo appetitus naturalis est magis actus elicitus in voluntate, quam appetitus naturalis in lapide.—Quid ergo est? Dico quod est inclination ad ipsam perfectionem, sicut in aliis non habentibus appetitum liberum. Et de isto appetitu loquitur Philosophus primo Physicorum, text. 81, quod materia appetit formam, sicut imperfectum appetit suam perfectionem. De isto appetitu non libero, sed naturali, apparet quod voluntas necessario, sive perpetuo et summe appetit beatitudinem, et hoc in particulari. Quod *necessario,* patet, quia natura non potest manere natura quin inclinetur ad suam perfectionem. Tolle ergo instam inclinationem, et tolles naturam; sed appetitus naturalis non est nisi talis inclinatio ad propriam perfectionem. Similiter voluntas ut natura necessario apetit suam perfectionem, quae maxime est beatitudo, et hoc appetitu naturali. Quod *summe* appetit, probatur quia summa inelinatio naturae est ad summam perfectionem. Si ergo natura appetat suam perfectionem, summe appetit summam perfectionem.... Cum igitur summa perfectio voluntatis sit beatitudo, sequitur quod voluntas ut natura summe appetit.... Quod *in particulari* sic naturaliter appetit beatitudinem, patet, quia ille appetitus est ad perfectionem, in qua voluntas realiter

The first point to note in this passage is the distinction between the will as free and the will as nature. These are not two distinct faculties, as Scotus observes elsewhere, but one and the same will viewed from different standpoints.[48] In the first case, the will is considered actively as the self-determining cause of its own acts. In the second, it is regarded passively as the recipient of its own immanent operations.[49] Scotus can make this distinction because he admits of no "natural" operations of the will, that is, acts which proceed necessarily *(per modum naturae)* from the faculty in question. Even in the beatific vision, the act whereby man loves God is free from any external or internal determination. Hence, for Scotus an elicited act of the will is always free. Consequently, the will as free can be equated with the will as active or the will as cause.

The natural appetite, then, is not an elicited act. It is simply an ontological relation that exists between the will and anything that is capable of perfecting it. As he puts it, "it is nothing more than the relation that arises in a faculty in reference to its proper perfection."[50] Basically, this appetite of the will is no different than "the natural appetite of a stone" or "the natural appetite of the intellect" or that of other beings "which have no free appetite."

Secondly, this natural appetite extends to anything and everything that perfects the will. A fortiori then it includes the loving fruition of God that follows vision, for "the highest perfection of the will is beatitude." (Beatitude, let us note, is understood here in a technical sense, namely that associated with the beatific vision.[51]) That this loving

---

perficitur; sed perfectio realis non est aliquid universale, sed singulare; igitur appetit beatitudinem in particulari. Item, illud *appetere* non est actus sequens cognitionem, quia tunc non esset naturalis, sed liber. Universale autem non est, nisi objectum intellectus, vel aliquid consequens operationem intellectus; igitur iste appetitus in voluntate est respectu beatitudinis in particulari.

[48] *Oxon.* 3, d. 17, q. un., n. 3; XIV, 654: Eadem potentia dicitur voluntas, cum tali respectu necessario consequente ipsam respectu propriae perfectionis, et dicitur libera secundum rationem propriam et intrinsecam, quae est voluntas specifice.

[49] *Ibid.*, n. 9; 655: Dico quod voluntas naturalis, ut sic, non est voluntas, neque potentia, sed tantum dicit inclinationem potentiae ad recipiendum perfectionem, non ad agendum, et ideo ut sic est imperfecta, nisi sit sub illius perfectione, ad quam illa tendentia inclinat potentiam; unde naturalis voluntas non tendit, sed est ipsa tendentia, qua voluntas absolute tendit, et hoc passive ad recipiendum; sed est alia tendentia in eadem potentia, ut libere et active agat, et tendat eliciendo actum, ita quod in una potentia est duplex tendentia activa et passiva; tunc ad formam argumenti dico quod voluntas naturalis secundum formale, quod importat, non est potentia vel voluntas, sed inclinatio voluntatis, et tendentia qua tendit in perfectionem.

[50] *Ibid.*, n. 3; 654: Voluntas naturalis non est voluntas, nec velle naturale est velle; sed naturale distrahit ab utroque, et nihil est nisi relatio consequens potentiam respectu propriae perfectionis.

[51] Cf. *Oxon.* 4, d. 49, 1. 2, n. 25; XXI, 49ss; *ibid.*, q. 5, n. 4; 175s: Quomodo distin-

union can be achieved only by supernatural intervention does not alter the fact that it does perfect the nature of the will. For, as Scotus continually points out, if we consider merely the recipient (in this case, the will) and what is received (the immanent operation or act of fruition), there is no supernatural. "Since the highest perfection of the will is beatitude, it follows that the will as nature seeks it above all."

That this natural appetite extends to the specific act of the beatific love that follows the vision of God's essence, Scotus infers from the fact that the will is not perfected simply by the love of what is good in general, but by a love of this or that particular being or thing. Hence, this "desire" or appetite is directed toward that specific perfection that results from the act of love whereby man is united to God in heaven. "A real perfection is not something universal but singular. Therefore, [the will] seeks beatitude in particular."

This "desire" is not something of which we are conscious. Like any other relation, it is known only when the two terms of the relation are known. Only after we learn that the beatific vision is actually the goal God has intended for us, do we know that we must possess a natural appetite for this perfection. Hence, this desire or appetite precedes all conscious activity and all cognition. It is present to the same degree in a newborn babe or a Cretin idiot as in a normal adult. "This seeking is not an act consequent upon knowledge."[52] And since we cannot demonstrate from reason alone that we do possess such a capacity for the beatific vision, neither can we know by natural reason that we have an *appetitus naturalis* in regard to it.

CONCLUSION

In view of the contemporary controversy over the tenability of a natural desire for the supernatural, we might make the following observations in conclusion:

Scotus' theory of the *appetitus naturalis* for supernatural beatitude

---

guantur fruitio beatifica et non beatifica? ... Imponitur hoc nomen beatitudo ad significandum fruitionem in determinato gradu, ita quod non infra; et illum numquam habet viator, nec secundum magis, nec secundum minus; sed sic habent illum diversi comprehensores, ideo unus eorum est beatior altero.

[52] *Oxon.* 4, d. 43, q. 2, n. 29; XXI, 57: Aut arguitur praecise de desiderio naturali proprie dicto, et illud non est aliquis actus elicitus, sed sola inclinatio naturae ad aliquid, et tune planum est, quod non potest probari desiderium naturale ad aliquid nisi primo probetur possibilitas in natura ad illud, et per consequens econverso arguendo de desiderio naturali minus proprie dicto, quod scilicet est actus elicitus, sed concorditer inclinationi naturali, tunc iterum non potest probari quod aliquid desiderium elicitum sit naturale illo modo nisi probetur, quod ad idem sit desiderium naturale primo modo.

seems to be nothing more than a conclusion drawn from the commonly accepted theological dictum that the supernatural does not destroy, but is built upon and perfects the natural. Applying the Aristotelian conceptions of act and potency, Scotus claims that a passive capacity for this supernatural perfection must exist in the nature itself. If he calls this supernatural perfection "natural," it is only in the sense that it is in accord with and does not do violence to that nature.

This passive capacity to receive such supernatural gifts as sanctifying grace or the beatific vision does not require the addition of some intermediary habit or quality by which the soul is proportioned, so to speak, to the divine causality. The soul is always in obediential potency to its creator, and this suffices. Referring specifically to the assent to the truths of faith, though what he says applies to all supernatural knowledge, he remarks:

> If you ask whether it is natural or supernatural, I declare that it is supernatural, if you understand it in reference to the agent.... When you infer that the intellect, then, is disproportional to it and must be made proportional through something else, I declare that of itself it is in obediential potency to the agent, and thus is sufficiently proportional to it to this extent that it can be moved by it. Likewise of itself it is capable of the assent caused by such an agent and that naturally.[53]

Now the principal objection to calling the beatific vision "natural," or admitting an *appetitus naturalis* in man for such a state, is that raised by Sylvester Ferrariensis and revoiced in our own day.[54] Were God the natural end of man in the sense that human nature is inclined towards the beatific vision and still this end could be attained only supernaturally, nature so to speak would contradict herself. Our natural desire would be in vain.

This raises an interesting question. Just how did Scotus understand the axiom, *natura nihil frustra fecit?* To take it in the sense of Aristotle or the "philosophers" of his own day was out of the question. If he had, either he must abandon the thesis of a natural desire for the

---

[53] *Oxon.* prol. q. 1; Assisi 137, f. 3ra: Cum ultra de illo alio quaeris an sit naturale vel supernaturale, dico quod supernaturale, sive intelligas de agente.... Cum infers: ergo intellectus est improportionatus ad illud, et per aliud proportionatur dico quod ex se est in potentia obedientiali ad agens, et ita sufficienter proportionatur illi ad hoc ut ab ipso moveatur. Similiter ex se est capax illius assensus causati a tali agente, etiam naturaliter capax.

[54] Sylvester Ferrariensis, *Comm. in Contra Gentiles*, I. c. 5, n. V, 2: Si Deus esset finis naturalis, idest in quem natura inclinat, se supernaturaliter acquirendus, sequeretur quod natura inclinaret suum subjectum ad aliquod ad quod esset impossibile ut perduceret. Hoc autem in omnibus naturis videtur falsum. Et etiam repugnat rationi; tunc enim naturalis appetitus esset frustra in natura, quia nullo modo per naturam adimpleri.

supernatural, or destroy the distinction between the natural and supernatural, a heresy which he himself labeled as "worse than the heresy of Pelagius." For, under pain of acting irrationally, God would be constrained to grant man grace and glory. They would be as "natural" as His conservation and concurrence with the laws of nature.

Since this "desire" of nature is nothing more than an ontological relationship of perfectibility, it is said to be in vain only if its realization involved an extrinsic impossibility, namely if no cause whatsoever existed—neither natural nor supernatural—that could impart this perfection.[55] Hence, his vehement opposition to the Aristotelian thesis that to every natural passive potency there is a corresponding natural active potency.[56]

Furthermore, the existence of this "desire" or appetite does not oblige God in any sense of the term to fulfill it on the score that He has created a nature and left it incomplete. Scotus brings this out very nicely in regard to the different degrees of grace and glory, for the same problem arises here as in the distinction between the natural and the supernatural. Not only does man possess a natural appetite for grace and glory in general, but he seeks the very highest degree possible, one that is actually given to the human soul of Christ alone.[57] In consequence, Scotus must maintain that no other created soul or angelic nature is fully satisfied. But does this imply frustration? Not at all. This "inclination" towards perfection is not the fruit of some intrinsic principle that demands fulfillment.[58] God does no violence to the nature whatsoever. Like the stone that "seeks" the heart of the earth, yet is perfectly content to rest on its surface, so too with the blessed. It is quite true that their natures desire the supreme degree of love and glory and in that alone will they be fully sated. Yet these same natures come to rest (quietari) and are satisfied with the very least.[59]

[55] Oxon. prol. q. 1, n. 25; VIII, 57: Dico quod potentia passiva non est frustra in natura, quia licet per agens naturale possit principaliter reduci ad actum, tamen ... potest per aliquod agens in natura, id est in tota coordinatione entium, puta per agens supernaturale complete reduci ad actum.

[56] Ibid.; Oxon. 4, d. 49; q. 11, n. 12 ad 3; XXI, 419.

[57] Scotus does not admit that grace can be increased sine fine, for the different degrees of grace or charity pertain not to the order of quantity but quality and that in the qualitative order there is an absolute degree that God Himself cannot exceed though He could create this absolute degree in more than one soul. Actually this maximum degree of grace was given to the soul of Christ. Oxon. 3, d. 13, qq. 1–2.

[58] Oxon. 3, d. 13, q. 4, n. 15; XIV, 471: Ista inclinatio non habet principium intrinsecum necessitans ad illud ad quod ipsa est, ita quod oppositum ejus non possit inesse nisi violenter.

[59] Ibid.: Inclinatur enim ad habendum gratiam summam et tamen potest quietari in minima. Ratio est quia non habet principium intrinsecum determinans eam ad aliquem gradum determinatum.

From all this it is clear that we are using metaphorical language in this connection. Translated into a more prosaic idiom, this natural desire for the highest glory means nothing more than that the "will could be naturally perfected by such glory."[60] Consequently, it is not required, Scotus assures us, that a natural appetite should have all the perfection of which it is ultimately capable.[61]

Lastly, we note that the existence of this natural desire for beatitude cannot be used to demonstrate the existence of the supernatural order. This is putting the cart before the horse. Only if we know that God has actually destined us for the face-to-face vision of Himself, can we infer with certitude that we possess a natural desire for the same. To ascertain either conclusively, revelation is required.

---

[60] *Ibid.*: Dico quod appetitus naturalis cujuscumque voluntatis est ad summam gloriam, hoc est, ista voluntas posset naturaliter perfici tanta gloria, nec tamen est ibi tanta inclinatio naturalis ad summam quod oppositum formae, i.e. non summa gloria, potentiae isti violenter insit.

[61] *Oxon.* 4, d. 50, q. 6, n. 3; XXI, 551: Non oportet quod appetitus naturalis habeat omnem perfectionem cujus est summe capax.

7 / Native Freedom of the Will as a Key to the Ethics of Scotus

Perhaps the most persistently recurring objection to the moral philosophy of John Duns Scotus is voiced most succinctly by Anthony Quinton in his article in the new *Encyclopedia of Philosophy*.[1] "Things are good because God wills them and not vice versa, so moral truth is not accessible to natural reason." I propose to show how Scotus would interpret the premise of Quinton's enthymeme and why he would not concede its conclusion. This can be done most effectively, I think, if we consider his teaching on the will's native freedom in relation to ethics, for although he developed this Anselmian notion with reference to a finite will, there is no doubt he regarded it as univocally predicable of God's will as well. What I hope will emerge as a by-product of the discussion is that Scotus did not consider 'to be radically and perfectly free' and 'to be guided by right reason' as antithetical or antinomic. On the contrary, he believed each notion logically entailed the other. In fact in his Metaphysics, he makes the paradoxical claim that only the will, not the intellect, is truly and essentially rational.[2] I will not go into his reasoning there since the wax nose of authority receives a

Reprinted with permission from *Deus et Homo ad mentem I. Duns Scoti* (Studia Scholastico-Scotistico 5), pp. 360–370.

[1] Anthony Quinton, *British Philosophy*, in *Encyclopedia of Philosophy*, edited by Paul Edwards, New York, Macmillan and Free Press, 1967, I, 373.

[2] *Quaestiones subtilissimae super libros Metaphysicorum Aristotelis*, lib. IX, q. 15, nn. 4–7; ed. Vivès, VII, 609–11. Unless explicitly noted otherwise, all references are to the Vivès reprint of the Wadding edition: *Joannis Duns Scoti opera omnia*, 26 vols., Parisiis, Apud Ludovicum Vivès, 1891–1895.

rather violent twisting. Suffice it to say that the substance of his argument is to show that Aristotle's distinction of active potencies into rational and irrational is acceptable and adequate only because it is reducible to Scotus' own basic division of *voluntas* and *natura*. It is this distinction I wish to take up first.

THE NATIVE FREEDOM OF THE WILL

Scotus deals with it in all his major works, but with varying shades of difference. In the Metaphysics, for instance, he argues for the basic character of this division of faculties or powers on the grounds that the way in which an active potency elicits its act is a more fundamental and essential characteristic than the way it is related to the other faculties it influences. On this score the will is set apart from the whole realm of nature or natural agents, because unlike the latter it is *ex se* undetermined, yet has the ability to determine itself. Its power indeed consists precisely in this. Natural agents by contrast have their action specified by what they are in themselves, and given the same set of extrinsic conditions or circumstances their action is uniform. Self-determination on the contrary presupposes two things: (a) logically alternative modes of behavior, specifically the possibility of acting or not acting (liberty of contradiction) or acting now this way, now that (liberty of contrariety); (b) in freely determining itself to one or the other of these several alternatives, the free agent acts *with*, but is not determined by, knowledge. In what is obviously a play on words, and yet contains a profound insight, Scotus writes: "If rational means to act *with* reason, then it is the will that is properly rational and it is concerned with alternatives both as regards its own actions and the actions of the powers it controls, but the alternative it selects is not determined by its nature (as is the case with the intellect which could not determine itself to act otherwise), but it acts freely."[3] In this basic and fundamental sense, he goes on to say, the intellect is only accidentally rational, as it were, namely as regards those actions it elicits which are subject to voluntary control.

In the Commentaries on the Sentences, however, when he deals with moral problems such as how moral goodness differs from the natural goodness of the will, or what constitutes the specific malice of Lucifer's or Adam's sin, and so on, a new dimension to his distinction of will and nature comes to light. It is in connection with his interpretation

---

[3] *Ibid.*, n. 7, p. 611.

of Anselm's distinction of the twofold inclination in the will, the *affectio commodi* and the *affectio justitiae*.[4]

Nature by contrast has a single inclination. According to Plato and Aristotle, it "desires" and seeks above all its own completion and perfection. With P. Rousselot we could call their theory of man's natural appetites and capacity to love "physical" in the original sense of that term.[5] As Plato poetically put it, "Penury or poverty is the mother of all love."[6] Expressed in less lyrical language, we could say all striving, all activity stems from an imperfection in the agent. As the etymological derivation of the word itself suggests, nature (from 'nascor', to be born) is literally what a thing was born to be, or more precisely, born to become, for nature as an active agent is essentially dynamic in a Faustian sense. It is restless until it achieves self-perfection. Since what perfects a thing is its good and since this striving for what is good is a form of love, we could say with Socrates that all activity is sparked by love. The peculiarity of such love, however, is that it can never be objective, to say nothing of being altruistic. It is radically self-centered in this sense, at least, that nature seeks primarily and above all else its own welfare. If at times we encounter what seems to be altruistic behavior in the animal world, for instance, it is always a case where the "nature" or "species" is favored at the expense of the individual. But nature, either in its individual concretization or as a self-perpetuating species, must of necessity seek its own perfection. Such is its supreme value and the ultimate goal of all its loves.

Such a theory presents a dual difficulty for a Christian. First, how can one maintain that "God is love" (I John)? Secondly, how can we love God above all things if self-perfection is our supreme value? As Rousselot points out, various solutions were suggested. Aquinas, we know, tried to solve the second problem within the framework of the Aristotelian system by developing the Stagirite's notion of how our love for others is an extension of selflove. Others had recourse to what

---

[4] Scotus' repeated appeal to this Anselmian distinction shows how basic he considered it to be to his ethical system. See, for example, the *Ordinatio* or *Opus oxoniense* II, d. 6, q. 2, n. 8 (XII, 353–55); d. 25, n. 23 (XIII, 222–23); d. 39, q. 2, n. 5 (p. 415); III, d. 15, n. 19 (XIV, 592); d. 18, nn. 5 & 16 (pp. 664 & 692); d. 26, n. 17 (XV, 340–41); IV, d. 29, n. 3 (XIX, 215); d. 49, q. 5, n. 3 (XXI, 172); q. 10, nn. 11–14 (379–81) as well as parallel passages in the *Reportata parisiensia*. Confer also W. Hoeres, *Der Wille als reine Vollkommenheit nach Duns Scotus* München, Max Hüber, 1962, 149–62; idem, *Naturtendenz und Freiheit nach Duns Scotus*, in Salzburger Jahrbuch für Philosophie II (1958), 95–139a.

[5] P. Rousselot, *Pour l'histoire du problème de l'amour du moyen âge*, Münster, Aschendorffsche Verlagsbuchhandlunger, 1908; in *Beiträge zur Geschichte der Philosophie des Mittelalters*, Bd. VI, Hft. 6, p. 3.

[6] Plato, *Symposium* 203.

Rousselot calls the "ecstatic theory of love"[7] which is almost the polar opposite of the "physical" theory in that in its love for God, at least, it is forgetful of self completely. Scotus, recognizing that will is an essential component of the angelic or human nature, and as such has a God-given drive or inclination to seek that which perfects it, tried a more balanced view which would incorporate Aristotle's insights without being limited to them. Appealing to Anselm, he argued that the will has a twofold attraction towards the good. One is the affection for what is to our advantage *(affectio commodi)* which corresponds roughly—so far as objects other than self are concerned—with the drive of nature described above. It inclines man to seek his perfection and happiness in all he does. If this tendency alone were operative, we would love God only because he is our greatest good and because man's perfected self (albeit perfected by union with God in knowledge and love) would be the supreme object of man's love. The latter would be the only thing that is loved for its own sake and would be that for the sake of which all else is loved. But there is a second and more noble tendency in the will, an inclination or affection for justice *(affectio justitiae)*, so called because it inclines one to do justice to the objective goodness, the intrinsic value of a thing, regardless of whether it happens to be a good for oneself or not.[8]

This affection for justice has several distinguishing features. One, it inclines us to love a thing primarily for what the latter is or has in itself (its absolute value) rather than for what it can do for us (its relative value).[9] This is what is meant by the expression "to love a thing for its own sake." Two, it leads one, consequently, to love God in himself as the most perfect and adorable of objects, irrespective of the fact that he happens to love us in return, or that such a love for God produces in man as an inevitable concommitant effect, supreme delight or happiness.[10] Three, it enables one to love his neighbor literally as himself (i.e. where each individual is of equal objective value). Finally, this love is not jealous of the beloved, but seeks to make the latter loved and appreciated by others. "Whoever loves perfectly, desires colovers

[7] Rousselot, *op. cit.* 56–87.

[8] Of the references in note 4, confer especially *Ordinatio* II, d. 6, q. 2, where Scotus theorizes about the sin of Lucifer.

[9] Cf. G. Stratenwerth, *Die Naturrechtslehre des Johannes Duns Scotus*, Goettingen, Vandenhoeck und Ruprecht, 1951. What he calls 'der Freiheit *zum* Wert' has also been recognized by such contemporary value philosophers as Dietrich von Hildebrand. See his *Phenomenology of Values in a Christian Philosophy*, in *Christian Philosophy and Religious Renewal*, ed. G. F. McLean, Washington, D.C.: Catholic University of America, 1966, p. 8.

[10] Scotus insists that man has the ability to love God in this way *ex puris naturalibus.* Cf. *Ord.* III, d. 27, n. 15 (XV, 368).

for the beloved."[11] Recall if you will the tendency to make others admire the beautiful, or the sorrow felt when something perfectly lovely is unloved, desecrated or destroyed.

If the *affectio commodi* tends to utter selfishness as a limiting case, the first checkrein on its headlong self-seeking is the *affectio justitiae.* "This affection for what is just," Scotus writes, "which is the first tempering influence on the affection for what is advantageous, and to this extent that our will need not actually seek that towards which the latter affection inclines us, nor need we seek it above all else,— this affection for what is just, I say,—is that liberty which is native or innate in the will, since it provides the first tempering influence on the affection for what is advantageous."[12]

Here we have a new description of the will's freedom, one that is not reducible to liberty of contradiction or contrariety. It is not a question of freely elicited acts, for neither of these affections, though they incline the will towards acting, and when the will does act, it elicits its act in accord with one affection or the other,[13] are elicited acts as such.[14] These affections are essential components or formal perfections of the will as a faculty. In an interesting passage of the *Reportata parisiensia,* he points out that while both inclinations are intrinsic to the will, it is the *affectio justitiae* that represents the ultimate specific difference, as it were, of the will as free. This native liberty or root freedom of the will, in short, is a positive bias or inclination to love things objectively or as right reason dictates. In the text cited above, it is described equivalently in what amounts to both a freedom *from* nature and a freedom *for* values. For as he goes on to explain, "From the fact that it is able to temper or control the inclination for what is advantageous, it follows that it is obligated to do so in accordance with the rule of justice that it has received from a higher will."[15] Native liberty was given to man for a purpose, namely that it might serve the interests of justice.

This brings us to the relationship of this conception of will to Scotus' ethical theory. If man had no free will but only an intellectual appetite, he would be ruled exclusively by the inclination for what is to his advantage and would be incapable of sin though subject perhaps to errors of judgment. Ethical behavior in short would be impossible. On

[11] *Ord.* III, d. 28, n. 2 (XV, 378); d. 37, n. 10 (p. 844).
[12] *Ord.* II, d. 6, q. 2, n. 8 (XII, 353).
[13] *Ibid.*, n. 5, p. 348.
[14] This is stated explicitly in regard to the *affectio commodi* or *inclinatio appetitus naturalis* (cf. *ibid.* n. 10, p. 355); but it is implied as regards the *affectio justitiae* as well.
[15] *Rep. par.* II, d. 6, q. 2, n. 9 (XXII, 621); see also *Ord.* II, d. 6, q. 2, n. 8 (XII, 354) and *Ord.* IV, d. 49, q. 5, n. 3 (XXI, 173).

the other hand, if the will's freedom meant nothing more than simple liberation from this inclination of nature, its actions would become irrational in a pejorative sense of the word, being governed by chance or caprice. What is needed is some counter inclination which frees man from the need to follow the *affectio commodi* exclusively and yet is in accord with right reason. When unimpeded by emotional considerations, human reason is capable of arriving at a fairly objective estimate of the most important human actions in terms of the intrinsic worth of their object, the goals attained, the effort expended, the consequences and so on. By reason of its affection for justice, the will is inclined to seek such intrinsic values even when this runs counter at times to man's inclination towards self-indulgence. But being physically free to disregard either inclination[16] or to follow the higher rule of justice, man becomes responsible for the good or evil he foresees will follow from his course of action.

The *affectio commodi*, as extreme forms of the ecstatic theory might seem to imply, is not something evil to be eradicated. For it too represents a God-given drive implanted in man's rational nature which leads him to seek his true happiness, the supreme degree of which is to be found in union with God. Consequently, both affections in their last analysis lead to God. It might be interesting to note parenthetically at this point, that the supernaturally infused virtues of charity and hope are interpreted by Scotus as perfecting the will's affection for justice and for the advantageous respectively.[17]

It is also clear, however, that since God has given each man this *affectio commodi*, to ignore our own perfection completely, if that were possible, or to give it no weight in our objective evaluation of things would be unjust. That is why, next to God, we ought to love ourselves more than others, all else being equal.[18] This too is in keeping with right reason. But what right reason also recognizes is that our self-perfection, even through union with God in love is not of supreme value. It enables man, in short, to evaluate objectively the purpose of his natural inclinations, to recognize that the drive for self-perfection paradoxically must not go unbridled if it is to achieve its goal, but must be channeled lest it destroy the harmony of the universe intended by God.

Though the counter inclination towards what is intrinsically and objectively good makes it easier for man to resist seeking self inordinately, Scotus does not regard free choice to be determined in a concrete

---

[16] *Ord.* II, d. 39, q. 2, n. 5 (XIII, 415).
[17] *Ord.* III, d. 26, n. 18 (XV, 341).
[18] *Ord.* IV, d. 50, q. 6, n. 8 (XXI, 557).

instance by the relative strength of these two inclinations. Physically speaking, the created will is free to follow either inclination, no matter how strong. But morally there is an obligation for man in eliciting his acts to follow the inclination of his native liberty, to the extent at least that he "moderate" this affection for what is advantageous lest he love it inordinately.[19]

This twofold inclination also figures in his analysis of moral goodness. There are several ways, he says, in which a thing in general and an action in particular may be said to be good.[20]

First there is transcendental goodness which is a property of all beings to the extent that they have any positive entity or reality. *Omne ens est bonum* was a medieval maxim. Though it may have expressed a profound truth for a Platonist, for the late thirteenth century scholastic it had lost much of its significance. It voiced only that obvious truth that only to the degree that it was something could anything be an object of desire or love. Not to be good in this uninteresting and trivial sense is simply not to be at all.

A more conventional meaning of goodness is that which Scotus calls *natural*. Since a given subject may either have or lack it natural goodness is described in terms of Aristotle's categories as an accidental quality. Like bodily beauty, Duns explains, it is a harmonious blend of all that becomes the thing in question. Actions too can have such a natural goodness. Walking, running and the like, for example, may be done awkwardly or with a certain grace or beauty. More generally an activity, an operation of mind or will can be "in harmony with its efficient cause, its object, its end and its form and it is naturally good when it has all that becomes in it this way."[21] Applied specifically to voluntary actions, natural goodness can be equated with perfecting the *voluntas ut natura* or as the seat of the *affectio commodi*. It should be noted however that since the will finds its ultimate perfection and supreme happiness when it functions in accord with the *affectio justitiae* or the *voluntas ut libera*, i.e. when it loves God for his own sake, this too falls under the heading of natural goodness.[22] But what differentiates the will's perfections as nature from the perfection of all other natural agents is that it can never be attained if it be sought primarily or exclusively: only by using its freedom to transcend the demands of its nature, as it were, can the will satisfy completely its natural inclination. We might note here parenthetically that since beatitude is a

[19] *Ord.* II, d. 6, q. 2, n. 9 (XII, 354).
[20] *Ord.* II, d. 7, n. 11 (XII, 386–87) d. 40–41 (XIII, 421–36). See also the parallel texts in the *Rep. par.* and *Quodl.*, q. 18 (XXVI, 228–258).
[21] *Ord.* II, d. 40, n. 2 (XIII, 424).
[22] *Ord.* IV, d. 49, q. 2, n. 24 (XXI, 42–43).

concomitant effect of this union with God in perfect love, there is a very real sense in which Scotus sees the friendship love of God in heaven and supreme human happiness as factually inseparable. One cannot be wanted realistically or honestly in complete isolation from the other. Yet God in himself and God as our good and source of delight are objects of distinct, but essentially ordered, voluntary acts. The first is an act of friendship love (*amor amicitiae*); the latter, an act of desire (*amor or velle concupiscentiae*) which presupposes the first act. The first is elicited in accord with the *affectio justitiae* and no way in accord with the *affectio commodi*. The second though it be in accord with the *affectio commodi*, also involves the *affectio justitiae*. "To want an act to be perfect so that by means of it one may better love some object for its own sake, is something that stems from the affection for justice," writes Scotus. "And so the good could have wanted happiness so that by having it, they could more perfectly love the supreme good."[23]

Moral goodness, however, goes beyond the natural goodness of a voluntary act. It implies that the action is performed in accord with the dictates of right reason. "Even as beauty of body is an harmonious blend of all that becomes a body so far as size, color, figure and so on are concerned," says Scotus, "so the goodness of a moral act is a combination of all that is becoming to it according to right reason."[24] Since the "dictates of right reason" and the "rule of justice" are logically equivalent terms, this is tantamount to saying that while a naturally good act is in accord with the will's *affectio commodi*, a morally good act must be elicited in accord with the *affectio justitiae*. Natural goodness, in this sense, is a necessary, but not sufficient condition, for moral goodness.

What justice or the dictates of right reason demand is spelled out most lucidly in the *Quodibet*, question 18.[25] There it becomes clear that to be morally good, the action must, in the judgment of the agent, have all that right reason says is suitable or should be present. This appropriateness or suitability, he explains, is twofold. The action must be suited to the agent and the act itself must have a suitable object (which determines the generic character—ex genere moris) and be performed under suitable circumstances (i.e. for an appropriate end, in a decent manner, at a becoming time and place). These circumstances, as it were, determine whether an action that is indifferent or only generically good, becomes specifically good, bad or indifferent morally.

---

[23] *Ord.* II, d. 6, q. 2, n. 12 (XII, 356).
[24] *Ord.* II, d. 40, nn. 2–3 (XIII, 424–27). *Ord.* I, d. 17, n. 62 (Vatican ed. V, 163–64).
[25] *Quodl.*, q. 18, nn. 3–8 (XXVI, 230–38).

Moral goodness requires that all these factors be becoming, whereas anything unbecoming on any count can introduce a degree of moral malice.

It is not our intention to spell out in detail what this entails except insofar as this is relevant to the general aim of this paper. Suffice it to say that Scotus insists that for judging this suitability of act to agent or object to act, nothing more is required of natural reason as premises than a knowledge of the nature of the agent and the faculty or faculties involved in the action and the essential character of the act itself.[26]

If one considers the nature of any rational being, the fact that he is endowed with free will as Scotus conceives this, and that there exists but one supreme good, infinitely perfect and the author of man, then it follows that no act is more becoming to such an agent or has a more suitable object than to love God for his own sake. This friendship love of God is the one will act that has all that is required for complete moral goodness by reason of the object alone or by reason of its generic goodness. Such love as it were contains its own good intention. It can never be ill-timed, out of place, or inordinate.[27] Here then, Duns declares, is our first moral principle, our primary ethical norm: "God is to be loved."[28] It precedes and is independent of any decision or determination on the part of God's will. This and its converse, "God must never be hated, dishonored, etc." are twin obligations that God himself could never dispense from.[29] Why? Because his will, precisely by reason of its native liberty or *affectio justitiae*, is "bound," so to speak, to render to the infinitely lovable divine nature what is its due. "His will," writes Scotus, "is determined by his rectitude to will that which is becoming his goodness, and this is, as it were, rendering what is due to himself, that is to say, to his goodness as something other [i.e. as an absolute or objective value and not as something relative or as a good for him]."[30] Put in another way, God is the one, absolute, intrinsic value that cannot be loved to excess. All other objects that could be loved by men or angels, however, are *ex genere* indifferent,

---

[26] *Ibid.*, n. 5, p. 236.

[27] *Ord.* II, d. 6, q. 2, n. 4 (XII, 346); IV, d. 26, n. 3 (XIX, 148); *Rep. par.* IV, d. 28, n. 6 (XXIV, 377–78): "Nullus tamen actus est bonus in genere ex solo objecto, nisi amare Deum, qui amor est objecti per se volibilis et boni infiniti, qui non potest esse moraliter malus, quia nullus potest nimis amare amore amicitiae, et propter se; et solus actus est ex genere malus, qui est oppositus isti actui, respectu ejusdem objecti, ut odisse Deum, qui nulla modo potest circumstantionari, ut sit bonus; ergo omnis alius actus est indifferens, qui est respectum alterius objecti, et potest esse circumstantionabilis bene aut male."

[28] *Ord.* IV, d. 46, q. 1, n. 10 (XX, 426); III, d. 27, n. 2 (XV, 355).

[29] *Ord.* III, d. 37, n. 6 (XV, 826).

[30] *Ord.* IV, d. 46, q. 1, n. 3 (XX, 400).

he argues.[31] That is to say, they are sometimes good, sometimes bad, sometimes indifferent morally, depending on circumstances. If they are commanded by God or other legitimate authority, they are obviously good; if forbidden, they are bad. If neither, they become good, if done for a good intention that relates them in some way to a moral obligation. For example, any action done for love of God is a fulfilment of that first moral principle: "God is to be loved." Similarly, actions done for love of neighbor, or to avoid sinning against the decalog, are related to what God has commanded.

This raises the question of how man can know the will of God as regards generically indifferent actions, which brings us to the second point. How is Scotus' statement to be interpreted: "Everything other than God is good because willed by God and not vice versa"—the premise of Quinton's enthymeme?

Good as Will-Dependent

The context in which this oft-quoted expression occurs is in reference to the merits of Christ and reads in full: "I say that just as everything other than God is good because it is willed by God and not vice versa, so this merit was good to the extent that it was accepted. Therefore it was merit because it was accepted. It was not the other way round, namely because it was merit and good, therefore it was accepted."[32] Though the specific application refers to the supernatural order and is theological, the principle from which it is inferred is undoubtedly metaphysical and philosophical and is open to a number of interpretations, in all of which the notion of God's native freedom figures largely. For if God's will tends to a good in terms of its intrinsic or objective value, then his infinitely perfect will can only be bound, so to speak, by its own infinite goodness.

Even in the case of God's intellect, Scotus argued that it would be derogatory to the perfection of the divine mind to be dependent for its knowledge on the intelligibility of a created object, for any such object is finite, limited, and to that extent, a mixture of perfection and imperfection. Like the poet or sculptor who first creates his masterpiece in his mind before putting it on paper or embodying in marble or bronze, God with his infinitely fertile intellect produces each possible creature as a thought object, thus giving it intelligibility. Hence, for Scotus, it is true to say, God does not know creatures because they are intelligible,

[31] Cf. note 27 *supra*.
[32] *Ord.* III, d. 19, n. 7 (XIV, 718).

but vice versa.[33] Creatures are intelligible because God knows them. In a similar way, he can say, the divine will moves with creative love towards a finite good not because it has any real goodness prior to or independent of the volition of God. It is at best a "possible good," i.e. something God can create by willing it to exist. One sense, therefore, in which this scotist maxim could be understood is of transcendental or ontological goodness.

But this is not all. Whatever God actually wills to create will also have a natural goodness about it. And this, I believe, is also a consequence of the native freedom of his will in a rather interesting way. Like the scholastics generally, Scotus distinguishes between the absolute and orderly will of God, the former being limited only by the principle of non-contradiction as it were. Yet if the *affectio justitiae* is a pure perfection and a constitutive element of the divine will, then the realistic possibilities of creation represents only a proper subset of the set of all purely logical possibilities, namely those that do him justice, we might say. Unlike Aquinas, Duns does not admit a twofold justice in God, one that impels him as it were to do justice to his own goodness and a second which impels him as it were to do justice to his creation. Following Anselm again, he sees only one justice in God, that which he owes to his own nature, but this justice, he insists, also affects his dealings with creatures for it "modifies his creative act," causing him to "give to natures such perfections as are due or becoming to them."[34] Properly speaking however, so far as creatures are concerned this is not so much justice as liberality. "Speaking simply, I say God is a debtor only to his goodness, that he love it; to creatures however he is a debtor out of his liberality, that he communicate to them what their nature demands, which exigency in them is set down as something just, a kind of secondary object of this justice."[35]

It has often been said of a fine artist or master craftsman that he cannot turn out a product badly done. I think this might serve as the model for what Scotus is saying equivalently. For God is obviously the most perfect of artists, a craftsman like no other. He owes it to himself that whatever he choses to create, will have a beauty and natural goodness about it. Yet no particular creation is so perfect, beautiful or good that it exhausts his infinite powers of creativity.[36] The goodness of creation is thus a consequence of the native freedom of his will. Yet no creation or creature is such that its goodness can be regarded, in a Leibnitzian sense, as a sufficient reason for its existence.

[33] *Ord.* I, d. 35, nn. 31–32 (Vat. ed. VI, 258).
[34] *Ord.* IV, d. 46, q. 1, nn. 4, 7–9 (XX, 404, 424–25).
[35] *Ibid.*, n. 12, p. 428.
[36] *Rep. par.* I, d. 43, q. 2 (XXII, 494); see also *Ord.* I, d. 44 (Vat. ed. VI, 363–69).

Neither must all evil or ugliness be absent, particularly that which stems from a creature's misuse of freedom. Like the darker shades and shadows on the canvas, these contribute by contrast to the beauty of the creation as a whole. And since the canvas on which God paints is a living, dynamic nature, these less perfect features are like the weakness of infant limbs or the temporary blindness of the newborn child. Pain, suffering and injustice are in part consequences of sin, but in part they are also the growing pains of a Christocentric universe.[37]

Finally, there is a sense in which moral goodness, like merit, is also will dependent, but with important qualifications. For as noted earlier, "God is to be loved," writes Scotus, "is a practical truth prior to any determination on the part of the divine will."[38] To the extent that the first table of the decalog reduces to this, God himself cannot dispense man from its obligation. Hence the meaning of the maxim here cannot be, these commandments bind only because God wills this. But since moral goodness is formally something inherent in a human act, namely its suitability or conformity to what right reason dictates, its existence as well as its possibility in some degree depends on the fact that God has freely created man not merely with an intellectual, but a free, appetite. But this reduces to the transcendental or ontological dimension of moral goodness, and is not a crucial issue for the critics of Scotus. But the will-dependence of the second table of the decalog is quite a different thing. It does not stem simply from the fact that God has contingently and freely chosen to create the kind of human nature he has. This determines only what will be naturally good or naturally evil. But the will as free cannot be bound automatically by nature as such. It can only be bound by an absolute good, which nature is not, or a higher will that has authority in the last analysis because it has authored man as free. And because the second table of the law is will-dependent, God can and has at times dispensed men from its obligation, says Scotus. This would be impossible if the moral obligation arose simply from nature being what it is. In the case of a dispensation, nature remains but the law and its obligation does not. Against Aquinas and others Scotus argues: "To dispense does not consist in letting the precept stand and permitting one to act against it. To dispense, on the contrary, is to revoke the precept or to declare how it is to be understood."[39] Nevertheless, the second table of the law, unless specifically

---

[37] *Ord.* IV, d. 46, q. 4, n. 19 (XX, 481): "Exemplum: melius fuisset caeco nato, de quo Joannis loquitur, a principio vidisse, non tamen melius in ordine ad manifestationem divinae sapientiae et bonitatis."

[38] *Ord.* IV, d. 46, q. 1, n. 3 (XX, 400): "Deus est diligendus...est veritas practica praecedens omnem determinationem voluntatis divinae."

[39] *Ord.* III, d. 37, n. 3 (XV, 785).

suspended, does oblige man, but it does so because human nature represents an expression of the will of God. And this brings us to our final point, why Quinton's conclusion does not follow.

THE MORAL LAW AS ACCESSIBLE TO REASON

What is often overlooked in the ethics of Scotus, and even more so, in that of William of Ockham, is that the notion that God reveals himself in nature as well as through the Scriptures was something the great scholastics took for granted. After all had not Peter Lombard formulated this basic principle in their theological textbook: "That the truth [about the *invisibilia Dei*] might be made clear to him, man was given two things to help him, a nature that is rational and works fashioned by God."[40] And Hugh of St. Victor, whose influence on the Franciscan school can hardly be overestimated, had even earlier made specific application of this principle to ethics and the will of God. "Was it not like giving a precept to infuse into the heart of man discrimination and an understanding of what he should do? What is such knowledge but a kind of command given to the heart of man? What was knowledge of what should be avoided but a type of prohibition? And what is the knowledge of what lies between the two but a kind of concession, so that it is left up to man's own will where either choice would not harm him? For God to command, then, was to teach man what things were necessary for him, to prohibit was to show what was harmful, to concede was to indicate what was indifferent."[41]

That Scotus accepted this principle is clear from what he says about the law of nature being, in the words of St. Paul, "written interiorly in the heart,"[42] of its precepts being *ex natura rei*,[43] and that "by natural reason man can see that each precept thereof must be observed."[44] It is expressed even more clearly in the *Quodibet* without benefit of metaphor that to infer whether an action is suitable to man as a moral agent and is therefore morally good we need premises that are certain.

---

[40] Peter Lombard, *Libri IV Sententiarum* I, d. 3, c. 1. Ad Claras Aquas, ex typographia Collegii S. Bonaventurae, 1916, I, 30.

[41] *De Sacramentis Christianae Fidei*, I, pars 6, c. 7 (PL 176, col. 268).

[42] *Ord.* I, prol. n. 108 (Vat. ed. I, p. 70). See also *Ord.* II, d. 28, n. 8 (XIII, 262): "Gentiles potuerunt juste vivere servando legem naturae, et tunc ipsi facti sunt sibiipsis lex, id est, per legem naturae scriptam in cordibus eorum interius direxerunt se recte vivendo, sicut Judaei per legem scriptam"; *ibid.* III, d. 37, n. 14 (XV, 851).

[43] *Ord.* II, d. 21, q. 2, n. 2 (XIII, 140).

[44] *Rep. par.* II, d. 22, n. 3 (XXIII, 104): "Man" is taken generally. Scotus did not believe that the precepts of the second table, at least in their finer details, were manifest to all. Cf. *Ord.* IV, d. 26, n. 9 (XIX, 160).

For this the knowledge of three things suffice, viz. the nature of the agent, the nature of the faculty by which he acts, and the essential characteristic *(ratio quidditativa)* of the action itself. And it is quite clear from what he says that he did not believe knowledge of this sort posed any problems.[45]

That is why for Scotus, as well as for Ockham who followed him, the substantive content of the natural law is basically the same as it was for the generality of the scholastics. It is only in their interpretation of why and how it binds that we discover a significant difference. It is a "law" and to that extent "obliges" inasmuch as it represents an expression of God's will in man's regard. But this itself introduces some important and subtle differences.

For one thing God can dispense from certain precepts, notably those of the second table of the decalog.[46] For while the precepts of the latter express what is *valde consonans* for the attainment of man's ultimate end as a spiritual and rational creature, they are not so indispensable that it would be a contradiction that this end be attained without their complete observance under all conditions.[47] Obviously God cannot dispense with the second table in its entirety for this would be equivalent to creating man with one kind of nature and willing him to act in another. But he could in specific instances and for good reasons, namely where the specific values for which the law was instituted can be obtained better in part at least under extraordinary circumstance than if all that is ordinarily prohibited were avoided.[48] This is itself in accord with right reason, as Scotus points out. That God does not act whimsically or arbitrarily in this regard is guaranteed by what we said of his affection for justice. *Quidquid Deus fecit, hoc scias, Deum fecisse recte.*[49]

The law of nature, in his system, loses something of its impersonal and inflexible character. Its personal dimension cannot be ignored. Where other scholastics, following Augustine who in turn was influenced by the Stoics, link it with the *lex aeterna* Scotus eliminates this last vestige of impersonalism.[50] To legislate or command is a function

---

[45] *Quodl.*, q. 18, n. 5 (XXVI, 236).

[46] *Ord.* III, d. 37, nn. 3–5 (XV, 785–826).

[47] Cf. Robert Prentice, *The Contingent Element Governing the Natural Law on the Last Seven Precepts of the Decalogue according to Duns Scotus,* in *Antonianum* 42 (1967), pp. 259–92.

[48] Scotus illustrates this in regard to marriage. Cf. *Ord.* IV, d. 33, qq. 1 & 3 (XIX, 358–64, 384–90).

[49] *Rep. par.* I, d. 44, q. 2 (XXIII, 498). See also *Ord.* IV, d. 4, q. 2, n. 3 (XVI, 390); "Dei perfecta sunt opera."

[50] Cf. G. Stratenwerth, *op. cit.* 5–7.

of will,[51] not of a nature as such, even if it be the most perfect of natures.

There is another important consequence that seems implicit at least in a scotistic approach to ethics. If nature's perfection is not an absolute value that must be placed above all else, then God, for whom a "thousand years are as one day,"[52] is under no constraint to see that it be attained at once. The conception of a nature that achieves its end or perfection only gradually and by an internal mechanism that allows for a trial and error method of progression does not seem foreign to or incompatible with the conception of God that Scotus held. Though he stated the principle of evolutionary development *Deus ordinate agens procedit de imperfecto ad perfectum*[53] in reference to God's supernaturally revealed law, there seems no reason why it cannot be extended to his promulgation of the law of nature as well, viz. to a gradual growth in moral awareness, protracted over a period of centuries or even millenia if you will. *In processu generationis humanae, semper crevit notitia veritatis.*[54]

[51] *Ord.* IV, d. 14, q. 2, n. 5 (XVIII, 52).
[52] 2 Peter 3, 8.
[53] *Ord.* IV, d. 1, q. 3, n. 8 (XVI, 136).
[54] *Ibid.*

8 / Duns Scotus on the Will as Rational Potency

John Duns's description of the will has both intrigued and puzzled philosophers to the present day.[1] *Newsweek* gave him center featuring over Socrates, Augustine, and Heidegger in a photomontage of Hannah Arendt's four philosophical heroes. The occasion was its review of her posthumously published *Life of the Mind*. The reviewer expressed surprise at her excitement over this medieval scholastic "whose originality she finds 'without precedent or sequel in the history of Western thought.' "[2] In the still most extensive study in English done half a century ago, C. R. S. Harris recognized that Scotus' "distinction between will and desire enables him to grapple more adequately with the psychological analysis of ethical problems and lends to his thinking a deeper insight into the facts of moral experience than was displayed by any Christian thinker since the days of Augustine."[3] But while he deplored simplistic categorizations of Scotus' ethical theory as extremely voluntaristic in view of his emphasis on the role of right reason, Harris argued to a "latent contradiction in Scotus' thought" and admitted he could find no "satisfactory solution to the antinomy."[4] Since subsequent sympathetic commentators on Scotus' moral philosophy often failed to see, or at least stress, its inner coherence, I was prompted to call attention to what I saw as the key to its unity—the Anselmian

[1] Work on this study was done when I was a research associate of the UCLA Center for Medieval and Renaissance Studies.
[2] *Newsweek*, March 20, 1978, p. 83.
[3] C. R. S. Harris, *Duns Scotus*, vol. II (Oxford: Clarendon Press, 1927), p. 303.
[4] *Ibid.*, p. 331.

doctrine he developed as to what he calls the "native freedom of the will," its bias or inclination to love things objectively according to their intrinsic value.[5] Yet in the very encyclopedia in which I first presented this view, Scotus' subtle position was dismissed elsewhere with a single sentence: "Things are good because God wills them and not vice versa, so moral truth is not accessible to natural reason."[6] It was to show how Scotus would interpret the premise of this enthymeme and why he could not concede its conclusion that I wrote my paper on the "Native Freedom of the Will as a Key to the Ethics of Scotus."[7]

What I would like to discuss here is Scotus' related paradoxical claim that only the will, not the intellect, is truly and essentially rational. I did not go into his reasoning before, since I thought at the time that "the wax nose of authority" was receiving "a rather violent twisting."[8] Careful study of Scotus' questions on the ninth book of Aristotle's *Metaphysics*, the context in which the above claim occurs, prompts me to revise that assessment, however. For one thing, the claim was not original with Scotus. We find it in Henry of Ghent, whose thought so often provided the springboard for Scotus' own speculations. Furthermore, Henry assumes this to be self-evident in virtue of Aristotle's own definition of rational versus irrational potencies.[9] The merit of Scotus' treatment lies in his systematic and sympathetic analysis, in fifteen questions, of Aristotle's notions of "act and potency" in the opening chapters of the *Metaphysics*, Book IX. Scotus ends with two especially interesting questions.[10] Number 14 challenges what many

---

[5] See Introduction of the present volume.

[6] "British Philosophy," *The Encyclopedia of Philosophy*, ed. Paul Edwards (New York: Macmillan and Free Press, 1967), vol. I, p. 373.

[7] *Deus et Homo ad mentem I. Duns Scoti* (Romae: Societas Internationalis Scotistica, 1972), pp. 359–70; cf. chapter 7, pp. 148–62, above.

[8] See chapter 7 of the present volume. The allusion to the late twelfth-century theologian Alan of Lille, who in stressing the need of rational analysis and a more formalistic methodology also pointed to the basic weakness of a purely authoritarian approach. "An authority has a wax nose, i.e. it can be bent to take on different meanings" (*De fide catholica*, lib. I, c. 30 [*Patrologia Latina* 210, col. 333A]).

[9] Henry of Ghent, *Summa quaestionum ordinariarum*, art. 36, q. 5 (Parisiis, 1520, photoreprint, St. Bonaventure, N.Y.: Franciscan Institute, 1953), fol. 237B: "Voluntas in homine dicitur potentia rationalis quia valet ad opposita." The intellect, by contrast, he calls "potentia naturalis" save insofar as it falls under the command of the will, where "natural" has the special meaning Aristotle assigned to "nonrational potencies" in *Metaphysics* IX, ch. 2, and *On Interpretation*, ch. 13. "Distinguitur potentia naturalis a rationali, quod potentia rationalis dicitur dicitur illa quae de se valet ad opposita: potentia vero naturalis ad unum tantum, ut vult Philosophus in locis praedictis" (*Summa, ibid.*)

[10] *Quaestiones subtilissimae super libros Metaphysicorum Aristotelis*, lib. IX (Vivès ed. VII, 529–617). In lieu of a critical edition of this work, we might note that the

followers of Aristotle considered an axiom—"Whatever is moved is moved by another"—but which many of Scotus' Franciscan predecessors since the time of Bonaventure had rejected on avowedly anti-Aristotelian grounds. Scotus, on the contrary, argues against the dictum from what he considered empirical data, reserving his dialectical skill to attack the cogency of the metaphysical proofs adduced in its favor. More remarkable is his castigation of those whose attachment to the universality of this metaphysical dictum leads them to reject the evidence that we are, as voluntary agents, patently self-movers. He writes:

> What is added about metaphysical principles being most universal is true enough, but none of them suffers exception in a particular instance. For the mark of true statements is the fact that they are illustrated in what is manifest. But how can that be called a principle from which so many absurdities follow? I don't believe Aristotle could have assumed any proposition to be—not a first, no, not even a *tenth* principle, which has in so many particular instances, such obviously absurd consequences. Also, if the following be a first metaphysical principle: "Nothing identical can be both in virtual act and still in potency to the formal perfection of which this virtual act is the effective principle"—if, I say, this be a first metaphysical principle, I know it is not inscribed in Aristotle's *Metaphysics*. If those who hold it have another metaphysics, how is it that they alone have the sort of intellect that can grasp the terms of this "principle," which everyone else is unable to comprehend?[11]

I call attention to this principle—the subject of an excellent analysis by Effler[12]—for two reasons: First, because the metaphysical possibility of self-movement or, more specifically, self-determination, is a logical presupposition for the theoretical view of the will Scotus defends. Second, because the above citation shows Scotus' high regard for and benign attitude toward Aristotle, a favor extended also to Avicenna. "Regarding the mind of these philosophers, Aristotle and Avicenna, I do not wish to attribute to them anything more absurd than they may actually have said or which necessarily follows from what they did say. And from their remarks, I wish to take the most reasonable interpretation I am able to give them."[13] We are reminded of Chenu's ob-

---

manuscript tradition ends with Book IX. The questions on the two additional books (pp. 622–712) in the Wadding-Vivès edition are of dubious authenticity. Hereafter references to this work are cited as QQ. in Meta.

[11] *Ibid.*, q. 14, n. 23, p. 600. Scotus' target here seems to be Godfrey of Fontaines. See J. F. Wippel, "Godfrey of Fontaines and the Act-Potency Axiom," *Journal of the History of Philosophy* 11 (1973), 299–317.

[12] Roy Effler, *John Duns Scotus and the Principle 'Omne quod movetur ab alio movetur'* (St. Bonaventure, N.Y.: Franciscan Institute, 1962).

[13] *Ordinatio* I, d. 8, n. 25 (Vat. ed. I, p. 294).

servation as to the theological technique of interpreting "authorities" (particularly the Fathers of the Church and the Scriptures).[14] Since the great Scholastics, Aquinas, Scotus, and Ockham among them, did not comment on Aristotle's works as bachelors of the arts, but rather after they had completed their commentaries on the *Sentences* as requirements for the Master of Theology, it is not surprising that they carried over the idea of *exponere reverenter* to a man they simply referred to as "the Philosopher." At any rate, Scotus, throughout his *Quaestiones subtilissimae in Metaphysicam Aristotelis*, uses his dialectical skill to interpret Aristotle as supportive of Scotus' own position. And this is particularly the case with question 15, which I should like to analyze in some detail.

The question reads: "Is the difference appropriate that Aristotle assigns between rational and irrational potencies, namely that the former are capable of contrary effects whereas the latter produce but one effect?"[15] And he introduces the question with the following text from the *Metaphysics* IX, chapter 2: "Clearly some potencies will be nonrational but others will be *with reason*; that is why all the arts, i.e., all the productive forms of knowledge, are potencies."[16] Aristotle proceeds to explain the difference in words that occasion the question: "Every potency with reason is capable of causing both contraries, but every nonrational potency can cause only one. For example, heat can cause only heating, but the medical art can cause sickness as well as health."[17]

Following the customary format for a Scholastic question, Scotus begins with six arguments for the opposition, which we may ignore except for his cryptic remark: "Against these is the text of the Philosopher." Scotus introduces the body of the question with the obser-

---

[14] M. D. Chenu, *Towards an Understanding of St. Thomas* (Chicago: Henry Regnery, 1964) in his chapter "The Procedures of Documentation" points out the dialectical rather than historical way in which the *auctoritates*, i.e., the citation from the Scriptures or the Fathers of the Church, were employed in theological argumentation. "The *auctoritates* have to be accepted, particularly in theological argumentation where they supply a traditional and decisive-in-itself support. Yet, these authorities display inadequacies, imprecisions, divergencies. They are, moreover, to be inserted within homogeneous thought constructions having their own systematic requirements. The solution, then, is to 'interpret' them, *exponere*," he says—and to do so "reverently," never outrightly contradicting them, but showing the rationale behind them. "*Exponere reverenter*: one should not entertain any illusions about the pious euphemism herein expressed. What it amounts to is an effective retouching of the text, or a noticeable redressing of it or again a discreet deflecting of its meaning. No medieval thinker, moreover, is duped in the process" (pp. 144–45).

[15] *QQ. in Meta.*, q. 15 (Vivès ed. VII, p. 606).

[16] Aristotle, *Metaphysics* IX, ch. 2, 1046b1–4.

[17] *Ibid.*, 1046b4–7.

vation, "If we are to hold the distinction to be well-made, we have to see first how it is to be understood, and then what is the rationale for it."[18]

THE SENSE OF THE DISTINCTION

In the initial questions on this ninth book of the *Metaphysics*, Scotus has clarified a number of linguistic ambiguities associated with "act" and "potency." Among those relevant to understanding the present question is that between potency as *principle* and potency as a *mode of being*, the former being probably more fundamental.[19] "Principle" here is understood as some sort of cause or originative source, but since for Aristotle "cause" is equivocal, Scotus gives linguistic grounds for limiting that term to efficient and material causes, and excluding the formal and the final. *Passive potency* can be equated roughly with the material cause or "matter" in a broad sense, and *active potency* with some form of efficiency. Even if we limit potency as principle to these two, there is still a further ambiguity in the notion of principle or cause. Sometimes it is taken as the subject as a whole *(principium quod)* or that by which the subject or agent causes *(principium quo)*. In the case at hand, the doctor is the cause of the cure or the patient's health, whereas it is his medical skill whereby he does so. Another point Scotus feels must be made is that Aristotle gives a physical rather than a metaphysical definition of "potency" in its primary sense.[20] "All potencies that conform to the same type are all principles of one sort or another, and are called potencies in reference to one primary kind which is the principle of change in another, or in the thing itself qua other."[21] Yet, Aristotle himself recognized that "potency" defined "in this strict sense is not the most useful for our present purpose. For potency and actuality extend beyond the cases that involve reference to motion."[22] And since in a subsequent chapter Aristotle explains this broader metaphysical sense of actuality and potentiality as referring to the existential or nonexistential status respectively,[23] Scotus, like the Scholastics generally, felt justified in broadening the notion of an active potency or principle beyond that of an agent that imparts motion to include that which gives being or existence as such to its effect. Yet

[18] Scotus, *QQ. in Meta.*, q. 15, p. 607.
[19] *QQ. in Meta.*, qq. 1–2, n. 2, p. 530.
[20] *QQ. in Meta.*, q. 4, nn. 2–8, pp. 543–48.
[21] Aristotle, *Metaphysics* IX, ch. 2, 1046a9–11.
[22] *Ibid.*, 1045b5–1046a4.
[23] *Ibid.*, ch. 6, 1048a30–33, "Actuality is the existence of a thing."

even here, Scotus insists, we are not down to a simple, unequivocal, notion of what "active potency" implies, because several subtly different relationships exist between the principle and what it does or effects.[24] For our purposes, it is enough to note that the rough description of an active potency as "what gives existence to something" has the merit of stressing that cause is cotemporal with its effect, and that the causal action is a continuous creative and sustaining productivity, as opposed to the Humean notion that views causality as a necessary temporal relationship between an antecedent and a subsequent event. Scotus needs this type of relationship if he is to clarify how the will as an active potency can create or elicit an action of volition or nolition, or how it can not only initiate but sustain a voluntary action such as singing or walking. For Aristotle clearly included under the notion of active potency the ability to do as we choose. But since we have mentioned "will" and "choose" in this connection, whereas the example Aristotle gives of a "potency with reason" is the medical art, and heat as an instance of a nonrational potency whose causality is limited to the action of heating, bear with me if I make one more observation. The skills or arts that Aristotle cites as instances of rational potencies were technically known as "habits," not in the sense that *habitus* or "having" is one of his ten categories, but as falling under the first species of the category of "quality." As the saying goes, the first act is the hardest, for its very performance makes the repetition of it easier; repeated actions become "second nature." The first subclass under the accident "quality," then, included *habits* and *dispositions* as its members. Inasmuch as a habit inclined one to act and made the acting easier and smoother in performance, an acquired habit was itself an active potency, for one meaning of this term was "a principle whereby one does something well or as he chooses."[25] Although voluntary actions may generate habits such as skills or virtues or vices, or what Aristotle called "productive forms of knowledge," these are distinct both from the will as an active potency and the act of volition it elicits that generates such habits or enables one to use them to produce opposite or contrary effects such as sickness or health, to use Aristotle's example. Habits as second nature must reside in some first nature as subject; acts of choosing, be they willing or nilling, volitions or nolitions, are in Aristotle's terminology qualitative accidents or a sometime thing. They themselves are transient qualities residing in some substance, and stemming from some cause. Language already distinguishes between the person or individual who acts, the nature of the

---

[24] Scotus, *QQ. in Meta.*, q. 4, n. 7, p. 547.
[25] Aristotle, *Metaphysics*, V, ch. 12, 1019a23.

agent that remotely specifies the sort of acts it can perform, and the specific capacity or potentiality that is actualized. In the case of a voluntary action, it is the person that is the *principium quod*; in the case of man or the angel, their human nature is regarded as the remote *principium quo* and the will as the proximate *principium quo* or faculty whereby the person acts, according to the technical language of the Scholastics. While one can consider these legitimate conceptual distinctions that enabled the bachelor opponents and respondents to perform creditably in the verbal duel that preceded the magisterial determination in the Scholastic debates that enlivened university life, there was great divergence of opinion as to what sort of ontological distinctions they were based upon. For Aquinas and others who appealed to the axiom that potency and act divide being and every category of being, the potencies or faculties of the soul or of any created nature had to be accidents of sorts, and hence really distinct from the substance of the soul, for the actualizations of these potencies (e.g., intellect or will) were themselves accidental forms (e.g., information or volition). In God alone were actual knowledge, intellect, and nature one in substance and only conceptually distinguishable.[26] Furthermore, in man at least, intellect and will were regarded as passive rather than active potencies.[27] Against this view, the Franciscan masters generally, influenced in part by Saint Augustine, down to Scotus' time stressed the real identity of the soul and its powers as well as the predominantly active character of these potencies.[28] Moreover, when Scotus calls powers "diverse perfections contained unitively in the same thing . . . but not in any real sense distinct,"[29] he is also summing up a long-standing Franciscan tradition that tried to mediate between an extremely re-

[26] Aquinas, *Sum. theol.* I, q. 77, art. 1 and art. 4.

[27] Cf. Odon Lottin, *Psychologie et morale aux XIIe et XIIIe siècles*, vol. I (Louvain/ Gembloux: Abbaye du Mont Cesar/J. Duculot, 1942), pp. 226–52, on the development of Aquinas' thought and the early Franciscan reactions to it.

[28] Cf. Ernst Stadter, *Psychologie und Metaphysik der menschilchen Freiheit: Die ideengeschichtliche Entwicklung zwischen Bonaventura und Duns Scotus* (München/ Paderborn/Wien: Verlag Ferdinand Schöningh, 1971). As for the intellect, Scotus adopts an intermediate position in *QQ. in Meta.*, q. 14, n. 13, p. 592: "Both knower and object are active in producing cognition . . . Thus we avoid the incongruities associated with the assumption that the intellect is wholly passive, or that it is wholly active, so that the object would do nothing."

[29] *QQ. in Meta.*, q. 5, n. 5, pp. 556–57: "Si autem per potentiam animae intelligatur illa perfectio, quae praecedit naturaliter actum sicut ratio elicitiva actus, sive receptiva motionis obiecti illa praecise dicit absolutum. Et tunc tenendo, quod potentia sint idem cum essentia, vel different praecise, sicut diversae rationes perfectionales in eodem unitive contentae . . . vel nullo modo realiter differunt sed tantum intentione vel ratione. Sed nec talis differentia cum sit completive in intellectu, et non in re, nisi in potentia, praecedat naturaliter differentiam actuum."

alistic and a purely conceptual analysis of the soul's structure. And when he speaks of its potentialities as something "absolute," he is countering Henry of Ghent's attempt to deal with them as purely relational aspects.[30] Active potencies, to be sure, have a relational aspect, which is real, but only when they are actually functioning or producing some effect, either in the agent itself (where the action is immanent as with volition) or in materials on which they are working (where the action is transient as with artifacts).[31] But Scotus regards the causal power as some positive entity or quasi form; something present in the soul, even when it is not actually functioning as such, and which is the originative source of that action. As such it has a nonrelational (i.e., absolute) aspect, in the sense that one can distinguish, formally at least, the term or foundation of a relationship from the relationship itself, inasmuch as the one is a necessary, but not sufficient condition for the other.[32] So much then for preliminary clarification of terms. Let us turn to what Scotus says of the rational-nonrational distinction itself.

If we look to the context of the *Metaphysics* in which this distinction of rational and nonrational powers occurs, we see it is concerned primarily with active rather than passive potencies.[33] This notion runs through the whole realm of nature whether it be causal activity characteristic of inanimate nature or of living things composed of body and soul. Moreover, there are various types of souls depending on whether the living thing is plant, animal, or endowed with reason. As the various medieval commentaries on this text of Aristotle point out, the potencies of bodies are nonrational. Also, because there are several sorts of souls, the potencies other than those of the rational soul are to be lumped together with the inanimate so far as their acting or being acted upon is concerned. For they act by an impulse of nature or in-

[30] Henry of Ghent, *Quodlibeta* (Paris, 1518; photoreprint, Louvain, Bibliothèque S. J., 1961), III, q. 14, fol. 66–71. Scotus, *QQ. in Meta.*, n. 2, p. 553–54. "Absolute" was not restricted to substance, but also included the two accidental categories of "quantity" and "quality," according to the Scholastics.

[31] Scotus deals with this question generally in *QQ. in Meta.*, q. 5, but brings the matter up again in q. 15 in clarifying the meaning of the distinction. Cf. n. 2, p. 607–8: "Et vocatur potentia activa non ipsa relatio quae numeratur secundum numerum correlativorum, sed natura absoluta, quae est relationum plurium, quae sunt ad oppositos effectus proprium fundamentum."

[32] The problem here is not unrelated to that which contemporary philosophers of science dealt with under the heading of "counterfactuals," at least where the active potencies were nonrational.

[33] See for instance Aquinas, *In duodecim libros Metaphysicorum Aristotelis IX, expositio IX*, lect. 2 (Taurini/Romae: Marietti, 1950), pp. 428–29; or Antonius Andreas, *Expositio in duodecim libros Metaphysicorum Aristotelis* (attributed to Scotus in the Vivès ed. VI, pp. 314–18).

stinct. Only the rational soul or rational portion of the soul has dominion over its acts, and this is the respect in which it differs from nonliving things or nonrational forms of life.[34] They go on to expand the examples of rational potencies to include not only the practical arts like those of the tanner or silver, gold, or coppersmith, but also to the practical moral sciences, such as prudence, where the activity does not extend to operations performed upon matter but upon one's own behavior.

With these distinctions and examples in mind, Scotus explains how "active potency," as an umbrella term for both natural and rational principles of acting, is to be understood. "Keep in mind that any sort of active potency, whether it results in an action or an artistic product, is so related to that result that so long as it remains the same in nature, it cannot be active in any other way than it is able to be of itself."[35] This formulation is meant to exclude diverse effects possibly resulting from the intervention of external factors. Heat may produce cold as in a gas operated refrigerator. The sun dried adobe bricks as naturally as it melted ice, not because it had any intrinsic ability to function differently in itself, but because of the different materials upon which it acts and which cooperate actively in their own peculiar fashion. Applying this general notion specifically to a potency with reason, we have this description:

> An active potency is said to be a cause of opposites, be they contrary or contradictory results, if—while remaining one in nature—its action first ends with something under which both opposites fall with equal measure.[36]

Aristotle had explained that, unlike a natural form, be it substantial or accidental, a "form" in the mind (a *ratio* or *logos*)

> explains both a thing and its privation, though not in the same way. For the conception applies to one essentially, but to the other in a kind of accidental way, because it explains the contrary by negation and removal.[37]

---

[34] Aquinas, *In duodecin Metaphysicorum Aristotelis* IX, lect. 2, nn. 1786–87, p. 428: "Principia agendi quae sunt in anima, manifeste differunt ab his quae sunt in rebus inanimatis. Et iterum animae plures sunt: quarum multae non multum differunt in agendo et patiendo a rebus inanimatis, quae instinctu naturae operantur. Nam partes animae nutritivae et sensitivae, impulsu naturae operantur. Sola autem pars animae rationalis est domina sui actus: in quo differunt a rebus inanimatis."

[35] *QQ. in Meta.*, q. 15, n. 2, p. 607.

[36] *Ibid.*

[37] Aristole, *Metaphysics*, IX, ch. 2, 1046b4–13.

One objection to the adequacy of Aristotle's description of a rational potency runs as follows: to choose contraries, it is not enough to know the alternative as a privation of the other; for each contrary has a positive nature of its own, and to make a rational choice, something more than this imperfect form of knowledge is required.

THE BASIS OR RATIONALE FOR THE DISTINCTION

One common explanation for the distinction is the difference between a natural form and the idea of a thing formed by the mind. "Form" according to Aristotle is not only the source of a thing's actuality, but determines the specific nature and what potentialities it has for acting or being acted upon. When we know a thing, we are "informed" about it, that is to say, we know the specific nature of a thing by reason of the conceptual likeness, the "species" or "form" of it in our intellect. Contrary forms, by definition, are such that no two such forms can coexist in the same subject. If a natural agent's activity stems from its form, it will act in accord with that form; the product will thereby be limited to something resembling its cause; and it will be incapable of itself producing contrary effects. The intellectual mind, by contrast, is able to conceive of many things. In principle, it is capable of knowing anything that is or can exist. And Aristotle called this information or rational account *logos*, which was translated *ratio*, which is rendered in English sometimes as "reason," other times as "notion," "essential definition," etc. Scientific knowledge, particularly practical rational knowledge, of anything would include not only an idea or conception of a thing, but how it behaves, how to make it, etc. Aristotle frequently made a point that the same science that treats of any particular subject also includes the knowledge of what is not that particular thing. If one recognizes when it is present, one also knows when it is absent. Thus, the same intellectual or intentional form is a principle for both knowing a thing and its privation. The same medical art enables the doctor to recognize both health and sickness. And, while wholesome food has but one natural effect, health, and unwholesome or poisonous edibles produce only sickness, the medical practitioner can cause either health or sickness, in virtue of the selfsame knowledge or medical art.

Many objections had been raised in the course of time to this explanation and echoes of them appear in the present question, probably voiced by the various student opponents and respondents, if this question was conducted, as it seems to have been, as a Scholastic exercise in the local Franciscan convent, with Scotus playing the role of regent master.

One was the hoary chestnut about the sun, whose natural form permitted it a wide range of disparate activities. Another was the point mentioned earlier that privative or negative knowledge of alternatives is not enough for one to produce opposite effects in any rational fashion. More serious, however, was the objection that if the whole rationale for this distinction lay in the difference between a form in nature and a form in the mind, then the intellect or its practical science represented the only active potency that "acts with reason," and thus the will would be excluded from faculties that are rational.

What lent this objection some measure of plausibility was the way in which Aristotle introduces desire or choice as the determining factor as to which of the opposite effects would be actually produced. Admittedly nothing results if the intellect or its knowledge alone is involved. As Aristotle expressed it in the *Ethics*, "The origin of action is choice ... Intellect in itself moves nothing!"[38] But he speaks of this as "something other than" the potency of opposites itself and that when a rational potency is determined by choice or desire it acts necessarily in one way just as an irrational potency does.[39] Thus the will does not seem to figure in as an integral component of the potency as a "principle for opposite effects." This exclusion of the will from active potencies that act "with reason" is not only counterintuitive but, as Henry of Ghent had already noted, it is at odds with the fact that the real potentiality for opposites lies in the contingency or liberty of the will. Hence Scotus presents his own interpretation of the rationale behind the distinction and shows how it can be reconciled with the statements of Aristotle.

THE SCOTISTIC DISTINCTION OF NATURE AND WILL

As Scotus views it, the basic distinction Aristotle wishes to make is between nature and art, between agents that function in a fixed, determinate, and necessary fashion, and intelligent man as a free creative artist. And if this be so, we are back to Scotus' earlier distinction between nature with its drives and appetites on the one hand and that which frees us to seek other values revealed by reason, and where the practical knowledge is a moral science, such as prudence, to be free to follow the dictates of right reason rather than the self-oriented demands of nature. In short, we are back to nature and will as the real rationale

[38] *Nicomachean Ethics* VI, ch. 2, 1039a32–36.
[39] Scotus, *QQ. in Meta.*, q. 15, n. 3, p. 608.

of this distinction of active potencies. But how does he argue for this? We must look, not primarily to the end product (whether it was an inevitable single effect or something deliberately intended that could have been otherwise), but rather to how the action began, how it issued from the "potentiality" as a source or causal principle. Thus, Scotus writes,

> You must keep in mind that the first distinction of active potencies is based on the diverse ways of eliciting their operation. The fact that they act on this or that—if it does in some sense distinguish them or reveal the distinction—is not so basic or immediate. For a potency is related to the object upon which it acts only by means of the operation it elicits and this it does either thus or so. But this manner of eliciting its proper operation can only be twofold generically. For either the potency is of itself determined to act so that so far as itself is concerned it cannot fail to act when not impeded from without; or it is not of itself determined, but can act by this act or its opposite, or even act or not act. The first potency is commonly called "nature," the second is called "will." Hence the primary division of active principles is into nature and will.[40]

That Aristotle was aware of this basic distinction between *per se* efficient causes is clear from *Physics* II where he uses only these to explain accidental causality—chance events being traced back to a coincidence of natural causes; and fortune, whether good or bad, to the unexpected and unintentional results of some voluntary action. But before explaining why Aristotle only hints of this distinction here, Scotus cites some objections to its basic character.

Since there is always a tendency to ask further questions, Scotus reminds us that we cannot ask reasons *ad infinitum*. And when we reach the distinction of will and nature we are back to primitive, irreducible notions. We can give no further reason save that it is the sort of cause that it is. Just as heat heats because it is heat, so will wills because it is will. The former does so necessarily, whereas the will acts contingently.

What evidence have we for this, asks Scotus? We have our immediate experience to fall back upon. "One who wills experiences that he could have not willed or nilled."[41] Elsewhere, he reminds us that "Some being is contingent" is a primary truth. As such it cannot be demonstrated by a demonstration of the reasoned fact, but only shown *a posteriori*. Nor is there need to demonstrate it. According to the Philosopher, "those who deny such manifest things require either senses or pun-

---

[40] *Ibid.*, n. 4, pp. 608–9.
[41] *Ibid.*, n. 5, pp. 609–10.

ishment,"⁴² or as Avicenna puts it, "Those who deny a first principle are to be flogged or exposed to fire until they concede that it is not the same to be burned or not to be burned, to be flogged or not to be flogged. So those who deny that something is contingent should be exposed to torment until they concede it is possible for them not to be tormented."⁴³

Scotus reminds us that contingent truths cannot be deduced from a set of necessary truths, and if there is some reason why the will wills A, for example, because it willed B, we cannot find necessary reasons for such truths. He does not expressly introduce his theory of intuitive knowledge at this point, though this would seem to be involved, since our certain assent to such primary contingent propositions appears ultimately to be based on some simple or nonpropositional awareness of the existential situation.⁴⁴

---

⁴² Aristotle, *Topics* I, ch. 11, 105a5–7.

⁴³ *Ordinatio* I, 38 and 39, n. [13] (Vat. ed. VI, 414).

⁴⁴ Ockham would surely say this. See for instance his *Ordinatio* I, prologue, q. 1 in *Opera theologica* I (St. Bonaventure, N.Y.: Instituti Franciscani Universitatis S. Bonaventurae, 1967), pp. 44–47. He attributes the same view to Scotus, quoting at length from the latter's *Ordinatio* IV, d. 45, q. 3, nn. 17–18 (Vivès ed. XX, 348–49). Scotus is arguing there that we remember our past acts of sense perception, because at the time they occurred our intellect was intuitively aware not only of the act but of what it was about. Proof of this, he says, is that "one knows contingently true propositions and from them infers things syllogistically. But to form propositions and to syllogize is something proper to the intellect. Now the truth about these concerns objects as intuitively known, namely under the aspect of their existence, under which they are known by sense." Scotus' doctrine of intuition, though it seems to have been the inspiration of Ockham's, differs from the latter's in several respects. Confer Ockham, *Ordinatio* I, prologue, q. 1, *Opera theol.* I, pp. 30–47; and *Ordinatio* I, d. 3, q. 6; *Opera theol.* II (1970), pp. 483–523. For Scotus the proximate object of recall, however, is the act—something known with the certainty equivalent to a *per se nota* proposition—and the sense perceptual object is the remote object, about the nature of which we may indeed be deceived, though not about the fact that we thought it to be the sort of thing it appeared to be. And under this proximate object fall also acts of intellection and volition, and the fact that we are responsible for our voluntary actions. Scotus continues: "Briefly then there can be a recalling of any object whose sense memory can be recalled, because that act which is the proximate object can be intuitively known when it exists and thus can be recalled afterwards. Also there can be a recalling of many proximate objects of which no recall by the sensitive memory is possible, such as that of past intellections and volitions. That man can recall such is proved because otherwise he could not repent of his bad volitions, nor could he also compare his past intellections as past with the future; and consequently neither could he, on the basis of what he had observed, arrange to consider other things that followed therefrom. In short, we could be destroyed in a multiplicity of ways if we did not recall past intellections and volitions. But no sense perception of them could be recalled because they do not fall under any sense." We can also recall past speculations about mathematical truths, where both the proximate and remote objects transcend sense perception. Intuitive knowledge or awareness of the existence of such acts and objects is an act of simple apprehension or intellection, of course, and is to be distinguished from the act of judging expressed in terms of affirmative and

One consequence of this being a primitive truth, however, is that it is futile to look for examples of the will's activity among natural causes. Scotus assures us, "No appropriate example could be given, because the will is an active principle distinct from the entire class of active principles that are not will in virtue of their opposite ways of acting. It seems stupid, then, to apply general principles about active principles to the will, since there are no instances of how it behaves in anything other than the will."[45]

But if the will is an active potency, undetermined of its nature, what reduces it from potency to act? This question was particularly pressing because of Bishop Stephen Tempier's condemnation at Paris in 1277 of some propositions that presumably stemmed from Aristotelian principles and were subsequently opposed by Franciscans.[46] Replying to the question, Scotus develops what we might call a positive, rather than a negative, notion of indeterminacy. One form of indeterminacy is insufficiency, which stems from passive potentiality and a lack of actuality, the sort of indeterminacy characteristic of matter that lacks form, whose potentiality needs to be actuated from without. But there is an "indeterminacy of superabundant sufficiency" arising from unlimited actuality such as that which characterizes God's relationship to possible created things. He has no need to be actuated from without; he himself determines what he shall produce.[47] Here we have "creativity" in its fullest form, and in God's will we have the ultimate basis of contingency in the world.[48] Elsewhere Scotus explains in what sense the ability to act freely and contingently is a pure perfection,[49] but here too he stresses that freedom for opposites is itself a measure of unlimitedness that mirrors in some fashion (quodammodo) what God possesses purely and simply (simpliciter). Even some material things, like fire, seem to have an inner source of energy—though, as he said above, there is no adequate analogy from the realm of nature. "But the indetermination here postulated of the will is not rooted in what is

---

negative propositions. This is the complex act of "composition or division." In the case of contingent propositions, as distinct from necessary ones, the knowledge of the terms in themselves does not justify either a positive or negative assertion. What Scotus and Ockham are maintaining is that the evidential basis in experience for such contingent assertions is the simple intuition of the existential situation of which we are conscious or aware.

[45] QQ. in Meta., q. 15, n. 8, p. 612.

[46] E. Stadter, Psychologie und Metaphysik der menschlichen Freiheit, p. 24, gives some of the specific propositions on the will from the condemnations of 1277 that may have been targets for the anti-Aristotelian or neo-Augustinian opposition of the Franciscan masters whose writings may have directly or indirectly influenced Scotus.

[47] QQ. in Meta., n. 5, p. 610.

[48] Ordinatio I, d. 2, nn. 79–88 (Vat. ed. II, 176–80).

[49] Ordinatio I, d. 38 and 39, n. [15] (Vat. ed. VI, 417).

material and imperfect, insofar as it is active, but rather in an excellence of perfection and a dominion (*potestas*) that is not tied down to a specific act."[50]

Though Scotus does not pursue the point, there is a striking analogy between the way in which the creativity of the will resembles our conception of God's creativity. If we can speak of the time continuum as being strung out as a horizontal line, God's and the will's causal action is vertically oriented. Both are non-Humean conserving types of causality: the creative action becomes identified really with the continued existence of the creature; the contingent causality of the will becomes identified concretely, where external actions are concerned, with the act of walking, talking, etc.; and even where the volition or nolition consists in "making up one's mind" or coming to a decision, the action is always "about something." Had Scotus pursued the question explicitly of how far an intuitive awareness—that we are the source of the action that gets verbally expressed in a descriptive contingent proposition—goes, perhaps he would have spelled out this peculiar nature of voluntary actions. But in one place in the present question he does make it clear that we are not first conscious of determining the will in the abstract. "I say it [the will] can [be] in act with no determination being understood before the act occurs so that the first determination, be it first in time or by a priority of nature, is in the placing of the act. And if one wants to say that the will is incapable of doing anything unless it is first determined, this is false."[51] The remark is in answer to an objection that the will behaves just like Aristotle's description of the intellect as a potency for opposites. It cannot do both things at once. Therefore, it does not seem to be able to do either without first being determined to one of the alternatives. And if it is so determined, then it no longer has the power over the alternative, but acts just as necessarily as something determined by nature to one mode of action. The objection occurs in a more subtle form in his discussion of Aristotle's principle of hypothetical necessity in *De interpretatione*, chapter 9—"Omne quod est quando est necesse est esse"—and Boethius' commentary on the same. The fact that '*p* implies *p*' is a necessary proposition does not mean that '*p*' is a necessary proposition. Where the fact that *p* is the result of a free or voluntary action, then at a deeper level than that of existence, there is still the potentiality for the opposite, so far as the nature of the will itself is concerned. And it is the nature of the *will*, not the act of nolition or volition, that is being designated as the active potency for

---

[50] *QQ. in Meta.*, q. 15, n. 5, p. 610.
[51] *Ibid.*, n. 13, p. 616.

opposites. If this potentiality for opposites were not always retained, even while the will is exercising one option, nothing would be truly contingent. As Scotus words it,

> If [the will] had no power over the opposite in that very instant and at that time when it is actually determined to something, then no effect that is being actualized would be contingent; but the consequent is false; therefore the antecedent is also false ... And the proof of the implication is that an effect is not said to be contingent or in potency except by reason of a cause that has power over the opposite; therefore neither is an effect contingent in act unless it is being caused by a cause that could be doing the opposite for that very now that it is causing its alternative."[52]

As Stadter pointed out in his interesting historical study of the notion of the will in the "middle Franciscan school" during the last quarter of the thirteenth century, Scotus' teaching about the will owes much to his predecessors. But while most of them regarded their views as anti-Aristotelian or neoAugustinian, Scotus—especially in this question on the *Metaphysics*—advances his as an authentic interpretation of the Philosopher himself. And this brings us to the final point.

The Will as the Only Truly Rational Potency

Why does Aristotle distinguish between nonrational and rational potencies rather than between nature and will? And why does he concentrate on the role of the intellect, or rather its practical knowledge, as an instance of a rational potency rather than the will? Scotus' complete answer is somewhat involved, partly because of the dialectical manner in which he develops this question. The first and most basic thing to realize is that Aristotle is not really talking about the essential nature of intellect or will as potencies, be they active or passive, but rather about the quasi-accidental relationship they exercise over man's subordinate powers under their control.[53] In this connection, he says much more about the intellect as a rational power than he does about the will, because the acts of intellect are better known, more common, and presupposed either as a sine qua non cause or precondition for the will's action. And Aristotle frequently begins his discussion with the more manifest, if less metaphysical analysis (as he did, for example, in defining active potency in physical rather than metaphysical

[52] *Ibid.*, n. 12, p. 615.
[53] *Ibid.*, n. 6, p. 610.

terms).[54] Thus, paradoxically, if by "rational" Aristotle means an active potency that acts "with reason" and whose power extends in the fullest sense to opposites, only the will is formally rational and free to create accordingly, whereas the intellect is essentially no different from other natural causes. Until choice enters in, man's practical knowledge represents only an incomplete rational potency.

To explain, Scotus says that intellect and will can be compared (i) either to the proper acts they elicit, or (ii) to the subordinate powers over which they exercise some causal control, the intellect by directing or showing what needs to be done and the will by inclining and commanding. So far as the first and obviously more essential is concerned, the intellect falls, strangely enough, under the general heading of nature and has no power to act in contrary ways. For when presented with an intelligible object it has no choice at this basic level but to grasp or understand it. Even where more complex or propositional knowledge is involved it is not free to affirm or deny in the face of contrary evidence. Thus, the intellect is as determined and necessitated in its action as is any natural form that is limited to one mode of action. The will on the other hand does have the capacity, when all conditions for acting are present, either to act or deliberately refuse to act. But Aristotle is not talking about this basic or essential operation (i). Certainly, he is not concerned with the essential operation of the intellect, because he considers it to be a passive potency that receives its information, and not an active potency of any sort, much less one concerned with opposites.[55] But neither is he talking about the will as potency, active or passive. For while much that he says allows one to infer something about the nature of the rational appetite and the originative source of *prohaeresis* or election, he never speaks of the will as a potency in so many words.[56] What Aristotle is concerned with is rather the way in which intellect and choice function in producing works of art or in rational (as opposed to instinctive or impulsive) behavior. If we restrict "rational potency" to the intellect or its practical knowledge, and eliminate the selective role of the will, nothing can happen, neither rational behavior nor works of art. Consequently, the intellect is not even a completely rational potency in regard to (ii) the extrinsic actions it directs. It is only rational in a restricted or qualified sense, namely that it is a prerequisite for the act of a rational power, which requires the further determination of the will. And this "collaboration" is not just an accidental combination, as some have tried to explain

[54] *Ibid.*, n. 11, p. 614; see also *supra* n. 28.
[55] *Ibid.*, n. 6, p. 610.
[56] *Ibid.*, n. 7, p. 611.

it. Rather the will, whose own act is not determined in any way, freely elicits an act and through it determines the intellect in its causal action as regards external behavior. Hence Aristotle admits that choice must enter in as an essential ingredient. That is why, Scotus concludes, if we take seriously what Aristotle says about nonrational potencies (*irrationales potentiae*) and potencies that act with reason (*cum ratione*)—namely "that every potency with reason is capable of causing both contraries, but every nonrational potency can cause only one"[57]— then "the will is properly rational, and has to do with opposites, both as to its own act as well as the acts of subordinate powers, and it does not act towards these after the manner of nature, like the intellect but does so freely, and is able to determine itself, and therefore it is a potency, because it is able to do something, for it can determine itself."[58] But the intellect, he goes on to say, properly speaking, is not a potency with regard to external things: for if it is concerned with opposites, of itself it cannot determine others; and unless it be determined, nothing outside can come about.[59]

[57] Aristotle, *Metaphysics* IX, ch. 2, 1046b4–6.
[58] Scotus, *QQ. in Meta.*, q. 15, n. 7, p. 611.
[59] *Ibid.*

9 / Duns Scotus on the Will and Morality

General Remarks

To show the inner coherence of Scotus' ethical theory and how he uses right reason to develop specific ethical conclusions, it seems well to begin with a brief account of the following presuppositions that underlie Scotus' ethical system. The first is his metaphysical notion of God; the second, his conviction that God must have free will and how it is to be understood; the third, how God's love for his infinitely perfect nature is both voluntary and steadfast, and hence is, in a special sense, necessary; the fourth, how this dual aspect of his will affects his relationship to creatures, with whom he always deals according to right reason and in some ordained and methodical way; and the last, in what sense God could be said to have revealed his will naturally to creatures, particularly in regard to the moral law. Once all this is properly understood, I think two points become very clear. First, Scotus had every reason to think moral truth was accessible to man's natural mental powers; second, his ethical philosophy as a whole is remarkably coherent.

Originally appeared in *Duns Scotus on the Will and Morality*, 1986. Reprinted in abbreviated form, with the permission of The Catholic University of America Press.

Scotus' Metaphysical Notion of God

Though an *ex professo* theologian, Scotus—like the generality of his university colleagues in the tradition of Anselm's *Faith Seeking Understanding*—made wise use of philosophy, which in his day included all knowledge acquired by natural reason. And living in an age that intellectually at least was pluralistic, embracing not only Jewish philosophers like Maimonides and Alfarabi but Moslem Aristotelians like Avicenna and Averroës, Scotus was concerned to separate out the rational component of his beliefs from those "that are the subject of belief, wherein reason is held captive—yet to Catholics, are the more certain since they rest firmly upon [revealed] truth and not upon our intellect which is blind and weak in many things.'"[1] Hence his attitude toward what reason could prove:

> If there are some necessary reasons for what we believe, it is not dangerous to set them forth, neither for the sake of believers nor for the sake of unbelievers. Not for believers, for Catholic doctors, inquiring into the truth of their beliefs and trying to understand them, did not intend thereby to destroy the merit of faith. Indeed Augustine and Anselm believed they labored meritoriously in trying to understand what they believed, according to that text from Isaiah 7:[9] (in the other [i.e., Septuagint] translation): "Unless you believe, you will not understand"; for as believers they inquired, that they might understand the reasons for what they believed... Neither is it dangerous so far as unbelievers are concerned. If one could find necessary reasons to prove the possibility of some fact, it would also be useful to confront unbelievers with such, because by so doing one might to some extent persuade them not to resist such beliefs as impossibilities. On the other hand, it could be dangerous to present such unbelievers with sophisms as demonstrations because by so doing one could expose the faith to derision (and this is also true of all other matters, also those which are [theologically] indifferent, such as geometry). Rather than proposing fallacious arguments in place of demonstrations, it is better for one who lacks knowledge to recognize that he is ignorant than to think he knows on the basis of such sophisms.[2]

Hence the theologians need for critical analysis rather than a fundamentalistic naivete or pietistic attitude. If you say, otherwise, that God gives such knowledge to whom he wills, then it would follow that we labor in vain in our study and inquiry into the truth. A far better and

---

[1] Wolter, *A Treatise on God as First Principle: A Latin Text and English Translation of the De Primo Principio*, 2d ed., revised with a commentary (Chicago: Franciscan Herald Press, 1983), p. 146.

[2] *Ord.* II, d. 1, nn. 138–39; Vatican ed., VII, pp. 69–70.

easier way of coming to theology would be to sit in church and ask God to give us this light.[3]

Because theology has God as its subject, Scotus was most interested in what philosophy could offer in the way of rational knowledge of God's existence and nature. John Duns felt that metaphysics, as the first and highest of the theoretical sciences outlined by Aristotle, had the most to contribute to his enterprise. Aristotelians like Avicenna and Averroës, however, had been at odds as to its subject and its goal. William of Alnwick, Scotus' secretary, gave the following edited account of John's own words as to why he sided with the former:

We must first see whether metaphysics, the first and highest of the naturally acquired habits [of knowledge or science] perfecting man's intellect in the present life, has God as its first object. On this point there is a controversy between Avicenna and Averroës. Avicenna claims that God is not the subject of metaphysics, because no science proves [the existence of] its own subject. The metaphysician, however, proves that God exists. Averroës reproves Avicenna in his final comment on the *Physics*, Book I, because he wished, by using the same major premiss against Avicenna, to prove that God and the pure spirits are the subject of metaphysics, and that God's existence is not proved in metaphysics, since it is only by means of motion, which pertains to the science of natural philosophy [or physics], that any kind of pure spirit can be proved to exist—It seems to me, however, that of the two, Avicenna has spoken better. Wherefore, I argue against Averroes as follows...If the philosopher of nature can prove that God exists, then God's existence is a conclusion of natural philosophy. Now if metaphysics cannot prove the existence of God in this way, then God's existence is presupposed as a principle of metaphysics. Consequently, a conclusion of natural philosophy is a principle of metaphysics, and therefore the philosophy of nature is prior to metaphysics...Now it is not just such properties of the effect as are treated in the philosophy of nature that are possible only on condition that God exists, for the same is true of the properties treated in metaphysics. Not only does motion presuppose a mover, but a being that is posterior presupposes one that is prior. Consequently, from the priority that exists among beings, the existence of the First Being can be inferred, and this can be done in a more perfect way than the existence of a Prime Mover can be established in natural philosophy. We can infer, then, in metaphysics from act and potency, finiteness and infinity, multitude and unity, and many other such metaphysical properties that God or the First Being exists...Hence I concede with Avicenna that God is not the subject of metaphysics. The Philosopher's statement (*Metaphysics*, Book I) that metaphysics is concerned with the highest causes, presents no difficulty.

[3] "Si dicas, quod non dat sic, sed cui vult (sc. Deus etc.), sequeretur quod laboraremus frustra in studio et inquirendo veritatem et esset multo melior via et levior veniendi ad scientiam theologiae sedere in ecclesia et rogare Deum, ut daret nobis illud lumen" (*Ord.* III, suppl. d. 24; Codex A, f. 167ra.).

For he speaks here as he did in the *Prior Analytics*, Book I, where he says: "First it is necessary to determine with what [Prior Analytics] is concerned and what it has to do. It is concerned with demonstration and has to do with the demonstrative branch of learning, that is with the general science of demonstrating or syllogizing." Hence "concerned with" denotes properly the circumstance of the final cause just as much as it does that of material cause. Wherefore, metaphysics is concerned with the highest causes as its end. In knowing them, metaphysical science attains its goal.[4]

Though he developed his metaphysical proof with slight variations in all his commentaries on the *Sentences*, its final form appears in what was to become a philosophical classic, his *Tractatus de Primo Principio*. Fittingly—since metaphysics has "being" as its subject— Scotus opens with a prayer to the God who revealed himself to Moses as "the I am who am." "Help me then, O Lord," he prays, "as I investigate how much our natural reason can learn about that true being which you are if we begin with the 'being' which you predicated of yourself." And in the closing pages he sums up what he thinks metaphysics can offer a believing Catholic:

O Lord, our God, Catholics can infer most of the perfections which philosophers knew of you from what has been said. You are the first efficient cause, the ultimate end, supreme in perfection, transcending all things. You are uncaused in any way and therefore incapable of becoming or perishing; indeed it is simply impossible that you should not exist, for of yourself you are necessary being. You are therefore eternal, because the span of your existence is without limit and you experience it all at once, for it cannot be strung out in a succession of events. For there can be no succession save in what is continually caused, or at least in what is dependent for its existence upon another, and this dependence is a far cry from what has necessary being of itself. You live a most noble life, because you are understanding and volition. You are happy, indeed you are by nature happiness itself, because you are in possession of yourself. You are the clear vision of yourself and the most joyful love, and although you are self-sufficient and happy in yourself alone, you still understand in a single act everything that can be known. At one and the same time you possess the power to freely and contingently will each thing that can be caused and by willing it through your volition cause it to be. Most truly then you are of infinite power. You are incomprehensible, infinite, for nothing omniscient or of infinite power is finite . . . Neither is the ultimate end, nor what exists of itself in all simplicity, something finite. You are the ultimate in simplicity, having no really distinct parts, or no realities in your essence which are not really the same. In you no quantity, no accident can be found, and therefore you are incapable of acci-

[4] Wolter, *Duns Scotus: Philosophical Writings* (Edinburgh: Nelson & Sons, 1962), pp. 9–12.

dental change, even as I have already expressed, you are so in essence. You alone are simply perfect, not just a perfect angel or a perfect body, but a perfect being, lacking no entity it is possible for anything to have. Nothing can formally possess every perfection, but every entity can exist in something either formally or eminently, as it does in you, O God, who are supreme among beings, the only one of them who is infinite. Communicating the rays of your goodness most liberally, you are boundless good, to whom as the most lovable thing of all every single being in its own way comes back to you as to its ultimate end.[5]

In describing how we form concepts of God,[6] Scotus points out that there are two ways in which we can speak and think of this infinite perfection. One is to enumerate all his perfections in the manner Scotus does above; the other is by using a simpler, but less perfect, concept (i.e., one that does not spell out formally all it implies), namely, "infinite being," which virtually includes all of the above. And in his *Quodlibet*, q. 5, he explains in some detail how we go about forming such a concept or how we give conceptual meaning to the term "infinite" as applied to God.[7]

The point of all this is that God, for Scotus, is equated with a being of infinite perfection, whether unqualified perfection be conceived of intensively or extensively. This will explain much of what he says about what is necessarily binding on God, both with respect to what he is and with respect to what he owes his own goodness, if and when he creates.[8] It also accounts for what will be binding in an absolute sense on whatever moral beings God might create.[9] And in all these matters, Duns will point out, God never acts contrary to what right reason or prudence would dictate, for God is always *ordinatissime volens*.

How Divine Free Will Differs from Ours

Equally certain to Scotus was the experiential fact that we possess free will[10] and that contingency exists in the world around us. He considered the latter to be a "primary truth not demonstrable *a priori*." Those who deny such manifest things, he says, quoting Aristotle, "need

[5] Wolter, *A Treatise on God as First Principle: A Latin Text and English Translation of the De Primo Principio*, ed. 2d, revised with a commentary (Chicago: Franciscan Herald Press, 1983), pp. 142–44.

[6] *Ord.* I, d. 3, n. 58; Vatican ed., III, p. 48.

[7] See Alluntis-Wolter, *John Duns Scotus, God and Creatures: The Quodlibetal Questions* (Princeton: Princeton University Press, 1975), pp. 108–12.

[8] *Ord.* I, d. 44, and IV, d. 46.

[9] *Ord.* III, suppl. d. 27, 28, 37, and 39.

[10] *Quaest. in Meta.* IX, q. 15.

punishment or senses," not argument." For as Avicenna puts it...
'Those who deny a first principle should be beaten or exposed to fire
until they concede that to burn and not to burn, or to be beaten and
not to be beaten, are not identical.' And so too, those who deny that
some being is contingent should be exposed to torments until they
concede it is possible for them not to be tormented."[11]

From the existence of our free will and the fact of contingency in
the world, he believed we could prove that God also has free will and
that this fact is a necessary condition, though not a sufficient reason,
why something is contingent. His proof for this was in the aforesaid
metaphysical argument for God, but is repeated in summary fashion
in dist. 39 of his lectures on the first book of the *Sentences*, where he
goes on to analyze in some detail how God's will must differ from
ours. This discussion appears in several forms, including that of the
original[12] and a substantially revised and expanded form that follows
the plan of the *Lectura*, but depends upon the *Reportatio examinata*
I, d. 38–40. The editors of the Vatican edition think this later version,
though expressing the most mature thought of Scotus, may have been
completed by a disciple using materials from Scotus' notebooks and
other sources no longer extant. Since it is found in all the principal
manuscripts in substantially the same form the editors believe they
all depend upon a single apograph, and they have prepared a critical
edition of this text in Appendix A of volume VI.[13] Scotus' argument
there runs as follows.

Granted contingency exists, what must we presuppose about God,
the first cause, as a necessary condition for the possibility of such
contingency? We must assume that he does not create, conserve, or
cooperate with the causes he creates in any necessary way. There must
be some positive cause or reason, which cannot be his intellect as such,
but must have its roots in his free will. To understand how we can
ascribe will to God we must first analyze what our own freedom involves. It has a triple aspect. First, we are free in regard to opposite
acts. This refers to what Scotus described in some detail in chapter 8,
namely, that our will is an active potency, and as such can do something, i.e., it can determine itself in opposite or contrary ways. Second,
as the root cause of such opposite acts of volition, it can also tend to
opposite objects, and third, produce opposite effects. The first sort of
freedom, as it exists in us, involves a certain imperfection, for we are
not only the cause of our volition but the recipient of this immanent

[11] Wolter, *Duns Scotus: Philosophical Writings*, p. 9.
[12] *Lectura*, Vatican ed., XVII, pp. 481–513.
[13] Vatican ed., VI, pp. 401–44.

action as well, and in causing it, we are changed from a state of not willing to willing. Passivity and mutability, then, are imperfections associated with this first sense of freedom. It will require further analysis, Scotus explains, to extract from this amalgam of positive perfection, passivity, and mutability what is a matter of pure perfection and hence could exist in God. Scotus finds this kernel of unqualified perfection to be what is implied in the will's peculiar character as an active potency or causal principle, namely, the positive or superabundant indeterminacy that enables the will to act in opposite or contrary ways. The second and third aspects of freedom, the will's ability to tend to opposite objects and produce opposite effects, is the sort of freedom required for artistic creativity and is also a matter of pure or unqualified perfection. The two aspects are separable, however, for one can love or hate something without necessarily producing or destroying it. Scotus describes the second aspect as characteristic of our freedom:

I maintain that one obvious power for opposites is associated with this freedom, for although it does not include the power to will and not will simultaneously (since this is nothing), it still includes the power to will after not willing, or a power for opposites in succession. This power for opposite acts in succession, however, is not peculiar to the will, but is characteristic of all mutable things. Nevertheless, the will has another, less evident power for opposites apart from any succession. For suppose that a created will existed for but one instant and had this particular volition at that instant, it would not have it at that moment in a necessary manner. Proof: If it did, then since it is a cause only at the instant it causes that volition, the will would cause it then in a simply necessary fashion. (For the present situation would not obtain, where the will is said to be a contingent cause, because prior to the instant it causes, it could either cause or not cause. Just as this being, then, when it exists, is necessary or contingent, so too a cause, when it causes, does so then either necessarily or contingently.) At this instant, then, [this cause which exists but for an instant] causes contingently, and hence has at that moment, in the absence of any succession, the power for the opposite of what it actually causes. And this real power (as first act [i.e., as actually existing]) is a power that is naturally prior to those opposites, which (as acts [i.e., as its actual volitions]) are naturally posterior. For the first act [i.e., something as existing]), considered in its natural priority to second act, gives to its effect, as contingent, its existence in such a way that, as naturally prior, it could just as well have done the opposite.

Concomitant with this real active power that is naturally prior to what it produces is a logical power, which is a compatibility of terms. For even when the will produces this particular volition, the opposite volition is not inconsistent with the will as first act [i.e., as an actually existing causal power]. The reason is twofold, first because the will is a contingent cause with respect to its effect, and second, insofar as the will is also the recipient subject of its immanent act, it is related to what informs it only contingently, because no subject is opposed to what inheres in it only as an "incidental accident."

Therefore, both a power for opposites in succession and a power for opposites at the same instant, are associated with the liberty of our will; or to put it another way, either of these real powers could exist without the other. But it is this second real power—as naturally prior to the concomitant third, or logical, power—that is the real cause of the volitional act. But the "fourth power"—viz., to have opposite acts simultaneously—is not associated with the will, because this represents no power whatsoever.

Using the logical tool of the distinction between the composite and divided senses, Scotus goes on to show both in what sense the ambiguous statement "When the will wills A, it can also not will A" can be both true and false and why Aristotle's controversial statement in *De interpretatione*. II, ch. 9 (19a23–24), that "whatever exists, when it is, must necessarily exist" needs qualification. Since Duns' detailed explanation is covered by what he says in chapter 8, we need not go into the matter further. Suffice it to say that just as we—at the instant we freely decide and will one alternative—have both a real and a logical potentiality for the opposite, so too does God. For this is what the essential perfection of free will implies. And while such coexists in us only with the imperfection associated with passivity and mutability, this factual mutability is lacking in God, who from all eternity freely decides to create, conserve, and cooperate with the free actions of his creatures in a contingent way. For despite the steadfastness of his free will, it always has at root its potentiality to have caused the opposite of what it *de facto* causes. This point is treated in *Ordinatio* I, 44, where Scotus deals with the absolute and ordained power of God.

God's Voluntary Self-Love as Both Free and Necessary

In *Ordinatio* IV, 29, we have Scotus' interpretation of the twofold "affection" Saint Anselm of Canterbury ascribes to the created will. The first is its affection for the advantageous (*affectio commodi*). This makes it a rational or intellectual appetite that seeks what the intellect shows is advantageous to the creature, particularly what makes it happy.[14] Under the aspect of its inclination for the advantageous we speak of a "natural will."[15] This refers primarily not to an elicited

---

[14] *Ord.* III, d. 17.
[15] *Ord.* III, suppl. 26.

action of the will, but rather to an inclination or bias the will has as a "nature." For like all natures, according to Aristotle, it seeks or "loves"—whatever perfects its nature. This affection for the advantageous is also characteristic of all human sense appetites. Hence it is not something proper or peculiar to a rational creature possessing intellect.

It is the second inclination that is proper to a rational being whose mind is governed by right reason, namely, its "affection for justice." This is essentially an inclination toward something intrinsically good (*bonum honestum*). By reason of this affection, the will is invited to love or tend toward that good "for its own sake." We experience such an objective attraction where beauty is to be found. There we are drawn out of ourselves, as it were, and are involved with and absorbed by the beautiful object itself. We "love it for its own sake" with a "love" that is neither private nor jealous, but rather one that inclines us to invite others to admire and share it with us. Richard of St. Victor was to develop this notion to explain the inner life of the Trinity,[16] wherein he was followed by Saint Bonaventure.[17] Scotus uses it primarily to show the rationale behind God's creativity.[18]

As Richard conceives of this "love," it has an aspect of necessity. Indeed, because this inner divine life is as necessary as is God's nature itself, Richard is convinced that he can give not just "probable but necessary reasons" why God is the sort of being he is.[19] Anselm's original approach is to stress the other aspect, the inner freedom or essential "liberty" of God's will-act or "love" of what is intrinsically good about himself. He had earlier corrected a common misconception about human liberty, viz., that our will is free because it has the capacity to sin, a *potestas peccandi* that permits it to depart from justice or what right reason dictates. As such, will cannot exist in God; neither is will in any unqualified sense a perfection (*perfectio simpliciter*). Hence, Anselm's revolutionary definition of "freedom" as a pure perfection, viz., as the capacity to preserve justice for its own sake (*potestas servandi rectitudinem propter seipsum*) and his definition of "justice" itself as "rectitude-of-will served for its own sake" (*iustitia est rectitudo voluntatis propter se servata*), cited by Scotus (*Ord.* IV, d. 46).

[16] Richard de Saint-Victor, *De Trinitate*, ed. J. Ribaillier (Paris: J. Vrin, 1958), pp. 136ff.

[17] Zachery Hayes, *St. Bonaventure's Disputed Questions on the Mystery of the Trinity* (St. Bonaventure, N.Y.: The Franciscan Institute, 1979), pp. 23–24.

[18] Wolter, "John Duns Scotus on the Primacy and Personality of Christ," in *Franciscan Christology*, ed. D. McElrath (St. Bonaventure, N.Y.: The Franciscan Institute, 1980), p. 157.

[19] *Ibid.*, p. 89.

Under this aspect, freedom is not opposed to necessity, for "necessary" and "necessity" are terms with many meanings, as we shall shortly see.

But before going into that, however, let us note that the rectitude and justice Anselm apparently had in mind was that supernatural or "gratuitous grace," something infused by God which so sanctifies the soul as to make it capable of sharing in the inner life of the Trinity in the hereafter. As such it liberates us from the need to seek God only as our ultimate perfection and happiness, and permits us to love him honestly for his own sake and above all else.[20] Scotus seemingly carried this notion of liberation even further than Anselm, for he described this "affection for justice" as "*libertas innata*," i.e., something inborn, native, or congenital to the human will. In fact he goes still further; not only is it an essential component of the will, but it represents what an Aristotelian would call the "ultimate specific difference" that elevates a rational appetite" and transforms it into an appetite that is "free." He refers to this "*affectio iustitiae*" either as an "*innata libertas*" (which I have translated as "native liberty") or as "*ingenita libertas*," which could be translated literally more properly as "unbegotten liberty" (but which I have translated, as characteristic of creatures, and man in particular, as "congenital"). Though it is a bias and an inclination, like the affection for the advantageous, and hence is not an elicited act as such, the affection for justice already introduces a measure of freedom from nature. For nature, according to Aristotle, always seeks its own perfection, either as concretized in the individual or as characteristic of the species. But liberty comes to its full perfection when the human will (which is physically free to elicit an act in regard to either inclination) freely determines itself in accord with this higher inclination and elicits an act that tends toward a good in an objective and honest manner, namely, in accord with the intrinsic value or goodness of the object as such. Where the human will is well ordered, its first act of love of any good, then, will be in accord with this affection for justice. But since man is finite in perfection and tends to perfect himself by actively acquiring what he needs to be perfect, he must also—to be true to himself and his God-given nature—will what is to his advantage as well as what is good in itself. Hence, secondarily, persons with well-ordered wills will love what most accords with their own perfection, namely, what fulfills their personal needs and thus brings happiness and contentment. Happiness itself can thus become a sort of reflex object of well-ordered love.[21]

[20] See *Ord.* III, suppl. d. 27.
[21] See J. Klein, "Intellect und Wille als die nächsten Quellen dersittlichen Akte nach

In the supernatural order, man is destined to be perfected by union with the Trinity, because God, as a perfect lover, wills that what he loves be loved by others, "willing others to love with him the very object of his love."[22] Hence the will's affection for the advantageous (*affectio commodi*) is perfected by the infused theological virtue of hope, whereas its affection for justice is perfected by the theologically infused virtue of charity or sanctifying grace.[23] In *Ord.* III, d. 27, art. 2, Scotus will explain how a well-ordered love can regard God under all three aspects, (1) as a good in himself, (2) as our good, and (3) as a source of happiness, and in that order of priority of values.

According to what was said in the previous section, God possesses whatever is a matter of pure perfection in our human will. Hence, the full conception of God's free will must include not only his ability to will opposites or to produce contrary effects (something Scotus thought was well described by Aristotle; see *Quaest. in Meta.* IX, q. 15), but also what Saint Anselm considered to be a pure perfection, i.e., the will's affection for justice.[24] Mutability, as we noted in the previous section, is an imperfection to the will, like the *potestas peccandi* that permits a finite agent to "depart from justice" and to will some finite good immoderately in one of the several ways Scotus explains that Lucifer might have sinned.[25] Mutability in this sense must also be lacking in God, where it would imply that he could cease to love his infinitely lovable divine nature with the objectivity that the affection for justice demands. If we can, and right reason dictates we should, love our own nature and whatever perfects it and makes us happy,[26] something we are already inclined by nature to do in virtue of our *affectio commodi*, then God too—in some analogous way—must also love this aspect of his infinitely lovable nature, namely, that it is good for him, and also a source of infinite happiness. For, according to our way of thinking, this dynamic unselfish love for what is intrinsically good also perfects his will and makes God happy in much the same way as our well-ordered love of God for his own sake has two other accompanying sorts of love for him, one because he loves and perfects us, the other because he is our ultimate happiness. Now, in the afore-

---

Johannes Duns Skotus," *Franziskanische Studien* 1916, p. 157; and *Ord.* III, suppl. d. 27.

[22] Wolter, "John Duns Scotus on the Primacy and Personality of Christ," p. 157.

[23] *Ord.* III, suppl. d. 27.

[24] See *Ord.* III, suppl. d. 26; also W. Hoeres, "Naturtendenz und Freiheit nach Duns Scotus," *Salzburger Jahrbuch für Philosophie und Psychologie* 2 (1958), pp. 95–134; and *Der Wille als rein Vollkommenheit nach Duns Scotus* (München: Verlag Anton Pustet, 1962).

[25] *Ord.* III, suppl. d. 28.

[26] *Ord.* III, suppl. d. 29.

said passage on Lucifer's sin, Scotus explains how the blessed in heaven can love their own happiness that results from the beatific vision and the love it engenders, and do so out of an affection for justice. In the same way Anselm explains that God could have necessarily loved what pertained to the perfection of his nature and satisfied his will, as it were, making it happy and content, with no compelling need to seek further perfection. For this is something that becomes his nature, and to fail to love himself, or to have the capacity we have of turning away from what we are most inclined to love by reason of our affection for justice, would imply an "infirmity" or weakness in God's essence, something metaphysically incompatible with the infinite perfection Scotus ascribes to it.

If such mutability is also lacking in God, then by the same token his will must have the pure perfection we call "firmness of purpose" or a "steadfast will." It is under this aspect that Scotus admits that, where God is concerned and with respect to his inner love life, the freedom associated with his "unbegotten liberty" (*ingenita libertas*) must also be associated with a certain immutability or necessity. It is this notion that he proposes in his *Quodlibet*, q. 16. We are indebted to William A. Frank for a critical reading of a portion of that text, which has been erroneously transcribed in all of our presently available editions. For *"firmitas est perfectio"* they have substituted *"libertas est perfectio"* where Scotus is explaining how *"libertas voluntatis et necessitas naturalis possint se competi in eodem respectu eiusdem actus."*[27]

The context in which the relevant passage occurs is as follows. Scotus has first shown that the act by which God loves himself is necessary in an unqualified sense, for "God is necessarily happy, and hence beholds and loves the beatific object." John Duns then undertakes to prove that this is not inconsistent with the essential freedom associated with every elicited act of God's will. No pure perfection excludes another pure perfection, says Scotus.[28] This need to love what is infinitely lovable, if we may call it a "need," is also a matter of pure perfection. Hence it is *per se* compatible, according to Anselm, with perfect liberty. Anselm explicitly tells us such, says Scotus, in chapter 1 of *Free Choice*: "Whoever has what is appropriate and advantageous in such a way that it cannot be lost is freer than he who has this in such a way that it can be lost." From this Anselm concludes: "The will then which cannot cease to be upright is freer."[29] Augustine too could be quoted in

[27] W. A. Frank, "John Duns Scotus' Quodlibetal Teaching on the Will" (Ph.D. dissertation, Catholic University of America, 1982), p. 215.

[28] See chapter 11, pages 273–74, of the present volume.

[29] Alluntis-Wolter, *God and Creatures*, p. 378.

confirmation, but—says Scotus—we can give rational proofs as to why this is so, the first of which is the one based on the notion of *"firmitas."* We might note that Scotus considers it a self-evident fact that "firmness" pertains to the perfection of such an action, because he speaks of the proof based on this notion as *"propter quid."* This is the sort of proof Aristotle says is not just a demonstration of the simple fact, but rather a proof that gives the essential reason why this fact is true.

The point of all this is to show why Scotus believed that in God, at least, the perfection of his love for his own nature is not only free but necessary. It is free, in the sense that it is a will-act, and *will as opposed to nature* never tends to anything except in the spontaneous, self-detemining, and liberated way that is peculiar to it as *will*. But it is also in some sense necessary. For "necessary"—he points out—is a multifaceted word with a multiplicity of meanings. And in addition to the ones that are cited explicitly in *God and Creature*,[30] we need to add the necessity entailed by "firmness of purpose" or a "steadfast will."

Finally, we should stress that this too is a consequence of God's "affection for justice," which, as Scotus points out in *Ord.* IV, d. 46, obliges him to do justice to his own goodness. And this brings us to our next point, how this dual aspect not only affects the relationship of God's will to his own goodness, but also modifies his creative act.

Right Reason Governs God's Relationship to Creatures

If God's will is infinitely perfect and all creatures have only a finite degree of being and goodness, then it is clear from an Aristotelian point of view that the finite goodness of a creature cannot be the final cause that moves God to give it existence, even if "moves" be taken in the metaphorical sense of a motive (*Finis movet metaphorice*). The Scholastics to a man rejected the theory of Abelard that anticipated in some sense Leibniz's belief that one could find a sufficient reason for God creating the world he actually did in the degree of goodness characteristic of this "best of all possible worlds." It is this conviction—rooted let us note in the fact that God's creative will is governed by right reason—that caused the Parisian theologians to reject the Averroistic necessitarianism that had invaded the arts faculty and prompted Bishop Stephen Tempier to issue the condemnations of "errors" in 1270 and 1277. Here is where we find the rationale of the controversial

[30] *Ibid.*, p. 379.

statement that "things are good because God wills them, and not vice versa."

The context in which this oft-quoted expression occurs is in reference to the merits of Christ and reads in full: "I say that just as everything other than God is good because it is willed by God and not vice versa, so this merit was good to the extent that it was accepted. It was not the other way around, namely, because it was merit and good, therefore it was accepted."[31] Scotus is concerned here specifically with meritorious goodness rather than natural or moral goodness as such. Since merit is dependent on grace or charity,[32] it has to do, not with the natural order, but with the supernatural state to which man has been gratuitously elevated by God. If any human act is to be rewarded with an increase of grace in this life and a face-to-face vision and love of God in the next, this is obviously a pure gift on God's part and transcends anything our human nature needs or requires. Hence, the particular application of this principle should not create any problem or appear as a violation of anything demanded by right reason. However, the principle itself is unquestionably broader in scope, and may even have a transcendental or metaphysical interpretation, as well as application to "moral goodness" in the broad sense in which this term is taken in *Ord.* II, d. 7. In either case, however, right reason and the affection of the will for justice seem to play a significant role. This will become clear if we consider how Scotus regarded natural goodness, and secondly, what moral goodness adds to the natural goodness of a voluntary act.

Natural Goodness Scotus is not denying that possibles by reason of their nature can have an essential or natural goodness; the same is true not only of substantive natures but also of actions, including voluntary acts that are elicited freely. In *Ord.* II, d. 7, for instance, he refers to "volition's natural goodness, which pertains to it as something positive and which is characteristic of any positive thing according to the grade of entity it has (the more the entity, the more the goodness; the less the entity, the less the goodness)." Obviously, such natural goodness, or the "primary or essential goodness" Scotus speaks of in *Quodl.*, q. 18—if these be the same—is not arbitrarily will-dependent. Otherwise, there would be no point in what he says about God as "*ordinatissime volens,*" something we shall take up shortly. What he is trying to rule out is the suggestion that this natural goodness somehow moves God's creative will in the way his own infinite goodness does, for no creature

---

[31] *Ord.* III, suppl. d. 37, n. 6.
[32] *Ord.* II, d. 7, nn. 28–39.

has a claim to actual existence simply in virtue of the sort of thing it happens to be.

In the case of God's intellect, Scotus has argued that it would be derogatory to the perfection of God's mind if it depended for its knowledge on the intelligibility of a created object. For any such object is finite, limited in perfection, and to that extent, it represents a mixture of perfection and imperfection, and as such it does not move God's intellect to know it. God is rather like the poet or sculptor, who first models his masterpiece in his mind before putting it on paper or embodying it in marble or bronze, for his infinitely fertile intellect mentally creates each possible creature as an object of thought, thus giving that created nature or essence its first intelligibility or *esse intelligibile*. Hence, for Scotus it is true to say: "God does not know creatures because they are intelligible; but vice versa, creatures are intelligible because God knows them."[33] If creatures have an ideal being or essence, they also have an ideal or essential goodness. But being finite in degree, it cannot force or compel the divine will first to give it being as a willed object (*esse volitum*) from all eternity, and then actual existence at some moment in time. Hence, when Scotus says that "everything other than God is good because it is willed by God and not vice versa," if natural goodness is meant, the statement can only refer to real or actual existing goodness. And it would mean nothing more than that the divine creative will is contingently related to whatever created good exists.

So understood, the controversial maxim would be a logical consequence of the fact that God's will is governed by an affection for justice. For this would mean it tends to something good in terms of its intrinsic or true value. Only where the good is infinite can it bind or necessitate God's infinitely perfect will. In all other cases, God is free to love or not to love creatively.

Does this mean God is free to deal with his creatures in a purely arbitrary and whimsical fashion? Does the affection for justice characteristic of his will impose any obligation on him as to what or how he will create? Scotus addresses himself to this problem in *Ord.* IV, d. 46, where he asks: Is there justice in God? and in *Ord.* I, d. 44: Could God have created things otherwise than he did?

In answer to the first question he points out in what sense God is just and upright both in respect to what he owes himself and in his dealings with others. To begin with, the law or practical truth "God must be loved" is prior to any decision on the part of the divine will. Furthermore, he is bound by his affection for justice to be true to his

---

[33] *Ord.* I, d. 35, nn. 31–32; Vatican ed., VI, p. 258.

own goodness. This obligation, if we can call it that, is also something anterior to any act on the part of his will. While he is obliged, so to speak, to love his infinitely lovable divine nature as an infinite good, he is not so necessitated toward any finite entity. Creative love is always a free gift on his part, something contingently given. But granted he does create, does God owe creatures anything in justice? Not in a strict sense, says Scotus, since these are finite and cannot compel or force an infinite will to do anything it does not freely choose to do. Nevertheless, the justice, that obliges God to be true to his own goodness does modify his creative act in regard to whatever he chooses to create. Scotus expresses this most succinctly when he writes in *Ord.* IV, d. 46:

> I say that God is no debtor in any unqualified sense save with respect to his own goodness, namely, that he love it. But where creatures are concerned, he is debtor rather to his generosity, in the sense that he gives creatures what their nature demands, which exigency in them is set down as something just, a kind of secondary object of this justice, as it were. But in truth nothing outside of God can be said to be definitely just without this added qualification. In an unqualified sense where a creature is concerned, God is just only in relation to his first justice, namely, because such a creature has been actually willed by the divine will.

God is obviously the most perfect of artists, a craftsman like no other. He owes it to himself that whatever he chooses to create will have a beauty and natural goodness about it. Yet no particular creation is so perfect, beautiful, or good that it exhausts his infinite powers of creativity. While the goodness of creation is thus, in some sense, a consequence of the affection for justice inherent in his will, no creation or creature is such that its goodness can be regarded in an Abelardian or Leibnizian sense as a sufficient reason for its existence.

This latter point is stressed in *Ord.* I, d. 44, which points out that God could always create otherwise than he actually has, since to do so is not self-contradictory. For though he has ordered things wisely, his absolute power extends beyond what he has actually ordained. And while absolute power is defined in terms of what is not self-contradictory, this does not mean—as an initial objection suggests—that "he could have made things inordinately." If what Scotus has just said of God's justice be true, then it would be simply self-contradictory if he did not do justice to his own goodness and in his generosity make creatures in a fitting way. And in the examined report of his late Paris lectures he says expressly, paraphrasing Saint Augustine: "Whatever God made, you know that God has made it with right reason."[34]

Put in another way, God is always "*ordinatissime volens.*" Scotus describes the actual order of creation as the theologian conceives of it:

> Everyone who wills in a reasonable way, first wills the end and secondly that which immediately attains the end, and thirdly other things that are more remotely ordered to the attainment of his end. And so it is [with] God, who is said to tend in different ways to the different objects ordered in some way to one another—first wills the end, and in this his act is perfect, and his intellect is perfect, and his will is happy. Secondly, he wills those things which are immediately ordered to him ... Hence, he first loves himself ordinately and consequently not inordinately in an envious or jealous manner. Secondly, he wills to have co-lovers, and this is nothing else than willing that others have his love in themselves ... Thirdly, however, he wills those things which are necessary to attain his end, namely, the gift of grace. Fourthly, he wills for their sakes other things that are more remote, for instance this sensible world in order that it may serve them, so that what is stated in the second book of Aristotle's *Physics* is true: "Man is in some way the end of all sensible things," for these are willed in the fourth place because of man's being willed in the second place. Also that which is closer to the ultimate end is customarily said to be the end of the sensible world, whether it be because God wills the sensible world to be ordered to predestined man or whether it is because his more immediate concern is not that the sensible world exist, but rather that man love him.

Even though he is speaking of a supernatural order, something beyond anything Aristotle dreamed of, there is no suggestion that the principle does not apply to the natural order as well. God is always "*ordinatissime volens*"—a most methodical lover. Grace builds on nature, after all, and the supernatural on the natural.

So much for natural goodness and meritorious goodness. But what of moral goodness?

Moral Goodness   Moral goodness is formally something inherent in a human act, namely, its suitability or conformity to what right reason dictates.[35] Hence its existence as well as its possibility in some degree depends on the fact that God has freely created man not merely with an intellectual but with a free appetite. One could interpret this reductively of course as meaning merely that a morally good act has a

---

[34] *Reportatio* I A, d. 44, q. 2; Vienna, cod. palatinus 1453, f. 122va: "*Quidquid Deus fecit hoc scias, Deum cum recta ratione fecisse.*"

[35] *Ord.* I, d. 17, nn. 62–67; *Quodl.* q. 18; *Ord.* II, q. 40.

special form of natural goodness. But Scotus apparently had something more in mind. As he points out in *Quodl.*, q. 18, *Ord.* II, d. 7, and *Ord.* IV, d. 46, moral goodness is something over and above the natural or essential goodness characteristic of a voluntary act, though it presupposes such antecedent goodness as a relational entity presupposes its relata and foundation for the relationship. The will's affection for justice or its native freedom liberates it in some degree from the servitude of human nature that always seeks its own individual perfection or that of the species. Consequently, one would suspect that the will too is not bound morally merely by some principle of self-actualization or obligation that arises automatically and exclusively from the fact that creatures are perfectible in certain ways. It can be bound only by an infinite or absolute good, or by a higher will that has authority because it authored man as free, i.e., with an inclination or affection for justice as dictated by right reason.

To explain. As ethicians have often argued, one cannot logically go from what is the case to what ought to be. Because justice determines what ought to be, Scotus sees the will as somehow morally bound by reason of what is essential to it as will, its affection for justice[36] and the fact that it is a "rational potency" or guided by right reason.[37] As such, it tends to things in terms of their intrinsic values, or what it owes to such. Where the value is absolute, such as in the case of the infinitely good God, "God should be loved" is an obligation according to right reason simply in virtue of the object to be loved. Scotus, in *Ord.* II, d. 7, distinguishes two grades of moral goodness antecedent to meritorious goodness. One is generic, the other specific; the former regards the object willed; the latter regards the attendant circumstances and particularly the end for which the object in question is loved or hated. Generic goodness is concerned with the question: "According to right reason is it suitable, appropriate, or just to love or hate such an object?" Specific goodness asks: "Is the purpose or other attendant circumstances such that according to right reason such and such an object should be loved or hated, sought or avoided? There is only one case where a voluntary act is completely good simply in virtue of its object or generic goodness, that is, where God is the object of friendship love (*amor amicitiae*). For by such a voluntary act, God is loved for his own sake, and thus, we could say, the appropriate end is built into the initial act itself. Furthermore, as an infinite good, God cannot be loved too much, or too often, or under any other inappropriate conceivable circumstance.

[36] *Ord.* III, suppl. 26.
[37] *Quaest. in Meta.* IX, q. 15.

As for generic goodness, this fitting relationship between the will-act and its object, like natural goodness, is not something that depends solely upon God's will. God wills such because it is good, and it is not good just because God wills it. Take the case where an act is generically good or bad by reason of the object alone, for example, love of God as an intrinsically good act, or hatred or disrespect of God as an intrinsically bad act. In *Ord.* IV, d. 46, referred to above, Scotus makes it clear that the "law" or "practical truth" "God should be loved" or "God must not be shown irreverence" holds good antecedent to any will or decision on God's part. It is on this score that Scotus concedes that "legal justice could be postulated of God if there were some other law antecedent to any decision of his will, with which law and its legislator' as other than his will, his own will could rightly agree." There is such a law, he goes on to say, namely, "'God should be loved'— if one ought to call it a 'law' rather than a practical principle of law." In any case, he insists, "it is a practical truth that is prior to any decision on the part of the divine will." If God's will itself is "bound by such a law," so too, *a fortiori*, is the free will of any creature he has authored.

But what is to be said of the other specific obligations that ethical philosophers agree are morally binding on man? All of these, unless they can be shown to follow logically from a law such as "God should be loved" or "God should not be hated," are indifferent *per se* generically, and become morally good or bad dependent on the circumstances. In regard to such actions, natural goodness becomes a necessary condition for generic moral goodness; generic moral goodness for specific moral goodness; specific moral goodness for meritorious goodness. Conversely, the absence of anything demanded by right reason suffices to induce some measure of moral badness or lack of moral goodness, according to the principle taken over from pseudo-Dionysius, namely, "Good requires that everything about the act be right."[38]

Like most of his contemporaries and medieval colleagues, Scotus equates the complete requirements of the moral law with what is enjoined on man by either natural law, divine positive law, or legitimate positive legislation imposed by proper ecclesiastical, civil, or parental authority. Obligations of divine positive law obviously depend upon the will of God; ecclesiastical or civil authority is legitimate if it is directly or indirectly sanctioned by God. The question of the will-dependence of the remaining obligations then comes down to how far the precepts of natural law can be said to be dependent on God's will.

In *Ord.* III, suppl. d. 37, Scotus explains at great length the two-

---

[38] *Ord.* II, d. 27.

fold meaning of "law of nature," reflected in its division into two tables. The initial three commandments that make up the first table concern our relationship and obligations toward God. The second table, comprising the last seven commandments, concerns our social and political relationship and obligations toward our neighbor. Now, the intrinsic and objective values safeguarded by the precepts of these two tables are vastly different. Inasmuch as the first table can be equated with this law, "God should be loved," God himself could not dispense man from its obligations. And hence in this sense, the actions commanded or prohibited by the first table are morally good or bad independently of the fact that God commands or prohibits such,[39] specifically the third commandment (regarding the obligation "to keep holy the Sabbath") represents positive divine law, explicating affirmatively how "God should be loved" is to be fulfilled, and to that extent this action is good because God wills it. But the first two precepts, insofar as they prohibit the worship of "strange gods" or any irreverence toward the true God, are precepts that "belong strictly to the natural law, taking law of nature as that which follows necessarily if God exists and he alone must be loved as God." Since God himself could never dispense from these two, the meaning of the controversial maxim cannot be that these commandments bind only because God wills such.

But what of the obligations imposed by the second table? Here, there were diverse opinions among the Scholastics as to how such commandments were expressions of the law of nature, and on what, if any, grounds God could dispense them. One thing all seemed to agree upon, however, was that only in its broad outlines was the natural law "written into the heart of man" and to that extent evident to all who had not sinfully blinded their intellect to the truth in the way Paul speaks of in the opening chapter of his Epistle to the Romans. We shall have occasion to refer to this again in the following section.

We might note here parenthetically, however, that many of Scotus' colleagues, following Augustine, made use of an idea borrowed from the Stoics. They considered the entire decalogue as a reflection of some impersonal "eternal law" that was written into nature, and saw it as binding on God by reason of what he is and the sort of created nature he decided to make. As we said above, Scotus—instead of making use of this Stoic conception—develops an insight of Saint Anselm; he sees the moral law as grounded rather in the

---

[39] See *Ord.* II, d. 21, q. 2, n. 3; Wadding reprint ed. XIII, p. 141; *Reportatio* II, A, d. 22, n. 3; Wadding reprint ed. XXIII, p. 104.

will's affection for justice; this native liberty frees it, to some extent, from what "nature" demands, and allows it to "moderate its affection for the advantageous."[40]

One could put this another way, by stressing that the values protected by the second table of the natural law cannot have the same absolute value as those preserved by the first table. They are not as independent of, or antecedent to, what God wills, in the way the values safeguarded by the precepts of the first table are. For the natural good each precept is intended to save or secure concerns some aspect of what is of individual, social, and political value to mankind. As such it represents only what pertains to man's natural perfection. Like human nature itself, this is only a finite good; furthermore, it represents an ideal for which one should strive, rather than the actual condition in which man exists. As a Christian theologian like his contemporaries, Scotus views man's actual condition as tainted by original sin. As he indicates in *Ord.* III, suppl. d. 27–28, man was destined for a supernatural end from which he fell, and to which he was restored through the merits of Christ. Now, none of the intrinsic or ideal natural perfections protected by the second table of the law are absolutely or necessarily connected with the attainment of man's actual supernatural end, which is union with God in the afterlife. Hence, Scotus maintains in *Ord.* III, suppl. d. 37, that while the second table represents what is *"valde consonans"* with natural law, certain aspects of the second table of the decalogue can be dispensed with according to right reason, when their observation would entail more harm than good. But God could obviously not dispense from all its precepts at once, for this would be equivalent to creating man in one way and obligating him in an entirely different fashion, something contrary to what he "owes to human nature in virtue of his generosity."

All of these aspects would have to be considered, Scotus would say, in answering whether some specific voluntary act was morally good or bad only because God willed such. The important qualification here is "only," for what is naturally good or evil, as we said, is a precondition for moral goodness or moral badness. And the natural goodness or badness of an act, as the subsequent section will make clear, is something we can reason to philosophically or logically. Natural goodness, as we said, does not automatically guarantee moral goodness, though the rational analysis of what constitutes such natural goodness can tell us much about the actual content of a law of nature.

[40] *Ord.* II, d. 6, q. 2.

If the will of God underpins it, then the law of nature, especially as regards the second table, loses something of its impersonal and inflexible character. Its personal dimension cannot be ignored. Where other Scholastics, following Augustine, who in turn was influenced by the Stoics, link it with the *lex aeterna*, Scotus eliminates this last vestige of impersonalism. To legislate or command is a function of will, not of a nature as such, even if it be the most perfect of natures.[41] However, this does raise a crucial question: How do we know the will of God? Does this not require a special revelation on his part?

The Moral Law as Accessible to Reason

What is often overlooked in the studies of the ethics of Scotus is that the notion that God reveals himself in nature as well as through the Scriptures was something the great Scholastics took for granted. That Scotus accepted this principle is clear from what he says about the law of nature being, in the words of Saint Paul, "written interiorly in the heart"[42] and in *Ord.* III, suppl. d. 37 (in answer to the initial arguments): "In every state all the commandments have been observed and should be observed. In the state of innocence also all were bound by these precepts which were either prescribed interiorly in the heart of everyone, or perhaps by some teaching given exteriorly by God." The same idea recurs in *Ord.* IV, d. 17, where the criterion of whether something belongs to the law of nature or not is whether it would hold for any state in which man existed. "The reason is that if [something] were a matter of natural law, the obligation would have held for any state of law—which is false. For no such obligation existed in the state of innocence or during the tenure of the Mosaic law."

But how far can human reason go in determining specific obligations of natural law, particularly something that pertains to the natural law only in the secondary sense that it is "*valde consonans*" or in harmony with those primary or self-evident principles that involve natural law in the primary sense. By way of answer, Scotus makes two points clear.

The first is that the human intellect, as such, has the capacity to reach reasonable conclusions about ethical matters, just as it has the capacity to reason to other theoretical or practical conclusions, beginning with principles that are more or less self-evident. In *Quodlibet*, q. 18, he explains how agents that act "by virtue of intellectual knowledge are suited by nature to have an intrinsic rule of rectitude for their

---

[41] See chapter 7, pp. 157–62, of the present volume. Cf. G. Stratenworth, *Die Naturrechtslehre des Johannes Duns Scotus* (Göttingen: Vandenhoeck und Ruprecht, 1951), pp. 5–7.

[42] *Ord.* I, prol., n. 108; I, p. 70; II, d. 28.

actions. Only they can have an act whose goodness is moral." He goes on to explain that to infer whether an action is suitable to man as a moral agent and is therefore morally good we need premises that are certain. For this, knowledge of three things suffices, viz., the nature of the agent, the nature of the faculty by which he acts, and the essential notion of the act ("*natura agentis et potentia secundum quam agit et ratio quidditativa actus*"). "If these three notions are given, no other knowledge is needed to judge whether or not this particular act is suited to this agent and this faculty," and hence is in accord with right reason. It is clear from all he says that he thought this sort of knowledge posed no particular problem, at least to a philosopher skilled in reasoning. Even the sort of dispensations Scotus sees God making, we might also note, are always in accord with right reason, and are something the human mind did figure out, or might have if emotions did not blind one's reason. For they concern such things as are good for man in relation to his fellow man, where there is a hierarchy of values involved, and where to obtain the principal value, certain aspects of lesser value may have to be sacrificed, in view of a less than ideal environmental situation. In short, Scotus in his analysis of the two specific areas where he believes God dispensed the Jewish patriarchs[43] is using right reason to clarify what he believes to be the objective priority of values.

The second point Scotus makes is that matters pertaining to the law of nature in the primary sense are far more clear, and universally agreed upon, than those pertaining to the second table of the decalogue. Scotus, like the Scholastics generally, did not think the finer details of what might be natural law were as readily discernible as were its broad outlines. Particularly is this true—he says—of those things that pertain to the second table. In *Ordinatio* IV, d. 26, n. 9, explaining why the indissolubility of marriage is not evident to everyone, he admits:

> Sed lex naturae etsi obliget ad indissolubilitatem vinculi praedicti, praemisso tali contractu, non tamen lex naturae evidentissima, sed secundo modo dicta. Illud autem non est de lege naturae nisi secundo modo, non est omnibus manfestum; ergo expedit necessitatem illius praecepti a lege positiva determinari ... Illa enim quae sunt remota a principis practicis legis naturae non apparent omnibus sicut ipsa principia practica quae sunt nota omnibus, quia non explicantur, et quia alii legislatores nesciunt talia explicare.[44]

This same notion comes through when Scotus explains why specific actions are sinful or not in accord with right reason. For theologians

---

[43] *Ord.* IV, d. 33, qq. 1, 3.
[44] Codex A, f. 248vb.

may often agree that something, such as lying, is sinful, yet the reasons they give why such is so differ widely.

Given the fact that Scotus, in determining what pertains to natural law, continually falls back on what is naturally good for human nature, it is not surprising that for him, as well as for Ockham, who followed him, that the substantive content of the natural law seems to be roughly the same as it was for the Scholastics generally. It is only in their interpretation of why and how it binds that we discover a significant difference. It is a "law" and to that extent "obliges" inasmuch as it represents an expression of God's will in man's regard. For as Scotus puts it, " 'To command,' I say, could only pertain to an appetite or the will."[45] A specific application of this way of thinking is found in *Ord.* II, d. 6, q. 2, where Scotus explains why we have an obligation to moderate our desire for happiness, even though it stems from a natural inclination. Scotus argues that Lucifer sinned when—despite his intellectual knowledge that it was morally wrong—he deliberately willed his own happiness in some immoderate fashion. For from the fact that Lucifer's free will, in virtue of its affection for justice, could moderate its affection for the advantageous, says Scotus, "it is bound to do so according to the rule of justice it has received from a higher will."[46] In other words, if we know from metaphysics that God exists and has made us, and we know from a psychological analysis of our affections that we have this capacity to moderate the affection for what is advantageous, we have thereby a moral obligation according to right reason to do so.

This refers to cases where the failure to do so would involve serious consequences, for Scotus points out that "though we are bound to God by creation in regard to whatever we are able to do, we are left free to do what we will so long as we keep the precepts of the decalogue."[47]

If we consider the above points carefully, we see that Scotus' system manifests a remarkable coherence, given the premises from which he begins. Before concluding these general remarks, however, it might be worthwhile to note the following points that make his moral philosophy interesting even to those who do not accept all his premises. Thus, although Scotus' ethical system does presuppose knowledge of the existence of God, it is in a sense independent of any particular

[45] *Ord.* IV, d. 14, q. 2, n. 5; Codex A, f. 230rb: "Hoc 'imperare' non convenit nisi appetitui vel voluntati."

[46] *Ord.* II, d. 6, q. 2.

[47] *Ord.* IV, d. 26; Codex A, f. 249ra: "Licet homo ex creatione Deo teneatur in omnibus quae potest, tamen Deus non tantum exigit ab homine, imo dimittit liberum eum sibi, solummodo exigens quod servet praecepta decalogi."

special revelation on the part of God. In the prologue to the *Ordinatio*, Scotus acknowledges that "the Philosopher, following natural reason, maintained that perfect happiness consists in the acquired knowledge of the pure Spirits, as he apparently wishes to say in Books I and X of the *Ethics*, or if he does not categorically assert that this is our highest possible perfection, at least natural reason can argue to no other."

Also, the fact that the second table of the decalogue is only *valde consonans* with man's ultimate (supernatural) end indicates that Scotus considered it more or less loosely connected with this, and consequently with what he believed a Christian theologian might accept as revealed knowledge of his ultimate destiny and how it might be obtained. As he explains in *Ord.* III, suppl. d. 28, I can have a basic love of my neighbor in the sense that I will that he attain God in heaven, without necessarily willing that he observe every item of what the last seven commandments require of him. Also, the Judaic or Moslem believer, or any other ethician who grounds moral obligation on the will of God as revealed to him by a rational analysis of human nature, might still agree with Scotus' fundamental conclusions about what is morally right in our dealings with our fellow men without necessarily accepting the whole of what he believed God had revealed to him through the Scriptures and positive divine law.[48] This is clearly illustrated in the obligation Scotus ascribes to the third precept of the decalogue and to the positive aspects of the first two commandments.[49] For it is only in their negative aspect that these precepts express what pertains strictly to the law of nature, namely, that God be not hated or dishonored or shown irreverence.

It also seems clear that one could use the same evaluative techniques that Scotus employs to solve particular ethical problems that fall under the second table of the law without necessarily agreeing with his reasons why they oblige morally. For what right reason tells us—according to the analysis he gives in the *Quodlibet*, q. 18—is what perfects man's human nature naturally, and this should suffice for the development of a rational ethics by those who claim man's moral behavior is not essentially dependent upon a divine command. That is why some who have developed a phenomenological axiology, like Dietrich von Hildebrand, find their concrete conclusions regarding what is morally good or morally bad in factual harmony with Scotus' ethical positions.[50]

In conclusion, I reiterate what I said in an earlier article:

---

[48] *Ord.* IV, d. 17.
[49] *Ord.* III, suppl. d. 37.
[50] Dietrich Von Hildebrand, "Phenomenology of Values in a Christian Philosophy,"

If nature's perfection is not an absolute value that must be placed above all else, then God, for whom a "thousand years are one day," is under no constraint to see that it be attained at once. The conception of a nature that achieves its end or perfection only gradually and by an internal mechanism that allows for a trial and error method of progression does not seem foreign to or incompatible with the conception of God that Scotus held. Though he states the principle of evolutionary development *Deus ordinate agens procedit de imperfecto ad perfectum* in reference to God's supernaturally revealed law, there seems no reason why it cannot be extended to his promulgation of the law of nature as well, viz., to a gradual growth in moral awareness, protracted over a period of centuries or even millennia if you will. In *processu generationis humanae, semper crevit notitia veritatis* [*Ord.* IV, d. 1, q. 3, n. 8; XVI, p. 136]."[51]

in *Christian Philosophy and Religious Renewal*, ed. G. F. McLean (Washington, D.C.: Catholic University of America Press, 1966), pp. 3–19.

[51]See chapter 7, page 162, of the present volume.

PHILOSOPHICAL THEOLOGY

10 / The "Theologism" of Duns Scotus

PART I

In his *Unity of Philosophical Experience,* Etienne Gilson devotes a chapter to a trend of philosophical thought which he calls "theologism." By this term he understands an overemphasis of the role of theology in philosophy so that the latter becomes "little more than theology clothed in philosophical garb." It is using "reason against reason in behalf of religion," and showing "that philosophy is unable to reach rationally valid conclusions on any question related to the nature of man and his destiny."[1] It confuses practically, if not theoretically, the distinction between philosophy and theology. Faith, for the Christian philosopher, becomes not merely the *sidus amicum* of which Pope Leo XIII speaks, but a *sine qua non* condition for constructing even a *natural* theology. It is an admission that the natural goal of reason lies above its natural powers so that unaided by faith, reason cannot hope to attain its proper object.

The classical representative of this tendency is St. Bonaventure,[2] of whom he writes:

Un aveu arraché a la raison qu'elle est incapable d'achever seule sa prope tache...Il est manifeste qu'a ses yeux la raison n'est pas competente dans son propre domaine si elle ne conserve son regard fixe sur des verites pour lesquelles elle ne l'est plus. Pratiquement, il n'y plus pour nous de

Reprinted, with permission, slightly altered, from *Franciscan Studies* 7 (1947) 257–73, 367–98.

[1] *Unity of Philosophical Experience* (New York, Charles Scribner's Sons, 1937), chapter 2, *passim.*

[2] *Ibid.,* p. 49.

domaine propre de la raison, et par là saint Bonaventure tourne le dos a la philosophie séparée des temps modernes.[3]

It is true that in the *Unity of Philosophical Experience*, Scotus is not expressly named as one of the "innumerable representatives of that tendency (theologism) whom I could quote."[4] But there can be little doubt that Gilson regards him as such, for he constantly describes the thought of the Subtle Doctor in terms of those characteristic doctrines and attitudes he has named theologism. While we find scattered references to the subject in many of his works,[5] it is developed most extensively, perhaps, in his *Les seize premiers theoremata et la pensée de Duns Scot.*[6]

This article represents a very ingenious attempt to conciliate Scotus' authentic writings with the first sixteen theorems of the dubious *Theoremata*. We are not particularly concerned with what Gilson says of the first thirteen theorems, for the latter seem doctrinally compatible with Scotus' genuine works. But theorems XIV to XVI cause considerable difficulty. They deal with the *credibilia*— truths known certainly by faith but indemonstrable from the standpoint of reason alone. Their doctrine has been a major factor in excluding the *Theoremata* as a whole from the corpus of authentic works. Theorem XV, for instance, calls the arguments for a First Cause coexistent with the series of its essentially ordered effects, mere probable proofs. Scotus himself speaks of them as demonstrations.

We are not interested primarily with the problem of the authenticity of the *Theoremata*, though we shall add a word of comment in the conclusion of this article. Neither are we concerned here with the question of how they may be reconciled with the genuine Scotus should they prove to be authentic. We do not wish to discuss whether theologism is as dangerous and indefensible as Gilson seems to believe,[7] or even, whether it colors the thought of Duns Scotus to a substantially greater degree than it does that of Maimonides or St. Thomas, the two "most balanced of all medieval theologians."[8] But we are troubled by the interpretation Gilson reads into Scotus' proofs for the existence of

---

[3] *La Philosophie de Saint Bonaventure*, 2ed. (Paris, J. Vrin, 1943), pp. 94,99.

[4] *Unity of Phil. Experience*, p. 49.

[5] *Reason and Relevation in the Middle Ages* (New York, Charles Scribner's Sons, 1946), pp. 85–87; *La philosophie au moyen âge*, 2ed. (Paris, Payot, 1945), *passim*; *God and Philosophy* (New Haven, Yale University Press, 1942), p. 69; "Metaphysik und Theologie nach Duns Skotus," *Franziskanische Studien*, XXII (1935), 209–231.

[6] In the *Archives d'Histoire Doctrinale et Littéraire du Moyen Age*, XII–XIII (1937–1938), 5–86.

[7] According to Gilson "scepticism always goes hand in hand with such theologies," *Unity of Phil. Exp.*, p. 48.

[8] *Ibid.*, p. 40.

God. For despite some of the excellent studies that have appeared recently on the latter subject,[9] there still seems to be a general distrust of Scotus' position among contemporary neoscholastics who persist in following Gilson's interpretation unquestioningly. Pegis, for instance, accepting the historical perspective suggested by Gilson finds the most striking characteristic of Scotus to be his attempt "to rescue philosophy from the errors of the philosophers by means of theology."[10] And Wellmuth, while admitting that Gilson's account of Scotus in *La philosophie au moyen age* is based in part on spurious works, suggests in view of his article on the Theoremata that "it would be premature to reject his (Gilson's) interpretation as too severe."[11]

Gilson succeeds in salvaging his original thesis in this latter work, however, only by departing from the obvious meaning of the authentic writings. Important as it is to interpret the doctrines of the great scholastics in their proper historical setting, it should be noted that the historical approach can be a two edged sword. When the "historical conception" of any philosopher becomes a hindrance rather than an aid in grasping his thought, when his clear cut distinctions have to be ignored and his categorical assertions toned down, when his whole intellectual stature has to be cut to fit the proverbial Procrustean bed, it may well be that the historical conception needs alteration. In the interests of historical truth we believe a reexamination of some of Gilson's basic assumptions in this connection are in order.

It may help to preface the discussion of these fundamental postulates with a brief summary of the stand taken by Gilson in his analysis of theorems XV and XVI.[12]

SCOTUS' THEOLOGISM

As we understand it, Gilson's thesis runs something like this. Scotus, like Aristotle, defines demonstration as a syllogism productive of sci-

---

[9] Confer for instance E. Bettoni, *L'Ascesa a Dio in Duns Scoto* (Milan, Società Editrice 'Vita e Pensiero,' 1943), esp. pp. 36ff.; Timotheus Barth, "De tribus viis diversis existentiam divinam attingendi." *Antonianum*, XVIII (1943), 91–117. While the latter gives simply a presentation of Scotus' position, Bettoni adds an extensive criticism of Gilson's interpretation. Only after we had completed our study were we able to obtain a copy of this work published during the war. We are in substantial agreement with Bettoni's critical comments. Our study is developed along somewhat different lines.

[10] Confer *Modern Schoolman*, XXIII (May, 1946), 228.

[11] Wellmuth, *Nature and Origins of Scientism* (Milwaukee, Marquette University Press, 1944), note 53. E. A. Moody's review of my study on Scotus' transcendentality is also colored by Gilson's interpretation. *Journal of Philosophy*, XLIV, 246.

[12] *Les seize premiers theoremata*, pp. 54–80.

entific knowledge (*scientia*). One condition for *scientia*, however, is that it must be a conclusion deduced from some necessary and evident principles which are related to it as cause to effect. Only a *propter quid* demonstration gives the cause or reason *why* the predicate of the conclusion inheres in its respective subject. Hence only the *propter quid* is a true demonstration. Now Scotus admits with St. Thomas that we cannot prove God's existence *a priori* or *propter quid*. Hence Scotus' argument in the *Oxoniense*, the *Reportata* and the *De Primo Principio*, based as it is on the impossibility of an infinite regress in essentially ordered causes, is no strict demonstration. At best it is a *necessary* proof, but not necessary *and evident*. In scholastic terminology, however, a conclusion from the necessary but not evident premises is not *scientia*, but *opinio*. And the corresponding syllogism is called *dialecticus* or *probabilis*, but not *demonstratio*. Now this is precisely the position of the author of the *Theoremata*.[13] He denies that in a series of essentially ordered causes, we can demonstrate the coexistence of the First Cause by a proof that is *simpliciter necessaria* and *mere naturalis*. Our proofs are only *probabiles*.

By *simpliciter necessaria*, Gilson tells us, Scotus means a proof that is both necessary and evident. That such proofs are beyond us becomes clear if we consider the position of metaphysics in the Scotistic system. Three sciences deal directly or indirectly with God, *theologia in se*, *theologia nostra* and *metaphysica nostra*. In the present state of existence we cannot hope to possess the first, for its object is *Deus ut hic* and is based on the intuition of the divine essence. *Theologia nostra*, however, is founded on revelation. Though it strives for the object of *theologia in se*, its success is but partial, for it grasps God not in himself, but only in so far as he can be known in the concept, *ens infinitum*. The third science (metaphysics) can deal only indirectly with God. Its proper object is being *qua* being, as Avicenna said—not God, as Averroes claimed. Consequently, when metaphysics enters the service of theology, it is doubly handicapped, for it lacks both intuition and revelation. Its struggle to become a theology is even more feeble than that of *theologia nostra*, since it can only attain *Deus ut hic* by first achieving the *ens infinitum*, which is properly the object of *our* theology. The metaphysician, therefore, is constantly trailing the theologian and translating into the language of being the truths of revelation. That is why reason can give us no *evident* conclusions about God. True, not

---

[13] *Theor.* XV, 1–2; Vivès, V, 51a: In essentialiter ordinatis est dare primum, quod sit unicum, et coaevum illi coordinationi. In omni genere causae est ordo essentialis. Istae duae propositiones petantur: quarum prima tres partes, secunda est simplex, utraque licet sit probabilis, tamen difficile esset, vel forte nobis impossibile eam simpliciter necessaria ratione, et mere naturali probare.

all necessary truths make the same demands on the metaphysician-turned-theologian. The absolute omnipotence of God, for instance, is less evident than his existence. But even the latter truth exceeds the competence of the philosopher. It is of cardinal importance, then, to remember that for Scotus *non omne necessarium est evidenter necessarium*.[14] It is with such truths that his metaphysics busies itself in its role as *ancilla theologiae*. Hence when he proves the existence, the unity, the infinity, intellectuality and other attributes from reason Scotus does not believe he has found proofs of absolute value. Technically speaking, they lack evidence. They compel reason without enlightening it. They are necessary, but not *simpliciter necessaria ratione*.[15]

But even here a distinction is necessary. If the metaphysician can give proofs that are in any sense of the word necessary, it is only because he has become a theologian. The philosopher unaided by revelation is even worse off. We said above that metaphysics has being *qua* being as its object. But even this must be qualified, for it presupposes that being *qua being* is the object of our intellect. But without faith we would be in Aristotle's position—convinced that sensible being alone was the proper object of our mind. Avicenna discovered the truth only because he was a good Mohammedan. But if revelation is required for a proper notion of being, is it not clear that all proofs based on the attributes of being derive their cogency from faith? What is this, then, but theologism?

> Ainsi, doublement déficient, et pour des causes qui relévent directment de théologie, notre connaissance métaphysique ne peut donc transcender l'être pour s'élever á Dieu, sans un secours de Dieu. C'est ce que disent les oeuvres authentiques de Duns Scot, c'est aussi ce que nos enseignent les *Theoremata*.[16]

Gilson elaborates on this distinction between the enlightened intellect and reason unaided by revelation. It becomes the key to solving the discrepancies between the two writings. Take the question of essentially and accidentally ordered causes. In both orders, Scotus claims we arrive at a First Cause coexistent with the series. The *Theoremata*, however, insists we can demonstrate it in neither instance. Apparently a radical opposition. Actually, Gilson assures us, they agree fundamentally. For both assure us that the order we take makes little difference. The validity (or invalidity) is the same in either case. The

[14] *Rep. Par.*, prol. q. 2, n. 18; XXII, 43b. (All references are to the *Opera Omnia Scoti*, Wadding-Vivès edition [Paris, 1891–1895] unless otherwise noted.)
[15] *Les seize premiers*, p. 61.
[16] *Ibid.*, pp. 66–67.

author of the *Theoremata* speaks as a pure philosopher, Scotus as a philosopher-theologian. The former finds only *probationes probabiles;* the latter *probationes necessarias.* Where the one fails, the other succeeds. Hence we have no reason to doubt the authenticity of the *Theoremata* on this score. Quite the contrary, it is only if we were to read there that

> la raison naturelle seule, *pro statu isto,* et sans aucun secours de la révélation, peut découvrir ce qui donne aux preuves de l'existence de Dieu leur vertu contraignante, un tel ecrit ne pourrait être de duns Scot et nous aurions grandement raison d'en suspecter l'authenticité.[17]

Even Gilson seems to realize that his explanation taxes the credulity of his readers considerably, for he hastens to call attention to the reason why the author of the *Theoremata* rejects the argument for the existence of the First Cause. As a father generates a son and then dies, so also the First Cause could conceivably produce another cause and go out of existence. If the continued existence of a father is not a necessary requisite for the continuance of generation, why cannot the same be said of the essentially ordered series of causes? Scotus himself, Gilson points out, found it very difficult to exclude this possibility. Speaking of Avicenna's theory that God does not immediately create all inferior beings, but only the first Intelligence, who in turn creates the second, Scotus remarks: *Difficile est prohibere, quin possit creatio competere agenti creato respectu multorum.* If Scotus finally succeeds, it is only because he is a Christian and can marshal the truths of revelation in support of reason. *Sed nos Christiani aliter ponimus.* Whence Gilson's conclusion:

> Les écrits théologiques de Duns Scot concèdent que, rationnellement parlant, on ne voit pas bien pourquoi certaines créatures ne seraient pas elles-mêmes capables de creér; or les *Theoremata* n'en demandent même pas tant pour construire leur critique... On ne voit pas quelle contradiction relever entre cette attitudé et celle de Duns Scot, ou, plutôt, c'est la même attitude, puisque c'est la même raison que l'on considére, tantôt réduite a ses seules resources, tantôt éclairée par la Révélation.[18]

Such in substance is the picture Gilson paints of the position of the *Doctor Subtilis,* a position essentially in harmony with the doctrine of the *Theoremata.* We may ignore the numerous minor details which require further substantiation and turn our attention to three assumptions which seem basic to his entire interpretation. The first and most far reaching in its implications concerns the Scotistic concept of demonstration. The second deals specifically with the proofs for the exis-

[17] *Ibid.,* p. 69.
[18] *Ibid.,* p. 73.

tence, infinity and unicity of God. The third involves the possibility of a creature creating independently of the existence of a first cause.

If we let Scotus speak for himself on these matters, I believe we shall come to a conclusion wholly at variance with that presented by Gilson. In this first installment, then, we shall consider the first of his fundamental postulates, that which has to do with his notion of Scotus' *demonstratio quia*.

ON THE NATURE OF DEMONSTRATION

Throughout his entire discussion, Gilson takes for granted that the *demonstratio quia* is no true demonstration. Only the *demonstratio propter quid* fulfills the requisites for scientific knowledge, since it alone yields conclusions that are both necessary and evident. We call this an assumption advisedly, first because Gilson himself offers no substantiating evidence for his assertion and, secondly, because Scotus' own statements give us every reason to maintain the contrary.

It is true, Scotus gives us no *ex professo* or exhaustive treatise on the subject of demonstration and consequently leaves a number of our questions on his exact position unanswered.[19] Nevertheless his passing remarks on this topic are amply sufficient to show how unwarranted is Gilson's interpretation.

The scholastics in general, and particularly the Oxford school following Robert Grosseteste, accepted Aristotle's definition of demonstration as a *syllogismus faciens scire*.[20] As we have no reason for suspecting that Scotus regarded it any differently,[21] we find no fault with Gilson for attempting to clarify the nature of demonstration from Scotus' concept of *scientia*. What do we object to, however, is his arbitrary interpretation of the latter.

Scientia, we might note parenthetically, is best translated by "scientific knowledge" rather than by "science." It is understood primarily of a single proposition which forms the conclusion of a demonstrative syllogism. Only secondarily is it understood of a body of such conclu-

---

[19] The *Commentary on the Posterior Analytics* where we should expect to find such a treatise is not regarded as a genuine Scotistic work. Probably it is the work of John of Cornubia. Confer Grajewski, "Duns Scotus in the Light of Modern Research," *Proceedings of the American Catholic Philosophical Association*, XVIII (1942), 180.

[20] *Analytica Posterior*, I, 2. 71b 17.

[21] *Super Universalia Porphyrri Quaestiones*, q. 1, n. 2: Dicendum, quod Logica est scientia, quae enim in ea docentur, demonstrative concluduntur, sicut in aliis scientiis; ergo sciuntur: quia *Demonstratio est syllogismus faciens scire*. 1 Posteriorum.

sions generically or specifically related in the sense that they deal more or less with the same subject matter.[22]

In several different passages, Scotus enumerates the four basic conditions for *scientia*. Though it is a matter of indifference which description we select, we quote the following from the prologue of the *Reportata*, since Gilson uses this as the basis of his speculation.

> Accipiendo scientiam prout *scire* 1 Posteriorum text 5, definitur, dico quod scientia est cognito certa veri demonstrati necessarii mediati ex necessariis prioribus demonstrati, quod natum est habere evidentiam ex necessario prius evidente, applicato ad ipsum per discursum syllogisticum. Prima conditio, scilicet quod est cognito certa, excludens omnem deceptionem, opinionem et dubitationem, convenit omni intellectuali virtuti quia virtus intellectualis est perfectio intellectus, disponens ipsum ad perfectam operationem, et perfecta operatio intellectualis est cognito veri certa; ideo omnis virtus intellectualis est habitus quo determinate verum dicimus, propter quod opinio et suspicio, quibus potest subesse falsum, non sunt virtutes intellectuales.—Secunda conditio, scilicet quod sit veri necessarii, sequitur ex prima quia si scientia esset veri contingentis, posset sibi subesse falsum, propter mutationem objecti, sicut opinioni. Si ergo scientia est essentialiter habitus cognoscitivus verus; ergo essentialiter non tantum includit relationem communem habitus ad objectum, sed specialem, scilicet conformitatis ad ipsum objectum. Nunc autem si objectum non esset verum necessarium, posset habitus idem manens quandoque conformari illi objecto, et quandoque non, propter mutationem illius objecti, et tunc posset esse quandoque verus, quandoque non verus... Tertia conditio, quod natum est habere evidentiam ex necessario prius evidente, est propria, distinguens scientiam ab intellectu principiorum, quia iste est veri habentis evidentiam ex terminis; ex primo Posteriorum text. com. 21 'Principia cognoscimus in quantum terminos cognoscimus;' scientia est veri habentis evidentiam ex principiis.—Quarta conditio est, quod sit notitia evidentiae posterioris causata a priore per discursum syllogisticum, et hoc est imperfectionis, nec est de per se ratione scientiae secundum se, sed tantum scientiae imperfectae, et non convenit scientiae, nisi in illo intellectu, cui convenit discurrere et procedere a noto ad ignotum.[23]

The first condition, then, demands certitude of the conclusion. Of course this implies that the premises from which it is inferred are also certain. On this score, *scientia differs* from *opinio*, which is the conclusion of a *syllogismus probabilis*.

Secondly, the proposition scientifically known must be a necessary truth, for purely contingent truths are incapable of demonstration.

Thirdly, this necessary truth is not immediately evident, but is

---

[22] *Metaphy.* 6, q. 1, n. 2, VII, 303a.

[23] *Rep.* prol. q. 1, n. 4, XXII, 7b–8b; confer also *Oxon.* prol. qq. 3 & 4 lat. n. 26; VIII, 183b; *ibid.* 3, d. 24, q. un., n. 13; XV, 44b; *Rep. Par.* 3, d. 24, q. un., n. 16; XXIII, 454ab.

known by reason of other necessary and evident truths. (Incidentally, this condition is one of the most difficult to fulfill in the case of a demonstration of God's existence. Most of the so-called classical scholastic arguments for God's existence failed to measure up to this requirement since they were based on contingent premisses.)

The fourth condition demands that the necessary and evident principle be related to the proposition scientifically known "per discursum syllogisticum," that is as the premisses of a valid syllogism are related to their respective conclusion. In this way the evident cause (the premisses) is applied to the conclusion (scientia). This last condition really involves imperfection and is characteristic only of a created intellect which proceeds step by step from the unknown to the known (discursive reasoning).

Scotus also accepted Aristotle's further distinction between the *propter quid and quia* demonstration.[24] The former, in so far as it gives the proximate cause as the middle term of the syllogism, provides the reason *why* the predicate of the conclusion inheres in the subject, whereas the *demonstratio quia* merely establishes the fact *that* it does so.

Now the question is, Do both the *propter quid* and the *quia* demonstrations produce scientific knowledge (*scientia*,) or is the former alone competent to do so? Gilson believes Scotus holds for the second alternative. Precisely where Scotus' *demonstratio quia* fails, he does not say directly. But if his comment on the Scotistic proofs for God's existence be any clue, the chief stumbling block would seem to be the third condition, namely:

> quod natum est habere evidentiam ex necessario prius evidente; et il ajoute aussitôt cette condition: 'scientia est veri habentis evidentiam ex principiis.' A partir de quel principe évident et antérier à Dieu pourrait-on acquérir l'évidence de l'existence de Dieu? Il n'en existe pas. Nous en arrivons donc a cette conclusion: Duns Scot ne peut, sans entrer en contradiction avec sa définition même de la science, prétendre nous donner une démonstration strictement nécessaire de l'existence de Dieu. Jamais nous ne pourrons en donner une démonstration *propter quid*; il faudra nous contenter d'une démonstration quia.[25]

It would be interesting to know on what grounds Gilson equates *simpliciter necessarium* or *strictement necessaire* with *evidenter neces-*

---

[24] *Quodl.* q. 7, n. 3; XXV, 283b: Prima distinctio est nota ex primo Posteriorum, quae est, quod demonstrationum alia est propter quid, sive per causam; alia quia sive per effectum. It is not clear whether Scotus equates *propter quid* and *a priori* on the one hand, and *quia* and *a posteriori* on the other or not. For Aristotle, demonstration through a remote cause (an *a priori* principle) is only a *demonstratio quia*. Confer *Analytica Posteriora* I, c. 13.

[25] *Les seize premiers theoremata*, p. 55.

sarium. As it is of no importance to our criticism, however, we shall let it pass. What is important though is his contention that the (1) *demonstratio quia* does not fulfill the requirements, (2) since its conclusions are necessary but not necessary and evident. Actually (1) and (2) are distinct, though related, problems. Let us consider Gilson's reason first.

Is it true that the *demonstratio quia* lacks premisses that are both necessary and evident truths, and therefore yields a conclusion that may be necessary but not evidently so? If it does, then Gilson is correct in consigning it to essentially the same category as the dialetical or probable syllogism. Scotus, however, seems to have different ideas on the subject than those attributed to him by the eminent historian.

Not only does he not remonstrate with Aristotle for discussing the *demonstratio quia* in the *Posterior Analytics* (it should have been treated in the *Topics,* if it were on a par with the dialetical syllogism), but in a classical passage of the seventh question of his *Quodlibet* he maintains the very opposite of what Gilson ascribes to him. Incidentally, we shall return to this question later, for to the discerning reader it provides a step by step refutation of Gilson's fundamental assumptions. Both the *propter quid* and the *quia* conclusions are based upon necessary and evident premisses. Consequently both have *evidentiam ex prius evidente.* We quote this interesting text in full.

> Prima distinctio est nota ex primo *Posteriorum,* quae est quod demonstratio alia est *propter quid,* sive per causam; alio *quia* sive per effectum. Probatur ista distinctio per rationem, quia omne necessarium verum, non evidens ex terminis habens tamen connexionem necessariam et evidentiam ad aliud, ut necessarium evidens ex terminis, potest demonstrari per illud verum evidens. Nunc autem, aliquod verum necessarium non evidens ex terminis, habet connexionem necessariam ad aliquod verum acceptum a causa, et aliquod ad verum acceptum ab effectu; non solum enim veritates de causis non possunt esse sine quibusdam veris de effectibus, sed nec e converso. Igitur potest aliquod verum demonstrari per aliquod verum evidens acceptum a causa, et tunc *propter quid,* vel per aliquod verum acceptum ab effectu, et tunc *quia.* Et videtur hinc sequi corollarium, quod principia immediata sive evidentia ex terminis, non possunt demonstrari demonstratione *quia;* quod si verum est, tunc quaedam media vera inter prima vera, et conclusiones ultimas, et solum illa sunt demonstrabilia, quia per vera ultima. Qualiter autem verum acceptum ad effectu possit esse evidens et tamen verum acceptum a causa non evidens, patere potest si aliquis consideret modum illum acquirendi scientiam 1 Metaphys. et 2 Posteriorum. Per experientiam est frequenter notum de effectu, quia est ex multis singularibus acceptis a sensu, et nondum scitur propter quid ita est, quia illud non habetur a sensu, nisi mediante ulteriore inquisitione.[26]

[26] *Quodlibet* q. 7, n. 3; XXV, 283b–284a.

We could wish for no clearer statement of our point. In every demonstration some necessary truth not known immediately from its terms is established by reason of its necessary and evident connection with an evident truth. *Omne necessarium verum non evidens ex terminis habens tamen connexionem necessariam et evidentiam ad aliud ... potest demonstrari per illud verum evidens.* This necessary and evident relationship holds not merely between premisses which express the ontological cause why the predicate of the conclusion pertains to the subject, but also where the premisses express an effect of the cause whose existence the conclusion establishes. The reason is clear, for *non solum enim veritates de causis non possunt esse sine quibusdam veris de effectibus, sed nec e converso.* Consequently demonstrations fall naturally into two classes, accordingly as the premiss is a necessary and evident truth accepted from the cause or one which is accepted from the effect. *Igitur potest aliquod verum demonstrari per aliquod verum evidens acceptum a causa, et tunc propter quid, vel per aliquod verum acceptum ab effectu, et tunc quia.* If it seems strange, Scotus goes on, that a proposition about an effect can be more evident than that about its cause, we need only remember that the source of evidence is experience. *Qualiter autem verum acceptum ab effectu possit esse evidens et tamen verum acceptum a causa non evidens patere potest si aliquis consideret modum acquirendi scientiam ... Per experientiam est frequenter notum de effectu quia est ... et nondum scitur propter quid ita est.*

Consequently, we should expect Scotus to admit two kinds of *scientia*, corresponding to the two types of demonstrations that fulfill the four requirements for scientific knowledge. And that is precisely what he does. He speaks frequently of the *scientia quia* and the *scientia propter quid.*[27] While the two differ in their relative perfection, as is obvious, nevertheless it should be noted that even the *scientia quia* is a truth that is both necessary and (mediately) evident. Hence, there is a vast difference between a *scientia quia* and *theologia nostra* which is neither *scientia quia* nor *propter quid*. Why Gilson has consistently minimized the one distinction and exaggerated the other, we fail to see. We find no evidence in the texts of Scotus himself. On the contrary, Scotus points out very clearly why *theologia nostra* at best yields conclusions that are *necessaria* but not *evidenter necessaria*. It is because the principles or premisses it uses are revealed and are not evident, either from their terms (*per se nota*) or from experience or from the evident principles of some higher science from which they can be inferred.

[27] Confer for instance *Metaphy.* 1, q. 1, *tota quaestio.*

This is clear from Scotus' criticism of St. Thomas. The latter, he claims, defended Theology as a strict science on the ground that its premisses, though actually known by revelation, can be regarded as derived from the superior science of vision which the Blessed in heaven possess. But the fact that the premisses we believe on faith are evident to the saints, does not make them either mediately or immediately evident to us. Averroes had essayed a similar solution when he made God the object of metaphysics, but eventually had to fall back on another natural source of evidence for the object of his science, namely, physics. And then, referring to the parallel the Angelic Doctor makes between the two theologies and natural sciences that are subordinated to one another such as metaphysics and optics (*perspectiva*), he makes the following interesting observation. It is true that the *subalterna scientia* (optics) can be developed as a true science, even by one who is not a metaphysician and is ignorant of the principles of metaphysics from which the first principles of optics are derived. But this is so only because the first principles of the subordinate science can be known evidently from another source, namely experience.[28] Such is not the case, however, with *theologia nostra*. It is necessary therefore that the first principles of a science be evident, either in themselves, or as derived from other principles known evidently, or because they are known directly from experience.[29]

Whatever else may be said about the *demonstratio quia*, from what has been noted so far it is clear that it cannot be excluded from the category of *syllogismi facientes scire* on the score that its premisses lack evidence. Referring specifically to the basis on which he will construct his proofs for the existence of God, Scotus remarks that it is *evidentissimum* and if any one were to deny it *indiget sensu et poena*.[30] Consequently, if the *demonstratio quia* fails against the third condition of *scientia*, namely, *quod natum est habere evidentiam ex necessario prius evidente*, it would be because the premisses were contingent and not necessary. Now there is some evidence, though it is not conclusive, that Scotus admitted a twofold division of the *quia* demonstration: one based on contingent though evident premisses, the other based on premisses that are also necessary. Obviously, only the

---

[28] *Rep.* prol. q. 2, n. 5; XXII, 35b: Possunt habere aliqua principia de quibus habent evidentiam per experientiam . . . Si sint autem alia principia in subalternata, quae non sunt nota per sensum et experientiam, oportet quod sciat ea reducere in alia principia priora. Ergo notitia, quae tantum supponit alia principia, et non propter quid, nec per experientiam cognoscit ista, illa non est scientia.

[29] *Ibid.*

[30] *Lectura Prima,* Cod. Wa, 1449, fol. 8b.

latter would fulfill the requirements for scientific knowledge and deserve the strict name of demonstration.[31] However that may be, the mere fact that reasoning proceeds from effect to cause is no sign that the conclusion has no *evidentiam ex necessario prius evidente*.

Gilson, apparently confuses the meaning of this third condition which demands that the evidence of the conclusion be derived from some anterior evident principle, or as Scotus puts it elsewhere: *quod sit per causam evidentem intellectui*.[32] If "causa" be understood ontologically, in the sense that one of the premisses is a proposition *de causis*, or to be more precise, if the middle term of the syllogism gives the cause—or at least some ontologically prior principle—why the predicate of the conclusion inheres in the subject, then *scientia* would be the fruit of a *demonstratio propter quid* alone. For only the latter gives the proximate cause *why* the predicate pertains to the subject. The *demonstratio quia*, on the contrary, is content merely to establish the fact *that* it does.

But why this unwarranted restriction? Certainly this is not the obvious meaning of "cause" in this connection. It is the premisses that are referred to, since they are the "cause" of the conclusion. For as Aristotle tells us, "the premisses of demonstrated knowledge must be true, primary, immediate and better known than the conclusion, which is *further related to them as effect to cause*."[33] The cause in question is not the precise reason *why the predicate inheres* in the subject, but *why we know* that the predicate is so affirmed. We are dealing here with logical, not ontological principles, with the order of knowledge, not with the order of nature. It is the premisses which constitute the principle (*necessarium prius evidens*) from which the conclusion flows. That is why Scotus says, *conclusio autem est certa per principium tamquam per causam suae certitudinis*.[34]

Consequently, Gilson's question should not read: A partir de quel principe évident et antérieur à Dieu pourrait-on acquérir l'évidence de l'existence de Dieu? For, posited in this way, it has no answer. Rather it should be, From what principle *known* evidently and anteriorly to any knowledge of God's existence, can we acquire knowledge of the

---

[31] *Rep. par.* 1, d. 2, q. 2, nn. 4, 6; XXII, 64b, 65b–66a; *Reportatio Magna*, Cod. Wb. 1454, fol. 12 (quoted from Bettoni, *op. cit.*, pp. 49–50): Respondeo quod in demonstratione quia, possum accipere praemissam de inesse vel de possibili. Si accipitur de inesse, est demonstratio contingens et non ex necessariis..., si autem accipiatur praemissa pro possibili esse sic: aliqua natura est possibilis fieri sive effectibilis vel productibilis, ergo aliqua natura est effectiva vel productiva, est demonstratio ex necessariis.
[32] *Oxon.* 3, d. 24, q. un., n. 13; XV, 44b.
[33] Post. Anal. I, 2, 71b 22:
[34] *Quodl.* q. 17, n. 11; XXVI, 220a.

existence of God? Framed in this way, the question is no longer mean-ingless as Scotus takes great pains to show.

Why does Gilson side-step this obvious interpretation? Why does he seek to limit Scotus' demonstration to the *propter quid?* We discover the answer in his *La philosophie au moyen âge,*[35] where Scotus is quoted as saying: *Nulla demonstratio, quae est ab effectu ad causam, est demonstratio simpliciter.* No reference is given! Boehner tells us he spent hours trying to find this quotation in the genuine works of Scotus.[36] We also wasted hours combing the accepted logical works and failed to find any doctrine faintly resembling the same. Turning to the commentary on the *Posterior Analytics,* a work whose authen-ticity has been rejected by the Scotistic commission, we finally located the text.[37] (Incidentally a great deal of unnecessary labor might be obviated and the task of clarifying the thought of Scotus simplified, if in the future commentators would indicate the exact source of their quotations from the Subtle Doctor!) But even this quotation, if read in its context, does not support Gilson's contention.

In all fairness to Gilson, however, it should be noted that many modern Scotistic commentators such as Van de Woestyne, Montefor-tino, etc., tend to limit demonstration in the strict sense to either the *demonstratio potissima*[38] or at least to the *propter quid.* But like Gil-son, these men have drawn heavily on works later rejected from the canon of authentic works. We know of no clear text in any of the authentic writings that would lead one to suppose that the *demon-stratio quia* is essentially incapable of fulfilling the four requirements for strict scientific knowledge.

On the contrary, we have every reason to suppose that it can. First of all in the passage quoted above, Scotus speaks of both the *propter quid* and *quia* as demonstrations without qualification.[39] Conse-quently, we find no confirmation of Wellmuth's contention that:

> Whereas St. Thomas holds, with Aristotle, that *a posteriori* demonstra-tions are real demonstrations, though inferior to those which are *a priori,* Scotus considers them to be demonstrations only in a modified sense.[40]

---

[35] *La Philosophie du moyen âge,* Paris, Vrin, 1925, p. 228.

[36] Confer Father Boehner's criticism of Wellmuth's *Nature and Origins of Scientism* in *Franciscan Studies,* V (1945), 311.

[37] *Post. Analy.* I, d. 11, n. 7 (*Opera Omnia Scoti,* Vivès ed., II, 227b–228a).

[38] The distinction between simple demonstration and the *demonstratio potissima* was admitted generally among the scholastics. The latter is an affirmative, universal, *propter quid* demonstration in the first figure.

[39] *Quodl.,* q. 7, n. 3; XXV, 283b. See note 24.

[40] Wellmuth, *The Nature and Origin of Scientism,* pp. 30–31.

Secondly, Scotus states expressly that it fulfills, or at least can fulfill, the second and third conditions of *scientia*, which are the only conceivable grounds on which one might be tempted to exclude it as a syllogism *faciens scire*.[41] Thirdly, it is implicit in what Scotus says of his demonstration of God's existence. (We shall deal with this more specifically later.) By way of confirmation, we might add a fourth reason.

It is well known that Ockham admired Scotus, even when he felt constrained to criticize him. Particularly did he respect Scotus *propter magnam notitiam quam habuit de Logica*.[42] In fact there are so many striking parallels between the logic of Scotus and Ockham that one wonders if the Venerable Inceptor did not merely set down in systematic form the logic which Scotus used so proficiently. Now Ockham leaves no doubt on the matter; both the *demonstratio propter quid* and *quia* fulfill all four conditions required to produce *scientia*.

> Restat nunc dicere de demonstratione. Est autem primo sciendum, quod cum dictum sit in principio, quod demonstratio est syllogismus faciens scire, accipiendo *scire* pro notitia evidenti et certa, ubi necessarium sequitur ex propositionibus necessariis, et talis syllogismus sit multiplex, necesse est quod multiplex sit demonstratio. Propter quod oportet scire, quod quaedam est demonstratio, cujus praemissae sunt simpliciter priores conclusione, et illa vocatur demonstratio a priori sive propter quid; quaedam est demonstratio cujus praemissae non sunt simpliciter priores conclusione, sunt tamen notiores sic syllogizanti, per quas devenit sic syllogizans in notitiam conclusionis; et talis demonstratio vocatur demonstratio quia sive a posteriori.[43]

Now Ockham tells us he differs with Scotus precisely in this, that the Subtle Doctor claimed that his proofs for the infinity and unicity of God were strict demonstrations.[44] If Scotus' concept of demonstration was not identical with that of his own, Ockham's criticism would have been simply pointless—particularly if Scotus had held the opinion Gilson ascribes to him. Unless, of course, we were to suppose that Ockham either misunderstood Scotus' position or deliberately misrepresented it. But it is inconceivable that one who knew Scotus' writings so thoroughly as Ockham and who was so well versed in the technicalities

---

[41] It is one of the two ways in which a necessary truth not evident from its terms can be inferred from a *verum evidens. Quodl.* q. 7, n. 3, XXV, 283.

[42] *Sent.* I, d. 2, q. 10, G.

[43] *Summa Logicae* III, p. 2, c. 17.

[44] *Quodlibetum* VII, qq. 17–23. Question 23 reads: Utrum demonstrationes philosophi 8 Phys. et 12 Metaphy. concludant Deum esse infinitum intensive . . . In ista quaestione dici Scotus dist. 2, quod sic . . . sed teneo oppositum quod illae rationes tantum probant Deum esse infinitum duratione. See Longpré, *La Philosophie du B. Duns Scot,* Paris, Société et Librairie S. François d'Assise, 1924, 34ss.

of medieval logic, should have mistaken Scotus' position on such a simple matter as demonstration. The second alternative is equally untenable, for as Boehner has indicated, Ockham is extremely careful to state Scotus' stand exactly whenever he differs with him.[45] Even apart from his great admiration for Scotus *qui excedit alios in subtilitate*, Ockham could not afford to do otherwise, dealing as he was with the doctrine of a man hardly ten years dead whose thought still lived on in scores of ardent defenders. Hence we have every reason to believe that Ockham not only gives his own definition of demonstration in the above text but that of Scotus as well.

From all this, it should be apparent that we have no reason for contesting the demonstrative character of Scotus' proofs for the existence, unicity and infinity of God on the sole ground that they are *demonstrationes quia*. Neither are we justified in asserting that in Scotus' eyes, they enjoyed no substantially greater validity than did his probable proofs for the omnipotence, immensity and ubiquity of God. But this brings us to Gilson's second assumption, which we shall deal with next.

Part II

Professor Gilson's second assumption is this: *Scotus did not*—in fact, could not consistently—*regard his proofs for God's existence, unicity, and infinity as strict demonstrations.*

He writes: "Pourtant quand tout est dit, Duns Scot croit-il avoir atteint des preuves de valeur absolue? Non, car elles ne possèdent qu'une nécessité pour ainsi dire formelle, mais sans évidence."[46] Obviously if his proofs yield only necessary, but not evidently necessary truths, Scotus' conclusions regarding the existence, unity and infinite nature of God are simply *credibilia*. They are substantially on a par with the conclusions regarding God's immensity, ubiquity and absolute omnipotence. For Scotus, the last named attribute, Gilson assures us, is simply "une autre vérité *nécessaire* dont on ne peut prouver que la probabilité."[47] It is true that within the realm of *credibilia* we can speak of various degrees of probability accordingly as the various truths are more or less removed from evidence. But even that which is least removed—the existence of God—forces man to transcend his natural

---

[45] "Scotus' Teaching according to Ockham," *Franciscan Studies*, VI (1946), 100–107.
[46] *Les seize premiers theoremata*, p. 63.
[47] *Ibid.* p. 61.

powers; hence 'notre connaissance métaphysique ne peut donc transcender l'être pour s'élever à Dieu, sans un secours de Dieu.'[48]

In adopting this interpretation, we believe Gilson has been unduly influenced by the interpretation of the seventeenth-century Scotists.[49] But from what has been said, there is little justification for relegating Scotus' proofs for the existence, unicity and infinity of God to the category of *probationes probabiles* simply because they are *demonstrationes quia*. As a historian, Gilson could hardly do so. As a philosopher, of course, he may; but then he would be condemning the arguments of St. Thomas even more severely; for based as the latter are on contingent premisses, they yield neither an evident (according to his assumption) nor a necessary conclusion. For that reason we prefer to keep the discussion on a purely historical level. And there we must confess our failure to see how Gilson has substantiated his position on the basis of any text from Scotus himself.

As to the additional confirmatory reasons he adduces, the following should be noted: 1) Scotus does not refer to his arguments simply as "preuves nécessaires." He calls them categorically demonstrations. Only when this fact is admitted, does the opposition of his contemporaries and successors become historically intelligible. 2) He does not reduce them to substantially the same level as the probable proofs (or if you wish to use Richard of St. Victor's terminology, necessary though not evident proofs) for the absolute omnipotence of God. On the contrary, he insists on the sharp chasm that separates them. 3) Scotus did not regard our metaphysics as a disgruntled philosophy or a disinherited theology struggling to regain what was lost through the fall and reach-

---

[48] *Ibid.* p. 67.

[49] In his commentary on the *Theoremata* (Vivès edit., V. 43), Maurice the Irishman writes: "Non obstat his ea quae habet in tractatu de primo principio, quia illa disputatio totalis praesupponit fidem, vel saltem non procedit a priori et ex simpliciter necessariis. Loquitur etiam de potentia creaturae et de facto, via attingentiae naturalis, non autem simpliciter de repugnantia capacitatis passivae, aliter contradiceret sibiipsi in quodlibet quaest. 7. et in Sententiis plerumque." Similarly Wadding in his comment on the *De Primo Principio* (Vivès edit., IV, 719) remarks: "Tractatus iste de primo principio vere aureus est, in quo Doctor, instar aquilae in altum volantis, quantum humano ingenio possibile esse videtur, naturam primi rerum principii, seu causae supremae indagat et scrutatur; quod non propriis naturae viribus, sed specialibus ejusdem primi principii adjutoriis confortatum praestitisse, testantur et persuadent, pecularis ejus in hoc tractatu prae aliis devotio, et veluti mentis in Deum continua ascensio." But both these Scotists, like Gilson, were interpreting Scotus' theory of demonstration in the light of the non-authentic commentary on the *Post. Analy.* and on the assumption of the authenticity of the *Tractatus De Creditis*. However, the real reason for the divergence of opinion in the *Theoremata* and the authentic works is not to be traced back to the difference of viewpoint between a pure philosopher and a philosopher-turned-theologian. It is a fundamental difference in the conception of the nature of essentially ordered causes, as we shall see later.

ing out for an object doubly transcending its natural powers like a child grasping for the moon.

If words mean anything, Scotus believed he had true demonstrations; not mere probable proofs. Assuring us he is seeking a knowledge of God, to which *possit pertingere nostra ratio naturalis*, and not with the *credibilia*, which he hoped to treat in a later work, Scotus claims he will demonstrate (*demonstrabo*) the existence of a First Being.[50] And even though he realized that many of his predecessors and contemporaries believed that the infinity and unicity of God are beyond the power of natural reason and are *credibilia*, Scotus professed his faith in the natural powers of the human intellect. Even in its fallen state, our reasoning faculty can establish God's unicity (which for Scotus presupposes a demonstration of God's infinity). *Ad quod ostendendum non puto deficere rationem.*[51]

The moment the demonstrative character of his proof is challenged, Scotus hastens to defend it.

> Ad secundam instantiam supra positam quae dicit quod ratio procedit ex contingentibus et ita non est demonstratio cum dico: aliqua natura vere est effecta ergo aliquid est efficiens. Respondeo quod posset sic argui: Aliqua natura est effecta, quod aliquod subjectum mutatur et ita terminus mutationis incipit esse in subjecto, et ita ille terminus vel compositum producitur sive efficitur; ergo est aliquod efficiens per naturam correlativorum et tunc potest esse secundum veritatem prima contingens sed manifesta.—Potest tamen sic argui probando primam conclusionem, sic: haec est vera: aliqua natura est effectibilis; ergo aliqua est effectiva.— Antecedens probatur, quia aliquod subjectum est mutabile, quia aliquod entium est possible, diffiniendo possible contra necessarium et sic procedendo ex necessariis. Et tunc probatio primae conclusionis est de esse possibili; non autem de existentia actuali, sed de quo ostenditur possibilitas ultra in conclusione tertia ostendetur actualis existentia.[52]

Curiously enough, Gilson tells us that Scotus merely means to defend his proofs as *necessary* and does not imply that they are *evidently* necessary. How he chanced upon this interpretation is difficult to see. First of all, it is a gratis assertion. Secondly, it ignores the meaning of words. Where does Scotus ever speak of probable proofs as *demon-*

---

[50] *De Primo*, c. 3. For "demonstrabo" the Mueller edition has "demonstrare," but the meaning is the same in either case.

[51] See note 49. The meaning of these passages is clear from the whole tenor of the *De Primo*, even if we did not have confirmatory evidence from the Commentaries on the Sentences and the *Quodlibetum* that he considered his proofs for the unicity of God demonstrations in the strict sense of the word. Scotus is obviously attacking the position of William of Ware (Sent. 1, d. 2, q. 1) and other contemporaries who denied that natural reason could demonstrate the infinity and unicity of God.

[52] *Cod. Assisiensis* 137, f. 15vb–16ra. See also *Opus Oxon.* 1, d. 2, q. 2, n. 15, VIII, 419ab (quoted from Bettoni, *op. cit.*, pp. 49–50).

strations! He calls the absolute omnipotence of God a *verum neces-sarium sed non evidenter necessarium*, but only because he believes it indemonstrable—, not merely by a *propter quid* but also by a *quia* demonstration. For both demonstrations, as he patiently explains by way of preface to the whole discussion, yield necessary truths that are mediately evident because based on evident principles.[53] Thirdly, this explanation does not seem to take into account the real historical problem at issue. Every scholastic knew that the strict Aristotelian demonstration is based on evident and necessary premises. To find evident premises for a proof of God's existence caused no problem at all. But where find a premiss that is both evident *and necessary!* On the one hand, if something contingent exists, it necessarily implies the present or past existence of a cause. Some would admit that the prop-ositions *Quod sit contingens* or *sit aliquid ens aliud a Deo* are some-how necessary. *Philosophi dicerent quod hoc est necessarium propter ordinem essentialem causati ad causam.*[54] Scotus, however, protests that such propositions of fact, based as they are, on the order of actual (contingent) existence are radically contingent propositions. This is clear from his criticism of the dubious principle: *Omne quod est, quando est, necesse est esse.*[55] This Aristotelian dictum could be in-terpreted in such a way as to confer hypothetical necessity on the proposition, *aliquod est effectum*, but only at the expense of affirming the necessity of the creative act of God. However, Scotus insists, we can prove that God creates contingently and that as a consequence, every such proposition *sit contingens respectu Dei tamen est contin-gens evidentissimum.*[56]

"I could begin with such contingent propositions of fact," Scotus tells us equivalently, "just as St. Thomas did. *Illae de actu . . . sunt contingentes, licet satis manifestae.*[57] But evident premisses are not enough, as every good Aristotelian knows, for *tunc prima ratio esset secundum veritatem contingentis, sed manifesta.*[58] But we are seeking a true demonstration, and therefore I have chosen premisses that are both evident and necessary."

It is precisely here that Scotus manifests his ingenuity. In his clas-sical refutation of Heracliteanism,[59] he revealed how the mind can

---

[53] Confer the text of *Quodl.* q. 7, n. 3 cited above.
[54] *Prima Lectura*, Cod. Wa, 1449, f. 8b.
[55] Confer the discussion on this problem by Boehner in *The Tractatus de Praedes-tinatione et de Praescientia Dei et de Futuris Contingentibus of William Ockham*, St. Bonaventure, N.Y., Franciscan Institute, 1945, pp. 70–88.
[56] *Prima Lectura, loc. cit.*
[57] *De Primo Principio*, c. 3, n. 1, Mueller ed., p. 38.
[58] *Oxon.* 1, d. 2, q. 2, n. 15, Fernandez-Garcia ed., I, 195.
[59] *Oxon.* 1, d. 3, q. 4, nn. 7–13; IX, 173–181.

discover an element of necessity in even the most radical and change-able entities. Here again he indicates how it is possible to attain a necessary proposition from a contingent fact, *quia ex contingenti sequitur aliquod necessarium, licet non econverso.*[60] This is done simply by shifting from the order of actuality to the order of possibility, from the order of existence to the order of essences. Such an inference is always legitimate according to the axiom *ab esse ad posse valet illatio.* But where, from the logical viewpoint, the actual existence of a fact is simply contingent, the possibility of such a fact is always necessary. If a man actually exists, it is, it always was and always will be true that he could exist at the time he actually did exist. Consequently Scotus uses as the premisses of his demonstration such a proposition *de possibili* as "Aliquod est effectibile." It is both necessary and evident. It is necessary, because *istae de possibili sunt necessariae.*[61] It is evident, because it can be immediately inferred from a contingent proposition which is *evidentissimum, quia ex tali contengenti... sequitur aliquod necessariium.* Hence Scotus' statement in the Lectura Prima:

> Ad illud quod secundo arguitur contra positionem praedictam ex contingenti, scilicet quod sit contingens vel sit aliquod ens aliud a Deo, philosophi dicerent quod hoc est necessarium proper ordinem essentialem causati ad causam; dico tamen primo sic: quia licet sit contingens respectu Dei tamen est contingens evidentissimum ut qui negaret *aliquod ens esse quod non sit aeternum,* indiget sensu et poena si negaret sensus, et ideo ex tali contingenti potest ostendi aliquid necessarium, quia ex contingenti sequitur aliquod necessarium, licet non econverso. Item dico quod licet alia a Deo actualiter contingentia respectu esse actualis, non tamen respectu esse potentialis unde illa quae sunt contingentia respectu esse actualis existentiae, respectu possibilis sunt necessaria; ut licet hominem esse sit contingens, tamen ipsum possibile esse est necessarium, quia non includit contradicitionem ad esse aliquid; igitur *possibile esse* aliud a Deo est necessarium, quia ens dividitur in possible et necessarium; et sicut enti necessario est necessitas, ita enti possibili ex sua quidditate est possiblitas; fiat igitur ratio quae prior cum possibilitate essendi et erunt propositiones necessariae.[62]

Furthermore, we find Scotus constantly referring to these proofs for God's existence, infinity and unicity as true demonstrations. They are to be differentiated from those probable, though necessary, proofs characteristic of the *credibilia.* For instance, he criticizes the statement that *Angelus est causabilis* cannot be demonstrated by natural reason, but is known certainly only because of revelation. Noting, first of all,

[60] *Prima Lectura, loc. cit.*
[61] *De Primo Principio, loc. cit.*
[62] *Prima Lectura,* Cod. Wa. 1449, f. 8b (quoted from Bettoni, *op. cit.*).

that '*Angelum esse ens a se' sit non tantum falsum, sicut patet, sed etiam valde absurdum, quia oppositum patebit*, he says:

> Dico ergo de ista minori: Angelus est causabilis, duo opposita praedictis: Primum quod *illa est demonstrabilis;* secundum, quod illud fuit ab Aristotele concessum. Primum probo sic, non possunt esse duae naturae intellectuales simpliciter infinitae; sed quaecumque natura intellectualis si est a se sive incausata, ipsa est simpliciter infinita; ergo non possunt esse plures naturae intellectuales simpliciter incausatae, alioquin non esset prima; ergo quaelibet alia est causata. Prima propositio istius deductionis probatur diffusus in quaestione de unitate Dei.[63]

Whatever is to be said of the proofs themselves, it is beyond the shadow of a doubt that when Scotus wrote the above question, he was convinced he had demonstrated the existence, the infinity and the unicity of God. And only because he had done so, could he further demonstrate that all other natures must be dependent and *causabiles*, whether they actually existed or whether they were merely possible. He did not have to take it on faith. He did not have to rest content with a merely probable, though necessary, proof. *Illa est demonstrabilis!* and why? Simply because the opposite is not merely false, but is *evidently* absurd (*sicut patet*).

Even those of his followers or his admirers who felt constrained to differ with him, disagreed with him as philosophers. They did not make the historical error of reading their own view into his writings, much as they would have welcomed the support of his authority. Ockham, for instance, agreed with Scotus that the existence of a First Being or Uncaused Cause can be demonstrated. But Scotus, he contends, goes too far in insisting that the unicity and infinity are equally demonstrable, and even suggesting that Aristotle himself (unenlightened by any revelation!) demonstrated the infinity of God considered *intensive*.[64]

If one were to accept Gilson's interpretation of the essential conformity of the *Theoremata* with the authentic writings he would have to ignore the clear-cut and unmistakable distinctions made by Scotus between what can be proved by reason and what can be known only by faith. Because Scotus lived in an age which was Christian enough to begin even a purely philosophical work with a prayer, Gilson tells us Scotus confesses the essential inadequacy of the human intellect unaided by revelation to discover any absolute proofs for the existence of God.[65] Similarly, he believes that Scotus regarded the unicity of God

---

[63] *Quodl.* q. 7, n. 38–39; XXV, 314a.
[64] Ockham, *Quodlibetum Septimum*, q. 23. Besides the Commentaries on the Sentences of Scotus, see *Quodl.* q. 7, n. 27ss; XXV, 306ss.
[65] Gilson, *Les seize premiers theoremata*, p. 63.

to be beyond the natural powers of reason because of what is said in the *De Primo Principio*.

> Il est vrai que, pour Duns Scot, l'unicité, et Dieu est démonstrable, mais dans quelles conditions? Dans le *De Primo Principio*, il nous déclare soudainement: Ici finissent les vérités rationnellement démonstrables, dans le traité suivant, *ponentur credibilia*. Pourtant, ajoute-t-il, il y en a un que je veux poser de suite avant d'achever mon traité: "Unum tamen est, quod hic pono, et in quo hoc opusculum consummabo; quod scilicet unus Deus sis, extra quem non est alter, sicut per Prophetam dixisti." Voilà donc l'unicité de Dieu rengée parmi les *credibilia*.[66]

There is little doubt that Gilson was misled by the poor reading of the Wadding edition. For if we take the critical text of Mueller, it is quite apparent that Scotus did not regard the unicity of God as one of the *credibilia*. It reads as follows:

> Praeter praedicta, de te a philosophis praedicata, saepe te Catholici laudant omnipotentem, immensum, ubique prasentem, justum et misericordem, cunctis creaturis et specialiter intellectualibus providentem, quae ad tractatum proximum differuntur. In hoc quippe tractatu primo tentavi videre, qualiter metaphysica de te dicta ratione naturali aliqualiter concludantur. In sequenti ponentur credibilia, in quibus ratio captivatur, quae tamen eo sunt Catholicis certiora, quo non intellectui nostro caecutienti et in pluribus vacillanti, sed tuae soldissimae veritati firmiter innituntur. Unum tamen est, quod hic pono et in quo hoc opusculum consummabo: quod scilicet unus Deus sis, extra quem non est alter, sicut per Prophetam dixisti; *ad quod ostendendum non puto deficere rationem*.[67]

In the preceding paragraphs Scotus has beautifully sketched the score of attributes that can be established by reason in addition to what he has just demonstrated. There are many other attributes of God which Catholics know by revelation such as God's absolute omnipotence, His immensity, and so on. In fact, Scotus tells us he intended to compose two tracts on God; one dealing with what can be proved by natural reason unaided by faith, the second treating those truths we know by faith alone. The first is the *De Primo Principio*. The second, apparently, was never completed.[68] From history, we know that many of Scotus'

---

[66] *Ibid.* p. 70.

[67] *De Primo Principio*, c. 4, concl. 11, p. 130; confer *Rep. Par.* 1, d. 2, q. 4, n. 3; XXII, 75a: demonstrative probatur conclusio.

[68] Some believe that the *Theoremata* represents this second work because of the *Tractatus De Creditis* (theorm. XIV–XVI) which it contains. Though the Wadding-Vivès edition reads: "In sequenti, scilicet in Theorematibus, ponentur credibilia," this reading is found only in two third-class 15th-century manuscripts. But a cursory reading of the

predecessors, contemporaries and successors regarded the unicity of God as indemonstrable. It could be established by faith alone.

> Sed dicunt aliqui, quod haec conclusio non est demonstrabilis, sed tantum accepta per fidem, et ad hoc auctoritas Rabbi Moysi ... quod unitas Dei accepta est a lege.[69]

But Scotus, though characteristically deferential to the weight of authority against him, disagrees. *Videtur tamen quod ista veritas possit ratione naturali ostendi.* And this is precisely what he means in the *De Primo Principio.* Before concluding this *opusculum,* which treats of what natural reason can demonstrate, and taking up the *credibilia* in the treatise which is to follow, I wish—says Scotus—to demonstrate the unicity of God, for despite what others may think, I do not believe this is beyond the powers of natural reason. *Ad quod ostendendum non puto deficere rationem.*

It is also interesting to note the basis on which he demonstrates the unicity of God in the *Opus Oxoniense.*

> Primo ex infinito intellectu, secundo ex infinita voluntate, tertio ex infinita bonitate, quarto ex ratione infinitae potentiae, quinto ex ratione infiniti absolute, sexto ex ratione necesse esse, septimo ex ratione omnipotentiae.[70]

But a distinction is made between these various proofs. The first six are demonstrable by reason, namely that God has infinite intellect, will, is infinite goodness, has infinite power (this is not the same as omnipotence, as we shall see shortly), etc. But when he comes to the last he says:

> De septima via, scilicet de omnipotentia, videtur quod illa non est per rationem naturalem demonstrabilis, quia omnipotentia (ut alias patebit) non potest concludi ratione naturali, ut Catholici credunt omnipotentiam, nec concluditur ex ratione infinitae. Tamen ex omnipotentia credita arguitur sic propositum: Si A est omnipotens, ergo potest facere circa quodcumque aliud, ipsum esse vel non esse, et ita posset destruere B, et ita fieret B nullipotens; ergo B non est Deus.[71]

Here as everywhere throughout his theological works, Scotus makes a clear distinction between the sphere of reason and of revelation.

De Primo and the *Tractatus De Creditis* will convince one that this interpretation cannot be correct, since many of the attributes which the *De Primo* asserts can be proved by reason are included in the *Theoremata* among those which cannot be proved except by revelation.

[69] *Oxon.* I, d. 2, q. 3, n. 2; VIII, 487b.
[70] *Oxon.* ibid. p. 488.
[71] *Ibid.* pp. 497–498.

Significantly, in the *De Primo*, a purely philosophical work, the proof based on omnipotence is dropped.[72]

In view of Gilson's belief that Scotus places his proofs for the existence of God on a par with those for His absolute omnipotence, it may be well to see what Scotus has to say on this point. Do the proofs in the two instances differ merely in degree, but not in kind? Is omnipotence simply *une autre vétrité nécessaire dont on ne peut prouver que la probabilité?*

The eminent historian has based his interpretation on what Scotus says in brief discussion in the commentary on the Sentences.[73] There he singles out a principle which he regards as a key to understanding Scotus, namely: *non omne necessarium est evidenter necessarium.* While we cannot see eye to eye with Gilson in regard to the importance of this principle, which is introduced simply to answer an objection based on the doctrine of Richard of St. Victor, this is of little moment. But the interpretation of this principle is important. And here it is necessary to read the seventh question of the *Quodlibetum* to discover its true significance. Incidentally there are few questions where Scotus displays the brilliance and precisiion of his logical mind to better advantage than in his careful treatment of the question: *Utrum Deum esse omnipotentem possit naturali ratione et necessaria demonstrari?* (*Quodl.* q. 7, Vivès, XXV, 283ss).

Suggesting that the interested reader pursue this discussion for himself, we content ourselves here with sketching its contents in so far as they pertain to our problem. First of all, Scotus explains the distinction between *demonstratio quia* and *propter quid* which we treated above. And as if anticipating Gilson's assertions, he reminds us that not only the *propter quid* but also the *quia* is based on *evident* premisses and not merely on necessary ones. Secondly, he distinguishes carefully between infinite power, which can be demonstrated by natural reason, and the Christian concept of omnipotence, which cannot be demonstrated.[74] And again anticipating Gilson, he distinguishes what can be demonstrated absolutely speaking, that is, by any intellect, and what can be demonstrated by the human intellect which has not yet attained the beatific vision. And even in regard to the *viator*, he

---

[72] It is true that the argument for the unicity of God based on His omnipotence is included in some of the manuscripts, but it appears to be a late addition. Of the eight manuscripts which give the original text, according to Mueller, only two include the argument. In the Madrid manuscript (Bibl. Pal. Nat. 411; 14th cent.) it is found in the margin added by a second hand. The 15th-century Merton College cod. 90 has it, but again with the marginal indication 'Extra.'

[73] *Oxon.* I, d. 42, q. un.; X, 714ss.

[74] *Quodl.* q. 7, n. 3; XXV, 284; see also *Oxon. loc. cit.*

further distinguishes between a human intellect supernaturally illumined (e.g. St. Paul's ecstacy) and one that is not so (e.g. Aristotle and
philosophi multi.)[75]

Remembering that the Christian conception of omnipotence implies
that God can create all possible beings *immediately* and not merely
through the agency of secondary causes, whereas omnipotence relatively speaking, or more exactly, *potentia infinita intensive*, asserts
merely that God as the first cause can produce all things either immediately or mediately through the agency of the secondary causes He
has produced, we can sum up Scotus' conclusions on omnipotence as
follows:[76]

(1) The omnipotence of God whether considered absolutely or relatively can be demonstrated *propter quid*, at least by an intellect that
has intuitive knowledge of the divine essence, such as that of the angels
or saints.

(2) That absolutely speaking it is not impossible for one who is still
in statu viae to demonstrate it *propter quid*, for God by His supernatural power could infuse in the human mind such knowledge of himself
that from this concept the mind could demonstrate God's absolute as
well as his relative omnipotence.

(3) For one who has no such supernatural revelations, but must rest
content with his natural and ordinary intellectual powers, neither the
absolute nor relative omnipotence of God can be demonstrated *propter
quid*.

(4) The absolute omnipotence of God (*licet videatur probabilis*) can
not be demonstrated by a *quia* demonstration by natural reason (*non
tamen esset Philosopho demonstratio*).[77]

---

[75] *Ibid.*, nn. 5ss; XXV, 286.

[76] *Ibid.*, n.3; 284b: De secundo articulo videndum est de demonstratione et primo de
demonstratione *propter quid*; secundo de demonstratione *quia*. De demonstratione *propter quid*, sunt tres conclusiones: Prima est ista: Deum esse ominpotentem, utroque
modo accipiendo omnipotentiam. est verum demonstabile in se demonstratione *propter
quid*. Secunda conclusio, istud verum est demonstrabile viatori stante simpliciter statu
viae. Tertia conclusio, istud verum non potest demonstrari viatori ex notis sibi naturaliter et de lege communi. De demonstratione *quia*, sunt duae conclusiones: prima est
ista: Deum esse omnipotentem omnipotentia respiciente immediate quodcumque possibile, licet sit verum, non tamen est a nobis demonstrabile demonstratione *quia*. Secunda conclusio: Deum esse omnipotentem omnipentia immediate vel mediate
quodcumque possibile respiciente, potest demonstrari a viatore demonstratione *quia*:
sic ergo sunt quinque conclusiones, ex quibus integratur solutio quaestionis.

[77] *Ibid.*, n. 19; 300a: Ista ratio, licet videatur probabilis, non tamen esset Philosopho
demonstratio. Contrast this with what he says of the next conclusion (n. 27, p. 306a):
Quinta conclusio principalis est ista, quod demonstrabile est viatori demonstratione
quia, Deum esse omnipotentem mediate vel immediate, hoc est, quod possit causare
quodcumque causabile, vel immediate, vel per aliquod medium quod subsit causalitati
ejus. Haec conclusio probatur per hoc quod necesse est statum esse in causis efficientibus,

(5) The relative omnipotence of God, namely, that He can create all possibles either mediately or immediately, can be demonstrated by us by a *quia* demonstration.

What strikes one in this analysis is the distinction made between the demonstrability of God, His infinite power considered *intensive* on the one hand (relative omnipotence) and of His absolute omnipotence on the other. The first can be demonstrated by reason and further, was demonstrated by Aristotle and himself. Absolute omnipotence, on the contrary, cannot be demonstrated. Our proofs are merely probable from a philosophical viewpoint. We may even speak of them in the language of Richard of St. Victor as necessary proofs. But they are not evident—neither in themselves nor by reason of an evident connection they have with relative omnipotence. For many a philosopher admitted the latter, yet denied the former. Many protested that God was all powerful in the sense that He created all beings, yet denied Him the ability to do so directly. Ecce Avicenna![78]

In the light of Scotus' statements in the *Quodlibetum*, it is difficult to see how Gilson can assert that both the existence of God and His absolute omnipotence are merely established by necessary but not evidently necessary proofs. For even in the text quoted by Gilson from the Oxford Commentary, Scotus' position is clear.[79] Before he asserts that proofs can be called necessary *tamen non evidenter necessariae*, Scotus points out that *two* sources of evidence must be excluded. *Non sunt notae ex terminis nobis notis, neque ex immediatis nobis notis possibile est hoc inferre.* Why does Gilson ignore the second alternative? For as we pointed out above, Scotus asserts we have contingent facts that are so evident that *qui negaret indiget sensu et poena si negaret sensu.* And from these immediately known facts *potest ostendi aliquid necessarium, quia ex contingenti sequitur aliquod necessarium.*[80]

Furthermore, Gilson's assumption that Scotus regarded metaphysics as a sort of disgruntled philosophy or disinherited theology warrants a re-examination. For it is based on a number of subordinate assumptions of dubious character. Scotus, we are told, was faced with the dilemma of Averroistic naturalism on the one hand and the Avicennian

---

et hoc probatur secundo Metaphysicae; et probatio Aristotelis, breviter nunc tangendo, stat in hoc: Tota universitas causatorum causam habet, non autem quae sit aliquid istius universitatis quia tunc idem esset causa sui; ergo aliquid extra totam universitatem illam. Si ergo in causis non ascendatur in infinitum, non solum quaelibet est causata, sed tota multitudo erit causata, et per consequens ab aliquo extra totam illam multitudinem; ergo in illo erit status, tanquam in simpliciter primo causante.

[78] *Ibid.*, nn. 29–32; 307b–309b.
[79] Gilson, *op. cit.*, pp. 61–62. See *Oxon.* 1, d. 43, q. un., n. 4; X, 716b.
[80] *Prima Lectura, loc. cit.*

metaphysics on the other. The former made God the object of metaphysics but was constrained to prove his existence by physics, which established a prime or cosmic agent having no relation to the Christian God. To make metaphysics a science of being, however, is to admit that a higher science exists which deals with God as its object. In either case metaphysics never really deals directly with God.[81]

Certainly this last statement is misleading. What is meant by "directly"? The only correct meaning we can give it is that metaphysics is not a *propter quid* science of God. But *quid ad rem?* Gilson introduces this lengthy analysis of the nature of metaphysics and theology according to Scotus to throw light on the fundamental problem. It will show why Scotus could not demonstrate the existence of God. It will make it clear why his proofs for an infinitely perfect being have no absolute value. It will tell us why the theorem: *in essentialiter ordinatis est dare primum, quod sit unicum et coaevum illi coordinationi* cannot be demonstrated but is at best probable. And what are we told? Scotus vehemently rejects the position of Averroës and sides with Avicenna. Metaphysics is the science of being. Hence it cannot deal directly with God. And therefore, by implication, it cannot prove the existence of God naturally by anything stronger than probable proofs.

Now anyone acquainted with the first question of the first book and the fourth question of the sixth book of Scotus' *Quaestiones Metaphysicae* will be mildly surprised, to say the least, at this conclusion. For the "principale propositum" Scotus sets for himself in the first question is to show *quomodo scilicet Deus potest esse subjectum metaphysicae.*[82] And the first error which Avicenna and Averroës committed was to believe that *nulla scientia probat suum subjectum esse,*[83] which in technical language means simply, they overlooked the fact that the *scientia quia* is a true science and the *demonstratio quia* is a true demonstration. And so Scotus goes on explaining how God can be regarded as a subject of metaphysics, *sed aliter est ponendum quam ponit Averroës.* Incidentally the very text Gilson quotes to prove that Scotus did not regard God as subject of metaphysics, Scotus himself adduces as a proof that he is.[84] Gilson suggests, however, that

---

[81] Gilson, *op. cit.,* p. 58.

[82] *Metaphy.* 1, q. 1, n. 39, VII, 31a.

[83] *Ibid.,* n. 34; 28ab: Primo enim ostendetur quomodo peccavit Averroës et Avicenna in opinionibus suis... Circa primum sciendum, quod Avicenna et Averroës habent hanc propositionem communem: nulla scientia probat suum subjectum esse.

[84] Gilson, *op.cit.,* p. 60: Pourquoi, demande-t-il, la métaphysique ne pourrait elle pas au moins s'ordonner vers Dieu comme vers sa fin, tout en conservant l'être comme objet? Parce que, répond-il, la fin d'une science, c'est de connaître son objet principal, et non un autre: 'Materia, circa quam principaliter agit scientia, est finis ejus.' Confer the context, *Metaphy. loc. cit.,* n. 45; p. 34b. It is true that Scotus apparently modified

Scotus is still undecided in this first question. Only in the sixth book is definite decision reached. *Tenetur igitur Avicenna!* But when we read this "decisive" question we receive another shock. True, Scotus breaks with Averroës. Metaphysics is not a *propter quid* science of God. It is a science of being. But why does he side with Avicenna? Because *only then can metaphysics demonstrate the existence of God (Primo, quia Deum esse probatur hic)!*[85] And not only his existence, but also something of his very essence (*concluditur tam esse quam quid est.*)[86] And why is Averroës wrong? Simply because he maintained that *naturalis solus probat Deum esse.*[87] And further, the God whose existence he established was at best a prime mover. But once metaphysics is conceded to be a science of being, we can do much better than that. By natural reason we are empowered to prove the infinite perfection of God itself.

> Item perfectior conceptus de Deo possibilis Physico est primum movens, possibilis autem Metaphysico est primum ens. Secundus est perfectior, tum quia absolutus, tum quia requirit perfectionem infinitam, nam pri-

---

this stand, when he said that metaphysics should rather be called the science of being from the standpoint of its starting point. But even in the *Oxionense* he made it clear that even if God was not the principal subject of metaphysics, no other natural science has a greater right to treat of his existence and essence. *Oxon.*, prol. q. 3, n. 20; VIII, 17la: Deus vero, etsi non est subjectum primum in Metaphysica, est tamen consideratum in illa scientia nobilissimo modo quo potest in aliqua scientia considerari naturaliter acquista. And similarly in the *Reportata Parisiensia*, prol. q. 3: Unde *circa* proprie notat circumstantiam causae finalis, sicut et causae materialis; unde Metaphysica est circa altissimas causae finaliter, ad quarum cognitionem terminatur scientia Metaphysicalis. What Gilson has consistently failed to do throughout his whole discussion is to distinguish between *scientia* in its primary meaning of the conclusion of a single demonstration and a body of conclusions that are related in some way among themselves. Metaphysics, considered as a body of conclusions, should properly be said to be the science of being. And the reason is simple. While it is true that the principle that no science proves the existence of its subject is not universally true, for otherwise the *demonstratio quia* would not be a science in any sense of the term, yet this principle is valuable in determining the *principle* subject of a science, in the sense of a body of conclusions. *Rep. ibid.*: Haec propositio *nulla scientia probat suum subjectum esse ...* vera est propter primitatem subjecti ad scientiam. But this does not say that none of the conclusions of the science of being qua being establishes the existence of God and his attributes, and that these particular demonstrations of God are true *syllogismi facientes scire* and their conclusions *scientiae* in the primary sense of the term.

[85] *Metaphy.* 6, q. 4, n. 1; VII, 348a.

[86] *Ibid.*, 1, q. 1, n. 41; 32a; *ibid.*, n. 39; 31a: Similiter potest esse [Deus] subjectum primo modo in scientia *quia*. Supposito enim quid dicitur per nomen, si tale est causa talis effectus, ex effectu potest concludi tale et esse ex esse, et hoc ex hoc tam quantum ad essentialia quam quantum ad proprietates, et hoc demonstratione *quia*. For Scotus, our demonstrations of God not only terminate in his existence but give us something of his very essence or quiddity. Hence Scotus insists that our concepts of God are also quidditative. *Oxon.*, 1, d. 3, q. 2, n. 5; IX, 16b–17a.

[87] *Metaphy.* 6, q. 4, n. 1; VII, 348a.

mum perfectissimum...Tenetur igitur Avicenna. Prima ratio ejus sic declaratur: *si est* praesupponitur de subjecto, non de actuali existentia, sed quod habet esse quidditativum, scilicet quod ratio ejus non est falsa in se. Tale *si est* ostenditur demonstratione quia a Metaphysico de primo ente. Ostenditur enim, quod primum convenit enti alicui, et ita quia ille conceptus, ens primum, qui est perfectissimus subjecti, si esset hic subjectum, non includit contradictionem. Ergo si aliqua scientia supponeret istum conceptum pro subjecto alia esset prior de ente, quae probaret praecedentem de primo ente, quia conclusio demonstrationis illius esset prior tota scientia de primo ente.[88]

Here we have the very opposite of Gilson's thesis. Because Scotus makes metaphysics a science of being, Gilson tells us, he *cannot* demonstrate the existence of God—his arguments are only probable. And Scotus himself says, because I make metaphysics the science of being I can demonstrate the existence of an infinite God. And this not because of any special illumination, revelation or supernatural theology. For this is *metaphysica nostra—quidquid sit de notitia naturali beati vel in statu innocentiae. Igitur sic potuit tradi a Philosopho.* It is the *prima scientia possibilis homini per rationem naturalem acquiri.*[89]

Furthermore, Gilson's description of metaphysics as struggling upwards for an object doubly beyond its natural powers puts Scotus in a false light. First of all the distinction of *metaphysics nostra* and *metaphysica in se* is not something over and above the distinction between *theologia in se* and *theologia nostra.* The first distinction is on the supposition that metaphysics be considered as a science which has God for its proper subject. Hence it is taken as *theology.* Metaphysics *in se* and theology *in se* are one and the same thing, both based on an intuitive knowledge of God as a supernaturally motivating object. But *theologia nostra* and *metaphysica nostra* are not identical. The former is not a strict science (neither *propter quid* nor *quia*). The conclusions it reaches are necessary but not evidently necessary truths, since the premisses are based on revelation. *Metaphysica nostra,* however, is a true science, but a *scientia quia.* It seeks to establish the existence and nature of God and is the *prima scientia possibilis homini per rationem naturalem.*

Secondly, this view pictures our metaphysics reaching out for the object of *theologia nostra* and through it to *theologia in se.* Having neither revelation nor intuition, it is doubly handicapped. This means in simple language that our metaphysics has as its *natural* object, something that is *beyond its natural powers.* This is all very interesting, but it ignores the fundamental difference between a *scientia quia*

[88] *Ibid.,* 348–349.
[89] *Ibid.,* 1, q. 1, n. 41; 32a.

and *propter quid*. The first establishes the existence of its natural object; the latter, presupposing both the *si est* and the *quid est*, demonstrates attributes of its subject. *Theologia nostra* truly reaches beyond itself simply because it has the form of a *propter quid* science, just as *theologia in se* has. But it fails to be a true science and does not yield demonstrative conclusions because its premises are not evident. But metaphysics, as a *scientia quia* of God, is based on both evident and necessary premises, and its purpose is to establish the existence and nature of God in so far as these can be known from creatures, a task which in Scotus' eyes is fully within its competence as a natural science.

Thirdly, it supposes that since revelation is required to know that being *qua* being is the adequate object of our intellect, revelation is somehow required to have a metaphysics of being. Hence as a science of being, metaphysics needs revelation to attain a proper concept of its object. Gilson's argumentation here is not clear to us. Why does the second assertion follow?

As we have pointed out elsewhere,[90] the problem of the object of the intellect and the subject of metaphysics are distinct in Scotus' mind. Despite the fact that natural reason is impotent to solve the problem of what the precise object of our intellect *qua intellect* is (it is very important to note the two ways in which an object may be said to be "natural" to a faculty!)[91] we cannot say, therefore metaphysics as a science of being requires the support of revelation. The univocal concept of being which can be predicated of God and creatures, substance and accident, is not the result of any supernatural revelation or natural illumination in the Augustinian sense. It is something naturally acquired by the abstractive powers of the intellect *in statu viae*. In fact, Scotus constantly insists that the *concepts* of the believer and unbeliever are not different. It is only that one gives his consent to certain *propositions* on the strength of God's authority whereas the other, lacking evidence, refuses such an assent. *Metaphysicus infidelis et alius fidelis eumdem conceptum habent.*[92]

Any science based upon the concept of being, as is Scotus' metaphysics, is an autonomous and purely natural science. And then Scotus' makes the surprising assertion—the very opposite of Gilson's interpretation—because we possess a *natural* concept of being *qua* being

---

[90] *Transcendentals and Their Function in the Metaphysics of Duns Scotus*, St. Bonaventure, N.Y., Franciscan Institute, 1946, pp. 73ss. Even from early times Scotistic commentators like John Canonicus and others have insisted that this distinction be kept clear.

[91] *Oxon.*, prol. q. 1, n. 20; VIII, 48ss; *Quodl*; q. 14, nn. 2, 11; XXVI, 2–3, 40.

[92] *Quodl.*, q. 7, n. 11; XXV, 293b.

and a *natural* science of metaphysics, we have grounds *from reason alone* for suspecting the Aristotelian thesis that material being is the proper and adequate object of the intellect.[93] What we do not know certainly from reason alone, and what revelation can answer definitively, is that anything of which being can be predicated, be it God or angels or the human soul, can directly motivate the human intellect to an act of simple apprehension—for this is what is meant by being *qua* being as the adequate object of the human intellect. This is what Avicenna discovered because he was a good Mohammedan. But this problem has not the slightest bearing on the principal problem of the validity of Scotus proofs for the existence of God. Consequently we believe Gilson's entire interpretation of the validity and the significance of Scotus' metaphysics, based as it is on this confusion of two distinct problems, needs a thorough re-examination.

CAN A CREATURE CREATE?

The third assumption upon which Gilson bases his theory is the different viewpoints of the *Theoremata* and the authentic Scotistic works. The author of the *Theoremata* views the problem of God's existence from the standpoint of a mere philosopher unaided by faith. The authentic Scotus treats the same problem from the standpoint of an enlightened philosopher, who has based his arguments on the data of revelation (theologism). Without revelation the pure philosopher is stranded. But where he fails, the other succeeds.

It is quite true that in his theological works (and we mean here supernatural theology), like all the medieval theologians, St. Thomas included, Scotus employs metaphysics as the *ancilla theologiae*. But to suggest that he did not admit the autonomy of metaphysics as a natural science, or that he considered that metaphysics *by its nature* was destined solely to serve a supernatural theology is quite unwarranted. It ignores the distinction between practice and theory. Scotus was primarily a theologian and consequently *used* philosophy to serve the ends of the theologian. But he recognized the essential independence of philosophy in general and metaphysics in particular. And even in his theological works, he clearly distinguishes what the philosopher

---

[93] *Reportata Par.* 1, d. 3, q. 1, n. 3; XXII, 93b: Si dicas quod hoc est creditum... arguitur per rationem naturalem sic: Nulla potentia cognitiva potest cognoscere aliquid sub ratione illimitatiori, quam sit ratio sui primi objecti, quia si sic, illud non esset objectum primum, et sibi adaequatum; sed intellectus viatoris potest cognoscere ens quod est illimitatius quidditate materiali, aliter non posset habere cognitionem metaphysicalem, ergo, etc.

can prove by reason alone. And apart from his commentaries on the philosophical and logical works of Aristotle, he has even essayed to determine just what the philosopher, using natural reason alone can know about God. When the *De Primo Principio* is stripped of the additions which well-meaning but theologically minded disciples contributed to the original draft, we see that Scotus has excluded any argument that supposes revelation or supernatural theology in any way. And then the meaning of the opening prayer becomes clear. He is not praying for a special illumination that reason may surpass its natural powers. Scotus is praying that God keep away any such special helps, that he may determine precisely how far natural reason can go toward approximating that picture God has given us of himself through revelation. *Adjuva me, Domine inquirentem ad quantam cognitionem de vero esse, quod tu es, possit pertingere nostra ratio naturalis ab ente, quod de te praedicasti, inchoando.*[94] Catholics, he reminds us, are certain of a great deal more than the unenlightened philosopher, but these truths he leaves for another work. *In hoc quippe tractatu primo tentavi videre qualiter metaphysica de te dicta ratione naturali aliqualiter concludantur.*[95] And from all we have said above, it is clear that Scotus was convinced that even in its fallen state a human intellect devoid of all revelation—even as that of pagan Aristotle—could demonstratively prove the existence of a unique Infinite Being, the first cause of the universe, coexistent with His creation.

To say, therefore, that "les *Theoremata* sont la contre-épreuve expérimentale de l'*Opus Oxoniense*: la même qui échoue sans la révélation, réussit avec elle,"[96] is to go contrary to the clear statements of Scotus himself.

Gilson, it is true, believes his assumption is confirmed by what Scotus says of the possibility of a creature creating. In order to reconcile the doctrine of the *Theoremata* with that of the authentic writings, it is of paramount importance to prove that the latter admit the possibility of a creature creating independently of the First Cause, or at least that such a possibility cannot be excluded by reason alone. The author of the *Theoremata* suggests that the first efficient cause may cease to exist after it has produced a second cause. Consequently it is impossible

---

[94] *De Primo Principio*, c. 1, pp. 1–2.

[95] *Ibid.*, c. 4, concl. 10, pp. 129–130. The "aliqualiter" does not mean that these conclusions made by the metaphysician are merely "probable," as is clear from the context of the *De Primo* and of the other authentic works as Gilson, Wellmuth, Heiser, etc. have inferred. A more simple and obvious interpretation is this. Scotus is contrasting the imperfect and partial, though valid knowledge we have of God in the present life with the perfect knowledge possible in the next. See for instance, *Oxon.*, I, d. 3, q. 1, where he discusses the imperfect character of our natural knowledge of God; also supra p. 274, note 44.

[96] Gilson, *op. cit.*, p. 69.

to demonstrate by reason that *in genere causae efficientis est dare unicum primum efficiens, quod nunc est in rerum natura.*

If we could prove from reason that no created cause can create or act in any way without the cooperation and consequent co-existence of its creator, it is obvious that the assumption of the *Theoremata* could not be maintained. Now just what does Scotus say on this matter? He is very clear and precise—both in the *Reportata*, which Gilson quotes in part, and especially in the parallel passage in the *Oxoniense*. Adverting to the difference between an instrumental and principal cause, Scotus states that to act or create as a principal cause can be understood in a twofold manner:

> Uno modo excludendo omnem causam superiorem agentem ut sic agere principaliter sit agere independenter a causa superiore agente. Alio modo potest intelligi agere principaliter, scilicet per formam propriam et intrinsecam agenti, licet in agendo per eam sit subordinata causae superiori agenti.[97]

And in the *Reportata* we read:

> Respondeo ergo ad quaestionem, quod creatio dupliciter potest accipi, uno modo proprie, excludendo a creante omnem aliam causam concreantem praeter causam finalem ... Alio modo accipitur creatio solum excludendo causam materialem concausantem, et isto modo creatio est productio alicujus de nihilo quia de nulla materia.[98]

Note, therefore, that to create in the first way implies that the actual exercise of the creative power is not dependent upon a higher cause. Scotus is clearly speaking here of a higher cause in an essential order of causes. If this were not already evident from the very use of the term *causa superior* (a characteristic of essentially ordered causes), the explicit statement that dependency is excluded *in actione sua* leaves no doubt in the matter. For only in a series of essentially ordered causes is the posterior dependent *in agendo* or *in causando.*[99]

Is it possible for a creature to create in this first manner? *It is clear,* Scotus answers, *that God alone* can act independently of any higher cause.

> *Patet* quod nihil aliud a Deo potest principaliter agere in quacumque actione.[100] Et isto modo concedo quod Deus solus creat. Licet enim quodcumque aliud a Deo posset aliud producere de nihilo, *necessario tamen praesupponeret aliud agens in actione sua, ut primam causam,* et ita non est possiblile isto modo aliquam creaturam creare aliquid.[101]

---

[97] *Oxon.*, 4, d. 1, q. 1, n. 26; XVI, 85b.
[98] *Rep.*, 4, d. 1, q. 1, n. 12; XXIII, 539a.
[99] *Oxon.*, 1, d. 2, q. 2, n. 12ss; VIII, 415bss.
[100] *Oxon.*, 4, d. 1, q. 1, n. 27; XVI, 86b.
[101] *Rep., loc cit.*

But we can understand "creation" in another way, namely, a production in the absence of a material cause; for creation after all is defined as a *productio ex nihilo sui et subjecti*. If a secondary and created cause were to receive from its Maker creative powers and were to exercise them with the cooperation and consequent co-existence of the first cause, it could still be said to create so long as it did not make use of any pre-existing matter. Note, this is a radically different assumption from that of the *Theoremata*.

What is to be said of the possibility of a creature creating in this sense?

> *Et hoc modo* accipiendo eam [sc. creationem] difficile est prohibere quin possit creatio competere agenti creato respectu multorum ut respectu formarum subsistentium, cujusmodi sunt Angeli, si sunt formae simplices, et etiam respectu formarum quae non educuntur de potentia materiae ut animae intellectivae, sive respecut formarum accidentialium, ut sunt fides, spes, intelligere, velle et hujusmodi.[102]

Here is the text quoted by Gilson to prove that Scotus held the same opinion as the author of the *Theoremata*.. What a difference it makes when read in its context.

But let us go on. Why is it difficult to exclude absolutely the possibility of a creature creating in this second manner? If we read the *Oxoniense*, the answer becomes clear. There is no dispute regarding the impossibility of a creature creating independently of the cooperation of a co-existing First Cause. The medieval schoolmen are agreed on its patent absurdity. They are likewise in agreement on the fact that a creature cannot create in the second way also. But—and here is the difficulty—can the impossibility of a creature creating in dependence upon a first cause be proved *from reason alone*. Some theologians, like Henry of Ghent, maintain that Avicenna's position can be disproved only by means of the data of revelation. Reason unaided is impotent to do so. A second group of theologians believe that reason alone suffices to show its absurdity. Scotus, after carefully weighing the two opinions, advances a third which, in a sense, mediates between the other two.

> Ideo dici potest tertio modo quod cratura non potest creare principaliter modo praedicto, scilicet per formam intrinsecam activam respectu termini in suo ordine agendi et hoc probatur *per rationem*, sed non communem omni creaturae sed per plures de diversis creaturis speciales.[103]

Scotus then proceeds to show by *reason alone* that: 1) a pure intellectual created nature, such as that of an angel, cannot create another

[102] *Ibid.*, 539b.
[103] *Oxon.*, *loc. cit.*, n. 26; XVI, 85.

substance, for intellection and volition in a creature are accidental. Only where these acts are substantial can they terminate in the creation of a substance. 2) No material form can be created by a creature. At most, creatures can cause a mutation of forms but not their creation or annihilation. 3) No material form, whether it be accidental or essential, can be a principle of creation. For if it depends on matter for its being, it will be dependent also in its causality on matter. Otherwise the term of its action would be of a more absolute character than the form and its activity itself. From these three conclusions, Scotus proceeds to prove that no angel can create a substance. Neither can it create any accidental form. No material substance can create anything, since it acts by reason of its form. It cannot produce matter alone nor create a form nor create the total effect *ex nihilo sui et subjecti*.

We are not particularly interested in the validity of Scotus' proofs as such. Our concern is the value he himself attributed to them. What did he think of Avicenna's position? He believed it could be disproved demonstratively and from reason unaided by faith. Not indeed by disproving *in general* the impossibility of a creature creating even in dependence on a First Cause, but by showing the impossibility for specific kinds of creatures. The impossibility, in other words, arises not because they are creatures but because they are this or that kind of creature. Hence his conclusion that reason finds it difficult to establish the universal impossibility of a creature creating.

But the important item to note is that this whole discussion of the competence or incompetence of reason arises only in regard to creation considered in the second way (*et hoc modo accipiendo eam difficile est prohibere quin possit creatio competere agenti creato*). In other words, only where the existence of a higher co-existing and cooperating cause is not excluded, is there any question, on a purely philosophical plane, of a creature creating. *Necessario tamen praesupponeret aliud agens in actione sua, ut primam causam.* Here we have the very opposite of the position in the *Theoremata* which assumes the possibility of a creature creating independently of the existence of the first cause. Yet Gilson assures us they are substantially the same.

To say that Scotus speaks here as a philosopher enlightened by faith while the *Theoremata* are written from the standpoint of a mere philosopher can hardly be justified by any sound principle of hermeneutics. If reason alone could not prove the impossibility of a creature creating independently of the existence of its own cause, *a fortiori* it could not do so in the second way. Why then does Scotus take such pains to make clear what reason can prove and cannot prove in regard to the latter, while dismissing the first as a patent absurdity? It is only because he has previously established the absurdity of an infinite series of either accidently or essentially ordered causes in his demonstrative proof for the existence of God—a proof, as we have seen, based on reason unaided by faith.[104]

We could point out other instances where Gilson has seemingly misinterpreted Scotus' thought. This, however, should suffice to show that the inner compatibility of the *Theoremata* with the authentic Scotus has by no means been established by the eminent historian, at least in regard to the proofs for the existence of God. Theologism with its incipient scepticism is foreign to that portion of his metaphysics.

THE THEOREMATA

We have not directly touched on the problem of the authenticity of the *Theoremata*. While the ultimate solution of this problem is one of the tasks of the Scotistic Commission, a few remarks may not be out of place. The arguments of Longpré, De Basly, and Balić pro and con are too well known to be repeated here.[105] Father Bettoni sums up the present status of the question very well, pointing out that external evidence unanimously favors the authenticity, while the doctrinal incompatibility is the strongest evidence against it.[106] As is clear from what has been said so far, Gilson's attempt to mitigate the doctrinal differences does not appear to be satisfactory. And the same can be said, more or less, of Baudry.[107]

As far as we can judge, a very strong and definite opposition exists between the position of Theorems XIV–XVI and that of the *Oxoniense, Quodlibetum,* and *De Primo Principio.* This in itself, however, is no proof against the authenticity of the *Theoremata.* There is always the possibility that Scotus changed his views on the matter in the course of time. Balić, however, argues for a late date of composition for both the *Theoremata* and the *De Primo.* When Scotus wrote the 7th question of his *Quodlibetum,* he was obviously still convinced of the demonstrative character of his proofs. Yet the *Quodlibetum* is one of his latest works, dating to the year of his regency as a Parisian Master of Theology.

---

[104] *Oxon.,* I, d. 2, q. 2, n. 12ss, VIII, 415bss; *De Primo principio, c.* 3 conclusio secunda.

[105] Longpré, *La philosophie du Bx. Duns Scot,* Paris, 1924, pp. 29–49; 289–291; De Basly, "*Les Theoremata* de Duns Scot," *Archivum Franciscanum Historicum,* XI (1918), 331; Balić, *Joannis Duns Scoti Doctoris Mariani, Theologia Marianae Elementa,* Sibenici, 1933, pp. cxxi–cxlv, etc.

[106] Bettoni, *Vent'Anni di Studi Scotisti* (1920–1940), Milano, 1943, pp. 19–22; *L'Ascesa a Dio is Duns Scoto,* Milano, 1943, c. 6, p. 104ss.

[107] L. Baudry, "E lisant Jean le Chanoine," *Archives d'hist. doct. et litt. du moyen âge,* X, 175–197.

Even if we grant the *Theoremata* in general are authentic, the additional problem still remains of determining how much of the present text given by Wadding and Vivès is original and how much represents the later interpolations. The Ragusa manuscript, for instance, contains only the first 13 theorems. While we can say with Balić that the *Theoremata* in general are little more than excerpts taken from the *Oxoniense*, this does not hold for the controversial *tractatus de creditis* (theorems XIV–XVI).

Balić offers a fruitful suggestion when he writes: *Tractatus de Primo Principio et Theoremata nihil aliud sunt quam duo excerpta ex Opere Oxoniensi quae Duns Scotus delineavit et alii perfecerunt.*[108] While in the case of the *De Primo* we have no reason to doubt that the final work received the approval of the master, the same cannot be said for the *Theoremata*. In fact, so far as the latter is concerned,

> valde nunc difficile est stabilire quamnam partem in opusculi confectione Duns Scotus habuerit. Non solum interest inter codices magna discrepantia, non solum saepius in variis codicibus elementa veluti per transennam posita, infecta apparent; verum etiam ubique deest quaevis adnotatio indicans Duns Scotum manu sua ad expoliendum et perficiendum hoc opus adlaborasse, cum haud paucae istiusmodi adnotationes occurrant in Ordinatione, quodlibet et in Metaphysica.[109]

Consequently we are faced with the problem of how much of the *Theoremata* is really Scotus'—granting the authenticity of the work as a whole. How much of the text in our present editions represents the additions of the scribe? How many marginal notes have been incorporated? Did Scotus ever see and approve the final draft? How can we rule out the possibility that the work itself was left unfinished at Scotus' death and completed by one of Scotus' secretaries? And if such be the case, would the latter have hesitated to amend those points where he believed his master had spoken less wisely?

In this connection, we would like to point out an interesting parallel between the doctrine of the *Tractatus de creditis* in the *Theoremata* and that of John de Bassolis, one of the earliest Scotists and perhaps even one of Scotus' secretaries. This comparison is of particular interest first of all, because it indicates a fundamental divergence of opinion among the immediate followers of Scotus regarding the demonstrative character of his proofs for the existence of God; secondly, because it indicates very clearly what the more critical group regarded as the weak point in the proofs of the master.

---

[108] Balić, "De Critica Textuali Scholasticorum scriptis accommodata," *Antonianum,* XX (1945), 289.
[109] *Ibid.,* pp. 295–296.

John de Bassolis

Let us take for instance, John's criticism of the argument for the three-fold primacy of efficiency, finality and eminence. To show that all three concur in the First Being, is Scotus' first step in demonstrating the infinity and unicity of God. Theorem XV challenges this position for it asserts:

> In essentialiter ordinatis est dare primum quod sit unicum et coaevum illi coordinationi. In omni genere causae est ordo essentialis.—Istae duae propositiones petantur; quarum prima tres partes continet, secunda est simplex; utraque licet sit probabilis, tamen difficile esset, vel forte nobis impossibile eam simpliciter necessaria ratione et mere naturali probare.[110]

In his commentary on the Sentences, John de Bassolis raises the question: *Utrum in tota universitate entium sit dare aliquod ens simpliciter primum actu existens?*[111] Prefacing his answer with a discussion of the meaning and mutual implications of essentially and accidentally ordered causes, he cites the arguments aduced *ad probandum quod est dare primum ens in universo*. They are simply a summary of the arguments given by Scotus in his authentic works. Then follows his personal evaluation of the latter. *Tertio dicam quid mihi videtur de rationibus utrum demonstrent vel non*. And what does he say?

> Et *videtur mihi quod sunt valde probabiles* et magis quam quaecumque rationes quae possunt adduci ad oppositum et quod difficile est ad eas respondere. Secundo *videtur mihi quod non sunt demonstrationes*, et quod possunt solvi probabiliter, ita quod non cogant intellectum ad negandum processum in infinitum in causis per se et essentialiter ordinatis.[112]

Here, in essence, is the position of the *Theoremata*. And there is no indication that the master himself agreed with his disciple's evaluation of his proofs. On the contrary, the *mihi videtur* would seem to indicate that he is differing with others on this matter. For we know that others, like Peter of Aquila, upheld the demonstrative character of Scotus' proofs.[113] In all probability, John is differing with Scotus himself. Cer-

---

[110] *Theor*. XV, 1, V, 51a.
[111] *Opera Joannis de Bassolis in Sententiarum Libros Aurea*, Paris, Franciscus Regnault et Joannes Frellon, 1517, liber 1, d. 2, q. 1. f. 45va. (n.b. The second book was published in 1516).
[112] *Ibid.*, 47rb.
[113] *Commentarium in 4 libros Sententiarum* I, d. 2, q. 2; Levanti, Conventus S. Assumptionis, 1905, t. 1, p. 55.

tainly he disagrees with the position expressed in the authentic works at least.

Now why does this disciple differ with the master? Why does he challenge the absolute validity of his proofs? Not for any of the reasons suggested by Gilson. No, he attacks the very point Ockham was to seize upon later—the validity of Scotus' distinction between essentially and accidentally ordered causes. For essentially ordered causes, he insists, can be understood in two ways. But only in one of the two can we argue to *aliquid simpliciter et perfectissimum*. In the other, the possibility of an infinite series cannot be excluded. Hence no basic difference in regard to accidentally and essentially ordered series exists on this count. What holds for the one holds for the other. *Ideo diceretur quod stante processu in infinitum in causis per se ordinatis stat in ordinatis per accidens.*[114] *Non est demonstratum aliquod ens esset incausatum.*[115]

Like the author of the *Theoremata*, John de Bassolis believes we cannot exclude the position of Avicenna.

> Potest dici quod non est demonstratum quod omnes causae causarent effectum, sed tantum causa immediata, licet illa causaretur ab alia superiori, et ita solum referretur effectus ad causam immediatam non ad omnes, sicut etiam nec est demonstratio apud eos quod deus causet omnia immediate sed quod secundam intelligentiam sibi demonstratam. Sed contra hoc est quia tunc non essent causae essentialiter ordinatae in causando; quia non omnes simul concurrerent ad causandum; sed de hoc non est vis facienda.[116]

The proofs for the existence of God have no greater validity than the proofs for His omnipotence. And what is said of the primacy in the order of efficiency holds for the order of finality and eminence as well.

> Ideo etiam eodem modo potest ad alias rationes de fine et de eminentia quia per idem incedunt. Et ita diceretur vel posset dici quod non est demonstratum esse aliquod ens simpliciter primum in universo, sed sola fide videtur hoc tenendum.[117]

Another interesting parallel between this disciple of Scotus and the position of the *Theoremata* is in regard to the possibility of a creature creating. After criticizing the position of St. Thomas, he takes up that of Scotus.

> Adducuntur ergo aliae rationes ad probandum eandem conclusionem, scilicet quod creatura nullo modo possit creare nichil presupponendo ex

[114] *Op. cit.*, f. 47vb.
[115] *Ibid.*, f. 50rab.
[116] *Ibid.*
[117] *Ibid.*

parte effectus quia planum est apud omnes et philosophos et theologos quod non potest creare nihil praesupponendo ex parte causae agentis quia sua actio inititur necessario actioni primi agentis eo ipso quod creatura est et agens secundum. Adducuntur ergo primo rationes in generali. Secundo in speciali...[118]

Then citing what are obviously the arguments of Scotus, plus some additional ones—probably of other Scotists—he concludes with this comment.

Si istae rationes valent valeant. Non puto tamen quod demonstrent. Tamen dico quod creatura creare non potest. Ad hoc est auctoritas Augustini... Ad hoc est auctoritas Damasceni... Ad hoc etiam est doctrina et sententia ecclesiae quia hanc conclusionem approbat.[119]

And he adds further:

Dico quod non est demonstratum ad creationem neccessario requiri infinitatem virtutis. Nec ex hoc probatur demonstrative quin creatura potest creare, licet probabiliter.[120]

On a number of other points, John de Bassolis differs with the position adopted by Scotus in the authentic writings and sides with the author of the *Theoremata*. For instance, in the *De Primo*, the *Opus Oxoniense*, the *Reportata* and the *Quodlibetum*, Scotus indicates his conviction that God's infinity, simplicity, unity, intelligence and free will are demonstrable by reason. Theorems XIV and XVI, on the contrary, place them among the *credibilia*. Here again, John argues against the position of Scotus on the grounds that

non est demonstratum an Deus aliquid intelligat extra se vel, si aliquid non tamen nisi per ea quae sunt praesentis universi et quae possunt constituere unum ordinem vel unum universum cum eis; non autem ad universum cui possideret alter deus, nec Deus ipsius, tunc solutum esset argumentum. Et similiter de casusalitate et potentia et volitione diceretur.[121]

The proofs of Scotus for the infinity of God, therefore, are without foundation, based as they are on the fact that God knows all intelligibles. Similarly the proofs for the unicity of God, are invalid since they presuppose in addition the infinite power of God, the fact that God possesses free will, and so on. Of free will, John insists that *si autem quod non est demonstratum Deum non velle de necessitate tunc non valet argumentum.*[122]

---

[118] *Op. cit.*, liber 2, d. 1, q. 2, 10ra.
[119] *Ibid.*, 10va.
[120] *Ibid.*
[121] *Ibid.*, lib. 1, d. 2, q. 3, f. 52rb.
[122] *Ibid.*, f. 52va.

If we insist that God possesses intellection, then we cannot demonstrate His simplicity, or if we assume His simplicity we cannot prove that God possesses intellection. *Non est demonstratum aliquod ens cujus substania sit unum intelligere.*[123]

Of the reasons adduced by Scotus for the existence of an *ens primum simpliciter infinitum actu intensive in perfectione et vigore,* de Bassolis has this to say:

Dico igitur quia licet demonstrari non possit, sicut dicam infra, quod Deus sit simpliciter infinitus, nec istae rationes adductae hoc demonstrant, licet sint multo probabiliores quam aliorum rationes probant quod sit finitus.[124]

Hence his conclusion:

Videtur mihi dicendum quod licet Deus sit infinitus secundum scripturam et sanctos, quia *magnus dominus et laudabilis nimis, et magnitudinis ejus non est finis, et sapientia ejus non est numerus,* tamen non videtur mihi hoc demonstratum ex apparentibus demonstratione cogente intellectum ex evidentia rei sic quod necessarium sit intellectum tali demonstrationi vel tali rationi propositae assentire.[125]

It is interesting to note that he uses the impersonal form in answering Scotus' arguments, creating the impression that others, like himself, were dissatisfied with their demonstrative character.

Ad primam diceretur quod non est demonstratum quia infinitum actu non repugnet enti, et per consequens cuilibet enti ... Ad secundum diceretur quod non est demonstratum quin infinitum sit modus intrinsecus vel passio omnis entis ... Infinitas actualis intensive non est demonstratum ... Non est demonstratum quin Deus sit in genere aliquo ... Demonstrative non potest probari quod sit infinita [natura] ... [126]

Since Scotus' arguments for the unicity of God presuppose a demonstration of God's infinite perfection, John de Bassolis is consistent in denying the demonstrability of this perfection also. Here again he cites Scotus' reasons, adding the significant comment *quarum aliquae reputantur demonstrationes.*[127] Then follows his personal verdict. *Dico*

[123] *Ibid.,* q. 2, f. 50ra.
[124] *Ibid.,* f. 49ra.
[125] *Ibid.,* f. 49va.
[126] *Ibid.,* f. 50rss.
[127] *Ibid.,* q. 3, f. 51ra; see also q. 2, f. 49va where John after citing Scotus' arguments for infinity adds: "Istae sunt rationes valde probabiles quantum ad aliquas quibus secundum aliquos ostenditur Deus vel primum ens actu existens in universo esse actu

quod non videtur mihi demonstratum quod sit tantum unus Deus, sed videtur hoc habetur ex fide, sicut dicit Rabbi Moyses.[128] And what is even more interesting, he attempts to argue that Scotus implicitly denied the absolute validity of these proofs from what he says in the *Quodlibetum*, quaestio quarta, regarding *relatio* and infinity. One wonders why John did not quote from the *Tractatus de creditis* where it is explicitly denied.

IN CONCLUSION

We have, then, a curious parallel between the position of John de Bassolis and that of Theorems XIV–XVI. It is in sharp contrast with that expressed by Scotus himself while he was yet a *Magister Regens* in Paris. For the seventh question of his *Quodlibetum* clearly indicates his firm conviction that a mind with no more supernatural aid than that which Aristotle possessed could demonstrate the unicity and infinity of God. His reference to his previous treatment of this problem in the Sentences manifestly proves he has not altered the position taken in the unfinished *Ordinatio*. We have no alternative, then, but to suppose that even at this late date he regarded his proofs of the triple primacy, the intellection, free will, unicity and infinity as valid demonstrations in the Aristotelian sense of the term. As such, they were not to be confused with such truths as could be established only on the basis of premises given by revelation. And if the *De Primo Principio* represents an even later work, then we must perforce maintain that at the time of its composition he had full confidence in the validity of his distinction between essentially and accidentally ordered causes, and consequently in his proofs for a being *simpliciter primum*. There is not the slightest evidence that he was at all aware of the distinction in essentially ordered causes made by his successors, a distinction that underlies the reasoning of the *Theoremata*.

For Theorem XIV, we know, assumes a conception of essentially ordered causes that is wholly foreign to the mind of the author of the *Oxoniense* and the *De Primo Principio*, for it assumes the possibility

---

infinitum intensive in perfectione et vigore: quarum aliquas multi reputant demonstrationes."—Scotus himself alludes to the different value of the various proofs for infinity. The argument based on the intellect of God he seems to have considered the strongest. In the *De Primo* he writes: "Infinitatem igitur tuam, si annuas ex dictis de intellectu tuo, primo conabor inferre; deinde alia quaedam adducam, an valeant vel non valeant ad concludendum propositum, inquirendo" (c.4, concl. 9, p. 90). Confer also his proofs in the *Ordinatio*.

[128] *Ibid.*, q. 3, f. 51vb.

of a creature creating independently of the coexisting "first" cause and declares we have no more reason for a *status* in an essential series than we have in an accidentally ordered one. No distinction is made by the author of the *Tractatus de creditis* between proofs for the omnipotence, immensity, etc. on the one hand and those of the unicity, intellection, free will, etc. on the other.

John de Bassolis, however, is in essential agreement with the *Theoremata*. Scotus' proofs are, in his opinion, *valde probabiles* but not demonstrations. Neither the proofs for the triple primacy, nor those of the infinity and unicity have any absolute validity. Yet this disciple does not challenge Scotus' argumentation on any of the grounds suggested by Gilson. It is not because we must be content with *quia* and *a posteriori* demonstrations. Neither is it because metaphysics has an object transcending its natural powers. Nor do Scotus' difficulties in determining the proper object of the intellect by reason alone enter into the discussion. It is Scotus' notion of the interrelation of essentially and accidentally ordered causes.

When Scotus wrote, apparently the greatest challenge to a demonstrative proof of God was the requirement of premises that were necessary as well as evident. With painstaking care he developed his demonstration to meet this demand. Yet, significantly, this whole aspect is ignored by John de Bassolis. The only objections alluded to center round the problem of ordered causes. In this early disciple, the beginnings of that opposition movement which culminated in Ockham is already in evidence. For it was this very point which caused the Venerable Inceptor to shift the argument for God's existence from the thorny field of causality to the Christian concept of conservation. In so doing he emphasized the very point which Scotus sought to establish by his distinction of essentially and accidentally ordered causes, namely, that the first cause must be coexistent with the whole series of secondary efficient causes, be they essentially or accidentally ordered among themselves. *Nulla enim difformitas perpetuatur, nisi in virtute alicujus permanentis, quod nihil est successionis.*[129]

What conclusions can we draw from all this? Is John de Bassolis himself a likely candidate for the co-authorship of the *Theoremata* or, perhaps, for the sole authorship of the *Tractatus de creditis* at least?[130] At the present writing, we are not inclined to think so. There appears to be a very marked general doctrinal agreement, it is true. On the other hand, however, certain differences appear. For instance, though

---

[129] *De Primo Principio,* c. 3, concl. 2, p. 43.
[130] Boehner has suggested de Bassolis as a possible author of the *Theoremata* in the *Tractatus de Praedestinatione et de Praescientia Dei et de Futuris Contingentibus of Wm. Ockham,* St. Bonaventure, N.Y., Franciscan Institute, 1945, p. 84n.

de Bassolis has the twofold distinction of essentially ordered causes, it does not seem to be completely identical with that which underlies the reasoning in Theorem XV. Further, it is not clear whether John would maintain that reason cannot exclude the possibility of a creature creating if the first cause ceased to exist. His criticism seems pointed specifically to the special reasons Scotus brings against Avicenna. For in introducing the arguments against the creation hypothesis, he says:

> Qua planum est apud omnes et philosophos et theologos quod non potest creatura creare nihil praesupponendo ex parte causae agentis quia sua actio inititur necessario actioni primi agentis eo ipso quod creatura est et agens secundum.[131]

However, this statement seems to be simply a statement of Scotus' stand rather than his own, particularly if we consider what he says elsewhere.[132]

The importance of John de Bassolis, however, would seem to lie rather in this. He indicates the existence of a divergent strain of thought among the early Scotists. Unlike Peter of Aquila, who accepted unquestioningly the validity of Scotus' demonstrations for the unicity of God, John falls back to the position of William of Ware and Moses Maimonides. From de Bassolis we learn the voice of opposition is already being raised and the position of the *Tractatus de creditis* was adopted by at least some of the earliest followers of the Subtle Doctor. But what is even more important from the standpoint of this study, the source of the difficulty is not to be found along the lines suggested by either Baudry or Gilson. And the consequent theologism Gilson reads into the authentic Scotistic proofs for the existence of God seems to be without foundation.

If any reconciliation between the *Theoremata* and the definitely authentic works is to be achieved, it would seem to be along the following lines. Perhaps the *de creditis* represents a later addition by one of the more critically or sceptically minded Scotists. It may even have been that the work was originally planned by Scotus but, being left unfinished, was "amended" according to the mind of the collaborator or scribe. This would explain why so many points contained in the *de creditis* are definitely placed by Scotus himself among the *metaphysica dicta ratione naturali* in his *De Primo Principio*. Mayhap the view of John represents an opinion which was already adopted by some of Scotus' disciples and was a topic of discussion by the master in his

---

[131] *Op. cit.*, lib. 2, f. 10ra.
[132] Confer note 115.

last years. Perhaps too, the whole treatise may be simply an example of the *ars dialectica* as the *petitiones* in Theorem XV would imply.

Be that as it may, we should not distort or pervert the clear statement Scotus gives in his authentic works of his position in regard to the proofs for the existence of God. No other medieval philosopher, to our knowledge, has taken such pains and devoted such care to establishing a proof for the existence of God that would meet the strictest requirements of Aristotelian demonstration. If he differs with Averroës and sides with Avicenna, it is because the latter leaves room for a rational metaphysics to demonstrate the existence of God. If he challenges the theory of the analogy of being, bred as it was in an Augustinian illuminationism, it is again because it places an insurmountable obstacle in the way of any Aristotelian demonstration of God. As philosophers we are at perfect liberty to disagree with Scotus on any of these points. But as historians we should not try to read theologism with its incipient scepticism into the thought of one who made such an effort to exclude this very position from his natural theology.

What Gilson once said of Scotus' reputed ontologism, might well be applied here to theologism.

> When we consider how often he has been accused of this, we might come to despair of any effort to be clear, since we see him saddled with that very theory... which most of all he detests and which his own metaphysics shows to be radically false.[133]

[133] Gilson, *Spirit of Medieval Philosophy*, New York, Scribners' Sons, 1936, p. 257.

11 / Duns Scotus and the Existence and Nature of God

Of the great scholastics, perhaps no one devoted more attention and care to developing a proof for the existence of God than did Duns Scotus. Unlike Aquinas, Bonaventure, Henry of Ghent and so many others, he made no attempt to exploit the multitude of ways he considered possible, but rather concentrated his efforts on a single proof incorporating into it what he believed to be the best elements of the arguments of his predecessors and contemporaries. From the time when he presented the first draft of his proof as a bachelor of theology at Oxford to the day some eight years later when death found him still busy revising his major works for publication, the Subtle Scot had reworked his proof no less than three times that we know of. The changes, aimed principally at economy of thought and greater logical systematization, left the major outlines of the argument unaltered.

In this chapter I have limited myself to sketching the general argument and touching some of the highlights of the proof. Indeed, I could do little more when the text of his argument in any one of its several versions would run into dozens of pages itself. If the title seems inappropriate to an essay of such restricted scope, may I add that Scotus did not believe you could really prove the existence of a God without by that very fact saying a great deal about his divine nature.

Those who seek in Scotus a ready made proof that may absolve them from any personal philosophical speculation on the subject of God's

Reprinted with permission, from *Proceedings of the American Catholic Philosophical Association* 28 (1954), 94–121.

existence may be disappointed in what I have to say. Perhaps we are inclined to agree with Canon Van Steenberghen who remarked at a lecture some years ago that none of the proofs of the great Scholastics taken at their face value and in the sense understood by their authors would be accepted as valid today. But if we share in his healthy optimism we may be convinced that many of them can be reworked into an acceptable form. Such as these may find much food for thought in a careful study of the Scotistic argument.

The final version in the *De Primo Principio* is in many ways the most interesting of all. But it is also the most technical, for the revisions of the man whom Ockham was to praise *propter magnam notitiam in logica* are not in the direction of elaboration but of greater brevity. For the purposes of this chapter I have followed the plan and the text of the *Ordinatio*, available now in the critical Vatican edition.[1] To clarify certain points, however, I have used the earlier Oxford lecture[2] and the *Reportatio examinata* of the Paris commentary,[3] as yet unedited, as well as the *De Primo Principio*.[4]

The *Ordinatio* of Scotus' Commentary on the sentences divides the second distinction of the first book into two parts, one dealing with the unity of the divine nature, the other with the Trinity of Persons. On the subject of unity, Scotus poses three questions: (1) Among beings does anything exist which is actually infinite? (2) Is the proposition "Something infinite exists" or "God exists" self-evident? (3) Is there but one God?

For anyone who believes that God's existence can be established only *a posteriori*, proper methodology would dictate that the second question be treated first, which is just what Scotus does. The two remaining questions then deal with the proof proper, and it is the substance of these two that are combined in the complete proof as we find it in the *De Primo Principio*. We shall consider the three questions in this order.

Is the Existence of God Self-evident?

The question is particularly pertinent in view of the objective Scotus sets for himself, *viz.* to prove that something actually infinite exists.

[1] *Duns Scoti Opera Omnia*, vol. 2 (Civitas Vaticana, 1950).
[2] *Lectura prima in I Sententiarum*, Vienna, bibl. nat., cod. lat. 1448, ff. 1ra–75ra.
[3] *Reportatio I A*, Vienna, bibl. nat., cod. lat. 1453, ff. 1ra–125va; Balliol College, cod. 205, ff 1r–185v; Merton College, cod. 59, ff 1r–192v.
[4] *The "De Primo Principio" of Duns Scotus*. A revised text and translation by E. Roche, O. F. M. Franciscan Institute Publications, Philosophy Series No.5 (St. Bonaventure, N.Y., 1949).

For the very notion of being actually infinite implies existence. Scotus' interesting discussion of this problem deserves careful study, particularly since the Subtle Doctor's proof is often referred to as "ontological" and said to begin with a concept.[5] Unfortunately, I can do little more now than to sum up what I believe to be the substance of his position. In the present life no notion we possess of God such as "necessary existence," "infinite being" or the famous Anselmian description "a being greater than which nothing can be conceived" will satisfy the requirements of the subject of a self-evident proposition "If you ask whether to be is predicable existentially of any (proper) concept which we conceive of God, so that the proposition in which existence is asserted of such a concept is self-evident. . . . I say no."[6] The basic reason is that all these notions of God are constructs. With all such notions we must first have the assurance that they can be predicated meaningfully in an existential proposition. How do we know that these notions are not what Aristotle called "false in themselves?" asks Scotus.[7] "That is false as a thing," says the Philosopher, "which either is not put together or cannot be put together, e.g. 'that the diagonal of a square is commensurate with the side' or 'that you are sitting'; for one of these is false always, and the other sometimes; it is in these two senses that they are non-existent."[8] Perhaps "meaningless" is the best modern equivalent of what Scotus understands by *in se falsum*. Any notion which cannot be predicated meaningfully within its respective realm of discourse is simply false in itself. And where the realm of the real is concerned (i.e., the set of all things that exist or can exist), existence can be predicated of a subject only if we know that there is such a thing and that this thing exists.[9] Even in the purely quidditative

---

[5] Such a statement *de virtute sermonis*, of course, is simply false and meaningless, since the *principium* or starting point of any demonstration can only be a proposition or set of propositions. What is meant, however, seems to be that all that is required to validate an existential proposition is the analysis of the intelligible content of an initial concept.

[6] *Ordinatio*, I, d. 2, pars 1, qq. 1–2, n. 26, pp. 138–139: Sed si quaeratur an esse insit alicui conceptui quem nos concipimus de Deo, ita quod talis propositio sit per se nota in qua enuntiatur esse de tali conceptu, puta de propositione cuius extrema possunt a nobis concipi, puta, potest in intellectu nostro esse aliquis conceptus dictus de Deo, tamen non communis sibi et creaturae, puta necessario esse vel ens infinitum vel summum bonum, et de tali conceptu possumus praedicare esse de eo modo quo a nobis concipitur,—dico quod nulla talis est per se nota.

[7] *Ibid.*, n. 30, p. 141: "Ratio in se falsa, est de omni falsa," says Scotus referring to the chapter *De falso* in the fifth book of Aristotle's *Metaphysica* (1024b 31–32).

[8] *Metaphysica*, V, c. 29 (1024b 17–22).

[9] *Ord., loc. cit.*, n. 31, p. 142: Ad veritatem propositionis enuntiantis esse oportet cognoscere partes rationis subiecti vel praedicati uniri actualiter.

order, a thing is real, if and only if, it is possible for it to exist.[10] The proposition *Homo irrationalis est animal* is not a self-evident proposition in the order of quidditative predication for the simple reason that the subject *homo irrationalis* involves a contradiction and is nonsense. The proposition *Homo albus est* is a self-evident proposition of the existential order, if and only if we know that a man actually exists and that this man is white. Otherwise, Scotus argues *Nihil est homo albus*, and conversely, *Nullus homo albus est*, therefore its contradictory *Homo albus est* is false.

Any notion that is not irreducibly simple, but can be broken down into other concepts, is not self-evident unless we experience an instance where the parts of the concept are actually united.[11]

If I understand Scotus correctly, then, nothing can be assumed to be meaningful *a priori*. Whenever the subject of a proposition is not irreducibly simple, that is, contains more than one intelligible note, let us say " x" and "y," its meaningfulness must be tested. Either we must experience a case where there is a thing and this thing is both an "x" and a "y," or we must demonstrate that there is a thing which is both an "x" and a "y." And if we are dealing with the set of the real, nothing is assumed to be meaningful unless we actually experience it, or are able to demonstrate that such a thing actually exists or at least can exist. Since a demonstration may never legitimately employ meaningless concepts, the ultimate test of meaningfulness either immediately or consequentially is experience. The net result of all this is to show that God's existence is anything but self-evident.

DOES AN ACTUALLY INFINITE BEING EXIST?

The proposition "An infinite being exists" cannot be demonstrated *a priori* by a demonstration of the reasoned fact, so far as we are concerned. But we can indeed demonstrate it *a posteriori* beginning with creatures. This limitation already indicates in general outline what the order of proof must be. For by such an approach we arrive first at the relative properties of such a being and only afterwards at its absolute

---

[10] *Ibid.*, "Oportet scire quantum ad praedicationes quiditativas quod partes rationis possint uniri quiditative, puta quod altera contineat alterum formaliter." Since a thing is a being only to the extent that it can exist *(ens, hoc est cui non repugnat esse)*, if it is impossible for it to exist it is nothing, and hence is something only in name *(quid nominis)*.

[11] *Ibid.*, p. 140: Nihil est per se notum de conceptu non simpliciter simplici nisi sit per se notum partes illius conceptus uniri.

properties.[12] Henry of Ghent, one of the great lights at the University of Paris when Scotus was beginning his study of philosophy, once declared that all the valid demonstrations of the existence of God developed by the great minds of the 13th century could be reduced to two basic ways, one which employs the principle of causality, the other way of eminence or relative perfection.[13] But where the Ghentian reduces the causal relations of God to the world to three, efficiency, finality, and exemplarity, Scotus points out that an exemplar cause is merely a subdivision of efficiency and implies that the cause in question is intelligent and does not act by a blind impulse of nature. Consequently, says Scotus, there are three ways or paths that lead from creatures to God that we can explore. Though these paths had been trodden many a time before, Scotus' use of them is unusual. He does not consider them as separate proofs but as integral parts of a single proof. For that reason it may be well to pause for a moment to outline the general plan of the argument.

The proof, as we said, falls into two principal parts, one dealing with the relative properties of the infinite being, *viz.* efficiency, finality, and eminent perfection; the second with the absolute property of actual infinity. The unicity of God, the subject of the following question, might be called the third part. Each of these parts includes several stages. There are three, for instance, in regard to the demonstration of the relative properties. The first stage consists in proving that each of the three ways (efficiency, finality, and relative perfection) terminates in an actually existing being that is first in that respective order. What is interesting to note is that Scotus, unlike Henry of Ghent, or for that matter St. Thomas, does not pause here to tell us that this first cause, or this ultimate end, or this supreme nature is God. In fact, he almost

---

[12] *Ibid.,* n. 39, p. 148: Ad primam quaestionem sic procedo, quia de ente infinito sic porcedo, quia de ente infinito sic non potest demonstrari esse demonstratione *propter quid* quantum ad nos, licet ex natura terminorum propositio est demonstrabilis *propter quid.* Sed quantum ad nos bene propositio est demonstrabilis demonstratione *quia* ex creaturis. Proprietates autem infiniti entis relativae ad creaturas immediatius se habent ad illa quae sunt media in demonstratione *quia* quam proprietates absolutae, ita quod de illis proprietatibus relativis concludi potest immediatius esse per ista quae sunt media in tali demonstratione quam de proprietatibus absolutis, nam immediate ex esse unius relativi sequitur esse sui correlativi; ideo primo declarabo esse de proprietatibus relativis entis infiniti et secundo declarabo esse de infinito ente quia illae relativae proprietates soli enti infinito conveniunt; et ita erunt duo articuli principales

[13] Henry of Ghent, *Summa quaestionum ordinariarum,* art. 22, q. 2 (St. Bonaventure, N.Y., 1953), I, f. 132, L. The first source drew its inspiration, according to Henry, from Aristotelian principles, the second stemmed from the Victorines and the *Monologium* of Anselm. It is interesting to see how Scotus attempts to give this "Augustinian" or "Platonic" approach an Aristotelian basis.

seems loath to use this term until he believes he has established the existence of a being so different and unique among existing things that we can attribute this name to it in a meaningful fashion. Consequently, in the second stage he proceeds to show that we can put an "equal" sign, as it were, between the heads of the three orders. A first efficient cause will also be an ultimate end and vice versa. A first efficient cause (and therefore an ultimate end) will be a supreme nature and vice versa. The third step is to show that this triple prerogative of being a first efficient cause, an ultimate reason, a supreme being in some hierarchy of things is not a trait that is common to several different kinds of beings, but is a relative property of but one kind of being. It never will be, nor can it ever be, characteristic of more than one kind of nature. It is not, in a word, a specific trait, or still less, a generic property. That it is in addition an individual property, Scotus puts off to the last question: Is there but one God or infinite being?

This being then can meaningfully be called the *Ens Primum*. The second part of the proof, then, attempts to go beyond these relative traits to reveal some of the absolute properties of this first nature. The goal of this portion of the proof is to demonstrate that "Some existing being is actually infinite." As preliminary steps to establishing infinity, Scotus essays to show that nothing can possess the relative attribute of the triple primacy without possessing knowledge and love or volition. Furthermore, this knowledge and love is identical with its substance. Finally, the knowledge of such a being is actually infinite. With these conclusions as premises Scotus sets up his proof that this being itself is actually infinite. The question "Does an actually infinite being exist?" then, can be answered in the affirmative. In the question that follows, he raises the problem: "Can more than one such being exist? or "Is there more than one God?" Contrary to many of the other Scholastics including his own teacher William of Ware,[14] Scotus believed that the unicity of God can be demonstrated. It is not simply an article of faith.[15] His proof is based on the contradictions that arise from the assumption of more than one infinite intellect, infinite will, infinite good, infinite power, infinitely perfect being, or one absolutely necessary being.

As we cannot hope to cover the whole of this proof, we shall limit ourselves to considering some of its more important aspects.

[14] Cf. P. Muscat, "Guillelmi de Ware Quaestio inedita de unitate Dei," *Antonianum*, II (1927), 335–350.

[15] *Reportatio Examinata*, Mert. cod. 59, f. 24r; Balliol, cod. 205, f. 23v: Credo quod conclusio ista potest demonstrari, scilicet quod sit unicum ens primum unitate numerali.

Part One. Proof of the Triple Primacy

Consider for example the proof for the existence of the triple primacy. The procedure in each of the three ways is the same. The first step is to show that it is possible to have a first being in the respective order, secondly that such a thing is completely uncaused, thirdly that it actually exists. Incidentally, we might note that the starting points of each of the three ways are also tied in with one another. I mean that Scotus claims that if you admit an order of efficiency you must also admit an order of finality as well as an order of eminence or relative perfection. The whole proof, then, is tightly organized so that, if you grant the validity of consequences, to admit the initial premiss, namely, that an effect is possible, you must also admit the actual existence of an infinite being.

Let us consider this starting point for a moment. I believe that it is rather frequently misunderstood. And Scotus himself is undoubtedly to blame for it, for he could have been much clearer on this point. But then he assumes that his readers are familiar with the theory of demonstration as understood in his day,[16] as well as his theory of truth and evidence in regard to propositions.[17]

Since demonstration is by definition *syllogismus faciens scire*, we may distinguish between the syllogistic discourse proper and the intellectual operations (including immediate inferences) that precede it. In practically all versions of the proof, Scotus concerns himself simply with setting up what he considers to be the demonstration proper. Only by accident, as it were, do we discover later why he began the way he did and what he considered to be the basis for the truth and evidence of his initial premise. I say initial premise, because the proof is in the form of an enthymeme, or rather a series of enthymemes.

The first conclusion he seeks to demonstrate is the possibility of an efficient cause which is first in the sense that it is not produced by any other efficient cause, nor does it depend on any such cause for the exercise of its causality. His proof runs as follows "Something can be effected; therefore it is either produced by itself or by nothing or by something other than itself; not by nothing, for nothing produces nothing; nor by itself, for nothing makes or begets itself; therefore it is produced by another. Call this other *a*. Now if *a* is a first efficient cause in the sense defined well and good, our thesis is admitted. If not, then it is dependent on another efficient cause for either its being or

[16] For a summary account of his theory of demonstration confer my article in *Franciscan Studies*, VII (1947), 263–273; cf. supra, pp. 215–224.

[17] Cf. P. Vier, *Evidence and Its Function According to John Duns Scotus* (St. Bonaventure, N.Y., 1951), p. 31ff, for his theory of truth and evidence.

its effectiveness. Call this other *b*, and proceed as before. Either it is first or it depends on another. Thus we have an infinite regress where every cause is itself secondary or dependent on some prior cause, or we have a first. But since a circle in causes is excluded and an infinite regress in an ascending order[18] is impossible, a primacy is necessary."[19]

In typical dialectic fashion, Scotus raises two objections to his argument. We shall consider only the second for the present since it throws light on why he began his proof the way he did. The proof, it would seem, proceeds from contingent propositions and consequently is not a demonstration, for the premises assume the existence of something caused, and every such thing exists contingently. So runs the objection.[20] In answer Scotus replies: "I could indeed argue that some nature is effected because some subject undergoes change and therefore the term of change comes into existence in the subject, and consequently this term or composite is produced or effected. Formulated in this fashion, the first argument would be based on contingent but manifest propositions. However, to prove our conclusion the argument can be reworded in such a way that it proceeds from necessary premises. Thus it is true that some nature is able to be effected, therefore, something is able to produce an effect. The antecedent is proved from this that something can be changed, for something is possible (possible being defined as opposed to necessary being)[21] and thus the conclusion follows from its essential or its possible being, and hence proceeds from necessary propositions."[22]

The original version of the proof in the *Lectura prima*[23] throws some light on what Scotus had in mind. A proposition such as 'The contin-

---

[18] That is, proceeding from effect to cause, or from what is posterior to what is prior.

[19] *Ordinatio,* n. 43, pp. 151–152.

[20] *Ibid.,* n. 45, p. 153.

[21] Cf. Aristotle, *Anal. priora,* I, c. 3 (25a, 36–39: The term possible is used in several senses [for we call possible both that which is necessary and that which is not necessary and which is capable of being]).

[22] *Ordinatio,* n. 56, pp. 161–162.

[23] *Lectura Prima,* Vienna, cod. 1449, fol. 8b: Ad illud quod secundo arguitur contra positionem praedictam ex contingenti, scilicet quod sit contingens vel sit aliquod ens aliud a Deo, Philosophi dicerent quod hoc est necessarium propter ordinem essentialem causati ad causam; dico tamen primo sic: quia licet sit contingens respectu Dei tamen est contingens evidentissimum ut qui negaret aliquod ens esse quod non sit aeternum, indiget sensu et poena, negaret sensus et ideo ex tali contingenti potest ostendi aliquid necessarium, quia ex contingenti sequitur aliquod necessarium, licet non econverso. Item dico quod licet alia a Deo actualiter contingentia [sunt] respectu esse actualis, non tamen respectu esse potentialis unde illa quae sunt contingentia respectu esse actualis existentiae, respectu possibilis sunt necessaria; ut licet hominem esse sit contingens, tamen ipsum possibile esse est necessarium, quia non includit contradictionem ad esse aliquid; igitur possibile esse aliud a Deo est necessarium, quia ens dividitur in possibile et necessarium; et sicut enti necessario est necessitas, ita enti possibili ex sua quidditate est possibilitas; fiat igitur ratio quae prior [est] cum possibilitate essendi et erunt propositiones necessariae.

gent exists' or 'Some being other than God exists,' says Scotus, the philosophers would say is necessary because of the essential order of what is caused to its cause. Undoubtedly it is the Avicennian necessitarianism to which he refers. "But I say," he continues, "that even though such a proposition is contingent, it is a most evident proposition so that anyone who would deny the existence of some being which is not eternal needs senses and punishment,[24] for he would deny his senses. From this contingent proposition, therefore, we can establish something necessary, for from the contingent, something necessary follows, but not vice versa. And I say that although things other than God are actually contingent with respect to actual existence, they are not contingent with regard to potential existence. Wherefore, those things which are contingent as regards their being in existence are necessary as regards their being possible. Thus for instance, though 'Man exists' is contingent, 'It is possible for him to exist' is necessary. Being is divided into what must exist and what can but need not be. And just as necessity is necessary to what must be, so possibility is of the very essence of what can but need not be. Therefore, let the former argument be formulated in terms of possible being and the propositions will become necessary."

Here Scotus expressly states that from an evident, though contingent, proposition of experience "we can show something necessary, because from the contingent something necessary follows." In virtue of the axiom of modal logic *ab esse ad posse valet illatio*, the contingent propositions *de inesse* can be transformed into necessary propositions *de possibili*. Even in the demonstration of the simple fact, as Aristotle explains,[25] we can demonstrate only necessary connections. The Arabic philosophers with their deterministic notion of creation believed that the very nature of God implied the necessity of the creature and conversely, the actual existence of the creature was a necessary consequence of the nature of God. No Christian, of course, could admit this. Yet in a true sense, the possibility of creatures is a necessary consequence of the nature of God. As Aquinas points out in discussing the omnipotence of God, active potency involves in its very definition the correlative notion of passive potency. God can produce something only

---

est possibilitas; fiat igitur ratio quae prior [est] cum possibilitate essendi et erunt propositiones necessariae.

[24] Cf. *Topica*, I, c. 11 (105a 4–7); also *Oxoniense* 1, d. 39, q. 1 (Vivès edition, vol. 10, p. 625b) where Scotus quotes Avicenna as saying: "Those who deny a first principle should be beaten or burned until they concede that to burn and not to burn, or to be beaten and not to be beaten are not identical." So too, he adds, should those who deny some being is contingent be exposed to torture until they concede that it is possible for them not to be tortured.

[25] *Anal. post.*, I, 13.

because something can be produced and vice versa. In virtue of this necessary connection, we can argue from effect to cause. But to be a demonstration, the premises must be necessary as well as evidently true. It is to meet this requirement that Scotus shifts the initial premise from a proposition *de inesse* to a proposition *de possibili*. "If you concede the premises about the actual, those about the possible are conceded, but not the other way around."[26] The evidence for either proposition in the last analysis, however, is based on a fact of experience, *viz.* that something is changed. So obvious and evident is this, says Scotus, that even Heraclitus would not deny it. The factual proposition as such, however, does not enter into the demonstration as a premise; it is only preliminary to the proof.[27]

The second objection Scotus raises to his demonstration is that the pagan philosophers and their followers admit that an infinity in an ascending order exists.[28] On the assumption that the world is eternal and process of generation and corruption of forms has gone on from

[26] *De Primo Principio*, p. 40: Sed malo de possibili proponere conclusiones et praemissas. Illis quipppe de actu concessis, istate de possibili conceduntur; non e converso.

[27] For similar reasons some neo-scholastics have tried to realize the requirements of Aristotelian demonstration by showing that every proposition *de inesse* that is true is also necessary at the moment it is true in virtue of the Aristotelian principle: *Unumquodque, quando est, oportet esse.* As Jan Lukasiewicz has pointed out, on the basis of a two-valued logic which assumes that every proposition must be either true or false, this proposition leads to two inacceptable conclusions, viz. *a posse ad esse valet illatio* and " If it is possible that p, then it is necessary that p." Cf. "Philosophische Bemerkungen zu mehrwertigen Systemen des Aussagenkalküls," *Comptes rendus des séances de la Société des Sciences et des Lettres de Varsovie*, XXIII (1930), 57. The Scholastics had already recognized this difficulty. As Ockham pointed out rather acutely, what Aristotle really meant is that the consequence, not the consequent is necessary. That is, it is necessary that p implies p, or conversely, it is not possible that p implies not-p. Worded thus, the Aristotelian principle states: If p, then the implication 'p implies p' is necessary. (This necessity of course is not logical but metalogical.) The net result is that we have only a necessary implication, but not a necessary proposition we can use as a premise for the demonstration. Cf. Boehner, *The "Tractatus de praedestinatione et de praescientia Dei et de futuris contingentibus" of William Ockham* (St. Bonaventure, N.Y., 1945), pp. 70–75. Scotus, on the contrary, declares that by using the principle *ab esse ad posse valet illatio*, we obtain not merely a necessary consequence but a necessary consequent. Thus, p implies 'p is possible' and 'it is necessary that p is possible'. On the assumption that p is true, we obtain a proposition which is necessary (viz. "p is possible") and unlike the necessary proposition (viz. "p implies p") it can be used as a premise. The necessity of course is metalogical, though valid and admitted by Aristotle. But there is no indication his requirement for scientific knowledge or demonstration was a purely logical necessity.

[28] In an ascending order we proceed from the posterior to the prior; in a descending order, from prior to posterior. That an infinity in a descending temporal order is possible, pagan and Christian agreed; as for an ascending order the Scholastics were not agreed. St. Bonaventure stigmatized the Aristotelian notion of perpetual movement and eternity of the world as "insane," whereas Aquinas admitted it as theoretically possible and Scotus left the problem undecided.

all eternity, as Aristotle claimed, the famous problem: Is the egg or the chicken first? is meaningless, for there was never a first egg nor a first chicken.

In answer to this objection, Scotus calls attention to the distinction between essentially and accidentally ordered causes. This is not the classical distinction between *per se* and *per accidens* causes, for the parents or parent is a *per se* cause of the child. The distinction regards not primarily the being but the act of causation itself. Any cause that needs the co-causality of a second cause in the act of exercising its causality, depends upon that second cause essentially and not accidentally. Such a relationship would obtain between the four classical causes of Aristotle. A material cause can not "matter" unless a formal cause "forms" and vice versa. These intrinsic causes in turn depend essentially on extrinsic causes and according to the Aristotelian and medieval conceptions a hierarchy of efficient causes essentially ordered also existed. In the Christian notion of the relationship of God to the world, all secondary causes are related to the First Cause by an essential order of efficiency, for God must cooperate with them or at least conserve them and their powers in being.

An essentially ordered series of causes differs from a series of accidentally ordered causes in three ways. (1) In the case of essentially ordered causes, the posterior depends on the prior for the exercise of its causality whereas in an accidentally ordered series the posterior depends on the prior for its being or something else but not for the actual exercise of its causality. Even though the parents depend upon grandparents for their being, they do not depend on them essentially for the exercise of their generative function, for parents can beget children when their own parents are dead. (2) The second difference, which Scotus considers to be a consequence of the first, is that in essentially ordered causes the causality of the prior cause is of a different type and order, for the superior cause is always more perfect. Such is not the case necessarily with accidentally ordered causes. Generation is essentially the same whether exercised by parent or grandparent. Underlying this distinction is the idea that to form a *per se* relation two things must differ in kind. For the scholastics, however, it was an axiom that whatever differs qualitatively must also differ by greater or less perfection. Hence one of the two elements in any *per se* combination must be superior to the other. (3) A third difference follows from the first. All causes that are *per se* and essentially ordered must coexist at the time the effect is produced; otherwise an essential causality would be lacking. Simultaneity, however, is not required for accidentally ordered causes.

Next Scotus sets up three propositions. First, an infinity of essentially ordered causes is impossible. Secondly, an infinity of accidentally ordered causes is impossible unless based on an essential order. Thirdly, if an essential order is denied, infinity is still impossible. The objection from the possibility of an infinite regress in causes then is invalid.

The proof of the first proposition takes the form of five arguments. From the *Reportatio* of his Paris lectures, it seems he considered only the first three as really cogent. They are: (1) the postulate of an infinite series of coexisting causes each of which depends on something prior, involves this absurdity. The series is both caused and uncaused; caused inasmuch as the causality of every cause within the series and consequently the causality of the series as a whole is dependent on something prior. Still the series as a whole must be uncaused for nothing is its own cause. Yet the very nature of essentially ordered series implies that it cannot be dependent on something beyond the series, because that on which it depends becomes a part of the series in virtue of this dependence. Hence the series as a whole is always dependent on something prior; yet, since nothing is prior to the series as a whole, it depends on nothing apart from itself. (2) In an essentially ordered series of causes, every cause must be actually existing (by virtue of the third difference); hence an infinite series would involve an infinite number of coexisting causes, a conclusion no philosopher would admit. (3) Since the superior cause exceeds the inferior in perfection and the series is infinite, some cause infinitely superior to the others must exist, and if it is infinitely superior in causality, it does not cause in virtue of another, for any such causality is imperfect.

To these three are added two other persuasive arguments, as he calls them. If nothing is first, then nothing is essentially prior to another. The second is based on the notion that, unlike formal or material causality, efficient causality does not of its nature involve any imperfection. Hence there seems to be no reason why it must always be imperfect. But if a perfect cause is possible this is all we need to prove. For later on, Scotus declares, we shall show that if such a cause is possible, it must actually exist.

The second proposition was this. An infinity of accidentally ordered causes is impossible if this series is not based on an essential order. Scotus does not intend to prove the absolute impossibility of infinity in accidentally ordered causes, for like St. Thomas he did not see a clear-cut contradiction to the idea of an eternally existing creation. All he seeks to show is that if such a series is possible, it is essentially dependent on something outside the series. Every succession, he argues, presupposes something permanent that guarantees the continuation of succession. *Nulla difformitas perpetuatur, nisi in virtue alicujus permanentis*. Since the principle of permanence might conceivably be a material cause (e.g. eternal matter of the philosophers) or a conserving efficient cause (i.e. *Deus convervans* of Ockham), it would be necessary to show that a material cause alone is not sufficient to guarantee or underwrite the perpetual generation of forms but also some continued efficient causality outside the series of temporal causes must be assumed. This gap in the version of the *Ordinatio* is expressly developed in the proof of the *De Primo Principio*.

The horizontal order of succession, then, presupposes a vertical order of dependence of a different kind. What is essentially a process, a *forma fluens*, must be dependent on something not a process and to that extent different and outside the series, yet coextensive with it in duration. A temporal series of causes as studied by Hume, then, would imply a relation to some type of cause to which it is essentially ordered, and in this direction infinity is impossible, as the proof of the first proposition revealed. Consequently, an infinite succession of causes is possible only if some first cause exists that is coeternal to the series.

The third proposition was this. If we deny that any essential order exists (either between the causes of the series, or between the chain of temporal causes as a whole and the guarantee of its perpetuity) infinite regress is still impossible. One cause at least is possible. This we know from the fact that something can be effected. Now either this cause is first or it depends on one that is first. If it is not first this is either because it depends on another cause for the exercise of its causality or because it depends on another at least for its existence. If no essential order of causes exists, however, it cannot depend on another in the first way. If it depends on another in the second way, we cannot push this dependence back *ad infinitum* because in this case an infinite series of accidentally ordered causes would exist. But by the previous conclusion, this is impossible if no essential order exists. Consequently, some possible efficient cause must be first in the sense that it was never produced by any other efficient cause, nor does it depend on any such for the exercise of its causality.

After this long digression then we see the necessity of the first conclusion.

(1) *It is possible that something is first in the order of efficient causality*. From this the second conclusion follows.

(2) *A cause that is first in this sense is wholly uncaused*. That it has no efficient cause is clear. But if that be so it can have no final, nor material, nor formal cause. The reason is based on the mutual implications of causes. Intrinsic causes imply extrinsic causes, a final cause exercises its proper causality only in metaphorically moving an efficient cause to produce the effect. Consequently, what is without

an efficient cause is wholly uncaused.[29] From these two conclusions, the actual existence of the first cause can be inferred.

(3) *Something first in the order of efficient causality actually exists, and some nature actually existing is first in this way.* This conclusion need cause no wonder, for it is a perfectly valid inference from the other two conclusions. What Scotus has established of his first cause by an *a posteriori* demonstration is precisely the fact that it is not impossible that such a cause exist actually. But the second conclusion, which follows from the first, is that such a being is totally uncaused. But only something that exists virtually in its causes can be possible without being actual. What has no cause consequently can be possible only by being actual. If a first efficient cause is possible, it must exist. *Ab oportere ad esse valet illatio.*

Three similar conclusions follow regarding the order of finality. First, an ultimate end is possible, secondly it is totally uncaused, thirdly it actually exists. We shall not go into his proofs but simply note that he employs the Aristotelian axiom used generally by the scholastics: *Omne agens agit propter finem.* Since an effect is possible only if an efficient cause is possible and efficiency implies finality, the initial premise of the first way also provides the starting point of the *via finalitatis.*

Since the end must exceed in perfection anything which was given existence only for the sake of the end, an order of relative perfection must also exist. In such a hierarchy a most perfect thing exists. Hence, Scotus draws three more conclusions. In the order of relative perfection a supreme nature is possible, secondly, it is uncaused, thirdly it actually exists.

With the establishment of this triple primacy, the *first step* in the proof of the relative attributes is achieved. The *second* is to show that each of these primacies implies the other.

Scotus does this by way of two conclusions,[30] the first of which is this.

(1) *A first efficient cause is also an ultimate end.* Proof is found in

---

[29] *Ordinatio,* n. 57, p. 163 f.: Causa finalis non causat nisi quia causa movet metaphorice ipsum efficiens ad efficiendum, nam alio modo non dependet entitas finiti ab ipso ut a priori; nihil autem est causa per se nisi ut ab ipso tamquam a priori essentialiter dependet causatum... Causalitas vero causae intrinsecae necessario dicit imperfectionem annexam, quia causa intrinseca est pars causati; igitur ratio causae extrinsecae est naturaliter prior ratione causae intrinsecae... Probantur etiam eadem consequentiae, quia causae intrinsecae sunt causatae ab extrinsecis vel secundum esse earum vel in quantum causant compositum, vel utroque modo, quia causae intrinsecae non se ipsis sine agente constituunt compositum.

[30] *Ibid.,* n. 70, p. 168f.

the way in which agent and end are related. "Every *per se* efficient cause acts for the sake of an end, and a prior cause for a prior end; therefore, the first cause acts for the sake of the highest end. But the first efficient cause does not act primarily or ultimately for the sake of anything other than itself; hence it must act for its own sake as for an end, and therefore the first efficient cause is the highest end. For if it were to act *per se* for the sake of an end other than itself, then something would exceed it in nobility, for if the end were anything apart from the agent intending the end, it would be more noble than the agent." The reasoning behind this argument is that if anything acts for the sake of something other than itself, it would not be self-sufficient, therefore not perfect. But that which is responsible *finaliter* for the action which the agent could not perform for its own sake, must have the missing perfection needed and therefore be more perfect than the agent.

(2) *The first efficient cause is also the supreme nature.* The proof is very brief. "Since the first cause is not a univocal but an equivocal cause with regard to the other efficient causes, it is therefore more eminent and noble than they, therefore the cause which is first is the most eminent."

The *third and final step* in the first part of the proof is to show that the threefold primacy is characteristic of but one kind of nature. The reason Scotus seems to have introduced this as a special conclusion is because of the notions the pagan philosophers held regarding the Intelligences. Some might object that these inferior "gods" could conceivably differ from one another in essence and nature and yet in regard to their immediate effects enjoy this triple primacy. Scotus draws a preliminary conclusion.

(1) *The efficient cause which possesses the aforesaid triple primacy is of itself necessary existence.* This follows from the fact that it has no cause and of itself it is not impossible. Hence, not only does it exist but it must exist of itself. If it were not necessary for such a being to continue to exist, this could be only because of something incompatible with it which would put it out of existence. This is clear says Scotus because no being can be destroyed except by something positively or privatively incompatible with it. But nothing can be positively or privately compatible with a being which exists of itself and is totally uncaused. This is proved as follows: "What is incompatible could exist either of itself or in virtue of some other being. If it can exist of itself then it actually does exist and then two incompatible entities will coexist, or rather neither will exist because each will destroy the other. Now this incompatible factor cannot exist in virtue of something else. For no cause is able to destroy something by reason of an effect in-

compatible with the thing it can destroy unless it is able to give a more perfect and intense existence to its effect that that which the thing to be destroyed possesses. Now the existence which a cause imparts to a being is never as perfect as that of a self-existent being, for the existence of what is caused is dependent whereas that of the self-existent being is independent."[31] From this first conclusion, the principal thesis of this part can be inferred.

(2) *The triple primacy is a property of but one kind of nature.* Three proofs are given. The first exploits the property of necessary existence. "If two necessary natures existed, some real character proper to each would distinguish one from the other. Let us call these differences A and B. Now either A and B are formally necessary or they are not. If we assume them to be necessary, then each necessarily existing nature will possess two formal reasons for its necessary existence, since in addition to A or B, each is formally necessary by reason of that part of its nature in which it is like the other. Now this is impossible, for since neither of the two reasons of itself includes the other, if either be excluded the being would still exist necessarily in virtue of the other and thus the being would be necessarily existent by reason of something which, if eliminated would still leave the nature existing as necessarily as before. On the other hand, if neither nature is formally necessary in virtue of these distinguishing characteristics, then the latter are not of the essence of necessary existence and consequently neither is included in a necessary being. For any entity which is not of itself necessary being is only possible [i.e. contingent] being. Nothing merely possible, however, is included in what exists necessarily."[32]

The other two proofs are drawn from the fact that the first nature is the first efficient cause and that it is the ultimate end. The universe cannot be the result of several efficient causes and ends that are not coordinated but are quite independent of one another. As the order of relative perfection requires a hierarchy so also does an order of efficiency or finality.

Scotus adds a confirmation to these proofs: "One and the same thing cannot be totally dependent upon two things, for then it would be dependent upon something which could be removed and still leave the thing in question as dependent as before. Hence, the thing would really not be dependent on it at all. Now other things depend essentially upon an efficient cause which is also their end as well as preeminent in perfection. Now these other beings cannot be dependent upon two such natures in just this triple way; consequently, there is but one nature

---

[31] *Ibid.*, n. 70, p. 170.
[32] *Ibid.*, n. 71, pp. 171–172.

on which beings depend in this fashion, and which therefore enjoys this triple primacy."[33]

Part Two. Proof of the Infinity of God

Though Scotus elaborated a number of proofs for God's infinity,[34] not all of which he considered of demonstrative force, the one that held the greatest fascination for him was one based on the intellect of God, or more precisely, on the knowledge required in a being that is both the first efficient cause and the last end. The argument obviously grew out of a constructive criticism of the Aristotelian argument for what we might call the 'infinity' of the first mover elaborated in the *Physics* and *Metaphysics*.[35] This argument from the "efficiency of the first mover," as Scotus calls it, maintains that the latter cannot be finite, "for it produces movement through infinite time, but nothing finite has infinite power."[36] The first, and most obvious weakness of this argument, or course, lay in the Aristotelian assumption that motion and time have had no beginning, which conflicted with the Christian belief of a creation in time. This difficulty, however, could be overcome if one could show that the first cause could have produced movement through an infinite time even though *de facto* it did not do so. But then, another difficulty appears. Since at any given moment, only a finite expenditure of energy is required, the prolongation of such a finite effect over an infinite period of time would only prove an "extensive infinity," not an "intensive infinity." If some agent has the power to lift a finite weight of say 10 grams, we cannot conclude from the fact that this agent can continue to lift 10 gram weights successively throughout an infinite period of time that it has the power to lift an infinite weight. We must first show that the power in question is intensively perfect or infinite, that is, at one and the same moment, it possesses sufficient power to produce the equivalent of the sum total of an infinite series of such effects. While Scotus tried to strengthen this argument from efficiency, it seems he was never fully satisfied with it and in the *De Primo Principio* it was finally relegated to the last place, among the arguments of doubtful efficacy. But if we assume that there is no limit to the possible creatures that God could create, even though at any given time only a finite number of such possibilities could be actualized why not apply the previous type of argumentation to God's intellect instead of God's power? So Scotus reasoned. For while

[33] *Ibid.*, n. 73, p. 173.
[34] *Ibid.*, n. 75–147, pp. 175–275.
[35] *Physica*, VIII, c. 10; *Metaphysica*, XII, c. 7.
[36] *Metaphysica, loc. cit.* (1073a 6–7).

we need not say that whatever God can create over a period of time, he can create at one and the same moment, we must say that he has to know all the possible creatures simultaneously. Only prove that the number of possible entities are infinite and that God knows distinctly each of these infinite possibilities simultaneously, and you have a God of infinite knowledge. Show further that this infinite act of knowledge is really identified with the essence or substance of the first being, and you have established the existence of an infinite being, for an infinite power cannot reside in a finite substance according to Aristotle.

With this thought in mind, Scotus introduces four preliminary theses or conclusions to pave the way for his proof for God's infinity. They are: (1) that the first being, whose existence has been established, has knowledge and volition; (2) that its self-knowledge and love, at least, are identical with its essence; (3) that no knowledge it possesses, even that of things other than itself, can be something accidental to its nature, and (4) that it knows everything other than itself that can be known and that this knowledge is necessary, eternal and prior onto-logically to the existence of the creatures themselves.

We cannot go into detail regarding Scotus' proofs for these specific points except to note in passing that he considers them to follow from what he has already established of the nature of the first being. One of his arguments for the existence of volition or free-will in God that is interesting, however, is that such a postulate is the only sound philosophical root for contingency in the universe. As his arguments elsewhere indicate Scotus also considered the free will of the First Cause to be the only adequate solution to the existence of evil or imperfection.

The proofs for these four introductory theses are derived in one way or other from the self-sufficiency of the first nature and the fact that it exceeds all others in perfection.

Once these preliminary conclusions are granted, the principal thesis is taken up. "From the fact that the first being knows distinctly every-thing that can be made, we argue as follows: The things that can be known are infinite, and they are all actually known by an intellect that knows all things. Therefore, such an intellect is infinite. But the in-tellect of the First Being is of such kind. I prove the antecedent and consequent of this enthymeme. Things potentially infinite or endless in number if taken one at a time, are actually infinite if they are actualized at one time. Now what can be known is of such a nature so far as a created intellect is concerned, as is sufficiently clear. But all that the created intellect knows successively, the divine intellect knows actually at one and the same time. Therefore, the divine intel-lect knows the actually infinite. I prove the major of the syllogism, although it seems evident enough. Consider these potentially infinite things as a whole. If they exist all at once they are either actually infinite or actually finite. If finite, then if we take one after the other eventually we shall know all of them. But if we cannot actually know them all in this way, they will be actually infinite if known simultaneously. The consequence of this first enthymeme, I prove as follows. Whenever a greater number implies or requires greater perfection than does a smaller number, numerical infinity implies infinite perfection. An example: a greater motive power is required to carry ten things than to carry five. Therefore, an infinite motive power is needed to carry an infinite number of such things. Now in the issue at hand, since to know A is a perfection and to know B is a perfection also, both A and B will never be known by one and the same act of knowledge unless the latter includes in a more eminent way the perfection of the other two. The same holds for three objects and so on *ad infinitum.*"[37]

A confirmatory proof of the same Scotus draws from the fact that the first being cannot depend upon creatures for its knowledge of them, yet knowledge of creatures it must have if it is truly the first cause in the sense established in the first part of the proof. The divine essence is so perfect an object of knowledge that it causes not only an intuitive vision of itself but of everything else as well, so that the presence of these secondary or lesser objects would contribute nothing to the perfection of the knowledge which the first being has of them by reason of the presence of its primary object. From this it follows that this primary object is infinitely knowable, for only if the superior object is infinite in cognoscibility, will it be impossible for the inferior object to add to it. But if it is infinitely knowable, then it is infinite in being, for according to Aristotle *unumquodque sicut se habet ad esse sic ad cognoscibilitatem.*[38]

In addition to this argument for infinity from the divine intellect, Scotus also examines other ways, e.g. from efficient causality, from finality and from eminence. From the use of such words as *suadetur, coloratur, roboratio, ultima probabilitas pro consequentia* and the like, all of

---

[37] *Ordinatio*, n. 125, pp. 201–203.

[38] *Ibid.*, n. 129, pp. 204–205: Notitia cuiuscumque nata est gigni ab ipso sicut a causa proxima, et maxime illa quae est visio sive intuitiva intellectio; ergo si illa alicui intellectui inest sine actione quacumque talis obiecti tantummodo ex virtute alterius obiecti prioris quod natum est esse causa superior respectu talis cognitionis, sequitur quod illud obietum superius est infinitum in cognoscibilitate, quia inferius nihil sibi addit in cognoscibilitate; tale obiectum superius est natura prima, quia ex sola praesentia eius apud intellectum primi nullo alio obiecto concomitante, est notitia cuiuscumque obiecti in intellectu eius. Ergo nullum aliud intelligibile aliquid sibi addit in cognoscibilitate, ergo est infinitum in cognoscibilitate. Sic ergo est in entitate, quia unumquodque sicut se habet ad esse sic ad cognoscibilitatem, ex II Metaphysicae.

which qualifying expressions are absent in the proof from the intellect, it would seem he regarded only the latter as strictly demonstrative. This is confirmed from the *De Primo Principio Principio*, where he prays: *Infinitatem igitur tuam, si annuas, ex dictis de intellectu tuo primo conabor inferre; deinde alia quaedam adducam, an valeant vel non valeant ad concludendum propositum, inquirendo.*[39]

IS THERE BUT ONE GOD?

The establishment of the existence of an infinite being represents as it were the peak of achievement of the human intellect in its upward striving from creatures to God. The fact that it comes at the very end of an *a posteriori* demonstration that began with creatures would already seem to indicate, says Scotus,[40] that in this notion God is set apart or distinguished most of all from creatures and to that extent, so far as our way of conceiving God is concerned, comes closest to describing the unique essence of the Supreme Being, who described himself in a language that the mind of mortals could understand as simply I AM WHO AM.[41]

It is true we can add more content to what is implied in this notion and thus form a kind of descriptive concept of God by bundling together all that is pure perfection and involves no shadow of imperfection such as wisdom, love, simplicity, actuality, and so on. By predicating all these perfections of God in an unlimited degree we form a cumulative notion of his infinity and it was in this sense that Damascene referred to him as a "sea of infinite perfections." Nevertheless, the notion "infinite being" though less perfect in this way is a simpler concept. Not that we can form any simple yet proper concept of this being who is simplicity itself, for all our notions are constructed mosaic fashion of various notes derived somehow from creatures. But what *ens infinitum* represents and signifies is so simple and one that if we could intuit God directly this perfection of infinite being would not cause two formally distinct notions in our intellect, as would for instance, those perfections of God we commonly call his attributes such as his goodness, truth, etc. Infinity, then, is not an attribute of being, like one or good. It is an intrinsic mode so one with being that if we prove for example that every being is true, or every being is good, it will

---

[39] *De Primo Principio*, p. 102.

[40] Wolter, "Duns Scotus on the Nature of Man's Knowledge of God," *Review of Metaphysics*, I (Dec. 1947), pp. 3ff.

[41] Cf. opening paragraph of *De Primo Principio*.

follow automatically in the case of God that he is infinitely true or intelligible, and infinitely good.

And as the notion of what a thing is may be used to demonstrate the attributes of that thing, so from the notion of infinite being we can prove all the other attributes that the human intellect unaided by faith can establish of God. If the pagan philosophers assumed they could prove many things which cannot be demonstrated such as the eternity of the world, the necessity of a hierarchy of intermediate beings between the all high God and the lowest of material beings, and so on, they erred in the other direction: *Multa non posuerunt quae tamen possunt cognosci per naturalem rationem.*[42] It is in this sense that he addresses himself to God in the *De Primo Principio* declaring that we can conclude through metaphysics "to many more perfections than the philosophers knew of Thee."[43]

"Thou art the first efficient cause, the last end, supreme in perfection, transcendent, uncaused and therefore without beginning or end, necessarily existing, eternal, a living God in the highest sense because intelligent and possessed of will. Thou art happiness itself, God of resplendent vision, of most joyful love, self-sufficient yet knowing at one and the same time all that can be known. Contingently and freely Thou canst will whatever effect is possible and by willing them bring them into existence. Truly of infinite power, omniscient, infinite, yet of the utmost simplicity, without real parts or accidents or quantity. Thou art perfect without blemish, lacking nothing that is simply perfect, the sun of goodness towards which all things turn as to their ultimate end, the first truth, being Thyself the perfect source of all Thy knowledge. All these things can the metaphysician establish of thee in a general way by natural reason."[44]

But of all these attributes that he could prove, Scotus at this point selects the one most pertinent to the subject at hand, God's unicity. And with this he concludes his proof for the existence of God.

Part Three. The Unicity of God

His method is to exploit the various contradictions that would follow by reason of the absolute attributes of the several infinite beings.[45] The

---

[42] *Reportatio Parisiensia*, II, d. 1, q. 3, n. 11.

[43] *De Primo Principio*, c. 4, p. 142.

[44] *Ibid.*, pp. 144–146. Because Scotus declares that in the *De Primo Principio* "tentavi videre qualiter metaphysica de te dicta ratione naturali *aliqualiter* concludantur" (p. 146) some believed that Scotus did not consider the metaphysician's proofs demonstrative. *Aliqualiter* is best translated "in a general way" as is clear from Scotus' quotation of Aristotle. "Oportet sapientem omnia cognoscere *aliqualiter* et non in particulari" (*Ord.* prol., q. 1, n. 14).

[45] *Ordinatio*, n. 163–181, pp. 225–236.

first of his six demonstrations is based on the fact that an infinite being has an infinitely perfect intellect. This means, first of all, that its knowledge extends to everything knowable; secondly, whatever such a being knows it knows most perfectly; thirdly, this knowledge is independent of the causality of anything outside itself. Now if two gods existed, each infinitely perfect, one or the other of these three characteristics would have to be denied. Suppose, he says, there were two gods, A and B, each with infinitely perfect knowledge. If A's knowledge extends to all that is intelligible, it cannot assuredly exclude the infinitely intelligible B. Yet it cannot in any way depend upon B for this knowledge for that would imperil its perfect independence. If it knows B at all, then, it must be by knowing its own self or substance, which is impossible of course for B must be wholly independent of A, and A can only know itself and what is contained therein either formally or virtually. Even if we assume, for the sake of argument that A and B are similar and therefore A by knowing itself has some kind of knowledge of B, A's knowledge would still be imperfect. For it would not be intuitive but by way of abstraction. In addition it would be a knowledge through universal or common notions so that the unique features which distinguish B from A would remain unknown. Furthermore, an additional difficulty arises for we should have to assume that one and the same act of knowledge has two adequate objects which are not only distinct but unrelated to each other by dependence, since by definition each god must be completely independent of the other.

Similar contradictions are developed in regard to the postulate of more than one infinitely perfect will, or infinite good, or infinite power, or infinitely perfect being, or more than one necessarily existing being. However, as the argumentation runs along the lines of the above we shall omit it in this summary account.

CONCLUSION

It would hardly be proper, I suppose, to close this exposition without adding a word of comment of some sort. Any extensive evaluation of course is out of the question in a chapter of this length so I will content myself with a few personal observations. For one thing, I find something fascinating in the way Scotus takes one of the simplest and most obvious facts to elaborate one of the most comprehensive notions of God. Using nothing more than the generally accepted metaphysical axioms of his day, he attempts to demonstrate the existence of an infinite being, perfect in knowledge and love, simple in substance, contingent in creating, unique in unity, transcending its creatures in perfection, yet immanent to the fluidity of their temporally transient existence as a conserving efficient cause and the ultimate answer to the why of their being. Only the actual existence of such a Being can guarantee not only the fact, but the very possibility of the change and contingency revealed by even the most primitive phenomenological analysis of the data of immediate experience.

I make no pretense of accepting all of his principles, though I am convinced that St. Thomas would have had no difficulty with the Scotistic proof on this score.[46] But for all that I believe that his proof might well serve as a model for one who inclines towards the "scientific," rather than a "sapiential" form of metaphysics, if I may borrow the Bonaventurian classification immortalized in the Aristotle and Plato of Raphael's "School of Athens."

In the *De Primo Principio* which seems to have been the last draft of this proof, reworked so many times, I see in germ what might be called a primitive attempt towards some kind of formalization of metaphysics. For those who believe in the possibility of an axiomatic metaphysics this trend might profitably be explored. In his analysis of *per se nota* propositions, he has recognized the need of testing the meaningfulness of any conceptual construct in terms either of its immediate verification by experience or as an ontological hypothesis conditioning what we know to be real. The distinction between essentially and accidentally ordered causes differentiates sharply between what I like to call metaphysical dependence or "causality" and the causality studied by Hume, Kant, and criticized by the contemporary physicist in its deterministic form. Where the latter extends horizontally through time and is itself one long temporal process, the atemporal dependence relation rises vertically, as it were, and terminates in the *Deus conservans* of Ockham or the Eternal Substance of Borgmann.[47] There are

---

[46] As far as I can judge, Scotus tried to free his proof of everything that bordered on the controversial. We have, for instance, one place where he rewrote a certain section lest his theory of univocity might prove a stumbling block to those who might disagree with it. (Cf. the note added by Scotus, *Ordinatio*, p. 141, line 10ff.) Most of the other characteristic differences of the Scotistic system such as the real identity of essence and existence in the actually existing being, the principle of individuation, the formal distinction, the theory of the divine ideas, and so on are significantly inconsequential so far as the presuppositions of his proof are concerned. Still less do I believe that the "essentialism" of Scotus would have created any serious difficulty for Aquinas. The issue of "essentialism versus existentialism" which many contemporary scholastics seem to consider the great metaphysical conflict of Thomas' day, as one writer well expresses it, "was one of which medieval thinkers were themselves largely unaware. Scotus does not consider his differences with St. Thomas as centering around the problem of existence, nor do fourteenth century thinkers describe him as the exponent of some subtle kind of 'realism', which, while not the same as 'essentialism,' is the closest thing to it in medieval vocabulary" (G. Lindbeck, *Review of Metaphysics*, VII, March, 1954, 430–431).

[47] P. Borgmann's interesting proof based on the temporal-eternal disjunctive as an

many other explicit or implicit traits of the proof that are worthy of comment, such as his excursion into the modalities, his reliance on logic, his theory of signification, and so on.

More important to my mind, however, than the letter of the proof itself is the spirit in which it was composed. In spite of its many revisions, I am not sure that he ever really considered it finished. Still less did he consider it to be the last word on the subject, though he obviously went out of his way to incorporate in it what he believed to be the most significant and sound contributions of philosophical thought down the ages. Anything but a relativist, Scotus at the same time recognized that truth as a quality of the individual mind as well as the corporate possession of the human race is not a static but a living growing thing. No philosopher worthy of the name, then, can afford to rest content with the achievements of his predecessors, for *in processu generationis humanae semper crevit notitia veritatis.*[48]

---

answer to contemporary actualism is obviously inspired by Scotus and Ockham. Cf. *Antonianum*, XXVIII (1953), 59–71.

[48] Scotus, *Oxoniense* IV, d. 1, q. 3 (Vivès ed., vol. 16, p. 136a).

12 / Is Existence for Scotus a Perfection, Predicate, or What?

Since the days of Kant, philosophers have criticized Descartes' 'ontological argument' for God on the ground that it mistakenly treats existence as a perfection or predicate. It is usually presumed that the "ratio Anselmi" in the *Proslogion* is simply an earlier version of Descartes' blunder. Both thinkers, it is said, were systematically misusing a language especially created for that purpose. English philosophers in particular were eager to suggest how such atrocious lapses in grammar might be prevented in the future and the general literacy level of the average philosopher improved.

Bertrand Russell, for example, showed that in the idealized language of the *Principia mathematica* the ontological argument cannot even be stated. In such an ideal symbolism, the true logical subject, the individual, is sharply differentiated from all descriptive terms predicable of that subject. None of the latter include words like 'existence', 'is' or 'being', nor phrases of the form 'There is' or ' There exists'. A special logical operator such as (∃x) or other syncategorematic term does the job of such expressions.

In his now classic essay *Is Existence a Predicate?*, G. E. Moore did a clever bit of ringmanship in putting a troup of tame tigers through their paces. In the statements 'Tame tigers exist' and 'Tame tigers growl,' the predicates 'growl' and 'exist' seem superficially similar but their linguistic behavior is quite different. 'Some tame tigers growl'

Reprinted with permission from *De doctrina Ioannis Duns Scoti*, vol. II (Studia Scholastico-Scotistico 2), pp. 175–182.

and 'Some tame tigers do not growl,' for example, both make sense. But while 'Some tame tigers exist' may be meaningful to a philosopher, although trivially true to a zoo-keeper, 'Some tame tigers do not exist' makes no sense at all unless one drastically alters the ordinary meaning of 'exist.' The upshot of Moore's circus performance was a recognition of the logical differences between 'exists' and the more usual type of predicate. To ignore such differences can only lead to statements that, if not nonsensical, are at best philosophically puzzling. Would it not strike you as strange, for instance, to find the book of Proverbs listing 'existence' among the perfections to look for in the ideal wife?[1]

In short, 'exists,' as Austin puts it, "is extremely tricky. The word is a verb, but it does not describe something things do all the time, like breathing, only quieter ticking over, as it were, in a metaphysical sort of way. It is only too easy to start wondering what, then existing is. The Greeks were worse off than we are in this region of discourse, for our different expressions for 'to be,' 'to exist' and 'real' they made do with a single word εἶναι. We have not their excuse for getting confused on this admittedly confusing topic."[2]

More recently N. Malcolm revived interest in the problem with his contention that Anselm has two versions of the ontological argument, the first regards existence as a perfection and is open to Kant's criticism on this score; the second treats 'necessary existence' as an attribute or perfection of God and this view can be defended.[3]

The modest aim of this chapter is to make some observations on what Scotus would have to say on the subject, beginning with Malcolm. From his remarks on why the triple primacy of efficiency, finality and eminence can only be found in one nature, it is clear Scotus considers "necesse-esse" to be a characteristic perfection or attribute of God. (Since contemporary analysts claim the descriptive phrase 'necessary being' is too muddled a notion to be of much service, let me say in passing that I think Scotus would regard "necesse-esse" as being logically equivalent to the conjunction of three other predicates: viz. able to be, unable to be produced, and eternal, i.e. always was and always will be. Though Scotus does not expressly mention the third component, it is clear from the *Lectura* version of the argument with its reference to Richard of St. Victor that he would exclude as nonsensical the possibility of anything being at once non-eternal and existing of itself.) But if Scotus would agree with Malcolm that "necesse-esse" can be treated as a perfection and introduced as a straight-forward sort

---

[1] *Prov.* 31, 10ss.
[2] J. L. Austin, *Sense and Sensibilia* (Oxford, 1962), 68, n. 1.
[3] N. Malcolm, "Anselm's Ontological Arguments," *Philosophical Review* 69 (1960), 41–62.

of predicate, he would go a step further I believe in his insistence that the possibility of existence itself is an essential trait.

'Necessary' is itself a modal expression. It seems intuitively clear that what *must be* the case, *is* the case, and what *is* the case, *can be* the case. In other words, "necesse-esse" entails facticity or *esse*, and facticity entails possibility or self-consistency. The reverse order of entailment is of course not valid.

It is quite clear that Scotus considers statements about the possibilities of any subject to be statements about the nature or what is essential to that subject. If you recall many of the earlier scholastics under the influence of pseudo-Denis, the Areopagite, declared with reference to God, that man could know that he exists, but not what he is; only what he is not or how he is related to the world (e.g. as creator or final end). If this seems strange to you as it did to Scotus, note that it can be expressed symbolically as follows: $(\exists x)\ \varphi x$. Read: 'There is an individual x such that it has the property φ', where φ represents any or all of the descriptive predicates one can assert of the subject. Statements of the "via negativa" such as 'There is an individual that is not finite' could be symbolized as $(\exists x) \sim Fx$ those of the "via causativa" such as 'There is a creator of the world' could be symbolized as $(\exists x)\ Rxw$ where R expresses the relation of creator, and w the world. Read: 'There is an individual x such that x is not finite' and 'There is an individual x such that x is related to the world, w, as creator'.

Scotus objects that it cannot be that all descriptive predicates are merely relative or negative. Relations presuppose relata, and it is a truism that while a "relatum" may be related, it is not itself a relation, but something absolute or non-relative. Thus though actual creation may be a contingent fact, the ability to create is an essential component of what God is and is identified with the attribute we call 'omnipotence'. If all descriptive predicates are negative, on the other hand, it becomes impossible to identify unambiguously what, if anything, the x refers to. If e.g. $(\exists x) \sim Fx$ ('There is an individual that is not finite') is taken to mean 'There exists in the real or extramental world something not-finite' then, Scotus argues, one could specify something about the nature or essence of the subject, viz. its ability to exist. That is why he insists that *ens* defined as "cui non repugnat esse," is an essential or quidditative term. It indicates the individual subject is capable of existing in the extramental world and hence differentiates it from the whole realm of mythical or fanciful entities such as chimaeras, gremlins or leprechauns.

Facticity, however, is not an essential attribute of any subject other than God, and here only because 'to exist necessarily' entails 'to exist always', and this in turn entails 'to exist now.'

What of something contingent ("ens contingens")? To say of something that it is contingent is to say by implication at least something about its nature or essence, viz. That is able to be but need not exist.

To sum up: to say of some individual that it is the sort of thing that *can* exist, or that *can* but *need not* exist is to say something about the nature of the subject. It represents an answer to the question: "Quid sit?" rather than "An sit?" Only if the answer to the first question is that the thing in question is the sort of thing that must be, do we also have the answer to the second. It is in this sense that Scotus says that 'Deus est' represents a proposition in the first mode of *per se* predication.

But what about 'exists' as a predicate of any other subject?

"Esse" itself is an 'umbrella term' covering a whole spectrum of irreducible meanings that have only a 'family resemblance' among themselves, to use Wittgenstein's description. Among the various meanings, Scotus devotes a lengthy discussion to Henry of Ghent's distinction between "esse essentiae" and "esse exsistentiae." Recall for example, question 2, distinction 1, in the second book of the *Reportatio Parisiensis*. More than once he uses the expression "essentia, eo modo quo distinguitur ab exsistentia" in a context suggesting that in creatures there is some kind of distinction between the two. It is obvious that he does not consider it a real distinction, and though some scotists have suggested it might be a formal distinction, there is no clear evidence this is the case. There is one cryptic remark in an "Additio" in the *Quodlibet*, q. 1—again in answer to the objection that essence, however it be distinguished from existence, seems to be potential with respect to existence as act. It reads:

> "Dici potest quod essentia et eius exsistentia in creaturis se habent sicut quiditas et modus, ideo distinguuntur. In divinis autem exsistentia est de conceptu essentiae, et praedicatur in primo modo dicendi per se."[4]

This has prompted the suggestion that the distinction is a modal formal distinction such as he proposes is to be found between 'infinite' and 'being' or "ens", or between 'whiteness' and its degree of intensity. Since the limits of the modal distinction are never systematically defined by Scotus it is obviously difficult to give a categorical yes or no to the question of whether this interpretation is correct.

I would like to point out some differences between what the mode of existence adds to its subject and what modes like 'finitude' (or 'in-

---

[4] *Quodl.* q. 1, n. 4 (ed. Vivès XXV, 9b–10a).

finite'), or 'degree of intensity' might be said to add to 'being' or 'whiteness' respectively.

Let me begin by saying that Scotus (not unlike Russell or the early
Wittgenstein) did believe that a careful study of the objective requirements for meaningful discourse or thought, could tell us something
about the logical form or metaphysical structure of the extramental
world.

Thus we find him insisting that unless one postulates some kind of
formal non-identity "a parte rei" or in the very nature of things, the
following set of statements cannot be simultaneously true: 'The Father
is God—the Son is God—the Father is not the Son' or again: 'The soul
is indivisibly simple—it is in essence both like and unlike an angel—
it is in essence both like and unlike the brute soul.'

On the other hand, it is clear that Scotus did not believe, as Wittgenstein once did, that thought or its linguistic expression to be meaningful must be a logical picture of what is the case. On more than one
occasion he warns against thinking that reality and our conceptual
descriptions of it are logically isomorphic. Because there is a superficial
resemblance between complex expression or concepts like 'thin man,'
'rational animal,' or 'infinite being,' we should not be so naive as to
think the objects they describe have a similar metaphysical structure.
If a fat man could take off weight without ceasing to be a man, but
could not shed his reason by any amount of slimming, this indicated
to his mind some fundamental difference in the way ' reason' and
'fatness' are related to their respective subjects. Thinking in terms of
their respective referents, Scotus would characterize the concept of
'thin man' as " non-simplex" in the sense of requiring several conceptual acts to do justice to the formal object conceived. 'Rational animal,'
on the other hand is a "conceptus simplex" but not "simpliciter simplex" as "ens" would be.[5] That is to say, one could grasp or understand
its conceptual content in a simple act of apprehension, but the content
could still be analyzed out in terms of a determinable (viz. 'animal')
and determining element (viz. 'rational').

The concept 'infinite being,' Scotus regarded as still more deceptive.
Though our concept is composed, what we intend to express is irreducibly simple.[6] Indeed, he argues, intuitive knowledge or face-to-face
vision would erase the distinction entirely. Recall the beautiful passage
in the Lectura[7] which is even clearer on this matter than the parallel
passage of the Ordinatio.[8] Only because we know God indirectly and
by way of abstract concepts in this life does it happen that the "una

[5] Cf. Lect. I, d. 3, n. 68 (XVI, 250).
[6] Cf. e. g. Collationes Paris. collat. 13, n. 5 (ed. Vivès V, 202).
[7] Lect. I, d. 8, n. 125 (XVII, 44–45).
[8] Ord. I, d. 8, n. 137–142 (IV, 221–224).

est realitas quae nata est facere istos duos conceptus in intellectu nostro."[9]

Now it is quite clear that we can also form an abstract concept of existence. In fact the notion "esse exsistentiae" is just that. And one could ask how this is distinguishable from the "esse essentiae." In the question on whether existence is the principle of individuation,[10] Scotus goes into this question, pointing out that while actual existence can be and often is referred to as "actus ultimus," it adds nothing in the way of descriptive predicates but is extrinsic as it were to them all. To the extent that it is outside of all substantial description including that of the primary substance or the individual, we might be tempted to speak of it as *quasi accidental*. Yet it is not really an accident, Scotus hastens to add, and rightly, because accidental features are after all descriptive. They add intelligible content and to that extent increase the conceivability of the subject in a straightforward sort of way. But the fact that something exists does not add to the concept in this way.

There is a particularly illuminating passage in the *De primo principio* (paralleled in the *Ordinatio*[11]) where he tries to extend or enlarge the usual meaning of 'a greater conceivable object' ("maius cogitabile") so as to make sense of the Anselmian formula 'What exists in reality is conceivably greater than what exists only in the intellect'. 'This is not to be understood', he insists, anticipating Kant's objection by some five centuries, 'in the sense that something conceived, if it actually exists, is by the fact of existing, conceivable to any greater extent. What it means is merely that for anything which exists solely in the intellect, there is some greater conceivable object which exists in reality.'[12] The point here is that given something that exists only in fancy or is only a fond hope of the future, one can always find a richer or more intelligible entity which actually exists. Thus anything which actually exists, *can* exist, and this does say something about the nature of the thing, viz. that it is not something that can exist only in one's fancy. And if the nature of contingent beings allows that they are able, but do not of necessity exist, the notion that something is not only able to exist, but must exist, does add something to our notion of what such a thing is, as we said earlier.

But still more interesting is his second "coloratio" of Anselm's argument: "A greater conceivable object is one which exists, that is to

---

[9] *Lect.* I, d. 8, n. 125 (XVII, 44).
[10] *Ord.* II, d. 3, q. 3.
[11] *Ord.* I, d. 2, pars. 1, q. 1–2.
[12] *De primo princ.*, c. 4, (ed. A. B. Wolter, *John Duns Scotus: A Treatise on God as First Principle* [Chicago, 1966], 124).

say, such an object is knowable in a more perfect way because it is visible [i.e knowable by intuitive cognition]... Now what can be seen or intuited is knowable in a more perfect way than something which cannot be intuited, but known only abstractively."[13]

Here I think we have the clearest description of what existence adds to essence according to Scotus. It is not properly a conceivable element at all, except at the level of abstract knowledge. But because Scotus did not restrict intuitive cognition to the sensory level, but regarded it as one form of simple intellectual awareness which went further than simple abstract intelligence, one could speak of a sense in which the former was more perfect and to that extent greater in terms of the information it provided about the object. Having experienced or confronted something intuitively, one can go on to consider the thing abstractively, prescinding from the question of whether it is or is not. But no amount of analysis of abstract conceptions will yield the information that the object of the abstract knowledge actually exists.

That is why I have suggested elsewhere,[14] that the more precise way of expressing how existence differs from essence in the concrete existing object, is in terms of the different objective requirements for intuitive and abstractive cognition.

There is one final note. Existence in creatures is a 'sometime thing.' Each moment can be logically distinguished from the other in the sense that existence at any one moment of time, while it excludes under pain of contradiction, non-existence at that identical moment, does not exclude non-existence at any other moment of time.

Consequently, I think Duns, like Ockham, would have been sympathetic to the view rejected by Austin. Austin's comment that 'exists' is not something things do continually, I submit, is a metaphysical opinion based on his idea of what things do or do not do. As theoretical considerations come to be associated in the mind of a physicist with the concept of light, e.g. it is a form of electromagnetic radiation, so I suspect medieval thinkers, especially after the Condemnations of 1277, tended to stress the idea of the essential contingency of existence in creatures, and that if asked, they might have answered like O'Meara. 'True, existing is not like breathing, in that for something to breathe, it must first exist. Nevertheless, why not say that existing is something things do intransitively all the time (while they exist)?"[15]

---

[13] *Ibid.*

[14] A. B. Wolter, "The Formal Distinction," in *John Duns Scotus, 1265–1965,* ed. J. K. Ryan and B. M. Bonansea (Studies in Philosophy and the History of Philosophy 3) (Washington, D.C., 1965); cf. chapter 1, pp. 27–41, above.

[15] W. O'Meara, "Actual Existence and the Individual According to Duns Scotus," *Monist* 49 (1965), 669.

13 / Scotus' Paris Lectures on God's Knowledge of Future Events

After the Parisian condemnations of 1270 and 1277 that stressed that God was not in any sense necessitated to create the world but did so freely, motivated only by his own goodness and liberality, Christian theologians laid greater emphasis on the fact that the world and all that is in it are basically contingent. On the other hand, they all accepted the traditional Scholastic doctrine that God's foreknowledge is both infallible and immutable. Where the prominent thinkers of the time differed, however, was in their theories as to how one might reconcile these beliefs.

Scotus' unique and intriguing approach was particularly influential on subsequent thinkers and continues to interest contemporary specialists in medieval history and philosophy. Their primary source of information, until the publication of the critical Vatican edition of Scotus' questions on Book I on the *Sentences*, both in their initial *Lectura* and final *Ordinatio* form, was the set of five questions with a common corpus published in the Wadding-Vivès edition as part of the second part of distinction 38 (which treats of God's infallibility) and distinction 39 (which treats of his immutability).[1] Though this group of questions is obviously a refined version of what he said in his early *Lectura*, the editors of the Vatican edition point out that Scotus himself did not compose this particular account, since he left a blank space here in his *Ordinatio* for his final solution to the problem. That

---

[1] *Joannis Duns Scoti opera omnia*, ed. Wadding-Vivès, vol. 10 (Parisiis: Apud Ludovicum Vives, 1893), pp. 612–56.

Scotus refers to distinction 39 elsewhere in the *Ordinatio* is no coun-
terargument, they claim, since he has done this elsewhere in cases
where he had a more or less clear idea of what his revision would look
like, for he planned here as elsewhere to follow the format of his earlier
Lectura. Had Scotus personally put together this account, they argue,
he would have included it in place of the blank. Since it exists in
substantially the same form in all the important manuscripts, however,
they contend these must have stemmed from some single "apograph"
composed by some disciple who not only knew Scotus' mind on this
subject but had access to sources over and above his initial *Lectura*
and the "examined report" of his Paris lectures.[2] Consequently, they
have given us a critical edition of this apograph and included it in an
appendix to volume VI of the Vatican edition of the *Ordinatio.*[3]
Whether or not it represents his latest thought on the subject, the fact
that Scotus did not incorporate it in his *Ordinatio* suggests he may
not have been completely satisfied with his treatment.

If this be true, it is worthwhile to review Scotus' controversial doctrine in the light of the Paris lectures, which may well have been his
last extent word on the subject, particularly since the original version
of these, examined personally by Scotus, are still unedited. The Scotistic Commission in charge of the Vatican edition of Scotus' *Opera
omnia* have to date identified five manuscripts containing this version,
which they call "Reportatio I A,"[4] and point out that what appears in
the Wadding-Vivès edition is only an abbreviated account of this report,
done by Scotus' disciple, William of Alnwick.[5]

Though the basic doctrine in the *Lectura, Reportatio* I A, and the
Apograph is substantially the same, their respective formats differ. Of

[2] See pp. 26*–30* of the "Annotationes" to vol. VI of the Vatican edition.

[3] *Doctoris Subtilis et Mariani Ioannis Duns Scoti Ordinis Fratrum Minorum opera
omnia* VI (Civitas Vaticana: Typis Polgylottis Vaticanis, 1963), pp. 401–44. I refer to this
hereafter simply as the Apograph.

[4] See [C. Balić's], "De Ordinatio I. Duns Scoti disquisitio historico-critica" (published
1950) in vol. I of the Vatican edition, p. 145*. The most important of the five seems to
be the fourteenth-century Codex Palatinus 1453 in the Nationalbibliothek of Vienna,
which ends with "Explicit Reportatio super primum Sententiarum, sub magistro Ioanne
Scoto, et examinata cum eodem venerando doctore" (fol. 125va). In this study I cite from
this manuscript. Where it is defective, however, I have inserted in brackets what is found
in other manuscripts.

[5] See, for example, p. 4* of the "Annotationes" to vol. VII of the Vatican edition,
published in 1973: "Ipse Wadding, intendens praebere quattour libros *Reportationis,*
quoad librum I erravit, nam ibi liber I non est *Reportatio* sed *Additiones magnae* a
Guilelmo de Alnwick compilatae." Though Alnwick generally presents the authentic
position of Scotus and often in words Scotus himself used, his abridged or edited account
is significantly shorter than the original "reportatio examinata." See A. Pelzer, "Le
premier livre des Reportata Parisiensia de Jean Duns Scot," *Annales de l'Institut supérieur de philosophie* 5 (1923), 449–91.

the three, the *Lectura* seems to represent Scotus' original approach to the problem of God's foreknowledge.[6] There Scotus raises five questions interconnected through a common corpus. The Apograph asks the same questions with a slightly different wording. They are: (1) Does God have determinate or specific knowledge of things according to every aspect of their existential condition, especially their futureness? (2) Is such knowledge of their existential conditions infallible? (3) Is God's knowledge immutable? (4) Does God know in a necessary manner about all change in things? Only the fourth is answered in the negative, for Scotus insists God's knowledge of contingent events must itself be contingent and not necessary knowledge. If it were necessary, one would have to deny the most obvious of experiential truths, that contingency exists in the world. Hence a fifth question arises: (5) Is the contingency of things consistent with God's knowledge of them?

To this we must add a sixth question from distinction 40: "Can one who is predestined be damned?" Since the question is raised simply to illustrate concretely the conclusion arrived at in the five preceding questions, we might say it forms an integral whole with the preceding five and in *Reportatio* I A it will replace Scotus' fifth question.

The distinctions associated with the various questions, however, differs in all three accounts. In the *Lectura* and the Apograph the five questions are linked respectively with distinction 39 alone, or with 38 and 39. In the Paris lecture the first two questions: Does God have specific or determinate knowledge of future contingents and if so, is such knowledge infallible? are treated as a unit under distinction 38. Under distinction 39 Scotus raises the two questions: Does God have immutable foreknowledge of future contingent events, and if so, does he know such in a necessary manner? Scotus' negative answer to the last, which prompted the fifth question in the *Lectura* and the Apograph, in the Paris lecture leads him to add the more concrete question of distinction 40: "Is it possible for one who is predestined to be damned?" This redistribution requires a corresponding split up of the material treated in the common corpus to the five questions of the *Lectura* and Apograph.

GOD FOREKNOWS FUTURE CONTINGENTS INFALLIBLY

In his answer to the two questions in distinction 38, Scotus points out that theologians are in general agreement that God has both definite as well as infallible knowledge about future contingents, but depending

---

[6] *Lectura* I, d. 39, qq. 1–5; *Opera omnia*, ed. Vat., XVII, pp. 481–510.

on their various theories as to how God knows, their explanations differ. Scotus cites two such theories.[7] The first is that held by Thomas Aquinas, among others, viz., that God knows the future because his eternity is coextensive not only with the past and present but also the future; the second theory (espoused by Saint Bonaventure among others) is that it is through his ideas that God knows all creatural events including future contingents. Scotus objects to the first because the future precisely qua future is nonexistent now and just as God's omnipresence does not extend to nonexistent places, so neither does the "now" of God's eternity coexist with the as yet nonexistent future. Scotus objects to the second, because ideas are in the divine intellect prior to any creative decision on the part of his will. Since the will is the reason why creation is contingent, these ideas alone cannot represent events that exist only contingently. Neither do they present what is future any differently than they do what is possible but may never exist. What is more they represent the future no differently than they do the present.

Scotus then sets forth his thesis that God knows specifically and infallibly every contingent event that will occur. Why this is so can be explained in this way, he says.[8] God could know definitely one of the two contradictory possibilities when that event actually occurs, because even we can do so then. But God knows nothing that is new, for otherwise he would undergo a change from not knowing to knowing. Since he is immutable, what he knows at the time it occurs he must also have known from all eternity. If you ask how is this so, Scotus replies:[9]

---

[7] *Reportatio* I A, d. 38, f. 113va: "Quidam enim hoc ponuntur propter infinitatem aeternitatis ambientis totum tempus et omnes differentias eorum quibus est praesens. Alii dicunt quod hoc est propter certam representationem idearum quas Deus habet de omnibus." See also *Lectura* 39, nn. 18–30; XVII, pp. 484–88.

[8] *Rep.* I A, d. 38, f. 114ra: "Respondeo ergo ad quaestionem quod Deus novit determinate et infallibiliter eventum omnem contingentem, non solum in generali quod futura evenient, sed in speciali quod hoc futurum eveniet. Quare autem ita sit hoc potest sic declarari: Deus potest scire alteram partem contradictionis determinate, quam etiam hoc possum certo scire, cum altera pars evenit. Sed Deus non potest scire hoc de novo, quia nihil est in eo novum; alias mutaretur; ergo ab aeterno novit vel altera partem contradictionis vel utrumque. Non utrumque, quia hoc nihil est noscere, quia tunc nosceretur idem esse hoc et non esse hoc, quae formaliter repugnant; ergo determinate novit alteram partem contradictionis cuiuslibet, et per consequens infallibiliter."

[9] *Ibid.*, f. 114rab: "Sed quomodo hoc sit respondeo. Dico quod omnis actus intellectus qui in Deo praecedit actum voluntatis est mere naturalis et non formaliter libera et per consequens quidquid intelligit ante omnem actum voluntatis est mere naturale. Ergo intellectus divinus mere naturaliter apprehendens terminos alicuius complexionis futurae contingentis est indifferens sive est de se neuter, quia non concipit veritatem alicuius complexionis nisi cuius veritas includitur in rationibus terminorum vel sequitur necessario ex veritate notitiae complexae. Sed offert terminos complexionis futuri con-

I say every act of the intellect in God that precedes the act of the will is not formally free and consequently, whatever he knows that is prior by nature to the act of his will is purely natural, and the intellect apprehending the terms of some proposition about a future contingent, sees this as indifferent and existentially neutral, for knowledge of the terms of a contingent proposition does not suffice to tell which of the contradictory possibilities will occur. But if the intellect offers both possibilities to the will, the will can freely choose one or the other, e.g. Socrates or Peter will be beatified, Judas will not be. Thus any such contingent proposition is either true or false, because its truth is first caused through an act of the will, and it is not because it is true that the will wills it to be true, but it is the other way around. And therefore once the determinate truth of the proposition is caused through an act of the will, the divine intellect then first knows one part of the two contradictory contingent possibilities is true.

In the *Lectura*[10] and Apograph[11] this solution appears as an answer to the fifth question, namely, why God's knowledge is consistent with the contingency of things. And that really is what Scotus is explaining here. Things are contingent because they depend upon God's creative free will and not upon any necessary emanation rooted in his essence or nature. Otherwise, what exists would be a necessary consequence of what he is. However, if the contingency stems from the fact that he creates contingently, then since he obviously knows what he does with respect to creation, there is no conflict between the contingency of creation and his knowledge of it.

There is nothing particularly startling or original about this explanation. Much of it can be found already in Henry of Ghent. It occurs, for example, in Henry's *Quodlibet* where he is concerned to show that God's invariable knowledge is not inconsistent with the variation char-

---

tingentis voluntati ut neuter de ea; termini autem futuri contingentis non includunt notitiam complexionis contingentis, quia termini non sunt causa talis veritatis, quia tunc esset immediata veritas, et ideo intellectus divinus de talibus terminus tantum habet cognitionem neutram ante actum voluntatis, sicut intellectus meus est neuter de ista complexione 'An astra sunt paria vel imparia.' Offerente autem intellectu huius complexiones voluntati, potest voluntas libere eligere unionem istorum terminorum vel non eligere et coniunctionem istorum terminorum contingentium vel divisionem illorum, ut Sortes vel Petrus beatificari, Iudam autem reprobari et ipsum ad beatitudinem non coniungi sed dividi et in eodem instanti quo voluntas vult Petrum et beatitudinem coniungi est haec primo vera et non ante "Petrus beatificabitur." Et ita quaelibet talis contingens est vera, quia veritas eius est primo causata per actum voluntatis divinae, et non quia vera, ideo voluntas vult eam esse veram, sed econtra; et ideo veritate causata in complexione talium terminorum determinata per actum voluntatis, intellectus divinus tunc primo novit unam partem contradictionem contingentium esse veram."

[10] *Lectura* I, d. 39, nn. 62–63, p. 500.
[11] Apograph, n. [23], VI, p. 428.

acteristic of the world of nature.[12] Scotus' discussion differs considerably from Henry's however, since Henry in this question intends to show the difference between speculative and practical knowledge in God. God's speculative knowledge is based on what he knows simply by reason of his essence apart from any decision to create, whereas the knowledge God has from all eternity as to what he has decided to create Henry regards as analogous to what we call practical knowledge, namely, knowledge that directs us as to what is yet to be done. Scotus, however, claims that strictly speaking God's knowledge is not practical if we follow Aristotle's definition. Practical knowledge is knowing how to do something correctly and it directs and justifies the action performed in accord with right reason. Scotus is willing to admit that when God acts in regard to creatures he knows as a fact that such action is in accord with right reason, but he objects to the claim that such knowledge is prior to and directive of the action and that it functions somehow as a justifying condition for the action to be correct.[13]

Obviously, if God's causal activity with respect to creation is contingent, his will must play a part, and knowledge of what he wills seems to be an obvious way of defending the independence of God's knowledge from any causation on the part of a finite created event, something all the late Scholastics agreed upon.[14] There are two ways,

---

[12] In Henry of Ghent's *Quodlibet* VIII, q. 2 (in corpore f. 300H–I), for example, we find the statement that "God, without any change in his knowledge, however, knows that a thing is when it is and is not when it is not, and that it will be when it will be and that it will not be when it will not be, and knows it was when it was and was not when it was not ... For the divine intellect knows what has to be done insofar as it has to be done, by knowing the determination of his completely unchangeable will, and not through the changing things outside, that come into existence in diverse ways, but according to the simple and invariable determination of the divine will, which at once from all eternity has determined all things and by this has constituted for himself a scheme of knowing what is to be done, and therefore, he knows all these things invariably."

[13] *Ordinatio* I, d. 38, q. unica: "Utrum scientia Dei respectu factibilium sit practica"; VI, 303–8.

[14] According to our way of thinking, if one accepts the Aristotelian model, as did Scotus and his contemporaries, knowledge depends causally upon the object. But where finite creatures are concerned, the Scholastics are in agreement that if God's intellect were even quasi determined by what is or is not the case, his intellect would be vilified. Saint Thomas in his *Summa contra Gentiles* I, ch. 67, writes: "Res autem, a Deo scitae non sunt priores eius scientia, sicut apud nos est, sed sunt ea posteriores." Henry writes (*Quodl.* VIII, q. 1, f. 299A): "Essentia divina est quoddam intelligibile ab ipso divino intellectu: ut intelligat seipsum ... Vero intelligendo se, intelligit omnia alia a se, dicente Avicenna in eodem. Quia ipse intelligit suam essentiam, per suam essentiam intelligit, et quicquid est post ipsum per hoc intelligit ... Propter suam illimitationem eminenter continet in se omnis esse et essentiae limitatae veritatem, ut non cognoscat alia a se ut propria obiecta, secundum quod alia sunt a se, sed secundum quod in se sunt ideae ipsi. Aliter enim per huiusmodi cognita intelligeret informatur ab eis recipiendo ab eis cog-

however, in which the will's decisions might conceivably influence God's knowledge.

One way is that the intellect, seeing the will and knowing it is omnipotent and its decision cannot be impeded, knows infallibly what will take place in the future. It is as if I were to see the determination of your will with respect to something you might do, says Scotus, and saw it could not be impeded. In such a case I would know indeed that this thing you could do will be produced definitely by you. And so it is in the case of the divine will with respect to a future contingent.[15] This is basically the interpretation Henry of Ghent gives and though Scotus in the *Lectura* seemed to regard it as probable, he suggests the second "perhaps is better,"[16] because there seems to be a discursive reasoning process involved.[17] In the *Reportatio* I A, however, he seems to go further, indicating his displeasure with Henry's solution not only because of the above reason, but because "according to this way it would seem that the divine intellect receives its knowledge from the will and is moved by it and not by the object or by its essence alone."[18]

He goes on to give a second way: "Given the fact that the will accepts one of the two contradictory alternatives, the union of these contingent terms presented to the will in their willed-existence is definitely known and the proposition expressing such is definitely true, and then the divine essence is the reason why this proposition is recognized by

nitionem in patiendo et vilesceret suus intellectus, secundum Philosophum XII *Metaphysicae*, dicente etiam Avicenna in eodem *Metaphysicae* suae." As Henry indicates, this notion is derived from Aristotle, and is supported by Avicenna. Only if one agrees that the divine essence itself determines, as it were, God's intellect, would this not be the case, for the infinitely perfect essence is infinitely knowable. The difference between Aristotle and Avicenna is that Aristotle's God knows nothing of the universe, whereas Avicenna's does. For knowing his own essence God, or the first Intelligence, knows everything that will emanate from it by necessity. Scotus, Henry of Ghent, and others simply adapt this idea of Avicenna by removing the necessitarian aspect and substituting the free decision of God.

[15] *Rep.* I A, d. 38, f. 114rb: "Sed dupliciter potest intelligi intellectum cognoscere illam veritatem determinate et infallibiliter. Uno modo quod intellectus, videns determinationem voluntatis suae ad unam partem contradictorum et quod ipsa ex omnipotentia sua est infallibilis et non impedibilis, novit determinate veritatem illius complexionis contingentis futuri determinate evenire et infallibiliter, sicut si ego viderem determinationem voluntatis tuae respectu alicuius operabilis et voluntatem tuam propter eius omnipotentiam non posse impedire, scirem utique illud operabile fore a te determinate producendum. Sic est in voluntate divina respectu futuri contingentis."

[16] *Lectura* I, d. 39, n. 65; XVII, p. 501.

[17] *Lectura* I, d. 39, n. 64, p. 501; see also the Apograph, n. [23]; VI, pp. 428–29.

[18] *Rep.* I A, d. 38, f. 114rb: "Vel si iste modus non placet, tum quia videtur ponere discursum in intellectu divino, tum quia secundum hoc videretur quod intellectus divinus acciperet notitiam suam a voluntate et moveretur ab ea et non ab objecto vel essentia sola, cuius oppositum dictum est prius quod a sola essentia divina movetur immediate intellectus, ut a primo obiecto . . . "

the intellect as true.'"[19] At first sight this seems to differ little from the first view; however, the way the second alternative is presented in the *Lectura* and the Apograph throws some light on the subtle point Scotus is concerned to make.

In the *Lectura* he states that

> when the will determines itself to one alternative, then this takes on the character of something that can be made and can be produced—and then the intellect, not through the fact that it sees the determination of the will, is simply aware of this propositional truth in such a way that the divine essence is the immediate reason why this truth is represented. I do not say the divine essence first presents the terms of this propositional truth to the divine intellect, and thereby the proposition itself (as happens with our intellect), for then the divine intellect would be vilified, but as was said at the beginning of this book, just as the divine intellect is the immediate reason why the divine intellect understands these terms, so too it is the reason why the intellect knows this propositional truth.[20]

In the Apograph we find the matter put much the same way:

> The will, choosing one part, viz. their conjunction in reality at some time—makes the proposition "This will exist at A" determinately or definitely true. But given that this propositional statement is definitely true, the essence is the basis by means of which the intellect understands this truth. And so far as the essence is concerned, this happens naturally in the following way. Just as it naturally understands all necessary principles, as it were, prior to the act of the divine will, because their truth does not depend on that act and they would be known by the divine intellect even if—to assume the impossible—[God's will] did not will; so the divine essence is the basis of cognizing those [necessary principles] at the prior instant, because they are true then. Not that those truths, or even their terms, move the divine intellect with the result that it apprehends such truth, for if they did, the divine intellect would be vilified, since it would be acted upon by something other than its essence. Rather the divine essence is the basis of knowing such propositional truths in the same way that it is the principle of knowing simple notions. But then these are not contingent truths, because as simples there is nothing to make them definitely true. But given the determination of the divine will, at the second instant [from all eternity], they are already true. And the same thing [i.e., the divine essence] will be the reason why the divine intellect will understand those that are true already at the

---

[19] *Ibid.*: "Sed iste, inquam, modus non placet propter praedicta. Potest dici alio modo, quod voluntate acceptante alteram partem contradictionis determinate scita [est] unio in esse volito istorum terminorum contingentium voluntati praesentatorum et complexio vera determinate, et tunc essentia divina est ratio intelligendi illam complesionem esse veram apud intellectum."

[20] *Lectura* I, d. 39, n. 65; XVII, p. 501.

second instant, and it would have known them at the first instant as well, had they existed at the first instant.[21]

To clarify the point still further Scotus gives this analogy. Suppose my eye had a visual act that always existed and it was the reason why I see whatever is put before my eye. If the colors presented vary, he argues, I would still see them by one and the same act, and the only difference would be that one object is presented first and another later. And if one were presented freely or contingently whereas the other were presented naturally, there would be no formal difference in my vision in virtue of which my eye would not naturally see both. Nevertheless, so far as their presentation went, one would be seen contingently and the other necessarily.[22]

Apart from the scientific inadequacy of the analogy, the point Scotus is trying to make seems clear enough. In God there is but one single eternal act of knowing, and his divine essence is—on the Aristotelian model of cognition—the only object that moves his intellect, as it were. And somehow in knowing that object, he knows not only his own divine nature but all creatural truths as well, both what is possible and what is actual. Neither is there any temporal priority or posteriority about what he knows.

According to our way of thinking, however, one can conceive of a conceptual or mental distinction among the objects known based on nonmutual implication. If knowledge of B implies knowledge of A, but that of A does not imply that of B, then the knowledge of A is conceptually prior to that of B. Scotus refers to this sort of priority and posteriority as "instants of nature" that can be numbered sequentially. Such nonmutual implication, Scotus claims, exists between what God knows simply as possible and what he knows will be actual at some moment of time and dependent on his volition.

With this in mind, we can understand better Scotus' distinction between the two ways in which one can understand the determination of God's will playing a causal role in regard to his actual knowledge. In the first way the reason for the "discourse" seems to be the fact that the intellect draws a conclusion from two premises, viz., (1) the will's decision (which is contingent and variable with respect to the essences) and (2) the fact that it cannot be impeded (a necessary premise). Furthermore, Scotus suggests it is the will, not the essence, that moves the divine intellect. In the second way, however, the intellect simply envisions the divine essence as it actually exists from all eternity, but that essence has a different character than it would have had

[21] Apograph, n. [23]; VI, pp. 428–29.
[22] Lectura I, d. 39, n. 65; XVII, p. 501; see also the Apograph, n. [24]; VI, p. 429.

if God had not chosen from all eternity to cooperate with secondary or created causes in the way he did. Nevertheless, that difference due to the decision of the will that makes certain propositional statements true and their contradictory statements false is presented naturally as part of the object. "Naturally" is Scotus' technical term for a quasi-automatic and nonvoluntary presentation. Hence, according to the first view the information is presented piecemeal, as it were, and it is the will that moves the intellect. Since it does so freely or contingently, this would be opposed to the necessary or "natural" movement of the essence. Natural refers here to the motivation of the intellect, however, rather than to the objects known. Otherwise, God's knowledge of what actually exists or will exist would not be contingent.

Although he does not introduce the visual analogy in this portion of the *Reportatio*,[23] Scotus does spell out the distinction he is making between the manner in which the intellect knows (which is identical for all knowledge, since the divine essence immediately moves the intellect to whatsoever knowledge it has) and the order or sequential difference of instants of nature that exists between what is known necessarily and what is known contingently. Put another way, though the reason why God knows—expressed analogously along the lines of the Aristotelian causal model—is the same in all cases, namely, it is the divine essence moving God's intellect, the truth value of any proposition about the future depends on what he has willed or not willed.[24]

In this 38th distinction of the *Reportatio* Scotus is concerned with

[23] He does give a modified form of the analogy, however, in the answer to the initial arguments of the first question he raises in *Rep.* I A, d. 39, f. 117rb: "Exemplum ad hoc est si semper et sine interruptione actus, si contingenter obiceretur mihi obiectum nunc unum, nunc aliud, contingenter viderem semper et non necessario, et tamen immutabiliter."

[24] Rep. I A, d. 38, f. 114rb-va: "Unde patet quod secundum istum secundum modum quod intellectus divinus non ideo cognoscit futura contingentia, quia videt complacentiam voluntatis sive omnipotentis, sed quia in illo instanti in quo complacet sibi voluntas, est primo verum tale contingens sic scitum et determinatum per voluntatem non impedibilem ad alteram partem contradictionis, et tunc cognoscat, sicut [cum] Deus videt me loqui, tunc primo cognoscit me loqui, et tamen ego non causo scientiam Dei, et sic quandoque hoc contingens est verum, essentia divina est causa huius veri determinati, quia Deus nihil cognoscat per aliquid nec per voluntatis determinationem, nec per aliquid quod fiat in me vel in re, nec per aliquid prius ex parte rationis cognoscendi.— Sed in hoc est differentia, quia Deus videt complexiones necessarias ante omnem actum voluntatis intellectione mere naturali, sed complexiones contingentium terminorum non nisi per voluntatem, vel cum voluntate complacente et acceptante, et in ipso instanti quo complacet, contingens est scitum verum determinate ad unam partem contradictionis.—Iste igitur ordo inter neutralitatem intellectus divinus et cognoscibilitatem certam est ex parte cogniti, non ex parte modi cognoscendi, et ideo non est discursus in divino intellectu, quia sua essentia est sibi immediate ratio cognoscendi omnia."

showing only that God's knowledge is both definite and infallible, and he concludes that whether one chooses the first or the second explanation as to how the will functions, the fact that it is both omnipotent and immutable suffices to guarantee that God's knowledge of the future is infallible.[25] The fact that such knowledge is also contingent and why this is so, he leaves for the next two distinctions.

GOD KNOWS CONTINGENT EVENTS CONTINGENTLY

Under distinction 39, Scotus raises two interconnected questions: Does God foreknow immutably future contingent events? And does he foreknow such in a necessary manner?

The second question is what primarily concerns him and he takes it up first, giving Thomas Aquinas' solution, viz., "Although the supreme cause is necessary, the effect may be contingent by reason of the proximate contingent cause . . . So likewise things known by God are contingent on account of their proximate causes, while the knowledge of God, which is the first cause, is necessary."[26] Thomas supports this view with a statement from Boethius that "the same future event is necessary with respect to God's knowledge of it, but free and undetermined if considered in its own nature."[27]

Scotus objects to this view of Aquinas on the grounds that, if God's initial causality is necessary, then secondary causes cannot introduce an element of contingency, particularly if one accepts the dubious principle that whatever is moved is moved by another. From this opinion, therefore, it follows that everything happens necessarily, for God is omnipotent, and consequently all possibles fall under his causality; therefore if he creates necessarily and all things are perfectly subject to him, everything will happen necessarily. Furthermore, if God is the first sufficient and perfect cause, then his causality is prior to that of all other causes. If, in that priori instant of nature, he causes necessarily, and all other causes move only because they are moved, whatever he

---

[25] *Ibid.*: "Sed quomodo infallibiter? Dico quod, sive ponatur unus modus vel alius, ratio infallibilitatis est quia voluntas Dei est immutabilis et non impedibilis et ratione omnipotentiae suae, et sic non potest non esse ut sit determinatum; vel secundum alium modum in Deo, infallibilis est divina cognitio ratione primi obiecti, scilicet essentiae divinae, et ideo non potest decipi circa contingentia sicut nec circa primum obiectum suum."

[26] Thomas Aquinas, *Summa theologica* I, q. 14, art. 13, ad 1; see also *Sent.* I, d. 38, q. 1. art. 5 (ed. Parma VI, 316b); *Summa contra Gentiles* I, c. 67.

[27] Boethius, *De Consolatione Philosophiae* VI, prosa 6 (PL 63, 861): "Respondebo namque idem futurum, cum ad divinam notionem refertur, necessarium,—cum vero in sua natura perpenditur, liberum prorsus atque absolutum videri."

moves immediately he will move necessarily, and if such a created cause is moved necessarily, it will in turn move necessarily, and the same will be true of every subsequent cause on down to the very last effect. Consequently, nothing will be contingent, but every effect will be necessary. Hence, it is impossible that any effect will be contingent because of its proximate cause if there is no contingency in the first cause with respect to its effect.[28]

If it is possible for some event to be caused contingently, this implies that its opposite was a genuine possibility at the time it came to be; otherwise it would be a necessary, not a contingent event. This is the substance of Scotus' thesis, and in the *Reportatio* he sets out to prove it with much the same detail that we find in both the *Lectura* and the Apograph. However, in the latter two works he deals with the fact, the nature and necessary conditions for contingency as he understands it, only after he has raised his fifth question: Is the contingency of things consistent with God's knowledge of them? In the *Reportatio* he introduces a more specific question that illustrates the same point, that which we find in distinction 40 of the *Lectura* and *Ordinatio*, namely, "Is it possible for someone who is predestined to be damned?" Paradoxical as a positive answer to the question may seem, Scotus will give that answer, for if the actual predestination is truly a contingent event, this implies that it is not an event that had to happen, and though it will in truth happen, its negation was also in some sense a real possibility. How to express this paradoxical fact will require the use of the distinction between the divided and composite senses.

PREREQUISITES FOR SOLVING THESE QUESTIONS

Having set forth these three interconnected questions, Scotus presents the prerequisites he needs for solving them.[29] Four points need to be

---

[28] *Rep.* I A, d. 39, f. 115rb: "Hic dicitur quod licet respectu Dei scientiae necesse sunt aliqua necessarie et necessario eveniant; non tamen respectu causarum proximarum est talis necessitas... Sed hoc non capio, quia ex hac opinione sequitur omnia necessario evenire, quod est impossibile, quia enim Deus est omnipotens, et ideo omnia possibilia subsunt imperio voluntatis suae et causalitate eius; ergo si in suo ordine necessario creat et [omnia] perfecte subsunt causalitate eius, sequitur quod omnia necessario evenient ...Deus enim est prima causa sufficiens et perfecta et prior omnibus aliis causis. Ergo in illo priori, si necessario causat vel movet, [causa quae movet] quia movetur, si necessario movetur, necessario movet, et sic de qualibet causa media usque ad ultimum effectum et, per consequens, nihil erit contingens, sed omnis effectus necessarius... Sequitur quod nihil causabitur contingenter in universo."

[29] *Ibid.*, f. 115va: "Ad solutionem istarum quaestionum quatuor sunt praemittenda: primo, si est contingentia in rebus; secundo, dato quod sic, inquirendum est ubi est

treated. First, is it a fact that things are contingent? Second, given that they are, what is the primary cause of this contingency? Third, granted this is to be found somehow in God, just how is he the primary reason for contingency? Finally, how are we to distinguish the puzzling propositions that have to do with this matter.

Are Things Contingent?

As for the first, Scotus claims we can distinguish a twofold contingency in things in contrast to two kinds of necessity, that of immutability and that of inevitability. The necessity of immutability is that which cannot be otherwise; we speak of God, in this sense, as a necessary being. Necessity of inevitability, however, is the sort of necessity characteristic of future events that depend upon the necessary action of inevitable natural causes. But since nature itself is a free creation on the part of God, natural inevitable events, such as that day follows night, or any other natural movements that we say are necessary, need not have existed or been created absolutely speaking. Hence, as regards any of these events, their nonexistence was a real possibility, and consequently, they are not necessary or immutable in an unqualified sense.[30]

By contrast to this dual necessity there is a double contingency in things. One is that characteristic of mutable things that can change or be otherwise than they are. The other is the contingency of evitability, which is characteristic of an event that can be avoided or impeded, and under this heading fall all the acts of the will itself as well as those that are subject to the command of the will, and hence are caused freely.[31] These two sorts of contingencies are basically dif-

---

prima causa contigentiae; tertio, quo in Deo possit inveniri ratio prima contingentiae; quarto, distinguendae sunt quaedam propositiones quae fiunt in hac materia."

[30] *Ibid.*: "Circa primum est notandum quod duplex est contingentia in rebus; sicut per oppositum duplex necessitas; quaedam enim est necessitas immutabilitatis et quaedam inevitabilitatis. Necessitas immutabilitatis est illa quae non potest aliter se habere, quomodo Deus est ens necessarium. Necessitas autem inevitabilitatis est illa qua eventus alicuius rei futurae dicitur inevitabilis, licet in se non sit immutabile nec necessarium, sicut solem oriri cras est necessarium necessitate inevitabilitatis, [et] alii motus naturales isto modo sunt, et tamen aliter possunt se habere, et non sunt simpliciter necessaria nec immutabilia."

[31] *Ibid.*: "Eodem modo per oppositum duplex est contingentia in rebus. Una mutabilitatis, qua aliquid in se potest aliter se habere, ut se habent mobilia et corruptibilia ista. Alia est contingentia evitabilitatis, cuius eventus et esse potest vitari et esse impediri, cuiusmodi sunt omnes actus voluntatis libere causati ab [ea]. Nec sunt istae contingentiae eaedem, quia non omne contingens primo modo, ut generabile quod in se est contingens, contingenter et in minori parte evenit; aliqua tamen ut generabilia et corruptibilia necessario eveniunt, et tamen in se non sunt necessaria sed contingentia.

ferent, for not everything contingent in the first way, is contingent in the second way. Rather some things, such as those that can come to be and can perish, occur necessarily in the sense that there is no freedom about their natural causes, though in themselves these causes could be impeded and hence the effects they produce are not strictly necessary but contingent. But things contingent in the second way, since they occur and are generated contingently by free agents, are in no way necessary in themselves. And inasmuch as such free agents can also impede or direct the action of natural causes, they impart to certain natural events an added measure of contingency.

In the *Lectura* Scotus insists that the existence of contingency in the world must be accepted as a primitive or self-evident truth, as it cannot be proved *a priori* through anything more knowable.[32] He makes the same point here, pointing out that though "contingent" and "necessary" in disjunction are immediate attributes of being, one cannot infer the existence of the contingent, given the existence of the necessary. The converse implication does hold, however, although it is not an *a priori*, but an *a posteriori*, form of inference.[33] Here, as in the *Lectura* and the Apograph, there is also the remark that one who denies such a manifest truth needs punishment, until he admits that the punishment he is receiving is contingent and that it is possible for him not to be punished—an allusion to Aristotle's distinction in the *Topics*[34] that "not every problem or thesis should be examined but only one which might puzzle one of those who need argument, not punishment or sense perception."[35]

Contingentia autem secundo modo, ut contingenter eveniunt et generantur, nec sunt in se necessaria. Utroque autem modo est contingentia in rebus. Nam ex motu aliqua contingenter producuntur et in se contingenter sunt."

[32] *Lectura* I, d. 39, q. 5, nn. 39–40; XVII, pp. 490–91: "Quod sit contingentia in rebus non potest—ut puto—probari per notius, nec a priori ... Accipiendum est tamquam per se notum quod sit contingentia in entibus,—et qui hoc negat, indiget sensu et poena."

[33] *Rep.* I A, d. 39, f. 115va: "Probare autem contingentia rerum a priori non video esse possibile, quia nec per definitionem sibi contingentis, scilicet, entis, cum non sit ordo, et ideo difficile est accipere medium ad hoc; nec per passiones eius; nec per passionem priorem, quia non habet priorem se, cum ipsum cum necessario condividat ens. Nec supposita altera passionis disiuncta, ut necessitate, potest probari contingentia, nisi ponatur sibi oppositi relative (quod non est verum), sicut causa et causatum in quantum talia sunt opposita relative. Non enim, si nobilius dividens est in universo, sequitur quod sit minus nobile; sed econverso bene sequitur, sed non a priori."

[34] *Topics* I, c. 11, 105a3–5.

[35] *Rep.* I A, d. 39, f. 115vb: "Et contra hoc negantes esset procedendum cum tormentis et cum igne et huiusmodi, et tam debent fustigari quousque fateantur quod possunt non tormentari, et ita dicere quod contingenter tormentantur et non necessario, sicut fecit Avicenna contra negantes primum principium. Tales enim secundum eum debent vapulari donec scirentur quod non est idem torqueri et non torqueri, comburi et non comburi."

Aristotle himself, Scotus points out, attempted no *a priori* proof that future events are contingent, though he did give an indirect or *a posteriori* argument for such, based on the fact that we should look out for ourselves and take counsel about our future, all of which would be entirely out of place if the future is beyond our control and that whatever is to happen will occur inevitably, despite what we do.[36] Scotus also suggests other *a posteriori* proofs based on what would follow if future events were not contingent but inevitable. Neither virtues nor precepts nor admonitions nor rewards nor punishment nor honors would be necessary, he points out, and in short all human social relationships would be destroyed.[37]

What Is the Primary Cause of Contingency?

Granting then that contingency exists in things, Scotus says, we must see secondly where the initial source of contingency is to be found. "To this I say that the first reason for contingency is in the divine will or its act as regards things other than self. I prove this, for if it were necessarily related causally to things other than self, [1] there would be nothing contingent in the universe; [2] also there would be no second cause in the universe; [3] third, there would be no evil in things—all of which things are absurd."[38]

Since his opponent admits the dubious principle that whatever is moved is moved by another, Scotus uses this *argumentum ad hominem*: "I prove the first in this way, because whatever is moved insofar as it moves, if it is moved necessarily, it moves necessarily; the first cause—according to you—moves necessarily and no secondary cause moves unless it is moved; therefore every secondary cause moves and causes necessarily."[39]

That no secondary or created cause could exist on this theory follows,

[36] *Ibid.*, f. 115va–b: "Philosophus etiam ponit contingentiam esse in rebus; non probavit hoc a priori sed a posteriori, quia, si non sit contingentia, non oportet negotiari nec consiliari; tantum enim vel plus est omnibus notum quod sit contingentia in rebus, sicut quod oportet consiliari et negotiari."

[37] *Ibid.*, f. 115vb: "Potest igitur probari a posteriori, quia aliter non essent necessarie virtutes nec praecepta nec monita nec mercedes nec poenae nec honores, et breviter, destrueretur omnis politia et omnis commiseratio humana."

[38] *Ibid.*: "Supponendo ergo contingentia esse in rebus, videndum est secundo ubi sit prima ratio contingentiae. Ad quod dico quod prima ratio contingentiae est in voluntate divino vel actu eius comparata ad alia a se. Quod probo, quia si necessario se haberet in causando alia a se: [1] nihil esset contingens in universo, [2] nulla etiam causa secunda esset in universo, [3] tertio non esset malum in rebus; quae sunt absurda."

[39] *Ibid.*: "Primum probatur sic, quia quod movetur inquantum movet, si necessario movetur, necessario movet; causa prima necessario movet per te et nulla causa secunda movet nisi inquantum movetur; ergo omnis causa secunda necessario movet et causat."

because "the first cause moves and causes naturally prior to the second; if therefore in that prior instant it causes necessarily and perfectly it cannot fail to produce its effect, and thus in the second instant the secondary cause can cause nothing, unless the same thing can be caused twice—which makes no sense."[40]

If God caused necessarily, no evil could exist, for "evil only exists in things because of a defect of some possible perfection which ought to be there... hence, if God would cause necessarily, since he is the first and most perfect agent, he would cause as much perfection in everything as he could cause and nothing would be wanting to any thing that could possibly exist in it."[41] Scotus is not concerned here to discuss the precise cause of evil, or to what extent God's permissive will is involved where moral evil or sin is introduced through a creature's abuse of free will.[42] For—as he will make clear shortly—God's will is not the sole source of contingency in the world, but is at most a necessary condition for any secondary causality, be it necessary or free.

Since none of these three consequences obtain, Scotus concludes

> it is manifest that the divine will is related contingently to everything other than itself to which it is immediately related, and that in the divine will the first reason for contingency is to be found. For if some other cause of the contingency were prior to it, it would be the divine intellect; but the divine intellect cannot be the first reason for contingency, because the intellect and its act, insofar as this precedes the will and its act, is merely natural, and a contingent effect cannot be traced back to a cause that is merely natural, just as the converse [viz., a necessary effect cannot be traced back to a cause that acts contingently or freely]. Therefore, the divine will is the first cause of contingency.[43]

[40] *Ibid.*: "Secundum sequitur, quia causa prima prius naturaliter movet et causat quam secunda; si ergo necessario causat in illo priori et perfecte, ergo non potest non producere effectum, et ita in secunda instanti causa secunda nihil potest causare nisi idem bis causaret, quod non est intelligibile."

[41] *Ibid.*: "Tertium etiam sequitur, quia malum non est in rebus nisi ex defectu alicuius debitae perfectionis possibilis haberi a toto vel a speciali ente; si ergo Deus causaret necessario, cum sit agens perfectissimum et primum causaret, in quolibet tantam perfectionem quantam posset causare et ita nihil deesset alicui rei quod esset possibile sibi inesse."

[42] See Scotus' question: "Is the power to sin from God?" in A. B. Wolter, *Duns Scotus on the Will and Morality* (Washington, D.C.: Catholic University Press, 1986), pp. 98–100, 458–63.

[43] *Rep.* I A, d. 39, f. 115vb: "Ergo cum haec illata sunt falsa, manifestum est voluntatem divinam contingenter se habere ad quodcumque immediate se habet aliud a se, et quod in ipsa est prima ratio contingentiae. Si enim aliqua alia causa contingentiae esset prior illa, esset intellectus divinus; sed intellectus divinus non potest esse prima ratio contingentiae, quia intellectus et actus eius, ut praecedit voluntatem et actum eius, est mere naturalis, et effectus contingens non habet reduci in causam mere naturalem, sicut nec econverso. Est ergo voluntas divina prima ratio contingentiae."

Scotus then goes on to make clear a most important point that tends to be obscured in both the *Lectura* and Apograph versions, namely, that the fact that although God's will is the first source, and is a necessary condition for any contingency in the world, it is not the only source, nor is it sufficient of itself to account for all that occurs in the created realm.

Some things have a second or additional cause of their contingency, he tells us, namely, anything involving a free act of our will. Although natural causes are contingent solely because God has freely willed them to exist and operate, the same is not true of our will. God has not only freely created and conserved it, but has endowed it with something of his own freedom, giving it the special power to determine itself.[44] Hence, he insists, "an act of our will has a double cause of contingency, one on the part of the divine will as the first cause and the other on the part of the will as second cause."[45] If natural events are contingent with respect to the first cause alone, they are necessary as far as the second and proximate cause goes. Hence, such natural events can be impeded by the divine will, but this is not true of us.

He goes on to comment on the various logical possibilities in which necessity and/or contingency might conceivably be associated. The first is that there are only necessary causes, whether they be divine or created. This was the theory condemned by the Paris theologians in 1270 and 1277. Though logically possible, Scotus considers this theory to be actually counterfactual, because it rules out any contingency in the world. The second is that God acts contingently and some created agents also act contingently, and this he considers to be true of all creatures endowed with free will. The third possibility is that which he ascribes to Aquinas and others, namely, "that something is contingent with respect to its second cause and necessary with respect to its first cause." This he too regards as impossible, for the reasons pointed out above. "The fourth member is also impossible, that something be contingent neither with respect to its first or second cause."[46]

---

[44] See especially his treatment in the last question in Book IX of his *Metaphysics*, where he stresses the will's "unlimited actuality" and "superabundant sufficiency" to determine itself. The text and translation can be found in Wolter, *Duns Scotus on the Will and Morality*, pp. 144–73.

[45] *Rep.* I A, d. 39, f. 115vb: "Sed aliquid potest dici dupliciter contingens ex parte suae causae, sicut actus voluntatis nostrae habet duplicem causam contingentiae, unam ex parte voluntatis divinae sicut causae primae et aliam ex voluntate ut ex secunda causa. Aliquid est contingens tantum respectu [causae] primae et necessarium quantum est ex parte causae secundae et proximae, ut illa quae possunt impediri a voluntate divina, ut sunt eventus rerum naturalium ex suis causis."

[46] *Ibid.*, f. 115vb–116ra: "Tertium membrum est impossibile, scilicet quod aliquid sit contingens respectu causae secundae et necessarium respectu causae primae, ut dictum est supra et probatum. Quartum membrum etiam est impossibile, ut quod aliquid sit contingens, et tamen non respectu causae primae nec causae secundae."

He then sums up his complete theory as to the root source of contingency in the universe. Not only does it embrace God as first cause, whose cooperative causality is involved in some way in whatever he creates and conserves, but it also includes free created causes that are moved contingently both on their part and on the part of the first cause with respect to which they are its contingent effects.

> Hence, in us, that is, in our will, there is contingency that stems both from ourselves and from God. In other things, however, such as all events produced by natural or nonfree causes, there is necessity on their part, but contingency on the part of God. In all effects, however, there is contingency in an unqualified sense with respect to the first cause upon which also all causes both necessary and contingent depend. Simple or unqualified necessity, however, is found in no effects, although there is qualified necessity in some, namely in every natural effect. But in every effect or thing willed by us as such there is no necessity but only contingency.[47]

It is true that in *Lectura*, and the same holds for the Apograph, this clear distinction between natural causes and free will is missing. The reason Scotus omits making any distinction, perhaps, is because he is speaking of contingency in general, and that includes—as the above passage indicates—all created causes whether they act naturally, that is, by a necessity of their nature, or whether they are free to determine themselves. Unfortunately, this omission on Scotus' part has led not a few incautious readers, who depend solely on the *Lectura* or the Apograph versions, to claim that the sole explanation of contingency in the case of free created agents is God's initial contingent action.[48]

[47] *Ibid.*, f. 116ra: "Inventa igitur causa contingentiae, res aliae moventur contingenter et ex parte sui et ex parte primae, respectu cuius erunt effectus sui contingentes. Unde in nobis, i.e. in voluntate, a se et a Deo est contingentia. In aliquibus autem [aliis] necessitas est a se, sed contingentia ex parte Dei. In omnibus vero effectibus est contingentia simpliciter respectu causae primae, a qua omnes etiam causae tam necessariae quam contingentes dependent. In rebus autem et in omnibus effectibus non invenitur necessitas simpliciter, sed tantum secundum quid, quia in comparatione ad causam proximam aliquis effectus est necessarius, scilicet omnis effectus naturalis, sed in omnibus effectibus vel rebus a nobis volitis in quantum huiusmodi, nulla est necessitas sed tantum contingentia."

[48] Thus D. C. Langston in his *God's Willing Knowledge: The Influence of Scotus' Analysis of Omniscience* (University Park: The Pennsylvania State University Press, 1986), p. 46, writes: "Scotus assumes the divine will does determine human wills, but that they are only contingently determined . . . Clearly both contingent and necessary determination are forms of determination in the sense that God determines the human will to will as it does. Nevertheless, if God only contingently determines the will to act in a certain way, the action of the agent is contingent. It is still logically possible for the human will to will something else; God merely needs to will it to will otherwise and it will so will."

This would lead to a deterministic interpretation so far as the created will is concerned, even though God's creative action is itself free or undetermined. This is obviously not Scotus' position, since he considers it a contradiction in terms that the will should be coerced.[49] In fact, he uses what we know about our will's own freedom to clarify how God's will operates, which brings us to the third problem.

How Is God the Free Cause of Contingency?

How are we to understand God's freedom? The *Lectura* first indicates how Scotus will solve this problem: "To understand how the divine will is the cause of contingency, we must first look to our own will to see how this is the cause of some contingent things."[50] Scotus then goes on to analyze what is perfect and imperfect about our volition, and ascribes to God what is perfect and eliminates what is imperfect, namely, whatever stems from our will's mutability. We find the same analysis made in even more detail in the Apograph.[51] In the *Reportatio*, however, Scotus gives a more concise account of his methodology.

Having seen how the divine will is the first cause of contingency in things and as a consequence, how our own will can also be a contingent cause with respect to its own acts, we must see just how the divine will functions as the first cause of contingency in all its effects, especially since both the divine will itself and what it effects through its decisions does not vary. What I plan to do here, says Scotus, is to take whatever is perfect about our will with respect to its volition and to eliminate anything of imperfection and to transfer those things that are matters of perfection in it to the divine will.[52]

---

[49] *Ordinatio* IV, d. 29 (Codex A, f. 250va): "Dico quod coactio non cadit proprie in homine in aliquo actu humano. Contradictio enim est voluntatem simpliciter cogi ad actum volendi."

[50] *Lectura* I, d. 39, q. 5, n. 45, p. 493: "Ad videndum autem quomodo voluntas divina est causa contingentiae, primo videndum est ex parte voluntatis nostrae quomodo ipsa est causa aliquorum contingentium."

[51] Apograph, n. [14], VI, p. 416: "Primam ergo contingentiam oportet quaerere in voluntate—quae ut videatur qualiter sit ponendo, primo videndum est in voluntate nostra, et ibi tria: primo, ad quae sit libertas voluntatis nostrae; secundo, qualiter istam libertatem sequatur possibilitas sive contingentia; et tertio, de logica distinctione propositionum, quomodo exprimitur possibilitas ad opposita."

[52] *Rep.* I A, d. 39, f. 116ra: "Viso quomodo voluntas divina est prima causa contingentiae [in rebus et per consequens voluntas nostra in actibus suis, videndum secundo quomodo voluntas divina potest esse causa prima contingentia] in omnibus effectibus, cum tam ipsa voluntas quam effectus eius sit invariabilis. Hic dico quod assumendo quae sunt perfectionis in voluntate nostra respectu sui actus et dimittendo quae est imperfectionis in ea, transferendo ea quae sunt perfectionis in ea ad divina, statim apparet propositum."

Now our will, he points out, is contingently indifferent (1) with respect to the various acts it can elicit, such as willing or nilling, loving or hating, and (2) it is also related through these acts to several different objects and effects. The first indifference is a matter of imperfection, since it implies that our will is passive and mutable with respect to the different acts of volition or nolition it elicits. The second sort of indifference, namely, with respect to the objects it wills or the effects it produces, is a matter of perfection and we must assume it exists in the divine. The indifference with respect to effects, which the *Lectura* and the Apograph treat as a third distinct type of indifference, however, is not the initial indifference in our will, because prior to this is its indifference to the objects that are willed or not willed. Our will's indifference both to objects and to the effects produced by willing diverse objects are matters of perfection, the *Lectura* insists. Only because the indifference of our will to diverse acts involves a succession of distinct volitions or nolitions is imperfection involved, for this implies that our will is not only an active potency, but it is also a receptive potency and, because of its limitation, its power to act has to be expressed through several acts. Hence, says Scotus, we may assume these things of imperfection are absent in the divine will. Thus the divine will is neither receptive with respect to its act of volition, nor need it, because of its limitation, tend to various objects through different distinct acts. Rather the volitional act of the divine will is one and simple, and yet through that selfsame act, though necessarily related to the divine essence as its first object, through the mediacy of that first object God's will is related to other things contingently. In this way, then, the divine will, in terms of what it wills formally to exist in actuality, is not indifferent to opposite acts—since it would be a contradiction for it both to will and nill A's actual existence at some given moment. Nevertheless, through its one simple act it will still be indifferent or contingently related to any given finite thing, and this because of its unlimited and infinite perfection. Because of this lack of limitation, then, it is able indifferently to both will A and not will A in one simple act, just as we are indifferently able to do this through a multiple act, inasmuch as in us to will and nill with respect to the same object would require distinct or diverse acts.[53]

---

[53] *Ibid.*: "Voluntas enim nostra indifferens est contingenter ad actus diversos, quam mediantibus est ad plura objecta et ad plures effectus. Prima indifferentia est imperfectionis; secunda est perfectionis et ideo ponenda est in divinis. Indifferentia ergo ad effectus non est prima indifferentia, quia alia est prior ea in ratione voliti vel non voliti; et nec illa indifferentia quae est respectu actuum diversorum, quia in hoc, i.e. in voluntate, est potentia receptiva respectu actuum. Similiter actus unius objecti. Amoveamus ergo ista quae sunt imperfectionis a voluntate divina, quae non est indifferens ad

There is another way in which our will resembles the divine will, for our potency to will opposites can be understood in two ways. Either our will is related simultaneously to opposites at the same moment of time, or, second, it is related successively to opposites at diverse moments. That potency with respect to opposites successively is something our will shares with other mutable things that can be changed from one state to another, and hence it is not something unique or proper to the will as a contingent agent in its own right. But there is another potency of our will to opposites, namely, that which at the same moment regards both objects indistinctly in a divided sense. This is not a potency to have both conjointly at the same instant, however, for this implies contradictory states.[54]

That our will has a dual potency for opposites that exist successively is evident and needs no proof, says Scotus. But less evident, and in need of proof, perhaps, is the fact that our will is also in potency in the second way, that is, it has the ability at one and the same moment to act in opposite ways in a divided sense. Scotus gives this proof: At the instant in which the will causes a volition or nolition with respect to some given object, it does so either necessarily or contingently. Hence, just as a being or an effect either exists necessarily or is something contingent when it has existence or is a being, so also it is true that a cause when it causes, either does so necessarily or contingently. But our will in that instant in which it elicits its act of willing, causes contingently (and this means that in the same instant in which it is a cause of its volition, it could will the opposite). For if that were not so, it would then, that is in that very instant, cause necessarily. And the situation is similar in the case of the divine will. For God can will nothing except in eternity, or more precisely, in what we call that one eternal instant. But by means of that single volition in that one eternal instant, God is only contingently, and not necessarily, the cause of

---

actus per quos respiciat obiecta diversa, quia hoc est imperfectionis in nobis, sed actus eius, scilicet divinae voluntatis, est unus et simplex et indifferens ad diversa objecta. Habet tamen se necessario ad actum primum et tamen mediante illo se habet ad alia contingenter. Sic ergo voluntas divina non est indifferens ad actus oppositos, ut est actu volens formaliter, sed per unum actum erit indifferens quia illimitatus et infinitus. Unde propter illimitationem indifferenter potest velle A et potest non velle A unico actu simplici. Sicut ego actu multiplici eo quod diversi actus sunt in nobis velle et nolle respectu eiusdem obiecti."

[54] *Ibid.*: "Aliud in quo assimilatur voluntas nostra voluntati divinae est quia potentiam esse ad opposita potest intelligi dupliciter: vel esse simul ad opposita pro eodem instanti temporis, vel, secundo, esse ad opposita successive et pro diverso instanti. Illa quae est ad opposita successive est in mutabilibus tantum sive ad mutari de uno ad aliud sicut patet in transmutationibus. Alia potentia ad opposita est voluntatis nostrae quae indistincte est ad utrumque oppositorum divisum tamen pro eodem instanti, non autem sunt pro eodem instanti coniunctim quia hoc implicat contradictoria."

A—just as if my will were to exist only for a single moment of time and at that instant were to elicit an act of volition or nolition, it would do so contingently and not necessarily. Such a contingent volition implies that the will could have been otherwise or altered, not because it preexisted at some other moment, but because at that very moment at which it elicits its act of volition or nolition, it does so freely and contingently. The divine will also functions in this fashion with respect to the effects it produces or wills to exist. In that instant of eternity in which it produces A, it is still true to say that A could have been nonexisting. Otherwise it would follow that when the divine will causes something, call it A, A would exist necessarily.[55]

But just what is this potency? Scotus asks. It does not precede its act durationally, he replies, because then it would exist together with mutability, but it is rather prior by nature to its contingent act. Hence, we can say that this dual potentiality, though durationally simultaneous with whatever volition or nolition the will actually elicits, is prior by nature to the elicited act.[56]

In both the *Lectura* and the Apograph Scotus raises three objections to what he has said. The first is based on the controversial text from the *De Interpretatione* that "Everything that is, must needs be when it is."[57] The source of the second is a rule of the obligatory art; and a third stems from the problem of how something in act can also be in potency to the opposite of that act. In *Reportatio* I A, Scotus raises these same three objections in a slightly different order, but adds a fourth, namely, if in that instant of eternity in which God wills A, he could not will A, it would seem he could will two opposites in the

---

[55] *Ibid.*, f. 116ra–b: "Probo de voluntate nostra quod sit talis potentia ad opposita; quantum ad primam potentiam, quae est esse successive ad opposita, patet. Quod etiam secundo modo voluntas nostra sit ad opposita per eodem instanti divisim, probo, quia in eodem instanti in quo causans causat, vel causat necessario vel contingenter. Unde sicut ens vel effectus, quando est ens, vel necesse est vel contingens, ita quando causa causat vel causat necessario vel contingenter. Sed voluntas nostra in illo instanti in quo elicit velle suum, causat vel contingenter, et in eodem instanti ut est causa eius, posset velle oppositum; alius tunc necessario causaret in illo instanti. Et isto [modo] est in voluntate divina. Deus enim nihil potest velle nisi aeternitate sive in instanti uno aeternitatis et mediante unico velle in illo unico instanti contingenter est causa ipsius A, sicut si voluntas mea non esse nisi in uno instanti temporis, contingenter et eliceret actum volendi in illo instanti. Posset moveri non quia praefuit in esse in alio instanti, sed quia libere et contingenter elicit talem actum volendi. Sic voluntas divina! In illo instanti aeternitatis in quo producit A, posset A non esse; alias sequeretur quod quando est causa, necessario esset A."

[56] *Ibid.*, f. 116rb: "Sed quae est ista potentia? Dico quod non praecedit actum suum duratione, quia tunc esset cum mutabilitate; sed est potentia prior naturaliter actu contingente; ergo prius naturaliter voluntas potest esse in opposito illius sed non ordine durationis."

[57] *De Interpretatione*, ch. 9, 19a23–24.

same instant, which is impossible. The solutions to the first three objections are much the same in all three works, and we need not dwell on them here where we are concerned primarily with what is peculiar to the Paris lecture.

To the specific objection unique to the *Reportatio*, Scotus counters as he often does with a general principle.[58] The crux of the objection comes down to the question: How can the will be said to have a potency for anything if that potency cannot be actualized? If it has a potency for the opposite of the act to which it is actually conjoined, it would seem that this also could be actualized as well as the other and then two opposites would coexist, which seems illogical. Scotus replies: "Whenever any two things are said to be possible with respect to some given third, it never follows that they can coexist with respect to it unless they are compatible with one another as related to it. Otherwise it seems that from the divided sense one could infer the conjoined sense." Scotus illustrates his general principle with two obviously fallacious counterexamples. "This body can be in this place and another body can be in the same place; therefore, the two bodies can coexist in the same place." Clearly the inference is invalid, for we have no evidence that the two bodies are co-compatible with respect to a given place. In the second example simultaneity is ruled out because of a lack of strength. "I can carry one stone at some given moment and I can carry a different stone at that same moment; therefore, I can carry both stones simultaneously." The situation in the case at hand is similar, says Scotus. The objector argues: "I can will A at this instant and I can also nill A at that same instant, therefore I can simultaneously will A and nill A." The reason this will not work, Scotus explains, is that in the composite sense, if I have a volition, I have to be willing something, and therefore, it is true to say I cannot both have the act and fail to have it, even though in the divided sense I can both will and not will. I can never actuate both possibilities at the same time,

---

[58] *Rep.* I A, d. 39, f. 116rb–va: "Quando dicitur quod potest simul velle opposita, si sit potentia coniuncta actibus, etc. dico quod quando duo comparantur ad aliquod tertium numquam sequitur quod sint simul respectu eius nisi compatiantur se respectu eius. Alias videtur quod ex divisis contingit inferre coniuncta. Exemplum: hoc corpus potest esse in hoc loco, et aliud corpus potest esse in eodem loco; ergo duo corpora possunt esse simul in eodem loco, non sequere, quia duo corpora non sunt possibilia in esse respectu tertium simul. Exemplum aliud, quando per quodlibet excluditur in ratione virtutis, tunc non sequitur simul ut possum portare unum lapidem et alium lapidem in uno instanti; ergo simul possum portare duos lapides non sequitur. Similiter est in proposito, possum velle pro hoc instanti ipsum A et possum nolle in eodem instanti ipsum A; ergo simul possum velle et nolle A. Non videtur quod ita possum velle quod si habeam velle, non possum non velle, sed utique possum divisim et ideo numquam ambo simul, quia hoc excludit primum velle."

however, for the simple reason that what I choose to do first, excludes my actual choice of the other possibility.

How Certain Puzzling Statements Are to Be Understood

This leads to his fourth and final prerequisite for solving these questions, particularly the third, as to whether one predestined can be damned, namely, how are we to distinguish and correctly understand certain propositions that predicate seemingly contradictory predicates of their subject. Take a proposition like this: "One who is willing A can not will A." We have to distinguish this according to the divided and composite sense, says Scotus. In one divided sense, the proposition is clearly true, namely that my will, willing A now, can subsequently will the opposite, since it does not act by rote, but can act in diverse ways at diverse times. Scotus calls this the will's "sucessive potency," namely its ability to act differently at successive moments of time. What of its "simultaneous potency"? There is one composite sense in which the above statement is manifestly false, namely: "One who is willing A is also nilling A simultaneously," and we can say this is simply impossible. There is a deeper or more basic level of potentially, however, where seemingly contradictory statements may be simultaneously true, but they need to be clarified according to composition and division. Take, for example, the statement: "My will, though willing A now, can also not will A now." This can be interpreted in either a composite or a divided sense. The composite sense unites "to will" and "not to will" conjunctively with "now" as an actual possibility, and on this interpretation, the proposition is manifestly false, for one contradictory state is predicated of the other. But there is another divided sense where we assert of "my will willing A now" that, since I am not willing A necessarily, it is possible for my will not to will A now. Or to put the meaning another way, that is, although my will is actually willing A now, it could have been not willing A now, and so in this divided sense the proposition is true, says Scotus.[59] And the

---

[59] *Ibid.*, f. 116va: "Quantum ad quartum principale quomodo sunt intelligendae propositiones quae fiunt in hac materia, dico quod haec propositio: 'Volens A potest non velle A' est distinguenda secundum sensum divisionis et compositionis. Sensus divisionis unus est manifeste verus, scilicet quod voluntas mea, volens nunc, potest velle oppositum potentia successiva. Alius est sensus compositionis manifeste falsum, scilicet quod 'Volens A sit nolens A simul' et ita dicat quod non est possibilis; est tamen impossibilis. Alius sensus est immanifestus quando sic dicitur 'Voluntas mea volens A nunc, potest non velle A'; et tunc haec propositio est distinguenda secundum compositionem vel divisionem. Unus sensus est iste: 'Voluntas mea potest non velle A nunc,' ita quod ista compositio sit possibilis uniens active 'velle et non velle,' cum 'nunc.' Et

Master (i.e., Peter Lombard) on this model designates how to distinguish propositions, like "The predestined can be damned" or "The reprobate can be saved," according to their composite or divided sense.[60]

As Scotus points out in distinction 40 of the *Lectura*[61] and *Ordinatio*,[62] in the composite sense, the subject of such propositions is not just the individual or person qua person, but that individual or person under the specific qualification of "predestined" or "reprobate," and it is manifestly false that one predestined "qua predestined" can be damned, or that "qua reprobate" one can be saved. In the divided sense, however, there are two categorical propositions affirmed of the individual or person qua person. One is existential or "de inesse," for example, that the individual in question is actually predestined to grace and glory; the other is a modal proposition "*de possibili*," namely, that this same individual " could be damned." In the *Reportatio* where this question of distinction 40 is combined with that of distinction 39 on the will, the application is made to the statements about the will rather than to those about the directly predestined.

In the divided sense, statements like "My will, willing A now, cannot will A now," or "My will, not willing A now, can will A now," reduce to two categorical propositions. One is *de inesse* asserting as actual, one opposite of the will (e.g., not willing A); the other proposition is *de possibili*, affirming the possibility of the other opposite (e.g., willing A) of the same subject, but qua undetermined by its "not willing A."[63] "Therefore," Scotus concludes, "when that proposition *de possibili* is implicit, as the Master says, it does not signify anything more than that for the same instant that one actually is *de inesse*, the opposite could be in it, so that one potency that is really the same is not determined now by the fact that this is in it; rather this choice is there contingently and the opposite choice could be existing there."[64]

---

sic dico quod est propositio impossibilis, quia hic sensus compositionis dicit oppositum praedicari de opposito. Sed alius sensus divisionis est sic: 'Voluntas mea volens A nunc,' de ea potest esse verum, 'non velle A nunc,' et sic est vera. Et Magister secundum hoc unum assignat istas propositiones distingui et intelligi secundum sensum compositionis et divisiones."

[60] Magistri Petri Lombardi, *Sententia in IV libris distinctae*, lib. I, dist. 40, c. 1; vol. I (Grottaferrata/Romae, 1971), p. 285.

[61] *Lectura* I, d. 40, nn. 7–8; XVII, p. 512.

[62] *Ordinatio* I, d. 40, n. 7; VI, pp. 310–11.

[63] Cf. note 59.

[64] *Rep.* I A, f. 116vb: "Quando ergo illa propositio praedicans de possibili est implicita, sicut dicit Magister, non plus significat nisi quod pro eodem instanti actualiter inest unum oppositum et aliud possibiliter inest, ita quod una potentia eadem realiter non est determinata nunc ut hoc insit ei; immo contingenter, et potest sibi inese aliud oppositum."

Reply to the Second Question

Having settled these preliminary problems, Scotus is prepared to answer the three questions he has posed with respect to distinctions 39 and 40, beginning with the second. That question, we recall, was whether God's knowledge of contingent events can be called necessary rather than contingent knowledge. Earlier he had criticized Aquinas' attempt to defend an affirmative answer on the ground that "things known by God are contingent on account of their proximate causes, while the knowledge of God, which is the first cause, is necessary." Now once more he refers to another argument used by Aquinas to claim God's knowledge of contingent events is indeed necessary knowledge, "because 'contingent' is used here only as the matter of the word, and not as the chief part of the proposition. Hence its contingency or necessity has no reference to the necessity or contingency of the proposition, or to its being true or false. For it may be just as true that I said a man is an ass, as that I said, Socrates runs, or God is; and the same applies to necessary and contingent."[65]

Scotus attempts to formulate the general principle Aquinas seems to be using, when he writes: "From these accounts one can form this sort of argument, which this doctor himself does not do. 'A rational act is not radically altered by the matter it is about; therefore, neither is the knowledge or volition of God radically altered by calling it contingent, because it is about something contingent.' But the divine knowledge is absolutely necessary. Hence, it is not impeded when it has to do with something contingent."[66]

Since this view makes no sense to him, Scotus declares that God knows contingent things just as these are in themselves, that is, as contingent. And by way of proof he argues that, so far as God is concerned, "to will that something exist" and "to know that it will exist" are logically coextensive, that is, not only does the truth of one mu-

---

[65] Thomas Aquinas, *Sum. theol.* I, q. 14, art. 13, ad 2; Scotus, *Rep.* I A, f. 116vb: "Dicit quidam doctor quod est necessarium Deus scit futurum contingens ita quod haec est necessaria secundum eum: 'Deus necessario praescit hoc fore ut te sedere cras,' quia contingens non potest ibi nisi ut materia verbi, et non sicut principalis et formalis pars propositionis, et ideo contingentia eius vel necessitas non refert ad hoc quod propositio sit vera vel falsa, necessaria vel contingens. Ista enim sic potest esse vera me dixisse materialiter hominem esse asinum sicut me dixisse 'Deum esse Deum,' est ita contingens est una sicut alia isto modo."

[66] *Rep.* I A, f. 116vb: "Ex his dictis potest formari talis ratio quae tamen ipse non format: 'Actus rationalis non distrahatur per materiam super quam transit; ergo nec scire vel velle Dei distrahitur ut dicatur contingens quia transit super contingens. Scire autem divina absolute est necessaria; ergo non impeditur quando transit super contingens.' "

tually imply the truth of another, but they have the same modal structure, so that one proposition cannot be contingent and the other necessary. The reason this is so is because prior to God's willing the existence of any created thing, it does not have any definite truth value, and hence it is not something that can be known.[67]

Furthermore, Scotus' previous discussion as to the source of contingency indicates that it does not derive from exclusively necessary presuppositions. Prior to God's creative act of volition, "his intellect is entirely neutral about the truth of any contingent proposition about the future, and so this proposition 'God wills A to be' does not prerequire the notion of the terms, but the notion of something willed or the notion of willing. At that moment, then, the divine will in regard to something contingent is contingent or all contingency in things must be denied. It follows that his intellect or knowledge about it is contingent."[68]

Scotus also rejects another attempt to defend the position that God necessarily knows that something contingent will exist on the grounds that the mode of necessity can determine either the act of knowledge itself apart from its term or that act in relation to the term known. The distinction is invalid, Scotus insists, because the members are not mutaully exclusive, since one includes the other. For God's knowledge of things other than himself is a transient act and implies that his intellect passes to the term, and hence there is no way one can abstract from the term and still have the act remain. And so, since the term is contingent, the act of knowing which formally terminates at such a term is also contingent. This is evident, says Scotus, since a transitive verb signifying to pass over to some term is specified by that term. Therefore, "God knows the contingent will occur" takes "know" as determined by that term; but that term is merely contingent; hence,

---

[67] Ibid., f. 116vb: "Sed hoc non capio. Et ideo dico quod Deus ita scit contingenter aliquid sicut ipsa sunt in se contingentia. Unde contingenter scit animam Antichristi [fore]. Quod probo sic, quia quando aliqua convertuntur in veritate non potest esse verum contingenter et aliud necessario verum, quia ex necessario non sequitar contingens, quia unum potest esse falsum et aliud verum. Sed 'velle animam Antichristus fore' et 'scire eam fore' convertuntur, ut prius probatum est, quia anima Antichristi non est prius scibilis fore nisi quia prius volitum a voluntate divina, sed velle eam fore est contingens, quia contingenter vult eam fore, [ergo contingenter scit eam fore]."

[68] Ibid.: "Item secundo sic, quod praesupponit contingens non est necessarium; sed Deum scire aliquid futurum contingens fore praesupponit illud esse volitum a Deo, quia ante acceptationem voluntatis divinae respectu illius intellectus eius est omnio neutrum de illo, et ita haec propositio, 'Deus vult A fore,' non praeexigit rationem termini, sed rationem voliti sive rationem velle; ergo tunc voluntas divina circa contingens sit contingens vel oportet negare omnem contingentiam in rebus. Sequitur quod intellectus eius sive scientia sit contingens circa illud."

God knowing such a contingent event will happen is something contingent and not necessary.[69]

This concludes the substance of Scotus' answer to the second question and, after answering the initial arguments against his position, he turns his attention to the first question, "Does God foreknow future contingent events?"

Reply to the First Question

To the first question one must say that God foreknows immutably whatever contingent thing will happen in the future, Scotus declares, because to understand and to will in him are the same as he is and thus are immutable, as was proved in the previous distinction 38.[70] The emphasis here is on the immutability of God's knowledge, since the initial counterarguments to the question stressed that if what God knew was truly contingent, this implied that it was possible that he might not have known this, and this would introduce some aspect of change and passivity in his intellect. Hence, Scotus gives this proof of the implication. The contingent object is presented to God's intellect not in its real existence (*esse reale*), but only according to the diminished sort of being or existence it has in the intellectual act of being known. Scotus calls this *esse intellectum*, or more generally, *esse intelligibile*. This being so, he concludes, the contingent object can only be otherwise, if it is otherwise in the act of understanding. But future contingents are not presented as objects except according to this *esse intellectum* they have in the act of being understood, because through the act of the intellect they are constituted in their being understood.

[69] *Ibid.*, 116vb–117ra: "Distinctio etiam aliquorum qua distinguitur haec propositio, 'Deus necessario scit A fore,' eo quod necessitas potest determinare actum scientiae in se vel in comparatione ad terminum, non valet, quia unum membrorum distinctionis est aliud, nam actus transiens vel transitivus non est talis actus nisi inquantum intellectus transire in terminum et ideo nullo modo potest abolvi a termimo manente tali actu, et sic cum terminus sit contingens, actus sciendi qui formaliter terminat ad talem terminum sit contingens, et hoc patet quia verbum transitivum significans transire super terminum specificatur illo termino. Ergo 'Deum scire contingens fore' accipitur 'scire' ut determinatum per illum terminum; ille autem terminus est mere contingens, ergo Deum scire talem contingens fore est contingens et non necessarium."

[70] *Ibid.*, f. 117ra: "Ad primam quaestionem dicendum quod Deus praescit immutabiliter quodcumque contingens fore futurum, quia intelligere et velle in ipso sunt idem quod ipse et ita immutabilia, ut probatum est distinctione supra. Ergo omne futurum in se contingens Deus novit immutabiliter. Probo consequentiam: obiectum quod non obicitur intellectui nisi secundum esse quod habet in actu intellectus non potest aliter se habere nisi aliter se habeat ut in actu intelligendi. Sed futura contingentia non obiciuntur nisi secundum esse quod habet in intelligendi, quia per actum intellectus constituuntur in esse intellecto; ergo si mutabiliter obiciuntur intellectui divino, mutabiliter se habent quae sunt in actu intelligendi; ergo actus intelligendi in Deo mutabiliter se habet, quod est falsum, quia ex opposito sequitur oppositum."

This is a point Scotus makes much of elsewhere, namely, that things are intelligible, that is, they have *esse intelligibile*, because God knows them, not vice versa.[71] Since God's act of understanding is not mutable, things are not presented in a mutable fashion to the divine intellect.

The difficulty in this question, Scotus explains, stems from the fact that God's intellect with respect to its contingent knowledge has the potency for knowing opposites inasmuch as it can know what it wills, but he thinks he has adequately explained this by distinguishing between the intellect's actual knowledge, at the factual level, and its deeper level knowledge of the will's potency for producing opposite effects. The root source of contingency in the object known stems in the last analysis from the will's logical and real ability to have willed otherwise than it did.[72]

In answering the initial arguments to the contrary, Scotus stresses that the intellect is not passive but active, and if as such it requires an object, it will be the divine will that presents what will be actual, and this object will be presented contingently, since from all eternity God could have presented its opposite. But if in the will "the object exists contingently in its being as an object, then also the act in regard to it exists contingently. The will, however, contingently projects this known as an object that is to be known contingently; however, it is projected immutabily, although not necessarily." And he adduces here the example of an uninterrupted act of vision that we referred to earlier.[73]

Reply to the Third Question

Finally, he gives his attention to the third and final question from distinction 40. "When it is asked whether it is possible for one who is

[71] *Ordinatio* I, d. 35, n. 32; VI, p. 258: "Deus in primo instanti intelligit essentiam suam sub ratione mere absoluta; in secundo instanti producit lapidem in esse intelligibili et intelligit lapidem"; see also my article "Ockham and the Textbooks: On the Origin of Possibility," in *Inquiries into Medieval Philosophy: A Collection in Honor of Francis P. Clarke*, edited by James F. Ross (Westport, Conn.: Greenwood Publishing Co., 1971), pp. 243–73.

[72] *Rep.* I A, f. 117rb: "Difficultas igitur in hac quaestione est propter potentiam ad opposita, quae est prius explicata et hic sufficiat ad solutionem quaestionem."

[73] *Ibid.*: "Ad aliud, quando dicitur quod illa potentia qua Deus potest scire A et non scire A vel est activa vel passiva, esto quod sit activa. Dico quod vis potentia operativa requirit obiectum et ideo, si obiectum se habet, ita contingenter in essendo obiectum et actus circa eum. Voluntas autem facit istud scitum contingenter obici ut objectum contingenter intelligendi, tamen immutabiliter obicitur licet non necessario, ut dictum est. Exemplum ad hoc est si semper et sine interruptione actus, si contingenter obiceretur mihi obiectum nunc unum nunc aliud, contingenter viderem semper et non necessario, et tamen immutabiliter. Sicut si viderem perpetuum esse beatum per obiectum beatificum quod est esse divinum, licet immutabiliter tamen contingenter, etc."

predestined to be damned, some say that one proposition must be distinguished and the other not, for that about the possible has to be distinguished, namely, this 'It is possible that one predestined be damned' or this 'It is possible that the predestined be saved.' The other *de inesse* need not be distinguished, namely 'God has predestined Peter to be saved,' because this is simply true."[74]

> But I say to the question that such propositions as "One predestined can be damned," and the like, are to be distinguished according to the composite and divided sense, as all participles imply or are implicative of both senses. And one must answer, however, as above, for in the divided sense, there are two categoricals one of which is *de inesse*, and expresses salvation, namely "Peter will be saved," whereas the other is *de possibili* and expresses damnation with possibility, that is, "It is possible for Peter to be damned," and each is true. For this is true: "Peter will be saved," and nevertheless this is true, "Peter can be damned."[75]

"But how can it be true," Scotus asks rhetorically?

> I say that God's knowledge is not opposed to the condition in the known, nor does the condition in the known militate against God's knowing it. That condition in the known is expressed in this proposition "Peter will be saved." I say that it is a contingent condition; likewise, there is also a contingent condition in the divine intellect as knowing; hence, that aspect of contingency is not opposed to the knowledge or to the object willed or known, but it includes such; therefore it can stand together with a potency for the opposite. Hence, if this is true that one predestined can be damned, and this is not opposed to the certitude of the knowledge or the divine predestination about those who will be saved (for contingency is known on the part of the object God knows), then it follows that it is not opposed to the divine knowledge itself nor to the certitude which God has about the predestined.[76]

---

[74] *Ibid.*: "Quando quaeri utrum sit possibile praedestinatum damnari, aliqui dicunt quod una propositio est distinguenda, et alia non, nam possibilis est distinguenda, scilicet, haec: 'Possibile est praedestinatum damnari,' vel ista: 'Possibile est praedestinatum salvari.' Alia autem de inesse non est distinguenda, haec, scilicet: 'Deus praedestinavit Petrum salvari,' quia simpliciter est vera."

[75] *Ibid.*: "Sed ego dico ad quaestionem quod tales propositiones sunt distinguenda secundum sensum compositionis vel distinctionis, ut praedestinatus potest damnari et huiusmodi, sicut omnia participia implicant vel sunt implicativa utriusque sensus. Et tamen dicendum est sicut supra, quia in sensu divisionis sunt duae categoricae quarum una est de inesse, 'Petrus salvabitur,' [quae] scilicet [enunciat] salvationem. Alia est de possibili et enuntiat damnationen cum possibilitatem, ut 'Possible est Petrum damnari,' et quaelibet est vera. Haec enim est vera 'Petrum salvabitur,' et tamen haec est vera, 'Petrus potest damnari.' "

[76] *Ibid.*: "Sed quomodo potest esse vera? Dico quod scientia Dei non repugnat conditioni in scito nec econverso, quae conditio est in scito in ista propositione, 'Petrus

Scotus then devotes himself to answering the initial arguments against his position, and though his answers are somewhat more detailed than in either the *Lectura* or *Ordinatio*, there is nothing particularly noteworthy about them so far as this study goes.

GOD'S CONCURRENCE WITH THE CREATED WILL

Perhaps the most important bit of information found in these Paris lectures that is absent from both the *Lectura* and Apograph accounts is Scotus' explicit statement to the effect that if the will of God is the first or initial reason why things are contingent, it is not the sole cause of the contingency found in created things. Our own will is free and accountable over and above those things willed or directly and immediately intended by God. Though the *Lectura* and Apograph do not call attention to this second source of contingency, the fact that the human will is free is implicit in both accounts, inasmuch as the analysis of our will's freedom in terms of what is a matter of perfection and imperfection is essential to Scotus' explanation as to how God's own will functions.

What needs to be clarified further, however, is how Scotus viewed God's concurrence with created causes, or more precisely, how can God as the first or prior cause interact with the created will as a second cause without destroying its freedom. In all his proofs of God's free will as well as in his accounts of how God knows future contingents, Scotus insisted that if God creates necessarily, then all things will be moved by him necessarily. This suggests that God somehow initiates the movement of the will, whether or not the priority is temporal or one of nature. Some have even gone so far as to credit him with the theory that God knows the future because he has freely predetermined it. It is true that Scotus might well have anticipated Banez's "praemotio physica" theory had he accepted the principle many ascribed to Aristotle, that "whatever is moved is moved by another." Scotus, however, had nothing but scorn for this so-called axiom of motion, and devoted an entire question in his *Question on the Metaphysics*[77] to

---

salvabitur.' Dico quod est conditio contingens; similiter in intellectu divino sciente est conditio contingens; ergo illa ratio contingentiae non repugnat scientiae nec obiecto volito vel scito, sed includit illam; ergo potest stare cum potentia ad oppositum. Si ergo ista est vera, quod praedestinatus potest damnari, nec hoc repugnat certitudinem scientiae vel divinae praedestinationis quam habet de salvandis—scitur enim contingentia ex parte obiecti quae scitur a Deo—ergo non repugnat scientiae divinae, nec certitudinem quam habet de praedestinatis."

[77] *Quaest. subt. in libros Metaphysicorum Aristotelis*, IX, q. 14, "An aliquid possit moveri a seipso" (Vivès ed., VII, 582–603); for an excellent analysis of this question see

refuting the claim by some of his colleagues that one version of it enjoys the status of a metaphysical principle.[78] The will in particular is singled out as a clear example of an active potency that can move or determine itself.[79]

Scotus' conviction that God does not move the will directly, however, is further obscured by the fact that, like most of the Scholastics, he accepts the general principle that whatever occurs through the agency of secondary or created causes involves God in some way as the first or prior cause.[80] The important thing, however, is to see how Scotus interprets "prior" in this connection, since the principle seems to conflict with his claim that the will determines itself and that it is a contradiction in terms to assert that God can violate its freedom.[81]

To find the answer we must turn to the *Ordinatio* II, d. 37, q. 2, where Scotus asks: "Is the created will the total and immediate cause of its own volition, so that God has no immediate efficacy with respect to it, but only a mediate efficacy?"[82] The solution of this question, introduced without initial arguments, is central to solving four other

---

R. R. Effler, *John Duns Scotus and the Principle "Omne quod movetur ab alio movetur"* (St. Bonaventure, N.Y.: The Franciscan Institute, 1962).

[78] Scotus, *Quaest. subt. in libros Metaphysicorum Aristotelis*, IX, q. 14, n. 23, p. 600: "Non credo quod Aristoteles potuisset aliquod complexum esse principium non solum primum, sed nec decimum, ex quo in multis singularibus evidentia absurda sequerentur. Si etiam illud est principium primum metaphysicum, scilicet nihil idem potest esse in actu virtuali et in potentia ad actum formalem, cuius ille virtualis sit principium effectivum, si inquam, est principium primum metaphysicum, scio quod illud non est in *Metaphysica* Aristotelis scriptum."

[79] *Ibid.*, n. 13, p. 592: "De appetitu intellectivo tenetur quod simpliciter est activus. Nec ponentes ipsum esse passivum mere ab ipso obiecto videntur veram vel totam salvare posse libertatem in homine, sed tantummodo, ut videtur, necessitatem sic procedendi, sicut et calor in calefiendo; aut solummodo a causa posse aliter esse, sicut dicuntur non esse in potestate nostra, quae cognoscenda primo occurrant. Sed haec de voluntate a multis multipliciter sunt improbata, quae non oportet hic in speciali, sed alibi explanare." See also q. 15, where he deals specifically with the freedom of the will.

[80] Against the idea that God's only concurrence is to create and conserve the will, but has no immediate causal influence on what the will does, Scotus quotes with approval the opening line of the *Liber de causis*: "Omnes causa primaria plus est influens super suum causatum quam causa secunda universalis." (Cf. *Ordinatio* II, d. 37, q. 2, ed. Wadding Vivès, VI, n. 5, p. 372.)

[81] See *supra* footnote 49; also *Ordinatio* II, d. 37, q. 2, Codex A, f. 136va–b: "Voluntas divina non potest impedire voluntatem meam nisi violendo eam si ex se determinetur ad unam partem, ex quo enim determinata est ad unam partem, non potest impediri nisi violentetur; sed voluntas violentari includit contradictionem; ergo Deus non potest volitum a voluntate mea impedire."

[82] *Ordinatio* II, d. 37, q. 2: "Ideo quaero sine argumentis utrum voluntas creata sit totalis causa et immediata respectu sui velle, ita quod Deus respectu illius non habet aliquam efficientiam immediatam, sed tantum mediatam." The question is found in the Wadding-Vivès edition, v. 13, nn. 1–18, pp. 368–81. We have corrected this text on the basis of Codices A (136rb–137), P (197ra–198vb), and S (143vb–145rb), which represent the first three of the ten manuscripts being used by the Scotistic Commission for Book II of the *Ordinatio*.

interconnected questions on sin that range over several distinctions of Lombard's second book of *Sentences*, namely, "Is sin caused by something good?" (d. 34); "Is sin *per se* a privation of good?" (d. 35); "Is sin the punishment of sin?" (d. 36); "Can sin be from God?" (d. 37, q. 1).

The Scholastics, following the suggestions especially of Augustine and Anselm of Canterbury, were concerned to make the created will of man or the angels accountable for sin, without directly involving God as a cause of the sinful action, and to do this it was necessary to attribute to the human and angelic created will a measure of independence. The question was how much independence is consistent with the idea that God is the primary cause of everything else that has entity or existence.

One ploy for exempting God from moral responsibility, where the action of the created will was forbidden and therefore morally wrong, was to claim that God's concurrence with its action was simply carrying out his original plan of creation, in conserving the native power of free choice he had bestowed on rational creatures. If this involved at least his permissive will, the sinful action did not necessarily receive his benediction or approval.

One version of this view that seems to have intrigued Scotus initially as a possible or even plausible solution was the claim that the created will is the immediate and total cause of its own volition, and that the only part played by God was to keep it in existence with its power to act as it chose to do. Though he eventually came to reject it as irreconcilable with his theory of God's foreknowledge, in the present question he still presents this opinion in considerable detail and defends it against some obvious objections. Its plausibility, for him, lies in the fact that it seems an obvious way to insure the will's freedom, or its unique character as an active potency with a contingency of its own; that it sharply differentiates the will from natural causes that act necessarily when given the opportunity; and above all, that it explains how sin is possible.[83] Each of these characteristics of the will provides its own argument in defense of the theory.

Consider first what freedom of the will implies. To begin with, the will is not truly free unless its volition is totally in its power. Either it is the sole cause of that effect, or if another cause concurs, that other cause is under its control. Originally—according to Alnwick—Scotus held that though our will could not act without knowledge of its op-

---

[83] *Ordinatio* II, d. 37, q. 2: "Ad istam quaestionem potest dici quod voluntas est totalis et immediata causa respectu suae volitionis, quod probatur per rationem. Primo, quia aliter ipsa non esset libera; secundo, quia aliter nihil contingenter causare posset; tertio, quia aliter non posset peccare; quarto, quia aliter omnino nullam posset habere actionem; quinto, ex comparatione eius ad alias causas creatas" (cf. Wadding-Vivès, n. 1, p. 368).

tions, such knowledge functioned only as a necessary condition, not as a partial efficient cause of its volition. Later he modified this view to allow the intellect, or its knowledge, to play a secondary and partial causal role, but under the control of the will.[84] For if the will does not choose to act, the knowledge remains ineffectual. But if God's immediate cocausation is required for our will's action, this is no longer something under our voluntary control.[85]

Furthermore, because this opinion was contrasted as the polar opposite of the predetermination theory, it suggested a second argument based on the will's freedom. If the human will is determined in any way by the divine will, it no longer has either its volition or what it effects completely in its power. Those who hold the motion principle also hold that the will is predetermined by the divine will to do what it does. Only in this way can one preserve the widely accepted theory that God's causation and that of creatures are interrelated somehow as essentially ordered causes. For, if neither moves the other, no essential order obtains between them.[86]

On the other hand, if the predetermination theory explains the essential order well enough, how can it be reconciled with the claim that the will is an independent source of contingency in the world? For an essential order seems to demand that one cause move the other, as the hand moves the pen. And if the higher cause determines how the inferior cause will act, then every inferior cause will be necessarily determined. For example, if my will was immutable and could not be

---

[84] C. Balić, *Les commentaires de J. Duns Scot sur les quatre livres de sentences* (Bibliothèque de la Revue d'Histoire Ecclèsiastique, I) Louvain, 1927, p. 282; see also his article "Une question inedite de J. Duns Scot sur la voluntate," *Recherches de théologie ancienne et médiévale*, 3 (1931), p. 191; the text Balić edited in this article (pp. 192–208) is now recognized to be Scotus' original *Lectura* version of d. 25, book II.

[85] Scotus, *Ordinatio* II, d. 37, q. 2: "Ex prima via arguitur dupliciter: primo sic: nulla potentia habet perfecte in potestate effectum, qui non potest causari ab ea immediate, nec ab aliqua causa, cuius causatio non est in potestate illius potentiae; causatio autem Dei non est in potestate voluntatis creatae, patet, sicut nec virtus agentis superioris est in potestate agentis inferioris alicuius; ergo si Deus necessario concurrat immediate, ut causa immediata respectu volitionis creatae, voluntas creata non habet plene in sua potestate illam volitionem. Propositio maior assumpta patet, quia quod habet in potestate sua perfecte effectum, vel potest ex se solo in illud, vel causatio cuiuscumque concurrentis est in potestate eius, scilicet quod ut causet vel non causet. Exemplum de intellectu, qui si concurrat ad causandum volitionem secundum tertiam opinionem dist. 25 huius libri, non tamen causat nisi voluntate causante, ita quod causatio eius est in potestate voluntatis" (cf. Wadding-Vivès, n. 1, p. 368).

[86] *Ibid.*: " Iuxta istam viam arguitur secundo sic: Quod ab alio determinatur ad aliquid non habet illud perfecte in potestate eius; voluntas creata determinatur ex hypothesi a voluntate divina ad hoc; igitur etc. Minor probatur quia aut una voluntas determinat aliam et non nostra divinam, quia temporale non est causa aeterni; aut e converso. Aut neutra aliam, et tunc neutra erit movens mota, nec erit inter istas ordo essentialis" (cf. Wadding-Vivès, n. 2, p. 369).

impeded, as God's will is, and I decided to write tomorrow, my hand would no longer be contingently related to writing or not writing then. But if God is the immediate cause of my volition, then his will must have chosen from all eternity one of two contradictory possibilities, and this determination on his part must necessarily be accompanied by my volition to act accordingly. Otherwise, God would decide or will something that would not take place. How, then, can my volition or what it effects be contingent?[87]

Or consider sin. If God is the prior and immediate cause of my volition, then in that prior instant either he causes immediately perfect rectitude in my volition or he fails to do so. If he does cause such, then in the subsequent instant my will does not sin, since it cannot cause the opposite of what the first cause causes. On the other hand, if God does not cause rectitude in my volition, it still follows that my will does not sin, for without God's help and grace it is impossible for it to will rightly. In neither case, then, is my will capable of sinning.[88]

Furthermore, if God immediately moves the will in this way, is my will really an active potency or an efficient cause in its own right? Is it not simply a passive potency as some claim? For if God is the prior and immediate cause of its volition, it would seem he is also its total cause, just as he is the total cause of immaterial or angelic creatures,

---

[87] *Ibid.*: "Praeterea ex secunda via arguitur sic: Illud non est contingens propter habitudinem sui ad aliquam causam, ad cuius eventum causa superior determinata est, cuius causae determinationem necessario sequitur determinatio omnium causarum inferiorum. Exemplum, si voluntas nostra esset modo determinata ad unam partem, de scribendo cras, et non esset impedibilis, nec mutabilis, non esset meum 'scribere cras' contingens ad utrumlibet ex habitudine sui ad manum, quia sicut voluntas est determinata modo ad alteram partem, ita ipsa virtualiter sunt omnes causae inferiores ad idem. Et similiter ex quo illud determinatum est ad cuius determinationem effectus esset determinatus, eventus illius effectus non est simpliciter indeterminatus ad utrumlibet, saltem non est eius esse contingens propter potestatem causae inferioris. Sed si voluntas divina sit causa immediata mei velle, iam est causa aliqua determinata respectu eius, quia voluntas Dei aeternaliter determinata est ad alterum contradictoriorum, et determinationem huius causae necessario concomitatur determinatio voluntatis meae respectu eiusdem; alioquin simul starent Deum velle hoc, et hoc non fore; ergo illud velle non est contingens ad utrumlibet propter potestatem voluntatis meae" (cf. Wadding-Vivès, n. 2, p. 369).

[88] *Ibid.*: "Ex tertia via arguitur sic: Si Deus sit causa immediata volitionis, constat quod erit causa prior voluntate; ergo prius natura influit ad effectum quam voluntas. Accipio ergo illud signum naturae in quo Deus causat velle inquantum est prius secundo signo, in quo voluntas agit ad illud velle; aut in illo signo Deus causat immediate rectitudinem perfectam in velle, et per consequens voluntas in secundo signo non peccat, quia non causat in effectu oppositum illius quod prima causa causat; aut in illo primo signo Deus non causat rectitudinem in velle, et sequitur quod voluntas in secundo signo non peccat, quia non potest tunc in velle rectum; in nihil enim potest ipsa in secundo signo nisi quod causa prior in primo signo producit; sed non habendo velle rectum, si non potest habere rectum, non peccat; igitur etc" (cf. Wadding-Vivès, n. 3, p. 369–70).

or is the total cause of what he creates from nothing. Hence, my will would not exercise any true efficient causality with respect to its own volition.[89]

And finally, how does my will differ from natural causes that act by the necessity of their nature. Surely, if any created cause is the total cause of what it immediately effects, this is the will, for admittedly it is supreme among all active causes. But if God immediately causes its volition, this seems no different than the way he causes the activity of natural causes. Neither does there seem any reason why one should exclude such power to the will, since it does not entail that the will is infinitely powerful nor does it seem to invest it with a measure of perfection inappropriate to a creature. Indeed, it seems to enhance the power of the creator if he can give the power to move itself to something he creates. Scotus cites a further proof, peculiar to the theory of physics current in his day, that natural subjects are in some way the immediate cause of their proper attributes: since these are considered proper accidents, they seem to be a necessary consequence of the nature God has created.

For these two reasons, then, there seems to be no reason why God should not give the will complete power to elicit its acts of volition or nolition, and confine his cooperation simply to creating and conserving it in existence. Furthermore, since there is no other cause that produces its effect in this unique way, the will would then be the total efficient cause of the choice it makes; otherwise, one would have to assume that two causes of the same sort produce identically the same effect. As he has indicated elsewhere, this would violate Aristotle's principle of economy that one should not introduce a plurality of hypothetical entities where there is no necessity for such.[90]

---

[89] *Ibid.*: "Ex quarta via arguitur sic: Si Deus sit causa illius volitionis erit totalis causa eius, quia volendo causabit eam; volendo autem est totalis causa perfectioris creaturae, puta angeli, vel cuiuscumque creati de nihilo; igitur, si volendo esset causa eius, esset totalis causa eius; sed cum totali causa alicuius nihil aliud potest causare cum illa in eodem genere causae; igitur voluntas nullam causalitatem haberet respectu sua volitionis" (cf. Wadding-Vivès, n. 3, p. 370).

[90] *Ibid.*: "Ex quinta via arguitur sic: Si aliqua est totalis causa activa respectu sui effectus, hoc maxime concedendum est de voluntate, quia ipsa est suprema inter omnes causas activas; sed aliqua potest esse totalis causa respectu sui effectus. Probo dupliciter: primo, quia hoc non repugnat creaturae; licet enim aliquid sit totalis causa caloris effectiva, hoc non ponit in eam aliquam infinitatem, nec perfectionem repugnantem creaturae. Si enim sit causa univoca non oportet quod excellat effectum in perfectione. Si autem aequivoca, non oportet in infinitum excellere effectum, sed in aliquo gradu determinato. Secundo probatur minor, quia illud est totalis causa alicuius quod, si esset omni alio per impossibile circumscripto, perfecte causaret; sed subiectum, si esset circumscripto omni alio, causaret suam propriam passionem; ergo subiectum est totalis

After citing some authorities from Scripture and the Fathers of the Church that seem to support this theory, he points out what he considers its great merit.

If this way were true, it would be easy to show why God is not the cause of sin. For whether one refers to the material cause of sin (i.e., the positive elicited act of free choice itself, something that can be or not be in accord with the will of God or not in conformity with it), or the formal cause of sin (i.e., the privation or lack of goodness that should be there, a goodness that stems from the fact that the act is in conformity with divine or human law), it is the created will that is the entire cause. Only in the sense that God has given to the created will something of his own power and perfection, can one say he is in any way responsible for sin's existence.[91]

What is more, Scotus even shows how two obvious objections to this view might be solved. For all the Scholastics generally, following Augustine, admitted that grace and glory are gratuitous gifts of God, since they imply something over and above anything that a created nature might deserve in virtue of being what it is. Consequently, no created action can merit such gifts in strict justice (iustitia de condigno), though God out of liberality accepts certain morally good actions as though they merited in some way (de congruo) a supernatural reward. But if merit is due to God alone and in no way is a natural effect of any action a creature can perform, why then is not sin also due to God as well?

Futhermore, most of the Scholastics were content to accept the first proposition of the Liber de causis, that where two or more causes are interrelated in an ordered fashion to produce an effect, the primary cause has a greater influence on the effect than any secondary cause. But the theory that God has no immediate causality with respect to the will's volition runs counter to this principle.[92]

---

causa respectu suae passionis. Ex hac minori dupliciter probata infertur conclusio quod voluntas potest esse totalis causa respectu suae volitionis, et ultra, cum praeter totalem causam nihil aliud causet in eodem genere causae, alioquin esset idem bis causatum vel causaretur ab aliquo sine quo posset non esse, et sequitur quod Deus immediate non causabit istam volitionem" (cf. Wadding-Vivès, n. 4, p. 370).

[91] Ibid.: "Si haec via vera esset, posset secundum eam faciliter assignari, quomodo Deus non sit causa peccati. Loquendo enim sive de materiali sive de formali in peccato, totum esset causatum a voluntate, sicut a totali causa, et ita nullo modo a Deo, nisi mediate, quia Deus produxit voluntatem talem, quae posset sic et sic velle" (cf. Wadding-Vivès, n. 5 bis, p. 372).

[92] Ibid.: "Sed contra istam viam obiciitur, quia ista via non salvaret Deum esse causam meriti, cum meritum sit ita liberum, sicut peccatum. Similiter non salvaret ordinem essentialem causarum quia secundum primam propositionem De causis: 'Omnes causa primaria, etc. [plus est influens super suum causatum quam causa secunda

To the first of these one could say that God is the cause of merit in a quite different way in which he could be said to be the cause of sin, for he is the immediate cause of the supernatural grace or charity that inclines in a quasi-natural way to make the act meritorious. When an agent acts in a natural way, this action stems from its form or the sort of nature it is. Quite different is the voluntary act which is elicited freely, and not as something that stems from the nature or form of the agent. Because of the conditions his ordained will has set up for the acceptance of an act as meritorius, if the voluntary act is performed under the influence of the supernatural habit of grace or charity, God is determined as it were, by reason of his ordained will, to accept the act as deserving of reward. But if the will, instead of eliciting its act in accord with right reason, to which it is primarily inclined by reason of its "affection for justice,"[93] abuses that freedom by eliciting a defective act, namely, one that runs counter to what right reason dictates, and is prompted exclusively by its "affection for the advantageous," this is something the will does on its own. And if it lacks rectitude or the justice that should be there, if it had freely chosen to follow right reason, it is solely because God has no intention by his ordained power to give such a gratuity to the defective act.[94]

To the second objection, he makes an important point that he will later use to explain his own theory of how God cooperates with our will. An essential order between two efficient causes need not be dependent on the fact that one cause moves the other in the way the hand moves the bat in hitting a ball. He refers to his theory of how the intellect and object coact as two essentially ordered causes to produce the act of cognition, yet the object does not give the intellect its power to act but only an occasion to exercise that power; similarly the intellect does not give the object the power to coact with it in producing knowledge, but only the opportunity for the object to exercise its specific causality. Nevertheless, the action of the intellect is more perfect and contributes more to the common effect than the action of the

---

universalis']. Sed secundum istam viam causa primaria nihil influeret in effectum nisi quia produxit causam aliam" (cf. Wadding-Vivès, n. 5 b 15, p. 372).

[93] For Scotus' theory of the two affections or inclinations of the will, see A. B. Wolter, *Duns Scotus on the Will and Morality* (Washington, D.C.: Catholic University of America Press, 1986), pp. 178–83; and for his view on the conditions for a meritorious act, see *ibid.*, pp. 49–51.

[94] Scotus, *Ordinatio* II, d. 37, q. 2: "Ad primam istorum potest dici quod Deus aliquo modo est causa meriti, quomodo non est causa peccati, quia immediate causat in animam gratiam vel caritatem, quae per modum naturae inclinat ad merendum, et quandocumque forma activa per modum naturae est ab aliquo agente, etiam actio formae est ab eo. Ex hoc etiam pateret quomodo aliter effectum aliarum causarum essent a Deo quam effectus voluntatis, quia istae causae determinatae acceperunt a Deo inclinationem et necessitatem eas ad effectus, non sic voluntas" (cf. Wadding-Vivès, pp. 372–73).

object. Yet each of the two cocauses acts immediately on the effect and not upon the other. Though the two together form the total cause of the act of cognition and function as a single principle, this sort of cooperation is quite different from the other case of two essentially ordered causes, where one cause (the hand) moves the other cause (the bat) to produce their common effect.

As for the other point that the primary cause contributes more to the effect than the secondary cause, this is certainly true of God and the created will, if for no other reason than that God created the will and gave it the power to work on its own. Furthermore, even though the created will specifies the kind of volition it will elicit, God still plays a creator/conserver role inasmuch as volition has an entity or being of its own.

To explain how several essentially ordered causes can simultaneously produce a common effect without one acting as the cause of the other, Scotus appeals to the pluriform theory of hylomorphism where several forms combine to produce a single substance. Each lower form conditions the matter to receive the next higher form, and by reason of the properties given to it by the lower form, that composite in turn becomes secondary matter with respect to the next higher form. And essential order obtains between the various matters and their respective forms for otherwise the resulting composite would not have any substantial or *per se* unity; yet not every form, but only the very lowest immediately informs primary matter.[95]

SCOTUS' PERSONAL VIEW OF GOD'S CONCURRENCE

Despite the intrinsic plausibility of this view, Scotus feels compelled to reject it in virtue of what he has said about God's foreknowledge of

---

[95] Scotus, *Ordinatio* II, d. 37, q. 2: "Ad secundum diceretur quod licet aliquando sit ordo principalium causarum et minus principalium, quarum neutra movet aliam, sicut se habet obiectum et potentia cognitiva respectu actus cognoscendi, ex distinctio 3 primi, aliquando sit ordo ita quod principalius movet minus principale vel ad actum secundum vel ad primum, ita tamen quod illae duae sint partiales et integrent per se unam causam totalem, sicut manus et baculus respectu motus pilae vel sicut sol et pater respectu filii, tamen in causis totalibus respectu suorum effectuum immediatorum potest etiam esse ordo essentialis ita quod causa secunda totalis sit et immediata respectu sui effectus, et tamen essentialiter sit secunda, quia secundum suam causationem, sicut secundum suum esse essentialiter dependet a prima, non tamen ita quod alia dependentia sit immediata effectus sui ad ipsamet ad causam priorem.—Et cum dicit illa propositio, quod causa prima plus causat, verum est, quia causat secundam. Exemplum huius poni posset in causis essentialiter ordinatis alio modo causandi. Si enim ponatur plures materiae ordinatae in composito, respectu ultimae formae, illa non materiae respectu ultimae formae, ita quod quaelibet earum perficiatur ab ultima forma, sed solum a prima materia, quaecumque autem prior sit perficiatur ab aliqua forma priore, quae constituit materiale respectu posterioris" (cf. Wadding-Vivès, n. 7, pp. 372–73).

contingent events. First of all, God would not have such foreknowledge by reason of how his will is related to his essence, given that the essence naturally moves his intellect. And second, God would not be omnipotent, at least as Catholics understand the term. For omnipotence in this sense implies that God could do immediately what he does through the causality of secondary causes. But if he has no influence on such causes save as their creator and conserver, then he is not omnipotent, save in some secondary or mediate sense that even pagan philosophers like Averroës or Avicenna admit can be proved from reason.

As proof of the first point he reviews briefly his theory of how God knows future contingents by reason of the decisions of his will. Only because that will has chosen from all eternity to cooperate with the free choice of his rational creatures does his intellect have certain knowledge of future contingents. For the will, together with its free decisions, is only formally distinct, but really identical with his simple essence, and hence it too is immutable, as well as unobstructable. But if the created will were the total cause of its effect, and was still only contingently related to its volition, the created will could will otherwise than God had decided it should will, and nothing could be inferred about the future from an analysis of the decisions of the divine will.[96]

As for divine omnipotence, Scotus gives a triple proof that if God's concurrence with the will were not immediate, he would not be omnipotent. The first reason is that whatever an omnipotent God would will, would occur; but if he willed that a particular act of mine would take place, and it still remained in my power as a total contingent cause to either perform or not perform the act in question, it could happen, if I chose not to act in this way, that something God willed to happen would not occur and thus he would not be omnipotent.[97] Second, Scotus considers it axiomatic that if our will is free, even God could not force it to act without doing violence to it, and to violate

---

[96] Ibid.: "Contra istam opinionem arguitur dupliciter: Primo, quia ex ipsa non sequitur quod Deus non sit naturaliter praescius futurorum; secundo, quod non sit omnipotens. Probatio primae consequentiae, quia non habet scientiam de futuris contingentibus nisi quia certitudinaliter novit determinationem voluntatis suae respectu eorum, quae voluntas sua est immutabilis et impedibilis. Sed si voluntas creata sit totalis causa respectu sui velle, et ipsa contingenter se habet ad illud velle, igitur quantumcumque voluntas divina ponatur determinata ad unam partem eorum, quae dependent a voluntate creata, poterit voluntas creata aliter velle et ita non sequitur certitudo ex cognitione determinationis voluntatis divinae" (cf. Wadding-Vivès, n. 8, p. 373).

[97] Ibid.: "Probatio secundae consequentiae tripliciter: Primo, quia quidquid vult omnipotens, hoc fit; sed si vellit volitionem meam fore, et ista est in potestate voluntatis meae, ut totalis causae contingenter se habentis ad illud; igitur ipsa potest determinari ex se ad unam partem vel ad aliam indifferenter, et ita potest non fieri illud aliud, ad quod voluntas divina eam determinavit." (cf. Wadding-Vivès, n. 8, p. 374).

the will, for him is a contradiction in terms.[98] Third, an omnipotent will could produce whatever it willed in the existence any time it willed to do so, for the divine will has no other act with respect to a created than to produce it in being. But if my will were total cause of its volition, God would have no power to give it existence.[99]

For these two sets of reasons, then, Scotus declares he cannot hold this view. Consequently, he must find another way to explain why the created will and not God is the cause of sin.[100] To do this, he first clarifies precisely what sort of cause is involved in sin, and refers back to the previous question of this distinction where he asked: Could God be the cause of sin? Before attempting to give an answer he defines what is meant by the word "sin," and concludes that formally it is a privation of something good, and that the authorities he has cited in the initial arguments to the contrary all agree on this point. Reason also confirms this, because an inferior agent is required to conform itself to its superior, and if it lies in its power to do so and it fails to conform to what it should, this is formally sin; hence, if the action is something forbidden by divine or legitimate human law and the will knowingly refuses to conform to the law, then the will sins. But the sin does not consist precisely or formally in the positive act it performs, for if that act under some circumstances could be in accord with the law or will of the superior, it would not be sinful. What is formally sinful, then, is not the act, but the fact that it is not in harmony but discordant with the law or the superior's will.[101]

He discusses three theories as to the precise cause of sin; the first is that of Bonaventure, which holds that sin is accidentally caused by something good, either because the accidentality is on the part of the cause insofar as it is defective, or second, the accidentality stems from the side of the effect, for the will intends something good in the effect to which some deformity is conjoined. The deformity is not wanted

---

[98] *Ibid.*: "Secundo, quia voluntas divina non potest impedire voluntatem meam nisi violendo eam si ex se determinetur ad unam partem ex quo enim determinata est ad [A 136vb] unam partem, non potest impediri nisi violenter; sed voluntas violentari includit contradictionem; ergo Deus non potest volitum a voluntate mea impedire" (cf. Wadding-Vivès, n. 8, p. 374).

[99] *Ibid.*: "Tertio, quia voluntas omnipotens [S 144va] producit volitum in esse pro tunc pro quando vult illud esse; non enim est alius actus voluntatis divinae respectu angeli vel alicuius alterius creati quo producitur in esse. Sed si voluntas mea est totalis causa huius volitionis, nullo modo producit istam volitionem in esse" (cf. Wadding-Vivès, n. 8, p. 374).

[100] *Ibid.*: "Propter ergo istas duas rationes de omnipotentia et omniscientia Dei, non tenendo istam viam, restat inquirere qualiter peccatum possit esse a voluntate creata quoad quaestionem primam, et quomodo non a Deo, quoad quaestionem quartam" (cf. Wadding-Vivès, n. 9, pp. 374–75).

[101] *Ordinatio* II, d. 37, q. 1, n. 3; Wadding-Vivès, n. 13, p. 353.

per se, but only incidentally as it happens to be associated with the desired good. The third view claims that since sin is not something positive, but a privation of some good, it does not stem from an effective cause, but from a defective one. Though each of these explanations may not stand on their own, it is possible to extract something good and correct from each and thus form one satisfactory integral explanation of the cause of sin.[102]

In sin there occurs a positive act that represents its material component, together with a privation of justice that ought to be there, but is lacking, and this privation constitutes the formal component of sin. With respect to this privation, however, there is no efficient cause, but rather a deficiency of causality, that is to say, some good ought to be produced but is not produced. The will ought to give righteousness to its act, and by not doing so, it sins. This deficiency, or lack of causation or failure to give the rectitude due to its act, which is something the will has the freedom to give, formally constitutes the sin, and it is due solely to the will, since it fails to do what it has the power to do.[103]

But where does the accidentality associated with the sinful act enter in? It stems from this fact, says Scotus. Though the will does not formally cause what is sinful about the act, but rather it is accountable for the privation through its omission of the righteous act it might have performed, it is accountable for the privation's presence. But the will effectively causes something positive, namely, a voluntary act to which privation is annexed, and thus the authorities cited by pseudo-Denis about the accidentality on the part of the effect are correct. There is also accidentality on the part of the cause, since it is not a proper cause with respect to the defect in question, just as being white is accidental to a bucket made *per se* to carry water. However, one needs to take "accident" in a somewhat broader sense, for instance, in the way one specific difference such as "rational" is said to be accidental to the genus "animal," for "animal" *per se* is indifferent to either "rational" or "nonrational." In a similar way, one could say that "will" in general is a pure perfection, for we posit will as a formal perfection

---

[102] *Ordinatio* II, d. 37, q. 2, n. 9: "Ex illis tribus viis, duabus scilicet quae ponunt causam per accidens respectu mali, et tertia quae ponti respectu eius causam deficientem, potest colligi una solutio integralis talis" (cf. Wadding-Vivès, p. 375).

[103] *Ibid.*: "In peccato concurrunt actus positivus ut materiale et privatio iustitiae debitae ut formale. Respectu huius privationis nulla est causa efficiens, sed tantum deficiens, secundam tertiam viam. Voluntas enim quae est debitrix dandi rectitudinem suo actui et non dat deficiendo peccat. Istud autem deficere, sed non causare vel non dare rectitudinem suo actui quae est debita, est a causa quae libere posset tunc causare, scilicet, libere dare rectitudinem suo actui, hoc est ergo formaliter peccare, causam talem liberam non dare debitam rectittudinem suo actui quam tunc posset dare" (cf. Wadding-Vivès, p. 375).

of God. But "will" in this general or common sense is not the cause of sin, for if it were then every instance of will would entail such an imperfection.[104] Rather it is "will" as contracted by "created" that represents the *per accidens* cause of sin, for "created" is accidental to "will" in general, and though "created" itself does not imply sin, Scotus tells us the term is a circumlocution expressing the fact that it is limited in perfection, defectible, and produced from nothing, and it is these imperfections that represent the reason why it is capable of sinning by omitting what it ought to do.[105] It still remains to show how this defectible sort of will is the cause of sin in a way the divine will is not its cause, for this—says Scotus—is how the fourth or previous question, viz., Can God be the cause of sin? is commonly answered.[106]

Scotus' solution comes down to the peculiar way God as the perfect cause concurs with the created cause which can fail to do what it has both the ability and obligation to do. The two causes are essentially ordered in the way he previously explained the interaction of the object and the intellect in the case of cognition; for he eventually came to believe a similar relationship existed between the intellectual knowledge of the object and the will as regards the act of volition. Hence, he writes: "when two partial causes concur to produce a common effect of both there can be a defect on the part of one without a defect on the part of the other. For example, the intellect and the free will concur

[104] *Ordinatio* II, d. 37, q. 2: "Ex hoc apparet illa via de causa per accidens, licet ista causa non causet formaliter quod est in peccato efficiendo, sed deficiendo causat tamen efficiendo aliquod positivum, cui annexus est iste defectus deficiendo causatus et ita stant auctoritates Dionysii de accidentalitate ex parte effectus. Est etiam accidentalitas ex parte causae non propriae, sicut album dicitur esse causa intendendi actualis accidentaliter et universaliter quando aliquid proprie accidit causae per se, ita quod facit unum per accidens cum eo, sed extendendo accidens ad quodlibet quod est extra per se rationem alicuius (quomodo differentia dicitur accidere generi) hoc enim modo illud quo voluntas nostra specifice est haec voluntas, accidit voluntati in communi, quia voluntas in communi est perfectio simpliciter, propter quod ponitur formaliter in Deo, et voluntas sub ista ratione non est proxima causa etiam contingens respectu peccati, quia tunc quodlibet inferius sub ea haberet talem rationem causalitatis, et ita voluntas divina" (cf. Wadding-Vivès, p. 375).

[105] *Ordinatio* II, d. 37, q. 2, n. 10: "Sed voluntas contracta per differentiam aliquam ad voluntatem creatam, quam circumloquimur per hoc quod est limitatum est proxima causa defectiva et per accidens respectu peccati, et ideo accidentialiter etiam ex parte causae, accipiendo voluntatem in communi pro causa, inquantum intelligitur ista differentia superaddi, accidit sibi per accidens, sicut si diceretur quod animal non est per se causa intelligendi, sed per accidens, quia animal perfectissimum intelligit" (cf. Wadding-Vivès, p. 375).

[106] *Ordinatio* II, d. 37, q. 2, n. 11: "Sed tunc restat videre quomodo voluntas defectibilis sit causa deficiens respectu peccati, aliter quam voluntas divina; immo quod ipsa sit causa et voluntas divina non sit causa, et hoc quantum ad solutionem quartae quaestionis, ubi dicitur et tenetur communiter quod voluntas divina non potest esse causa peccati" (cf. Wadding-Vivès, p. 376).

in the act of volition, according to the third view presented in distinction 25 of this book. This voluntary act can be defective because of a defect in the will, although it is not preceded by any defect in the act of cognition." In like fashion when the divine will and created will concur in producing the created act of volition, the defect can arise on the part of the created cause, because it could give righteousness to its act and is in fact bound to do so, where the alternative is sin, but it fails to do so. One might object that it is God, the uncreated cause, not the created will, that gives the righteousness to the act. Strictly speaking that is so, but whatever God gives antecedently, says Scotus, he always gives consequently unless some impediment is placed by the other cause. By creating the human will with a positive bias or affection for justice, he gives the will the ability to moderate its affection for the advantageous lest this induce it to act against what right reason dictates. In addition, he gives it supernatural grace or charity that enables it to perform righteous and meritorious works. In so doing, he bestows rectitude on every act of the will so far as his antecedent will is concerned. And if the will does its part, that is, if it acts in accord with this inclination for justice and in virtue of its supernatural habit of charity, then God, by his consequent will, bestows righteousness upon it. If righteousness is not bestowed, it is because the will has failed to act in the way it could and should have acted. And thus the defect in the effect of the two causes does not stem from the superior cause, but from the inferior or created cause. It is not that the superior cause produces rectitude in the effect, and the inferior cause distorts it. Rather it is because the superior cause would cause it, if the inferior cause did its part, and therefore, the rectitude is not caused precisely because the second cause did not cause or do its part.[107]

---

[107] *Ordinatio* II, d. 37, q. 2, n. 14: "Dico quando duae causae partiales concurrunt ad effectum communem ambarum potest esse defectus in productione effectus ex defectu utriusque causae concurrentis praecise et non alterius. Exemplum: quantum ad velle secundum opinionem tertiam. dist. 25 huius, concurrit intellectus et voluntas libera; potest esse defectus in actu isto ex defectu voluntatis, licet non praecedat defectus in cognitione.—Ita igitur si ad velle voluntatis creatae concurrunt voluntas creata et voluntas divina, potest esse defectus in ipso velle ex defectu alterius causae, et hoc, quia ista causa posset rectitudinem dare actui et tenetur dare, et tamen non dat; alia autem licet non teneatur eam dare, tamen quantum est ex se daret si voluntas creata cooperaretur. Universaliter enim quidquid Deus dedit antecedenter, daret illud consequenter quantum est ex se nisi esset impedimentum. Dando autem voluntatem liberam, dedit antecedenter opera recta quae sunt in potestate voluntatis, et ideo quantum est ex parte sui dedit rectitudinem omni actui voluntatis, et voluntati ex consequenti daret, si ipsa voluntas, et voluntati ex consequenti daret, si ipsa voluntas quemcumque actum elicitur recte ageret ex parte sui. Est ergo defectus in effectu duarum causarum non propter defectum causae superioris, sed inferioris, non quia causa superior causet rectitudinem in effectu, et inferior obliquitatem, sed quia causa superior quantum est de se causaret,

If one objects that in this cooperative venture the divine will must enjoy some priority, at least of nature, if not in time, Scotus denies this to be so. When the four Aristotelian causes (material, formal, efficient, and final) coact to produce a common effect, they do so in one and the same instant of nature. Matter does not matter by any priority of nature, before the efficient cause effects, or vice versa. The only priority or posteriority that exists between these essentially ordered causes, is one of relative perfection. But none can cause without the other three cocausing, and thus there is no priority of nature with respect to their common effect; they all cause in one instant of nature. In a similar way, says Scotus, two efficient causes cocause in one instant of nature, where neither can cause without the other. In bestowing rectitude God only acts according to his ordained power and according to this ordination he cannot act if the created agent fails to do its part. Hence, Scotus says, if the effect is not rightly caused, this is not now because a prior cause of itself would cause rightly, if the second caused, but because of a defect in the second cause which had it in its power to either cause with the first cause or not cause with the first cause, and if it did not cocause with it, as it was bound to do, then no rectitude exists in the common effect of the two causes.[108]

If a quibbler should ask, why cannot the uncreated will be the first reason why the act is defective, Scotus replies.

> If God did not freely cause the righteousness that should be in the act of the created will, and this because of his liberty of will, and not because of any defect in the created will for not voluntarily cooperating, there would be no sin in the created will, for it would lack no justice that should be there. For there is no lack of due justice in the created will

---

si causa inferior secundum suam causalitatem causaret et ideo rectitudinem non causari est propter hoc, quia causa secunda quantum ad se pertinet non causat" (cf. Wadding-Vivès, pp. 387–79).

[108] *Ibid.*, n. 15: "Et si obiciatur de illis duobus instantibus naturae, sicut obiectum est, quod in primo Deus daret rectitudinem actui, respondeo. Dico quod prioritas quae includit posse esse sine invicem absque contrdictione, non est ordo in causis ut causant effectum communem, sed simul causant; sicut enim loquendo de diversis generibus causarum, non prius natura materia materiat quam efficiens efficiat, quasi sine contradictione possit esse materiatum et non effectum, vel e converso, sed tantum prius natura, hoc est perfectius una causat quam alia; ita in eodem genere causae diversae causae ordinatae licet habeant ordinem secundum perfectius et imperfectius causare, non tamen habent prioritatem naturae, quae dicat posse esse sine invicem respectu tertii. Immo, sicut in uno instanti naturae materia materiat et efficiens efficit, ita duae causae efficientes ordinatae in uno instanti naturae causant effectum communem, ita quod neutra tunc causat sine altera. Sed quod effectus non rectus causetur, hoc non est tunc propter causam priorem, quae quantum est ex se recte causaret, si secunda causaret, sed propter defectum secundae, quae in potestate sua habet concausare causae primae vel non concausare, et si non concausat illi, ut tenetur, non est rectitudo in effectu communi amborum." (cf. Wadding-Vivès, p. 379).

unless it is in its power to act rightly. Thus we can think of nothing that could be taken away from the prior cause that would prevent the created will from willing rightly; hence if God were the prior cause that failed to give righteousness, the nonrighteous act [of the created will] would be no sin.[109]

CONCLUSION

From all of the above, it seems that Scotus' basic argument expressed in syllogistic from, comes down to this:

> God knows what the human will will do *at the time* it wills.
> But God's knowledge is unchangeable.
> Therefore, God knows what the human will will do from all eternity.

The major premise is what Scotus regards as given and uncontroversial. If we know what a person wills at the time he wills it, *a fortiori* God does. The point that is never discussed, but would seem essential to the argument, is how does God know how to cooperate with the will's specific choice unless that choice plays some determining role with respect to that knowledge? Scotus, however, simply falls back on the commonly accepted Scholastic doctrine that God's knowledge of the creature does not depend upon the creature in any way but is self-contained and this secondary knowledge stems somehow from his primary knowledge of his own essence. This is the real question Scotus left untouched. It was the subsequent discussions of Banez and Molina that attempted to explain more precisely how God knew, one by the "preamotio physica" theory, the other by means of a "scientia media."

However, let us leave this question open for the present and simply concentrate on the fact that this is Scotus' basic principle from which his entire subsequent discussion depends. Since, according to him, principles or premises in an argument have a priority as to evidence and certainty over the conclusion, we can say that foreknowledge is of secondary importance in this whole discussion. The basic point is

---

[109] *Ordinatio* II, d. 37, q. 2, n. 17: "Sed quare in aliqua voluntate increata non potest prima ratio deficiendi?—Respondeo: si Deus non causat libere rectitudinem, quae deberet esse in actu voluntatis creatae, et hoc propter libertatem voluntatis suae, non autem propter defectum voluntatis creatae non voluntarie cooperantis, non est tunc causa peccati in voluntate creata, quia non est carentia iustitiae debitae. Non enim est iustitia debita a voluntate creata nisi inquantum in potestate eius est recte agere, ita quod nulla prius intelligitur subtractatio causae prioris, propter cuius defectum non posset voluntas recte agere; si ergo Deus esset prima causa non agens rectitudinem, actus non rectus non esset peccatum" (cf. Wadding-Vivès, p. 380).

that God's knowledge—and the same will be true of his volition—is primarily concerned with the present, not the past or future. It is here-and-now oriented.

If this be so, then the fact that God had this here-and-now oriented knowledge from all eternity is a secondary or incidental aspect of the knowledge. What is primary or essential and is the starting point of Scotus' argument is that God knows at the time the will wills. But since the present continues indefinitely, this knowledge is an ongoing thing, and hence extends to everything that occurs. By calling the foreknowledge secondary or incidental, I mean that it is not basic, but is a conclusion that follows, if and only if one accepts the additional thesis that God is essentially unchangeable, and that his knowledge as really identical with his essence is also unchangeable. As a matter of fact, not all theists admit that God is completely unchangeable, at least as regards what he knows or wills. Hence, they could not argue that just because God knows what is going on at present, he also knew this from all eternity.

The point I wish to make, however, is that if the foreknowledge is secondary, then the fact that God foreknows cannot be in any sense the reason why the present is what it is. What Scotus has given us in short is only a proof of the simple fact that God foreknows, he has not given us an argument for the reasoned fact except in a limited sense, that given the simple fact that God always knows the present, we can find a reason why he foreknows the present. But since the argument for the reasoned fact rests upon a premise of the simple fact, the entire argument is one of simple fact.

From this standpoint let us review the role of the will in God's knowledge. We could construct a similar syllogistic form of Scotus' argument in this way.

> When the creature acts voluntarily, God cooperates with the specific act so that the effect is the result of their combined causality.
> But God's specific cooperation was given from all eternity, for otherwise he would be mutable.
> Therefore, God willed to cooperate in this specific way from all eternity.

Let us examine the major premise more closely. Scotus' clear analysis of how God's causality and that of the creature are interrelated makes it clear that God's cooperation in no way determines what the creature does. In other words, it does not specify the act. The act could have been otherwise. This is precisely where the second reason for contingency enters in, that which stems from the creature's free will and ability to determine itself. The essential order that obtains between God's causality and that of the creature is literally that of a "concursus," not that of a "primum movens" or "praemotio physica." This was the point that I said got obscured by the fact that Scotus first argued that if God did not create contingently, then no cause—whether natural or free—would act contingently.

That God is the primary cause of the combined act means nothing more than where an essential order exists between two or more causes in producing a common effect, one action may be more perfect than the other. The priority is one of eminence, not of dependence. In short, the essential order between the cocauses is not like that of the hand moving the pen, where the hand as the primary cause initiates the movement, and the secondary cause, the pen, would not move unless the hand first moved it. The interrelationship is rather like that of the four Aristotelian causes or that of intellect and object. Each of the four causes must exercise its respective causality simultaneously or no effect is produced. Similarly, intellect and object must each play their respective causal role simultaneously or no concept or knowledge results. Scotus insists that in such cases there is no priority of either nature or time involved. In other words, when the creature wills, God also wills. God does not initiate or move the created will. To do so would violate its freedom, something Scotus considered to be a contradiction in terms.

This is Scotus' primary or basic assumption. God's volition insofar as it is concretized in a created effect always concerns the present. Its effectiveness is simultaneous with that of the created cause. That God's volition, as really identical with his immutable essence, was given from all eternity is again a secondary or incidental conclusion. It follows only because what God wills now, he would have to have willed from all eternity; otherwise he would be mutable.

Putting it another way, we can say that although God's knowledge and volition are from all eternity, terminatively they always have to do with the present, with what is going on here and now. If in the here-and-now God's cooperation did not determine the human will, then the fact that, so far as he is concerned, he gave that cooperation from all eternity, cannot in any way determine or predetermine the human will.

It is this nondeterminative cooperation, willed from all eternity, that God knows somehow either (1) because he knows what he wills and realizes that his omnipotent will cannot be impeded (Henry of Ghent's view), or (2) because that volition is really identical with God's essence and in knowing that essence he knows also the way he has willed (Scotus' preferred view).

This is essentially Scotus' theory as to how the will functions in regard to God's foreknowledge. If it is true that as creator and conserver he gave each created cause its nature and therefore its power, his role as cooperator is distinct from the creator/conserver role. Having given the created will the power to determine itself, God respects that in his cooperation. Hence, Scotus can legitimately claim that although God's volition is the primary cause of contingency, it is not the sole cause of contingency except in the case of natural causes. Where free agents are concerned, however, it is essentially the created agent that determines what the effect will be. God simply cooperates with whatever action the creature chooses to perform. Hence in the last analysis, although God knows what the effect will be because of his willed cooperation, the effect is contingent in the sense of being what it is rather than something else because of the determination of the creature, not because of God's determination.

What is left open, of course, is the question as to how God knows how to cooperate in the specific way he does at the moment the creature acts. Scotus does not attempt to offer any answer in the way that Banez and Molina later tried to do. At most, he makes the point that God's knowledge is not a series of acts; there is but one infinite act that extends to all possible situations. In a similar way, he claims there is not a series of acts of God's will. Rather there is but one act of the will whereby he necessarily loves himself and yet contingently loves whatever he has willed to create. And in the case of the human will, that one infinite act extends, as it were, to all his specific cooperative acts. We are thus left with a basic mystery.

What begins to look like an explanation of how God knows what he knows, (a demonstration of the reasoned fact) ends up as a simple proof that he knows (a demonstration of the simple fact). What Scotus seemed primarily concerned to prove was that the two most competing accounts in his day as to how God knows the future, namely, through the ideas or through the fact that eternity is coextensive with the whole of time, are inadequate, and that the divine will—as Henry of Ghent insisted—must be taken into consideration. Scotus' whole analysis, therefore, as in the case of many similar problems, seems to be a development of an idea he found in Henry.

A Bibliography of Allan B. Wolter, O.F.M.

1942

1. M.A. thesis. "The Mechanism of the Nineteenth Century in the Light of Aristotelian Philosophy." The Catholic University of America, 1942.

1945

2. Rev. of *Fact and Fiction in Modern Science*, by Henry Gill. *New Scholasticism*, 19 (1945), 258–60.
3. Rev. of *Physics in the Twentieth Century*, by Pascal Jordan. *New Scholasticism*, 19 (1945), 260–62.

1946

4. Ph.D. dissertation. "The Transcendentals and Their Function in the Metaphysics of Duns Scotus." The Catholic University of America, 1946.
5. *The Transcendentals and Their Function in the Metaphysics of Duns Scotus*. Franciscan Institute Publications Philosophy Series, No. 3. Ed. Philotheus Boehner and ABW. St. Bonaventure, N.Y.: Franciscan Institute, 1946. Publication of 4.

1947

6. "Duns Scotus on the Nature of Man's Knowledge of God." [Intro., text and trans.] *Review of Metaphysics*, 1 (1947), 3–36. Revised version in 72, pp. 14–33.
7. "The 'Theologism' of Duns Scotus." *Franciscan Studies*, 7 (1947), 257–73, 367–98.
8. Rev. of *L'Ascesa a Dio in Duns Scoto*, by Efrem Bettoni. *Franciscan Studies*, 7 (1947), 511–12.

Updated and reprinted with permission from *Essays Honoring Allan B. Wolter*, ed. William A. Frank and Girard J. Etzkorn (St. Bonaventure, N.Y.: The Franciscan Institute, 1985), 351–63.

9. Rev. of *Vent'Anni di Studi Scotisti*, by Efrem Bettoni. *Franciscan Studies*, 7 (1947), 515.

1948

10. Rev. of *The Philosophy of the Alfarabi and Its Influence on Medieval Thought*, by Robert Hammond. *Franciscan Studies*, 8 (1948), 89–90.
11. Rev. of *The Thomistic Philosophy of the Angels*, by James Collins. *Franciscan Studies*, 8 (1948), 214–16.
12. Rev. of *The Nature and Unity of Metaphysics*, by George M. Buckley. *Franciscan Studies*, 8 (1948), 305–7.
13. Rev. of *General Biology and Philosophy of Organism*, by Ralph Stayner Lillie. *Franciscan Studies*, 8 (1948), 310–12.

1949

14. "Duns Scotus on the Natural Desire for the Supernatural." *New Scholasticism*, 23 (1949), 281–317.
15. Rev. of *The Driving Forces of Human Nature and Their Adjustments*, by Dom Thomas Verner. *Franciscan Studies*, 9 (1949), 79–81.
16. Rev. of *Thomas-Lexikon*, by Ludwig Schuetz. *Franciscan Studies*, 9 (1949), 457–58.
17. Rev. of *A Lexikon of St. Thomas Aquinas* by Roy J. Deferrari et al. *Franciscan Studies*, 9 (1949), 457–58.
18. Rev. of *The Renaissance Philosophy of Man*, by E. Cassirer et al. *New Scholasticism*, 23 (1949), 449–50.

1950

19. "Ockham and the Textbooks: On the Origin of Possibility." *Franziskanische Studien*, 32 (1950), 70–96. Reprinted in 99.
20. Duns Scotus. *Proof for the Unicity of God*. [Text and trans.]. (pro manuscripto). St. Bonaventure, N.Y.: Franciscan Institute, 1950. Slightly revised version printed in 73, pp. 83–95.
21. Duns Scotus. *On the Spirituality and Immorality of the Soul*. [Text and trans.]. (pro manuscripto). St. Bonaventure N.Y.: Franciscan Institute, 1950. Revised version printed in 73, pp. 134–62.
22. Rev. of *Man's Last End*, by George M. Buckley. *Franciscan Studies*, 10 (1950), 198–202.

1951

23. "Duns Scotus and the Necessity of Revealed Knowledge; Prologue to the *Ordinatio* of John Duns Scotus," [Intro. and trans.], *Franciscan Studies*, 11 (1951), [237–72].
24. Duns Scotus. *Concerning Human Knowledge*. [Text and trans.] (pro manuscripto). St. Bonaventure, N.Y.: Franciscan Institute, 1951. Slightly revised version in 73, pp. 97–122.

1952

25. "The Recognition of Miracles." *In Philosophical Studies in Honor of the Very Reverend Ignatius Smith*, O. P. Ed. John K. Ryan. Westminster, Md.: Newman Press, 1952, pp. 233–56.
26. "Professor Renoirte's *Cosmology*." [Review article]. *Franciscan Studies*, 12 (1952), 139–47.
27. Select Problems in *The Philosophy of Nature*. (pro manuscripto). St. Bonaventure, N.Y.: Franciscan Institute, 1952. Revised version in 70.

28. "Explanation of the Third Order Regular Rule." *The Cord* [published in 22 parts], 2 (1952), 16–19, 35–41, 60–66, 81–88, 107–10, 131–36, 181–86, 204–7, 231–34, 273–77; 3 (1953), 14–19, 71–76, 103–7, 136–40, 158–65, 190–99, 257–62, 286–91, 324–32; 4 (1954), 86–92, 148–57, 182–84. Revised for book form in 36.

1953

29. "The Christian Philosophy of Love." Aquinas Lecture. Cleveland, Ohio: Notre Dame College, 1953.
30. Rev. of *Idea Men of Today*, by Vincent E. Smith. *Franciscan Studies*, 13 (1953), n. 1, 67.
31. Rev. of *Marc de Toledo, Traducteur d'Ibn Tumart*, by M. T. D'Alverny and G. Vajda. *Franciscan Studies*, 13 (1953), n. 4, 131–32.
32. Rev. of *Thomism and Aristotelianism*, by Harry Jaffa. *Philosophy and Phenomenological Research*, 14 (1953), 130–32.

1954

33. "Duns Scotus and The Existence and Nature of God." In *Existence and Nature of God*. Proc. of American Catholic Philosophical Association, 28 (1954), 94–121.
34. "Doctrine of The Immaculate Conception in the Early Franciscan School." *Studia Mariana*, 9 (1954), 26–69.
35. "The Theology of the Immaculate Conception in the Light of 'Ineffabilis Deus'." *Marian Studies*. Proc. of the 5th National Convention of the Mariological Society, 5 (1954), 19–72.
36. *The Book of Life: An Explanation of the Rule of the Third Order Regular of Saint Francis*. St. Bonaventure, N.Y.: Franciscan Institute, 1954. Slightly revised edition, in book form, of 28.
37. Rev. of *Philosophisches Wörterbuch*, by Walter Brugger. *Franciscan Studies*, 14 (1954), 114.
38. Rev. of *Ens et unum convertuntur. Stellung und Gehalt des Grundsatzes in der Philosophie des hl Thomas von Aquin*, by Ludgen Oenig-Hanhoff. *Franciscan Studies*, 14 (1954), 445–46.
39. Rev. of *Dusquesne Studies I–III*, ed. Andrew G. Van Melsen and Henry J. Koren. *Franciscan Studies*, 14 (1954), 448–52.
40. Rev. of *La preuve réele de Dieu, Étude critique*, by Joseph Defever. *Franciscan Studies*, 14 (1954), 452–54.
41. Rev. of *Aristoteles Werk und Geist*, by J. Zürcher. *Modern Schoolman*, 31 (1954), 137–39.
42. Rev. of *Ontologie*, by Caspar Nink. *Modern Schoolman*, 31 (1954), 139–43.
43. Rev. of *Metaphysica generalis in usum scholarum*, by Gerard Esser. *Modern Schoolman*, 31 (1954), 139–43.

1955

44. "The Atomic Nucleus." *Franciscan Studies*, 15 (1955), 350–83.
45. "The Mystery of the Atom." In *Nature: The Mirror of God*. Report of the 36th Annual Meeting of the Franciscan Educational Conference. Washington, D.C.: Franciscan Educational Conference, 1955, pp. 74–89.
46. "Duns Scotus and the Predestination of Christ." [Intro. and trans.]. *The Cord*, 5 (1955), 366–72.

1956

47. "The Monthly Conference: Human Destiny." *The Cord*, 6 (1956), 1–8.
48. "The Monthly Conference: Our Destiny as Children of God." *The Cord*, 6 (1956), 33–38.
49. "The Monthly Conference: Our Destiny as Religious I." *The Cord*, 6 (1956), 65–77.
50. "The Monthly Conference: Our Destiny as Religious II." *The Cord*, 6 (1956), 97–106.
51. "The Monthly Conference: The Queenship of Mary." *The Cord*, 6 (1956), 129–35. Reprinted in 68.
52. "The Monthly Conference: Sin, the Betrayal of Love." *The Cord*, 6 (1956), 161–69.
53. "The Monthly Conference: The Challenge of Sin." *The Cord*, 6 (1956), 193–200.
54. "The Monthly Conference: Transformation in Christ." *The Cord*, 6 (1956), 225–33.
55. "The Monthly Conference: Blessed Are the Poor in Spirit." *The Cord*, 6 (1956), 257–66.
56. "The Monthly Conference: Blessed Are the Pure of Heart." *The Cord*, 6 (1956), 289–99.
57. "The Monthly Conference: Blessed Are the Pure of Heart II." *The Cord*, 6 (1956), 321–31.
58. "The Monthly Conference: The Grace of Guadalupe." *The Cord*, 6 (1956), 353–59. Reprinted in 67.

1957

59. "Monthly Conference: The Two Final Beatitudes." *The Cord*, 7 (1957), 5–13.

1958

60. *Life in God's Love*. Chicago: Franciscan Herald, 1958. Reprint in book form of 47–58.
61. *Summula Metaphysicae*. Milwaukee: Bruce, 1958.
62. "Causality (Presidential Address)." In *The Role of the Christian Philosopher*. Proc. of American Catholic Philosophical Association, 32 (1958), 1–27.
63. "Christian Philosophy of Love." *Alumni Bulletin* [of Quincy College], 10 (1958), 3–5, 6–8, 11 (1958).

1959

64. *A Brief Commentary on Ludwig Wittgenstein's Tractatus Logico-Philosophicus*. (pro manuscripto). St. Bonaventure, N.Y.: Franciscan Institute, 1959.
65. "Monthly Conference: Mental Prayer." *The Cord*, 9 (1959), 257–63.

1960

66. "The Unspeakable Philosophy of the Late Wittgenstein." In *Analytic Philosophy*. Proc. of American Catholic Philosphical Association, 34 (1960), 168–93.
67. "The Grace of Guadalupe." *Our Lady's Digest*, 15 (1960), 194–201. Reprint of 58.

1961

68. "The Queenship of Mary." *Our Lady's Digest*, 16 (1961), 31–37. Reprint of 51.

69. "Chemical Substance." In *St. John's University Studies: Philosphical Series*, No. 1. Jamaica, N.Y.: St. John's University Press, 1961, pp. 87–130.
70. *Select Problems in the Philosophy of Nature*. Revised ed. (pro manuscripto). St. Bonaventure, N.Y.: Franciscan Institute, 1961. Revision of 27.
71. *Duns Scotus. The Oxford Lectures on the Existence of God*. [Text and trans.]. (pro manuscripto). St. Bonaventure, N.Y.: Franciscan Institute, 1961. Trans. printed in 84, pp. 157–88.

1962

72. "The Realism of Scotus." *Journal of Philosophy*, 59 (1962), 725–36.
73. *Duns Scotus. Philosophical Writings: A Selection*. [Intro., text and trans.] Edinburgh: Thomas Nelson, 1962. Intro. and trans. reprinted, 81. Intro., text, and trans. reprinted, 146.
74. "Toward a Theory of Real Knowledge." In *Philosophy and The Integration of Contemporary Catholic Education*. Proc. of the Workshop on Philosophy and the Integration of Contemporary Catholic Education at The Catholic University of America, 16–27 June, 1961. Ed. George F. McLean. Washington, D.C.: Catholic University of America Press, 1962, pp. 44–74.

1963

75. "The Ockhamist Critique." In *The Concept of Matter in Greek and Medieval Philosophy*. Ed. Ernan McMullin. Notre Dame, Ind.: University of Notre Dame Press, 1963, pp. 124–46.
76. "Comment" [on Weisheipl's "The Concept of Matter in Fourteenth Century Science"]. In *The Concept of Matter in Greek and Medieval Philosophy*. Ed. Ernan McMullin. Notre Dame, Ind.: University of Notre Dame Press, 1963, pp. 342–43.
77. "Scotism." In *Teaching Thomism Today*. Proc. of the Workshop on Teaching Thomism Today at The Catholic University of America, 15–26 June, 1962. Ed. George F. McLean. Washington, D.C.: Catholic University of America Press, 1963, pp. 64–80.
78. "Thomism and Ecclesiastical Approbation: A Comment on Father Ashley's Paper." In *Teaching Thomism Today*. Washington, D.C.: Catholic University of America Press, 1963, pp. 111–17.
79. "Philosophical Analysis." In *Teaching Thomism Today*. Washington, D.C.: Catholic University of America Press, 1963, pp. 183–93.
80. "Linguistic Analysis." In *Teaching Thomism Today*. Washington, D.C.: Catholic University of America Press, 1963, pp. 368–70.

1964

81. *John Duns Scotus. Philosophical Writings: A Selection*. [Intro. and trans.] Indianapolis: Library of Liberal Arts, Bobbs-Merrill, 1964. A 1964 reprint of trans. of 73.

1965

82. "The Formal Distinction." In *John Duns Scotus, 1265–1965*. Ed. John K. Ryan and Bernardine M. Bonansea. Studies in Philosophy and the History of Philosophy, 3. Washington, D.C.: Catholic University of America Press, 1965, pp. 45–60.
83. "Parapsychology." *The Catholic Encyclopedia for School and Home*. 1965 ed.

1966

84. *John Duns Scotus. A Treatise on God as First Principle. A revised Latin text of the De primo principio translated into English along with two related questions from an early commentary on the Sentences.* Chicago: Forum Books, Franciscan Herald Press, 1966. Rev. text and trans. of *De Primo*, with commentary, in 138.

1967

85. "Bacon, Roger." *The Encyclopedia of Philosophy.* 1967 ed.
86. "Boehner, Philotheus Heinrich." *New Catholic Encyclopedia.* 1967 ed.
87. "Bonaventure, St." *The Encylopedia of Philosophy.* 1967 ed.
88. "Duns Scotus, John," *The Encyclopedia of Philosophy.* 1967 ed.
89. "Efficient Causality." *New Catholic Encyclopedia* 1967 ed.
90. "Knowledge, Infused." *New Catholic Encyclopedia.* 1967 ed.

1968

91. "Is Existence for Scotus a Perfection, Predicate or What?" In *De doctrina Ioannis Duns Scoti.* Vol. II. Rome, 1968, pp. 175–82.
92. Discussion of Roy Effler's "Is Scotus' Proof for the Existence of God an Essentialist Proof?" In *Scotus Speaks Today, 1266–1966.* Southfield, Mich.: Duns Scotus College, 1968, pp. 134–40.

1969

93. *Medieval Philosophy: From St. Augustine to Nicholas of Cusa.* Ed. ABW and John F. Wippel. Readings in the History of Philosophy, ed. P. Edwards and R. Popkin. New York: Free Press, 1969.
94. "Clare, Saint." *Encyclopedia Britannica.* 1969 ed.
95. "Francis, Saint (of Paola)." *Encyclopedia Britannica.* 1969 ed.
96. "Giles, Saint." *Encyclopedia Britannica* 1969 ed.
97. "Monte Corvino, Giovanni di" (*in part*). *Encyclopedia Britannica.* 1969 ed.

1970

98. "Duns Scotus on the Omnipotence of God." [Intro. and trans.]. Allan B. Wolter and Felix Alluntis. In *Ancients and Moderns.* Studies in Philosophy and the History of Philosophy, 5th ed. John K. Ryan. Washington, D.C.: Catholic University of America Press, 1970, pp. 178–222. Trans. reprinted in 111, pp. 159–97.

1971

99. "Ockham and the Textbooks: On the Origin of Possibility." In *Inquiries into Medieval Philosophy.* Ed. J. F. Ross. Westport, Conn.: Greenwood Publishing Co., 1971, pp. 243–73. Reprint of 19.
100. Rev. of *A Wittgenstein Workbook,* by Christopher Coope et al. *Thomist,* 35 (1971), 551–52.
101. Rev. of *The Elusive Mind,* by H. D. Lewis. *Review of Metaphysics,* 25 (1971), 357–58.
102. Rev. of *G. E. Moore. Essays in Retrospect,* ed. A. Ambrose et al. *Review of Metaphysics,* 25 (1972), 567–68.

1972

103. "Native Freedom of the Will as a Key to the Ethics of Scotus." In *Deus et*

Homo ad mentum I. Duns Scoti. Rome: Societas Internationalis Scotistica, 1972, pp. 360–70.

104. Rev. of *The Logic of Plurality*, by J. E. J. Altham. *Review of Metaphysics*, 25 (1972), 549.

105. Rev. of *The Basic Quidditive Metaphysics of Duns Scotus as Seen in his De Primo Principio*, by R. P. Prentice. *Review of Metaphysics*, 25 (1972), 565.

106. Rev. of *Philosophy of Logic*, by Hilary Putnam. *Review of Metaphysics*, 25 (1972), 565–66.

107. Rev. of *Collected Papers*, by G. Ryle. *Review of Metaphysics*, 25 (1972), 567–68.

108. Rev. of *Prototractatus* by Ludwig Wittgenstein. *Review of Metaphysics*, 25 (1972), 575–76.

1973

109. Rev. of *Causality and Scientific Explanation*, by William A. Wallace. *Review of Metaphysics*, 26 (1973), 549.

1974

110. "Duns Scotus, John." *New Encyclopedia Britannica.* 1974 ed.

1975

111. *John Duns Scotus: God and Creatures, the Quodlibetal Questions.* [Trans., intro., notes and glossary.]. Allan B. Wolter and Felix Alluntis. Princeton: Princeton University Press, 1975.

112. Rev. of *The Historical Constitution of St. Bonaventure's Philosophy*, by J. Quinn. *Review of Metaphysics*, 29 (1975), 145–48.

1976

113. Rev. of *William of Ockham*, by Gordon Leff. *Review of Metaphysics*, 29 (1976), 552–53.

114. *Rev. of Concepts of Space and Time*, ed. Milic Capek. *Review of Metaphysics*, 29 (1976), 728–29.

115. Rev. of *Causal Powers*, by Rom Harre and E. H. Madden. *Review of Metaphysics*, 29 (1976), 735–36.

116. Rev. of *Ockham's Theory of Terms*, [by Wm. Ockham], trans. Loux. *Review of Metaphysics*, 29 (1976), 742–43.

117. Rev. of *Guillelmi de Ockham. Opera philosophica I. Review of Metaphysics*, 29 (1976), 742–43.

118. Rev. of *Theories of the Proposition*, by Gabriel Nuchelmans. *Review of Metaphysics*, 29 (1976), 742–43.

1978

119. Rev. of *Amerikanische philosophie von den Puritanem bis zu Herbert Marcuse*, by E. F. Sauer. *Review of Metaphysics*, 32 (1978), 370–71.

120. "An Oxford Dialogue on Language and Metaphysics." *Review of Metaphysics*, 31 (1978), 615–48 and 32 (1978), 323–48.

1979

121. *Duns Scotus. Questions on the Metaphysics, Book Nine: Potency and Act.* [Trans. of a corrected text.] (pro manuscripto). Washington, D.C.: Catholic University of America, 1979. Available through Translation Clearing House, Department of Philosophy, Oklahoma State University, Stillwater, Oklahoma 74078.

122. Rev. of *The Twelve Patriarchs, The Mystical Ark, Book Three of the Trinity,* by Richard St. Victor. *Review of Metaphysics,* 33 (1979), 445–47.
123. Rev. of *Guillelmi de Ockham. Opera philosophica II. Review of Metaphysics,* 32 (1979), 766–68.

1980

124. "John Duns Scotus on the Primacy and Personality of Christ." [Intro., annotated bibliography, text and trans.] In *Franciscan Christology.* Ed. Damian McElrath. Franciscan Institute Publications Franciscan Sources, no. 1. Ed. George Marcil. St. Bonaventure, N.Y.: Franciscan Institute, 1980, pp. 139–82.
125. Rev. of *The Dissolution of the Medieval Outlook,* by Gordon Leff. *Catholic Historical Review,* 66 (1980), 673–76.
126. Rev. of *Universals and Scientific Realism I–II,* by David M. Armstrong. *Review of Metaphysics,* 33 (1980), 615–16.
127. Rev. of *Guillelmi de Ockham. Opera philosophica III. Review of Metaphysics,* 33 (1980), 645–47.
128. Rev. of *Guillelmi de Ockham. Opera theologica IV. Review of Metaphysics,* 33 (1980), 645–47.

1981

129. "A 'Reportatio' of Duns Scotus' Merton College Dialogue on Language and Metaphysics." In *Miscellanea Medievialia.* Band 13/1. *Sprache und Erkenntnis im Mittelalter.* Ed. Albert Zimmermann. Berlin: De Gruyter, 1981, pp. 179–91.
130. *John Duns Scotus. Six Questions on Individuation from the Oxford Lectures, Book III, Distinction 3* [Trans.] (pro manuscripto). Washington, D.C.: Catholic University of America, 1981. Available through Translation Clearing House, Department of Philosophy, Oklahoma State University, Stillwater, OK 74078.
131. Rev. of *Disputed Questions on the Mystery of the Trinity,* by St. Bonaventure; intro., trans. by Z. Hayes. *Review of Metaphysics,* 35 (1981), 117–8.
132. Rev. of *Guillelmi de Ockham. Quodlibeta Septem. Review of Metaphysics,* 35 (1981), 147–48.

1982

133. "A Scotistic Approach to the Ultimate Why-Question." In *Philosophies of Existence Ancient and Medieval.* Ed. Parviz Morewedge. New York: Fordham University Press, 1982, pp. 109–30.
134. "Duns Scotus on Intuition, Memory and Our Knowledge of Individuals." In *History of Philosophy in the Making: A Symposium of Essays to Honor Professor James D. Collins on His 65th Birthday by His Colleagues and Friends.* Ed. Linus J. Thro. Lanham, Md.: University Press of America, 1982, pp. 81–104.
135. Rev. of *You, I and Others,* by Paul Weiss. *Review of Metaphysics,* 35 (1982), 638–39.
136. Rev. of *William of Ockham,* by Gordon Leff. *International Studies in Philosophy,* 4 (1982), 102–4.
137. "Duns Scotus' Parisian Proof for the Existence of God." *Franciscan Studies,* 42 (1982), 248–321. (With Marilyn McCord Adams.)

1983

138. *John Duns Scotus. A Treatise on God as First Principle. A Latin Text and English Translation of the De Primo Principio.* 2d ed., rev., with a commen-

tary. Chicago: Forum Books, Franciscan Herald Press, 1983. Revision of text and trans. of 84, with new extensive commentary.

139. Rev. of *Ockham's Theory of Propositions: Part II of the Summa Logicae*, trans. by A. J. Freddoso and H. Schuurman. *Thomist*, 47 (1983), 614–15.

140. Rev. of *The Philosophy of Robert Grosseteste*, by James McEvoy. *Journal of the History of Philosophy*, 21 (1983), 440–502.

1984

141. Rev. of *Guillelmi de Ockham. Opera theologica V. Review of Metaphysics*, 37 (1984), 633–34.

142. Rev. of *Guillelmi de Ockham. Opera theologica VI. Review of Metaphysics*, 37 (1984), 633–34.

143. Rev. of *The Writings of Charles S. Peirce: A Chronological Edition*. Vol. I: 1857–66. *Review of Metaphysics*, 37 (1984), 643–45.

144. "Philotheus Boehner: In Memoriam." *Francisan Studies*, 44 (1984), vii–x.

1986

145. *Duns Scotus on the Will and Morality*. [Intro. texts, and trans.] Washington, D.C.: Catholic University Press of America, 1986.

1987

146. *John Duns Scotus: Philosophical Writings. A Selection*. [Introd. text, and trans.] Indianapolis: Hackett, 1987. Reprint of 73. 2nd edition.

147. Rev. of *God's Willing Knowledge: The Influence of Scotus' Analysis of Omniscience*, by Douglas Langston. *Theological Studies*, 48 (1987), 182–85.

1988

148. *Duns Scotus: Four Questions on Mary*. [Intro., text, and trans.] Santa Barbara, Calif.: Old Mission, 1988.

149. "Scotus' Ethics." *Essays in Medieval Studies: Proceedings of the Illinois Medieval Association*, 5 (1988), 17–31.

1989

150. *Duns Scotus: Political and Economic Philosophy*. [Intro., text, and trans.] Santa Barbara, Calif.: Old Mission, 1989.

151. Rev. of *Richard Rufus of Cornwall and the Tradition of Oxford Theology*, by Peter Raedts. *Catholic Historical Review*, 75 (1989), 152–53.

Forthcoming

152. "Scotus' Theory of Individuation." In *Individuation in Scholasticism: The Later Middle Ages and the Counter-Reformation*. Ed. Jorge Gracia. Munich: Philosophia Verlag.

Updated and reprinted with permission from *Essays Honoring Allan B. Wolter*, ed. William A. Frank and Girard J. Etzkorn (St. Bonaventure, N.Y.: The Franciscan Institute, 1985), 351–63.

Index of Names

Index of Subjects

Abstraction
  "Augustinian" abstraction, 65
  definition by abstraction, 64
  four kinds distinguished, 62–66
  precisive abstraction, 62
  subjective/hypostatic abstraction, 62
  See also Cognition
Action
  distinct from active potency whose a.
    it is and from habits derived from it,
    168
  qualitative accidents inhering in some
    substance, 168
Action, morally good
  generic and circumstantial suitability,
    distinguished, 156, 198
  generic goodness not solely dependent
    on God's will, 199
  must accord with *affectio iustitiae*,
    190
  must conform to the dictates of right
    reason as regards both its objects and
    its circumstances, 155
  no created object renders an act m.g.
    ex genere, 156–57, 198–99
  whether or not love of created objects
    is m.g. depends on whether it is
    commanded by God or another legit-
    imate authority, and the end for
    which it is sought, 157, 199

Action, voluntary
  the person is the *principium quod*
    thereof, 169
  the will is the proximate, the person
    the remote *principium quo*, 169
Affection for justice (*affectio iustitiae*)
  in creatures checks inordinate self-
    seeking, 152–53
  in creatures constitutes a native free-
    dom from nature and for values, 152
  in creatures strengthened by infused
    charity, 153, 191
  inclination to value a thing for its own
    sake as right reason dictates, 18, 151,
    152, 189
  infused for Anselm, innate for Scotus,
    190
  leads to friendship-love (*amor amici-
    tiae*) or benevolence (*amor benevo-
    lentiae*), 19, 155, 198
  makes altruism possible, 18, 151, 189
  must be followed for act to be morally
    good, 155
  not jealous, but seeks other lovers for
    the beloved, 18, 151
  proper to rational beings, 189
  used to explain inner life of Trinity,
    189
  used to explain rationale of Divine
    creativity, 189

Library of Congress Cataloging-in-Publication Data

Wolter, Allan Bernard, 1913–
    The philosophical theology of John Duns Scotus / Allan B. Wolter :
Marilyn McCord Adams, editor.
      p. cm.
    Includes bibliographical references.
    ISBN 0–8014–2385–6 (alk. paper)
    1. Philosophical theology—History of doctrines—Middle Ages,
600–1500. 2. Duns Scotus, John, ca. 1266–1308. I. Adams, Marilyn
McCord. II. Title.
BT40.W64 1990   89–46162
210'.92—dc20